EU ENVIRONMENTAL PRINCIPLES AND SCIENTIFIC UNCERTAINTY BEFORE NATIONAL COURTS

This comparative book explores the dynamics driving how courts across Europe and beyond understand and analyse scientific information in nature conservation. The Habitats and the Birds Directives – the core of EU nature conservation law – are usually seen as the most 'uniform' parts of EU environmental law. This book analyses the case law from 11 current and former EU Member States' courts and explores the dynamics of how, and crucially why, their understandings of scientific uncertainty on the one hand, and EU environmental principles on the other, vary.

The courts' scope and depth of review, access to scientific knowledge, and scientific literacy all influence such decisions – as does their interpretation of norms and principles. How have the courts evaluated scientific evidence, encompassing its essential uncertainties? This book answers this and many more questions pertinent to EU environmental law, comparative environmental law, administrative law, and STS studies.

Co-edited by experienced leaders in the field, and with outstanding contributors, this book is an essential guide to the dynamics of nature conservation law.

EU Environmental Principles and Scientific Uncertainty before National Courts

The Case of the Habitats Directive

Edited by
Mariolina Eliantonio
Emma Lees
and
Tiina Paloniitty

•HART•
OXFORD • LONDON • NEW YORK • NEW DELHI • SYDNEY

HART PUBLISHING

Bloomsbury Publishing Plc

Kemp House, Chawley Park, Cumnor Hill, Oxford, OX2 9PH, UK

1385 Broadway, New York, NY 10018, USA

29 Earlsfort Terrace, Dublin 2, Ireland

HART PUBLISHING, the Hart/Stag logo, BLOOMSBURY and the Diana logo are trademarks of Bloomsbury Publishing Plc

First published in Great Britain 2023

A catalogue record for this book is available from the British Library.

A catalogue record for this book is available from the Library of Congress.

ISBN: HB: 978-1-50994-819-2
ePDF: 978-1-50994-821-5
ePub: 978-1-50994-820-8

Typeset by Compuscript Ltd, Shannon

TABLE OF CONTENTS

CONTRIBUTORS

Richard Broadbent is Director in Freeths LLP's Environmental Law team.

Catherine A Caine is Senior Lecturer in Law at the University of Exeter.

Roberto Caranta is Professor of Administrative Law at the University of Turin.

Dacian Dragoş is Professor at the Center for Good Governance Studies, Faculty of Political, Administrative and Communication Sciences at the Babeş-Bolyai University in Cluj-Napoca.

Floor Fleurke is Associate Professor of European Environmental Law at Tilburg Law School, Tilburg University.

Agustín García-Ureta is Professor at the University of the Basque Country, Bilbao.

Konstantinos Gogos is Professor of Administrative Law at the Aristotle University of Thessaloniki.

François-Vivien Guiot is Lecturer in Public Law at the College of European and International Studies of Pau University.

Mariolina Eliantonio is Professor of European and Comparative Administrative Law and Procedure at Maastricht University.

Michał Krajewski is an Inquiries Officer at the European Ombudsman. He holds PhD in Law from the European University Institute, Florence (Italy). Previously, he worked as an Assistant Professor at the University of Maastricht and a Postdoctoral Research Fellow at the University of Copenhagen. The chapter that he co-authored reflects his personal views only and cannot be attributed to the European Ombudsman.

Wolfgang Köck is Head of the Department of Environmental and Planning Law at the Helmholtz-Centre for Environmental Research in Leipzig, Professor of Environmental Law at the Law Faculty, University of Leipzig, and Member of German Advisory Council on the Environment.

Emma Lees is Chair in Transnational Law at the School of Transnational Governance, European University Institute and Professor of Environmental and Property Law, University of Cambridge. She is the Peter Wilson Fellow, Fitzwilliam College, Cambridge.

Till Markus is Senior Researcher at the Helmholtz-Centre for Environmental Research in Leipzig and senior lecturer at the University of Bremen.

Bogdana Neamţu is Associate Professor at the Center for Good Governance Studies, Faculty of Political, Administrative and Communication Sciences at the Babeş-Bolyai University in Cluj-Napoca.

Hanna Nieminen-Finne (LL.D.) is Administrative Judge (currently on leave) and Senior Specialist at the National Courts Administration in Finland.

Tiina Paloniitty (LL.D.) is Postdoctoral Researcher of Sustainability and Environmental Law at the Helsinki Institute of Sustainability Science and Faculty of Law, University of Helsinki.

Jurgita Paužaitė-Kulvinskiene (LL.M.) is Professor and Head of the research group for Administrative and Administrative Proceeding Law at Vilnius University as well as Vice-Dean for Research at Law Faculty.

The Hon Justice Brian J Preston FRSN SC FAAL is the current Chief Judge of the Land and Environment Court of New South Wales, Australia, having practised as a solicitor, barrister and senior counsel. He is a Visiting Professor at Durham University (UK), and an Adjunct Professor at three Australian universities, the University of Sydney, Western Sydney University and Southern Cross University.

Áine Ryall is Professor at University College Cork and Chair of the Aarhus Convention Compliance Committee.

Katalin Sulyok is Assistant Professor in Environmental Law and International Law at ELTE Eötvös Lorand University, Budapest. She is Chief Legal Advisor to the Hungarian Ombudsman for Future Generations.

Indrė Žvaigždinienė is Judge of Vilnius Regional Administrative Court and Associate Professor of Environmental Law at Vilnius University Law Faculty.

TABLE OF CASES

EU

Court of Justice

General Court

Australia

Finland

France

Council of State

Administrative Courts of Appeal

Administrative Courts

Germany

Federal Constitutional Court

Federal Administrative Court

Greece

Hungary

Constitutional Court

Supreme Court

Courts of Appeal

Lower Courts

Ireland

Italy

Court of Cassation

Sicilian Council of Administrative Justice

Council of State

Regional Administrative Tribunals

Lithuania

Romania

United Kingdom

ECHR

TABLE OF LEGISLATION

Regulations

Directives

Australia

Federal Legislation

New South Wales

Primary Legislation

Secondary Legislation

Finland

Constitution

Legislation

France

Laws

Decrees

Ordonnances

Germany

Constitution

Legislation

Administrative Regulations

Greece

Constitution

Code

Legislation

Decrees

Ministerial Decisions

Hungary

Code

Decrees

Ireland

Constitution

Legislation

Regulations

Italy

Constitution

Laws

Legislative Decrees

Royal and Presidential Decrees

Lithuania

Constitution

Legislation

Ministerial Orders

Netherlands

Romania

Constitution

Legislation

Emergency Ordinances

Governmental Decisions

Ministerial Orders

England and Wales

Primary Legislation

Statutory Instruments

Northern Ireland

Scotland

Introduction

MARIOLINA ELIANTONIO, EMMA LEES AND TIINA PALONIITTY

I. Aims of and Justification for Comparative Analysis

A full understanding of how courts handle complex scientific questions is essential to appreciating the dynamics of environmental law. The Habitats Directive (HD) and Wild Birds Directive (WBD) represent the core of European Union (EU) nature conservation law.[1] This comparative volume analyses the case law from current and former EU Member States' (MS) courts, European courts, and from one non-European jurisdiction, Australia. It explores the dynamics of how, and crucially, why their handling of scientific information and solutions to scientific uncertainty vary. The courts' scope and depth of review, access to scientific knowledge, and scientific literacy all influence answers to this overall question – as does their interpretation of norms and principles. How have the courts evaluated scientific evidence, encompassing its essential uncertainties?

We have chosen to focus on scientific uncertainty as environmental governance relies on precaution. Environmental impacts of planned projects must be evaluated in advance in various decision-making processes. As with any forward-looking activity, environmental impact assessment is inherently uncertain. Such uncertainties can be approached as scientific or technical questions (entailing 'factual' considerations), and scientific practice has its own mechanisms for reducing the uncertainty of its outputs. However, there is always the 'residual uncertainty' that is evaluated as legal question, entailing the application of environmental principles, such as the precautionary principle: is the uncertainty of detrimental impacts such that the precautionary principle needs to be employed and planned projects revised or rejected?

In this context, the extent of the courts' review, their access to scientific knowledge, and their scientific literacy is prone to influencing where the courts draw the line between factual and legal questions, and, as a consequence, their interpretation

[1] Council Directive 92/43/EEC of 21 May 1992 on the conservation of natural habitats and of wild fauna and flora [1992] OJ L206/7 and Directive 2009/147/EC of the European Parliament and of the Council of 30 November 2009 on the conservation of wild birds [2010] OJ L20/7. To avoid unnecessary repetition, the remaining chapters will not give full details of these two Directives in their footnotes. Rather, the long title and official journal information appear here, and in the table of legislation found at pp xxv–xliii.

of the applicable norms and principles. Thus, examining the science/ law interface unveils a critical aspect of EU environmental law, its effectiveness and application.

This volume explores the following five subthemes: (a) how constitutional underpinnings affecting assessment of scientific information might produce variation in practice in MS notwithstanding a static and uniform EU law underpinning; (b) the significance of those underpinnings for how science is used in court; and (c) how the judiciary constructs and handles scientific questions to allow resolution of disputes notwithstanding uncertainty in the factual underpinnings. In comparative terms, we study (d) how the judicial system of 'findings of fact' (ie something becoming proven) operates where 'proof' is impossible; and from the EU law perspective, we analyse (e) how all these aspects influence the effective enforcement of EU law, for the differences in the legal and scientific uncertainty assessments may result in uneven implementation of the EU environmental law. The variation that the comparative analysis unveils originates from procedural, substantive, constitutional and cultural differences that define the legal landscapes of each judicial system studied. As the concluding comparative chapter of this book explains, these variations are perhaps even greater than originally anticipated.

At its most fundamental, our analysis is about the separation of powers, modulated through the specific setting of EU biodiversity law as it is realised in individual courts. When these courts adjudge matters with significant scientific uncertainties, they divide power between themselves, administrative authorities, expert consultants, and the public at large. The courts establish lines between the political, the legal and the scientific, negotiating their way across this triangle in the way found preferable in each legal system. The values they abide by, constitutional or otherwise, define the way the decisions are made. As explained in the first chapter of this book:

> The decision what is scientific information, and what is not, and therefore whether uncertainty is scientific, or not, is determined not by some pre-determined and objective standard, but by an on-going and developing dialogue between context, understandings of the judicial role, and constitutional principles in any particular jurisdiction.[2]

II. The Thematic Landscape

The volume at hand discusses and cross-pollinates four separate themes: science and technology in courts, environmental principles, comparative law on judicial review, and application of EU law at the national level.

First, by exploring in depth the ways in which scientific information is integrated into decision-making processes surrounding the WBD and HD, the book contributes to the existing literature regarding the uses of scientific information in court in an environmental context. Whilst this topic has been the study of a number of

[2] See chapter one of this volume by Emma Lees and Tiina Paloniitty at page 27.

general works – most prominently, for example, Jasonoff's work on the role which science can (and cannot) play in the judicial process,[3] and Fisher's exploration of science in environmental law more generally[4] – and some more specific studies – including Ky's analysis of merits review and science in an Australian context,[5] and Fisher et al's exploration of scientific review in the context of the United States[6] – the topic has been mainly tackled in jurisdictions with broad scopes of review. This book does not limit itself to legal systems with broad and deep review, but gathers new knowledge on the way in which courts deal with scientific uncertainties and environmental principles, and the constitutional constraints of their actions. Importantly, it has become apparent in this study that a binary distinction between legality and merits review does not accurately describe or explain the variation in the legal systems we have addressed.

Most importantly, the question of scientific and technical uncertainties in judicial review has not been considered comparatively in a systematic and detailed way. Indeed, as the *Oxford Handbook of Comparative Environmental Law* emphasised, there is lack of depth of analysis in some comparative environmental law.[7] This volume intends to continue to push the analytical richness of comparative environmental law by looking at the critical question of the role of science within different jurisdictions, but within the same legal framework to make such comparison as rigorous and as informative as possible. Specifically, the choice of the WBD and HD is very revealing in showing how constitutional underpinnings of judicial review of administrative action shape the implementation and techniques of environmental law more than might be assumed given the ostensible homogeneity of the legal test being applied. Earlier, Emma Lees and Ole W Pedersen have explored the relationship between the 'avenues' of adjudication in the processes employed by courts, and found that the constitutional underpinning of this avenue has an enormous influence on how environmental law is 'done'.[8] By looking at the WBD and HD as a comparative case study, it becomes apparent to what extent the cultural baggage associated with different constitutional set-ups adjusts how

[3] See Sheila Jasanoff, *Science at the Bar: Law, Science and Technology in America* (Harvard University Press, 1997) 42; Sheila Jasanoff, 'The Idiom of Co-production' in Sheila Jasanoff (ed), *States of Knowledge: The Co-Production of Science and Social Order* (Routledge, 2004) 3; and Sheila Jasanoff, 'Just Evidence: The Limits of Science in the Legal Process' (2006) 34 *Law, Medicine and Ethics* 328.

[4] Elizabeth Fisher, *Risk, Regulation and Administrative Constitutionalism* (Hart Publishing, 2007); Elizabeth Fisher et al, 'Understanding Environmental Models in their Legal and Regulatory Context' (2010) 22 *Journal of Environmental Law* 251; and Elizabeth Fisher, 'Sciences, Environmental Laws, and Legal Cultures' in Emma Lees and Jorge E Viñuales, *The Oxford Handbook of Comparative Environmental Law* (Oxford University Press, 2019).

[5] Patrick Ky, 'Qualifications, Weight of Opinion, Peer Review and Methodology: A Framework for Understanding the Evaluation of Science in Merits Review' (2012) 24 *Journal of Environmental Law* 207.

[6] Elizabeth Fisher et al, 'Rethinking Judicial Review of Expert Agencies' (2015) 93 *Texas Law Review* 1681.

[7] Emma Lees, 'Value in Comparative Environmental Law – 3D Cartography and Analytical Description' in Lees and Viñuales (n 4).

[8] Emma Lees and Ole W Pedersen, *Environmental Adjudication* (Hart Publishing, 2020).

science is handled in the tripartite relationship between adjudicator, administrator and scientific advisor.[9] Up until now these constitutional and procedural realities of environmental litigation have been discussed primarily in studies on single jurisdictions but less so in a comparative setting.[10]

Second, our analysis contributes to the principles discourse by analysing the role of principles and scientific uncertainty in science-intense environmental matters, mapping the dynamics between science and law in environmental judicial review. Environmental principles are often portrayed as a unifying feature of fragmented and piecemeal environmental regulation.[11] Environmental law has been keen to adopt them and scholars have produced rich literature on the principles.[12] The environmental law research community has, however, started to become more aware of the contingent and culturally dependent nature of the principles.[13] This volume builds on this context/ contingency focus, drawing especially on the work by Eloise Scotford, who emphasises the contingent nature of the principles, their vagueness, and the little content they have in the abstract.[14] We elaborate on one aspect on which the contingency hinges, namely the way in which scientific information is handled by courts. By doing so we unveil the mechanisms with which courts strike a balance between the applicable legal principles, gradually in-/decreasing scientific uncertainty, and the procedural constraints within which they operate. Thus, our comparative analysis manages to avoid the two most common pitfalls of being at a high level of generality or focusing on a single jurisdiction or legal provision.

Third, by exploring the procedural rules applicable before these courts, we contribute to the much overlooked area of comparative law of judicial review.

[9] Emma Lees, 'Allocation of Decision-Making Power under the Habitats Directive' (2016) 28 *Journal of Environmental Law* 191.

[10] See, eg, Fisher et al (n 4); Tiina Paloniitty and Niina Kotamäki, 'Scientific and Legal Mechanisms for Addressing Model Uncertainties: Negotiating the Right Balance in Finnish Judicial Review?' (2021) 33 *Journal of Environmental Law* 283. A comparative element is included in some accounts: eg Brian J Preston, 'Characteristics of Successful Environmental Courts and Tribunals' (2014) 26 *Journal of Environmental Law* 365.

[11] This common presumption of principles' unifying nature is deconstructed in Eloise Scotford, *Environmental Principles and the Evolution of Environmental Law* (Hart Publishing 2017) 2–3, 46–48, 59–60. See also Ole W Pedersen, 'The Contingent Foundations of Environmental Law' (2018) 30 *Journal of Environmental Law* 362.

[12] See, eg, Jacqueline Peel, 'Precaution' in Lavanya Rajamani and Jacqueline Peel (eds), *The Oxford Handbook of International Environmental Law*, 2nd edn (Oxford University Press, 2021); Brian J Preston, 'The Judicial Development of the Precautionary Principle' (2018) 35 *Journal of European Planning and Environmental Law* 123; Rene von Schomber, 'The Precautionary Principle: Its Use within Hard and Soft Law' (2012) 3 *European Journal of Risk Regulation* 2; Caroline E Foster, *Science and the Precautionary Principle in International Courts and Tribunals* (Cambridge University Press, 2011); Elizabeth Fisher et al (eds), *Implementing the Precautionary Principle: Perspectives and Prospects* (EE, 2006); Nicolas de Sadeleer, 'The Precautionary Principle in EC Health and Environmental Law' (2006) 12 *European Law Journal* 139.

[13] Pedersen (n 11) 359; Scotford (n 11); Ceri Warnock, 'Environment and the Law: The Normative Force of Context and Constitutional Challenges' (2020) 32 *Journal of Environmental Law* 365.

[14] Scotford (n 11).

While some studies have tackled questions of standing in comparative perspective or have compared systems of judicial review, these contributions have remained fairly general, aiming at providing only overviews, or discussing systemic similarities and differences between various legal systems.[15] The book at hand provides thorough and comparative knowledge of procedural rules concerning evidence in judicial review of administrative action. Along the same lines, we contribute to shedding light on the different intensities of review used by the national courts when reviewing the administrative action.

Fourth, by discussing adjudication of specific provisions of EU law before the national courts, we contribute to the growing body of literature on the application and enforcement of EU (environmental) law at the national level.[16] In the EU's system of decentralised enforcement, environmental law is mostly applied and enforced by the national authorities and courts – but the application and enforcement of EU law by MS authorities and courts has remained largely unexplored. In this context our contribution has dual identity: we both elucidate the conflict produced by uniformity in application of EU environmental law failing to reflect the constitutional underpinnings in the MS and, at the same time, consider whether these very characteristics lead to the uniform application of EU environmental law becoming critically endangered.

III. Structure

The book consists of three parts: Part I – Courts, Science and the Habitats and Wild Birds Directives; Part II – Reviewing Science and Law in the Member States' Courts; and Part III – Broadening the View. Part I covers the basic dilemmas which are at the core of this book, namely: how do we understand the interplay between constitutional constraints on judicial and administrative action, between scientific and 'value-based' information and decisions, and between environmental law and the wider administrative context.

Chapter one explores the four elements of decision-making under the HD in respect of how science is handled. It looks at the identity of decision-makers, the

[15] Susan Rose-Ackerman and Peter Lindseth (eds), *Comparative Administrative Law*, 2nd edn (Elgar, 2019); Chris Backes and Mariolina Eliantonio (eds), *Cases, Materials and Text on Judicial Review of Administrative Action* (Hart Publishing, 2019); Jurgen de Poorter et al (eds), *Judicial Review of Administrative Discretion in the Administrative State* (Springer, 2019); Guobin Zhu (ed), *Deference to the Administration in Judicial Review* (Springer, 2019); Tiina Paloniitty and Mariolina Eliantonio (eds), 'Special Issue: Scientific Knowledge in Environmental Judicial Review: Safeguarding Effective Judicial Protection in the EU Member States?' (2018) 24 *European Energy and Environmental Law Review* 108.

[16] See, eg, Michal Bobek and Jeremias Adams-Prassl (ed), *Air Passenger Rights* (Hart Publishing, 2016); Andrea Keessen et al, 'European River Basin Districts: Are They Swimming in the Same Implementation Pool?' (2010) 22 *Journal of Environmental Law* 2; Bettina Lange, *Implementing EU Pollution Control: Law and Integration* (Cambridge University Press, 2008). See also Mariolina Eliantonio et al (eds), *EU Soft Law in the Member States* (Hart Publishing, 2021).

nature of information required to meet the tests in the HD, how this information is processed, and what this means for the level of scrutiny applied by a court to such information and processes. The chapter advocates for a greater focus on specificity as a solution to the gridlock of scientific knowledge, scientific uncertainties and environmental principles that have confused and restrained legal scholars, judges and practitioners alike. Further, it shows why it is far too simplistic to rely only on a distinction between merits review on the one hand, and legality review on the other, as being determinative of how science is considered in the adjudication process.

This part will then zoom in towards the case study of our collection, namely the WBD and HD, which are examined in chapter two. This chapter offers a short introduction to the Directives. Second, and more importantly, chapter two examines the Court of Justice of the European Union (CJEU) case law on the matters dealing with those Directives. By doing so chapter two offers the EU law context to the ensuing analysis on individual MS. With its focus on the European court it also adds to the volume's diversity by covering the transnational level, enabling even more exhaustive analysis in the concluding comparative chapter at the end of the volume.

In Part II, the 11 national chapters discuss the general rules on evidence, expert knowledge and intensity of review performed by the national courts in light of the constitutional understandings of the division of labour between courts and administrative authorities. Thereafter, the chapters discuss the relevant cases which can shed light on how courts tackle scientific uncertainties in cases falling within the scope of application of the above-mentioned Directives. In particular, the chapters consider how courts distinguish questions of fact from questions of law; how the courts discuss the scientific uncertainty at stake; and how prone they are to question the scientific choices made by the authorities and to ask available technical expertise for help.

Lastly, Part III provides an additional perspective on the topic of scientific uncertainties in environmental litigation by providing an insight into how similar questions are dealt with outside the EU. The first chapter of this Part examines Australian case law, including rulings from the Land and Environment Court of New South Wales, which is known to be at the forefront of an intense review of scientific uncertainties in environmental litigation. The second chapter of Part III tackles the EU level as a system of judicial review and discusses how the Union courts approach scientific uncertainties when reviewing the choices made by the EU administration. While the first chapter of Part III broadens the view geographically, the second chapter does so thematically, as the cases discussed do not deal with conservation law.

The three parts are followed by a concluding chapter where the comparative results are summarised and the overarching research questions are answered.

PART I

Courts, Science and the Habitats and Wild Birds Directives

1

'Science' in Court – The Importance of Specificity

EMMA LEES AND TIINA PALONIITTY

> Scientific truth-making, in particular, as human beings engage in it, is always a social enterprise. It is situated in particular places and circumstance; it is context-specific, purposive and culturally embedded. As such, even scientific claims are subject to distortion, through imperfections in the very human systems that produced them. In attempting to render justice, the law's objective should be, in part, to restore to view these potential shortcomings, instead of uncritically taking on board a decontextualised image of science that ignores its social and institutional dimension … When science enters the courtroom, it should do so as an adjunct to the law's need for credible but meaningful story-telling. In a court of law, science cannot hold itself out as simply science, the source of transcendental truths; most modestly, and with appropriate caveats, it can be the source of just evidence.[1]

I. Introduction

Analyses of environmental law as context-dependent, culturally-shaped and specific, are now mainstream in environmental scholarship.[2] The main message of such accounts is that the specific matters. Generalisations may lack depth, and worse, create a false impression of neatness or homogeneity. To generalise about

[1] Sheila Jasanoff, 'Just Evidence: The Limits of Science in the Legal Process' (2006) 34 *Law, Medicine and Ethics* 328, 339.

[2] OleW Pedersen, 'The Contingent Foundations of Environmental Law' (2018) 30 *Journal of Environmental Law* 359; E Scotford, *Environmental Principles and the Evolution of Environmental Law* (Hart Publishing, 2017); and Ceri Warnock, 'Environment and the Law: The Normative Force of Context and Constitutional Challenges' (2020) 32 *Journal of Environmental Law* 365. For discussion of legal culture more generally, see David Nelken, 'Using the Concept of Legal Culture' (2004) 29 *Australian Journal of Legal Philosophy* 26. Lees has argued elsewhere that the notion of contingency can be taken too far if it becomes a barrier to analysis, resulting in paralysis. See Emma Lees, 'Value in Comparative Environmental Law – 3D Cartography and Analytical Description' in Emma Lees and Jorge E Viñuales, *The Oxford Handbook of Comparative Environmental Law* (Oxford University Press, 2019).

the role of science in conservation law is therefore to underplay the importance of the specific. Analyses of the role that science plays in environmental regulation may blur the boundary between how courts do use such information (because the landscape is too complex and large) and how they should do so, without recognition that the normative balance shifts enormously with the specific context of a dispute.[3] Indeed, the very goal of this book as a whole is to provide a three-dimensional appreciation of how scientific information and uncertainty is handled by courts in a very specific context so as to allow us to capture and make sense of some of this complexity.[4]

The Wild Birds Directive (WBD) and Habitats Directive (HD) provide our focus.[5] As explained in the Introduction, the book raises three questions. First, we ask how might the text and form of the Directives shape the outcome of scientific uncertainty in adjudication relating to these Directives? Second, do judicial decisions in a range of courts show variation in how scientific uncertainty is managed in such adjudication? Third, what role do – on the one hand – environmental principles, and – on the other – constitutional principles of the national and EU legal order more broadly, as well as the national procedural framework, play in explaining or containing that variation? This first chapter looks at the first of these questions. Subsequent chapters in this book address questions two and three.

In answering this first question, three further sub-questions emerge:

i. What tests are generated by the Directives and where might scientific uncertainty generate challenges in relation to these?
ii. What does this tell us about the nature of decisions, and the identity of decision-makers under the Directives before we consider the modulation of the Directives through the pressures of the specific legal system in which it operates?
iii. How should we properly understand what scientific uncertainty *is* within adjudication?

This chapter looks closely at the text of, and tests established by, the HD to examine what kinds of scientific information and expert opinion are relevant, and when, and what this means for the consequences that scientific uncertainty may have for adjudication. By doing so we offer an analytical account of not only the distribution of powers – between the executive and the judiciary – in the specific contexts we examine, but also of the operation of power within the judicial branch.[6]

It does so, in section II, by examining the text of the HD itself in order to show how at different points within the tests established by the Directive, we would

[3] Elizabeth Fisher, 'Sciences, Environmental Laws, and Legal Cultures' in Lees and Viñuales, *ibid* 752.

[4] We are thus, too, 'complicating further the "and society" aspect of legal studies', Emilie Cloatre and Martyn Pickersgill, *Knowledge, Technology and Law* (Routledge, 2015) 3–4.

[5] For full details, see the Table of Legislation or the Introduction.

[6] Bettina Lange, 'Foucauldian Inspired Discourse Analysis: A Contribution to Critical Environmental Law Scholarship?' in Andreas Philippopoulos-Mihalopoulos (ed), *Law and Ecology: New Environmental Foundations* (Routledge, 2011) 39, 48–49.

expect judicial actors to refer to, handle and examine scientific information in different ways. In section III, it considers 'science' and scientific uncertainty, and how this essentially contested term can be unpacked and understood. It will be shown that the consequences of scientific uncertainty on decision-making under the Directive will be determined not only by the kind of uncertainty in the scientific information, but also by the allocation of power to overcome or 'move on from' that uncertainty, and by the specific question that a court or administrative authority is addressing in the particular case. Within the Directive 'science' plays a multifaceted role, and like a kaleidoscope, the number of facets increases once viewed through the lens of individual national legal systems. In the concluding chapter to this book we consider whether this fragmented picture is problematic.

II. The Habitats Directive and Scientific Tests

When we begin to think about decision-making under the Directive, and in particular the role which scientific uncertainty plays in the process of adjudication in Member State and other courts, it is natural to divide approaches according to whether what is undertaken is a legality-focused judicial review or a more intensive merits or substance review. But such a classification underplays the degree to which individual questions and issues in the tests established by the Directive can be disaggregated. Furthermore, significant patterns of variation exist within this binary classification (a theme which emerges very strongly through the chapters of this book). It is necessary therefore to examine the Directive itself (and particularly arts 6 and 12 which are the main focus of the case law this book examines) in order to set up a framework to organise our thoughts.

Through this process of disaggregation we build a map of decisions which the Directives require of administrative authorities and of courts. This map is underpinned by mandatory information processes, by decision-making expertise, and by allocations of power. Furthermore, this exercise begins to hint at the importance of the range of meanings which can be attributed to 'science' in regulation and in practice, as well as revealing the subtly different emphases that may be placed on such information in a variety of contexts, a theme which is addressed in section III.

This section looks at the Directive from two perspectives. First, it looks at the text of the Directive itself, for even in the kinds of tests that are established, it is apparent that uncertainty in scientific evidence will be more or less significant for the outcome of the case. In the second part, it considers four perspectives on the Directive: people, process, information and level of scrutiny.

Before embarking on this discussion, however, it is useful here to briefly discuss the jurisprudence of the Court of Justice of the European Union (CJEU) on the impact that uncertainty in science has on the operation of the Directive. This case law, as is well known, relies heavily on the precautionary principle to insist that in cases of uncertainty developments risking protected sites should not be authorised. This case law is discussed in detail by Garcia-Ureta in chapter two of this book so that discussion will not be repeated here. However, it is part of the argument of this book that because scientific uncertainty can be of many kinds, and manifest itself in different ways, practice around the Directive shows that this precautionary approach does not, and cannot, solve the problem of uncertainty.[7] Instead, it shifts the question. It tells us what action to take *if* there is uncertainty, it does not identify uncertainty.

A. People, Process, Information, Scrutiny

To explore the consequences of uncertainty in respect of the HD, it is useful to unpack four aspects of the Directive. These can be summed up as: people, information, process and scrutiny. To explain these four perspectives in more detail, the easiest way is to present them as a series of four questions:

1. Who gets to decide?
2. Upon which information will their decision be based?
3. What processes must be undertaken so that this information is of recognised legal quality?
4. To what extent will the decision-maker interrogate decisions or information provided by an alternative decision-maker?

Before explaining these further it is useful to explore an example. As we explain below, the question of the existence of effects from a development on the environment is one where scientific information, clearly, has a central role to play. Scientific information is needed to establish the causal link between the act, and the protected species or habitat. Imagine a case involving the felling of woodland, and a survey designed to ascertain the effects of such felling on the fauna of the woodland: thus, because the wood was felled, x number of badgers lost their habitats. That this causal link exists is something which a judge cannot know or determine. A judge is unlikely to know much if anything about the consequence of felling on badger habitats beyond the most general and obvious. This means that for this sort of causal link it is essential to engage with scientific information of some form. In cases of prediction, as here, this will usually mean reliance not on data from the particular site, but on the informed opinion of experts. There may be competing expert opinions, in which case the judge will decide which of

[7] See Brian J Preston, 'The Judicial Development of the Precautionary Principle' (2018) 35 *Environmental and Planning Law Journal* 123. Paloniitty and Kotamäki have clarified the legal and non-legal applications of the principle, Tiina Paloniitty and Niina Kotamäki, 'Scientific and Legal Mechanisms for Addressing Model Uncertainties: Negotiating the Right Balance in Finnish Judicial Review?' (2021) 33 *Journal of Environmental Law* 283–308.

two expert opinions to follow, but the answer 'there is an effect' is provided by the expert, not by the judge. If the expert is unsure of their conclusions such that the scientific information is uncertain, the court will need to decide how to proceed in the face of this uncertainty in reviewing an authorisation by an administrative authority based on such evidence.

By contrast, when asked whether the loss of habitat for x badgers is '*significant*', whilst the expert can say they think it is significant because the number of badgers is very high, for example, the meaning of significance, and its connection to the wider legislative context, is a matter for the judge. The judge will decide whether the loss of habitats for a large number of badgers is significant, not the expert. However, there may be uncertainty over the scale of this significance (eg one expert may say the loss is 100 per cent of the badgers occupying the woodland, and the other that it is more like 50 per cent – the court is faced with scientific uncertainty on the background to its judgment regarding significant). The lines here are fine. But different questions place the bulk of the burden of determining whether the facts meet the legislative tests more or less on the shoulders of those providing expert opinion and more or less on the shoulder of the judge. This has consequences for the ways in which uncertainty prevents or facilitates decisions. Similarly, the information required to assess whether a test is met or not will vary. Establishing the causal link requires analysis of predictive modelling, for example, whereas the question of significance requires the integration of non-scientific information into the process, including information about the political ambitions of the legislation. This simple example shows how the impacts of uncertainty in science in court will not be homogenous but instead are specific and context-driven. It is for this reason that specificity in analysis as explained here is so important and also why it is so useful to keep the angles of people, information, process and scrutiny in mind, when thinking about the operation of the Directive as a whole.

Thus, 'people' refers to *who* makes a decision; who decides the level of scrutiny to be applied; who generates information, etc. In respect of uncertainty, therefore, who decides whether there is uncertainty in the scientific position will either (a) trigger the precautionary principle or (b) thinks it is more appropriate to divest decision-maker power to someone else (eg a court determines that the scientific position is unclear, knows that its generalist judges cannot solve this problem, and therefore requests support of an expert). Which of these options they choose and when will be a question of their constitutional role and the divisions of power within the legal system.

'Information' refers to the kinds and forms of information needed to evince the factual situation before the court. This information might be information available to both administrative authority and to the court, only to the administrative authority, or only to the court. Nevertheless, it is important to think about the kinds of information generated in connection to the Directive, and required by the Directive, as this will impact upon the ways in which uncertainty is made manifest. For example, judicial decisions about the admissibility of evidence will be hugely significant in determining whether or not a challenge to an authorisation under the HD can succeed.

'Process' refers to the ways in which decisions are made and challenged, including the interplay between judge, judicial hierarchies and precedent, and the rules concerning cross-examination of witnesses, reviews on paper only and the like. In respect of uncertainty, we could see a tendency to hide uncertainty behind a focus on the process followed in an appropriate assessment, or a judicial process which encourages or discourages the expression of doubt in documents provided to the court.

Finally, there is the question regarding the level of scrutiny being applied. This can be seen as being made up of merits versus legality review, but it is more and less than this distinction. As will become apparent across the course of this book, the merits or legality review distinction is not particularly illuminating in revealing how much a court will explore scientific information to unearth uncertainty, and what they will do if uncertainty is found. The level of scrutiny is twinned with the subject of that scrutiny. For example, can/ does/ should a court examine the qualifications of one providing expert evidence? It is better to think of scrutiny broadly, as being a question of the degree to which a judge will examine an assessment made by others. This less precise but more comprehensive approach to scrutiny will be especially useful in reading the country chapters.

In sum, when thinking about the role that science plays in the adjudication of disputes arising under the WBD and the HD, keeping in mind these four perspectives is useful. However, a more fundamental point must also be kept in mind. Judicial conclusions around uncertainty in science is not a binary choice – either a judge identifies some uncertainty in 'the science' or they conclude the science is perfect and absolute. Rather, uncertainty may be present, and even acknowledged, but rendered peripheral by a variety of judicial techniques. The courts might, for instance, in cases of uncertainty demand not an improved scientific assessment, but rather expect a more robust expression of reasons from an administrative authority. In such cases, it is not the uncertainty *per se* which renders the challenge to an authorisation successful, it is the administrative authority's inadequate response to the fact of that uncertainty in terms of the way they have justified their decision which becomes legally problematic. One of the key lessons of this book, and we discuss this in more detail in the conclusions, is the range of techniques that courts employ to transform (deliberately or otherwise) what on its face appears to be a scientific question of the scope of risk, into a legal question about the process followed, the logic of an administrative authority's approach, or the adequacy of their reasons. Scientific uncertainty shapes these outcomes, but is not front and centre of how the court itself is reasoning.

Finally, before moving onto the Directive itself, it is useful to emphasise that courts will utilise scientific information in different ways. The courts have different methods for how to assess the presence or absence of uncertainty in such information. Two prominent pieces in this vein are Ky and Fisher et al. Both produce an analysis of the methodology of handling of scientific information in court in their respective contexts. Thus, Ky argues that there are four different means by which a court can handle scientific questions: 'merits review bodies adopt four approaches when evaluating scientific reliability: the Qualifications, Weight of Opinion, Peer Review and Methodology Approaches'.[8] It is of critical importance to note that Ky restricts his gaze here to merits review bodies. Second, Fisher et al examine the handling of scientific information in the context of United States Environmental Protection Agency decision-making:

> In overseeing scientific challenges, the courts appear to serve as a necessary irritant, encouraging the agency to develop much stronger administrative governance and deliberative decisions on complex science-policy issues. Conversely, in developing stronger decision-making processes, the resulting agency efforts have a reciprocal, positive impact on the courts' own standards for review. The courts and agencies thus appear to work symbiotically through their mutual efforts on the establishment of rigorous analytical yardsticks to guide the decision process.[9]

In both of these instances the focus is on a single jurisdiction, and this means that there is a single legal culture in the background. In the case of this book as a whole, these different methodologies will feed into judicial decision-making around people, process, information and scrutiny, and will vary according to jurisdiction.

How can we draw all of these threads together into a framework which allows us to make sense of the legal landscape in this book? Elsewhere, one of us has argued that adjudication in its function as a power-broker dividing decision-making powers between players in the wider administrative state, is often at its most powerful in situations where adjudicators (and particularly judicial adjudicators) are required to define the scope of their own powers.[10] Thus, in judicial review, what constitutes legitimate judicial action in such cases is decided *not* by statutory provisions, but on the basis of precedent developed by the judiciary themselves. Similarly, the fact/ law distinction which is of such critical importance in common law administrative law is not determined on the basis of a series of statutory tests, but is instead a judicial pronouncement of the limits of judicial power. When we think about this self-determined power-broker effect in respect of the four questions above, it becomes clear that how an adjudicator envisages the role that science should play in answering these questions is of central importance, and that, in turn, depends on two things: what they think science *is* and how central they think that should be to answering the question at hand. To put this another way, keeping in mind the four potential perspectives above, and the fundamental points raised about judicial techniques and evasions, and methodology for

[8] Patrick Ky, 'Qualifications, Weight of Opinion, Peer Review and Methodology: A Framework for Understanding the Evaluation of Science in Merits Review' (2012) 24 *Journal of Environmental Law* 207, abstract.

[9] Elizabeth Fisher et al, 'Rethinking Judicial Review of Expert Agencies' (2015) 93 *Texas Law Review* 1681.

[10] Emma Lees, 'Allocation of Decision-Making Power under the Habitats Directive' (2016) 28 *Journal of Environmental Law* 191, 201.

engaging with information, means that in each case the court has a lot of power to define not only the effects of the WBD and HD in terms of the natural world, but also to define and determine where true power sits in this system.

B. Effect, Spectrum and Categorical Tests

The above analysis shows how the significance of uncertainty will vary according to the kind of question a court is answering. However, this is not the whole picture. The precise wording of the legislation under consideration also impacts upon the consequences emerging from uncertainty. This is apparent from the badger example above in the different treatment which the 'effects' and 'significant' tests require. However, we have a methodological challenge here. In exploring 'the Directive', we have to acknowledge in our comparative perspective that there is not *one* version of the Directive. There are multiple interpretations of the Directive in the CJEU and in the courts of Member States. How can we explore the tests in the Directive 'in itself'? This is the very challenge addressed by one of us in exploring the value of comparative methodology in respect of context-driven law.[11] There it was argued that in order to build a map which demonstrates the hills and dales of the legal landscape emerging in respect of a particular environmental question – here, the WBD and HD – it is necessary to accept that a map cannot reproduce the entirety of the landscape it surveys. The very usefulness of maps is that they are a simplification with only important details retained. The goal of comparative law in this sense is to retain the important details to allow the contour lines of the landscape to reveal the overall picture. In other words, when, in this chapter, we discuss the Directive itself, we are aware of the fact that these terms, as we attempt to categorise them, will not be categorised in the same way in all of the jurisdictions we look at. The categories here do not exist in the jurisprudence. Instead, they are included here to help the reader navigate through the country studies, and we return to them in conclusion to see how the range of norms in the Directive plays a role in shaping the outcomes we see in subsequent chapters.

Here, we examine the text of arts 6 and 12 HD for the purposes of demonstration. Article 6(2)–6(4) is reproduced, followed by a table categorising some of the different terms within the Directive according to whether they are 'cause', 'spectrum' or 'categorical' questions. These terms, and their significance, will be explained below. This is followed by the text of art 12 and a similar table. It should be acknowledged here also that readers may very reasonably disagree with the categorisation of some terms here. Indeed, the example of 'natural' and 'wild' is instructive for whether a court sees these as terms which exist on a spectrum (more or less natural) or as a category (natural state) will influence how they reason in

[11] Lees (n 2) 42.

a particular case. Nevertheless, demonstrating the broader point, that there are different types of assessment, is the 'takeaway' from this discussion.

> 2. Member States shall take appropriate steps to avoid, in the special areas of conservation, the deterioration of natural habitats and the habitats of species as well as disturbance of the species for which the areas have been designated, in so far as such disturbance could be significant in relation to the objectives of this Directive.
>
> 3. Any plan or project not directly connected with or necessary to the management of the site but likely to have a significant effect thereon, either individually or in combination with other plans or projects, shall be subject to appropriate assessment of its implications for the site in view of the site's conservation objectives. In the light of the conclusions of the assessment of the implications for the site and subject to the provisions of paragraph 4, the competent national authorities shall agree to the plan or project only after having ascertained that it will not adversely affect the integrity of the site concerned and, if appropriate, after having obtained the opinion of the general public.
>
> 4. If, in spite of a negative assessment of the implications for the site and in the absence of alternative solutions, a plan or project must nevertheless be carried out for imperative reasons of overriding public interest, including those of a social or economic nature, the Member State shall take all compensatory measures necessary to ensure that the overall coherence of Natura 2000 is protected. It shall inform the Commission of the compensatory measures adopted.
>
> Where the site concerned hosts a priority natural habitat type and/or a priority species, the only considerations which may be raised are those relating to human health or public safety, to beneficial consequences of primary importance for the environment or, further to an opinion from the Commission, to other imperative reasons of overriding public interest.

Table 1 Categories of Terms in Art 6 of the Habitats Directive

Cause	Categorical	Spectrum
Avoid	Natural	Appropriate
Effect	Plan	Beneficial
Implications	Project	Coherence
Ascertained	Assessment	Significant
Affect	Opinion	Directly
Obtained	General public	Necessary
Protected	Solutions	Likely
Deterioration	Compensatory	Adversely
Disturbance	Measure	Integrity
	Considerations	Negative
	Human health	Imperative
	Public safety	Overriding
	Environment	

Article 12 HD states:

> 1. Member States shall take the requisite measures to establish a system of strict protection for the animal species listed in Annex IV (a) in their natural range, prohibiting:
>
> (a) all forms of deliberate capture or killing of specimens of these species in the wild;
> (b) deliberate disturbance of these species, particularly during the period of breeding, rearing, hibernation and migration;
> (c) deliberate destruction or taking of eggs from the wild;
> (d) deterioration or destruction of breeding sites or resting places.
>
> ...
>
> 4. Member States shall establish a system to monitor the incidental capture and killing of the animal species listed in Annex IV (a). In the light of the information gathered, Member States shall take further research or conservation measures as required to ensure that incidental capture and killing does not have a significant negative impact on the species concerned.

Table 2 Categories of Terms in Art 12 of the Habitats Directive

Cause	Categorical	Spectrum
Impact	Natural	Strict
Destruction	Range	Protection
Disturbance	Prohibiting	Significant
Killing	Deliberate	Negative
	Specimens	
	Wild	
	Breeding	
	Rearing	
	Hibernation	
	Migration	
	Sites	
	Place	

Let us consider these categories in more detail. In the first category, questions of causal link, the evidence before a decision-maker – whether that be court, tribunal, national panel or administrative agency – is to demonstrate a causal or other connection between a relevant act and a relevant outcome. In general terms such questions can be predictive, or responsive to facts as they have played out. Both are present in the Directive. Thus, responsive questions here include assessment as to whether a particular agency has 'obtained' the opinion of the general public or not. To show they have obtained it, they will need to present information demonstrating actions from some period in the past. This is not a scientific question (see later for a definition of scientific evidence) but it is a question demanding *evidence* taken from historical events to prove a link between those actions, and a categorical outcome.

Some of these are predictive, such as 'avoid' or 'affect' where the decision-maker is required to review evidence before them to establish whether, on the balance of that evidence, a particular act *will* lead to a particular categorical outcome. The question in all these cases is to show the connection between the act (adoption of a plan, for example) and the outcome (adverse effect on the integrity of a site). To prove the connection, evidence will need to be produced which can assign causation on the balance of probabilities, or will need to predict causation on the balance of probabilities.

Second, there are categorical questions. The issue here is not whether something has or will happen, but whether something which has or will happen meets a certain categorical test. Is this coffee finished, or not? The status of being finished, or not being finished, is an either or. It does not exist on a spectrum – if a coffee is nearly finished, it is not, by definition, finished. One can spend a good deal of time constructing a definition by which one judges that status of coffee being finished or not, but once a definition is reached, the coffee will determinatively be either finished or not finished. Similarly, one may spend a good deal of time deliberating on what constitutes 'public opinion' but once you have decided a definition of public opinion for the purposes of the legislation, something cannot be more or less public opinion, just as it cannot be more or less 'a measure', 'a plan' or 'a project' once those terms have a definition.

But this can be contrasted, finally, with spectrum issues. These are questions where even once defined, as a matter of linguistics, something can *still* be more or less. It makes sense to say something is 'more' significant or 'less' significant, however one defines significant. Similarly, it makes linguistic sense to say something is more or less likely, even once likely has been defined. There is a threshold issue: this is likely (if it is not likely, it must, by definition, be *un*likely), but even once you've got over the threshold into likely, in a collection of events some will still be *more* likely, and others will still be *less* likely, even if all are likely. Similarly, two events, both significant, can be more or less significant than each other. Something cannot be 'more' a plan than another thing which is also a plan. A coffee cannot be 'more' finished. If it is finished, it is finished, and all other finished coffees are equally finished.

Why does this categorisation of questions matter? It matters because different approaches are needed to adjudicate on these questions, and the judgment required kicks in at different points. There is also an important difference in respect of whether scientific information forms part of the definition of something – eg habitat, or whether it is used to answer the question – eg significant, because then the role of the science will shift. In one it is being used to define a question of law, and in another it is being used to define question of fact. As a result, uncertainty in the evidence as to these questions will have different consequences. Uncertainty as to whether a site is a breeding site will, if the precautionary principle is adopted, mean that no development can take place. Uncertainty as to *how* significant the impact will be is irrelevant if the threshold of significance is passed. In the first situation, scientific uncertainty must somehow be overcome to make a decision.

In the second, the uncertainty can persist without affecting the decision-making process. This is why understanding the different kinds of test in the Directive is so important to understanding how courts handle uncertainty and where and why that varies.

C. 'Science'

Consideration of the operation of the Directive is not the end of the story, however. We need to complete the other side of the picture. What is scientific information, and scientific uncertainty? Again, let us commence this discussion with an example. The role which different understandings of the idea of 'science' may play is exemplified (on one reading) by the arguments concerning anthropogenic climate change. Whilst much, if not most, climate change denial emerges for entirely different reasons, for some, the denial of anthropogenic climate change is (on the accepted consensus amongst the majority of qualified researchers) to misunderstand of what scientific 'proof' consists. On this version of the climate change sceptic model, science is not science 'worthy of the name' if it is not generative of absolute facts, certain and unchallenged and unchallengeable.[12] (Of course, there are some for even the most 'absolute' of scientific propositions – such as the roundness of the Earth – are unproven on the basis that the evidence, on their view, is artificially constructed.) On the more mainstream model which accepts the anthropogenic nature of the current changes in climate, science is not understood as representing a search for that which is absolutely proven (even if the scientific consensus does see this as a proven fact). Rather, it engages a process, the results of which gives a deeper understanding of natural and other phenomena, but which at no point makes a claim to absolute truth.[13] Some people who disagree about climate change disagree, at least in part, over what it means for 'science' to constitute evidence.[14]

The traditional paradigm for the use of scientific information in court is as forming discussion centred around competing scientific reports, provided by each side to a dispute, with a judge sitting as adjudicator attempting to navigate potentially unfamiliar terminology and concepts to establish, on the balance of

[12] Chalmers makes a similar point about 'creation science', emphasising that arguments regarding the inclusion of such in education syllabuses is at its heart an argument about whether or not creation science is *science*, the implication being that if it is 'science' then it is automatically on a higher level of rightness or quality which would justify its inclusion. Alan Chalmers, *What is this Thing Called Science*, 4th edn (Open University Press, 2013) Introduction.

[13] This argument, taken to its apotheosis, renders scientific knowledge on a par with myth, giving it a force derived not from the quality of the information obtained or the processes followed, but by the faith of those hearing the information on the nature of the source. See Chalmers, *ibid*, considering Paul Feyerabend, *Against Method: Outline of an Anarchistic Theory of Knowledge* (New Left Books, 1975).

[14] Jasanoff discusses the distinction between science as immutable knowledge, and science as a fair source of evidence in the judicial process. Jasanoff (n 1).

probability, which version of 'the science' is correct.[15] Thus, in medical negligence cases, the appropriateness of a particular treatment is demonstrated by reliance on scientific evidence on one side, and contested by reliance on scientific evidence on the other.[16] On such a model, scientific uncertainty is an intractable problem for good governance of environmental problems because of how challenging it is for courts to assess the scientific reports before them (although one may cogently argue that the same is true of medical negligence cases).[17] Decisions to prefer one scientific account over another may be made more or less on a whim, particularly when a judge is contending with their own lack of scientific understanding, and making their decision through the assistance of advocates, where similarly few, if any, will fully understand 'the science' they are interrogating.[18] The interaction between science and law in environmental problems, if understood in this way, does not sit easily within an adjudicatory paradigm of opposition and argumentation.

When we come to environmental problems, therefore, the paradigm shifts, if not by necessity, then at least often in practice. It does so not because there has been a conscious decision to treat science differently in such adjudication in many cases, but rather because the overall governance framework within which adjudication is taking place is different. The additional layers that emerge from, for example, local decision-making authorities, nature conservation bodies, independent and partisan scientific reports, public consultation, and expert and non-expert or specialist and non-specialist judges mean that the 'simple' choice between expert report A and expert report B melts away into a complex web of decision-making powers.[19] The different way science is handled in environmental cases then is not only a consequence of more or less certain science; but also of more or less expertise embedded within a decision-making process; of more or less experience with the science, and, most importantly, is a consequence of the *type of decision* being made. The differences come too from the purpose to which the scientific information is being put. And this directs us to the fundamental point: science in court is not an immutable 'one single thing' but rather an enormous range of forms of information tackling a range of issues and kinds of questions at different stages in

[15] In this traditional paradigm, lack of specificity can result in either vilifying or romanticising either group of actors, judges or scientists, David S Caudill and Lewis H LaRue, *No Magic Wand: the Idealization of Science in Law* (Rowman and Littlefield, 2006) 50.

[16] On judges' difficulties with medical controversies see, eg, Jaakko Taipale, 'Judges' Socio-Technical Review of Contested Expertise' (2019) 3 *Social Studies of Science* 310.

[17] See, eg, Emma Lees and Ole W Pedersen, *Environmental Adjudication* (Hart Publishing, 2020). See also Elizabeth Fisher, *Risk, Regulation and Administrative Constitutionalism* (Hart Publishing, 2007) and David Bazelon, 'Science and Uncertainty: A Jurist's View' (1981) 5 *Harvard Environmental Law Review* 209.

[18] Pasky Pascual et al, 'Making Method Visible: Improving the Quality of Science-based Regulation' (2012) 2 *Michigan Journal of Environmental and Administrative Law* 429, 433.

[19] This can be so to the extent that the decision-making becomes co-productive, Maria Lee and others, 'Techniques of Knowing in Administration: Co-production, Models, and Conservation Law' (2018) 45 *Journal of Law and Society* 427.

a decision-making process. The variation in legal questions asked and scientific answers given, and the dynamics they create, is thus extensive, as the chapters in this book elucidate.[20]

The consequence of this is that our approach to what science is cannot ignore its multiplicities. Furthermore, whilst there are boundaries – not everything is 'science', the boundaries around the concept of science are essentially contested. When persons disagree in their approach to defining 'science' often neither will be wrong. That science is problematic to define is well-documented in the literature,[21] but to consider it thus an *essentially contested* concept adds an additional dimension to the general definitional approach. In relation to such terms, ideological standpoints will create constellations of meaning, which give a (more) static definition to such terms and allegiances to build in respect of such meanings. In law, these allegiances will build in adjudication taking account of the judge's own conceptions of the limits of their power, of rule of law, and of science.[22] This does not mean that law is politics in a simplistic sense, but rather that the judicial perception of the proper judicial role influences what different judges understand to be 'science' (and therefore without their province) and 'law' or legally-relevant, and therefore within the scope of their decision-making power. And in doing so these differences do not mean that one or other judge is wrong because it is not possible to ring-fence scientific information.

The parts which follow develop this argument further. First, section III, A explores the potential definitions and roles of science in law and adjudication. Second, section III, B considers further the consequences of the blurriness of these definitions for adjudication. Finally, this section concludes by emphasising that the essentially contested nature of 'science' means that the definitions and approach to scientific information adopted by a court can be seen as as much an expression of other values within their personal or constitutional code, as it is about their view on the value of scientific information to environmental decision-making.

III. Defining 'Science'

Policy-makers and government officials, especially in recent times, habitually describe themselves as following 'the science' or being led by or engaging with 'science'. As is well-documented, this is a meaningless notion, for 'science' is not an immutable and static wellspring of 'facts' which dictate action. Rather, we can

[20] Lena Wahlberg, *Legal Questions and Scientific Answers: Ontological Differences and Epistemic Gaps in the Assessment of Causal Relations* (Lund University, 2010) 15, 16, 27.

[21] Chalmers (n 12).

[22] As Tegner Anker and others have put it, 'The expertise reflected in the composition of the courts as well as the experience gathered by the courts may thus be important factors for their scope of review in practice'. Helle Tegner Anker et al, 'The Role of Courts in Environmental Law – a Nordic Comparative Study' [2009] *Nordisk Miljörättsliga Tidning* 9, 17.

pick apart aspects of 'science' and handle them in different ways. Attempts to do this abound in the literature. The purpose of this section is not to provide a full articulation of these attempts. Rather it is designed to draw the link between some of these definitions and the consequences each may have in terms of how science is handled in court.

A. Forms of Information

First, we can think about defining science from the perspective of the kind of information it generates. For example, the distinction between scientific information, that is to say information generated through the application of scientific method of proof based on evidence generated in order to test a theory by experiment, or through calculations and interrogations of data generated outwith a laboratory environment; and the opinions of experts based on their own understanding, experience and interrogations of that scientific information, already shows how 'science' in court may mean at least two radically different forms of information.

The first (hypotheses proved though the scientific method) may well produce scientific fact, at least in the long run, albeit that in the short run peer opinion, scientific consensus and repeated proofs may be absent such that the line between information and opinion can become narrow. The second however does not make a claim to generate facts *per se* but rather leaves questions of judgement to those who are in a good position to make such judgements. A useful way to think about these two forms of science is to consider how one would test for quality: in the first case, quality will be determined by the reliability of the methodology and the robustness of the conclusions; in the second, it will be the level of expertise of the opinion-giver, and to a certain extent the degree of peer engagement and agreement with the opinion they are giving. It would also involve examination of what kinds of scientific information of the first sort were used in allowing the expert to generate their opinion, and thus an examination of the quality of the first kind of information is relevant too in the second case. In some situations of course, a highly qualified expert, who is respected in their field, may be asked to provide a scientific opinion in the almost complete absence of scientific information in the first sense.[23] In such cases, the opinion is the scientist's best guess, in effect, but that guess is premised upon expertise in general. When we talk about science in court, therefore, there will be (at least) a tension between science as the information generated through experimentation, and science as the opinion (well-founded or otherwise) of scientists.

[23] In such cases, the legally relevant limits of scientific information have become central, revealing the epistemic gaps between the fields, and scientific information in the first sense cannot offer answers, Wahlberg (n 20) 15.

Of course, in some cases, and often in instances of legal dispute, the distinction between what is opinion and what is a more or less proven/provable fact on the basis of information gleaned through the scientific method, is narrow or indistinguishable. The definition, explicit, or more likely implicit, of sufficient expertise, sufficiently robust mythology, large enough data set, and the like, will all influence the degree to which any adjudicator examining/following this scientific information should be bound to follow the conclusions presented and accept them as true.[24] The more novel or uncertain a situation, the more both the qualifications of the expert, and their personality and mode of presentation will be relevant in swaying the minds of those assessing whether to follow their opinion or not.[25] In environmental law, novelty will be a particularly prominent characteristic, from which emerges uncertainty. Thus, when we think about how courts engage with science, it is apparent from this discussion that whether or not the question relates to information of the first sort, or opinion of the second, or both, will change how adjudicators will engage with scientific information and it will shape the court's approach to deference, the exercise of discretion, the important or relevance of cross-examination, etc.

B. The Role of Information

A second approach to considering questions of definition of science is to look not at the kind of information, but at the role the information is playing. In doing so, however, we must be cautious. As Fisher has argued, the monolithic conception of science which sees it as something entirely 'other' from the legal process, sitting outwith governance and regulation, is a false one: 'whilst the sciences are distinct areas of disciplinary practice, their relationships with law are close and entangled. This understanding of the sciences as "Science" threatens the development of effective and valid in environmental law'.[26] This viewpoint is also shared by Jasanoff in the quotation at the opening of this chapter.[27]

Rather, Fisher emphasises that 'scientific practice' (that is the *process* of generating both information and expertise), whilst recognisable as a process, is never purely 'scientific' in the sense of being free from the cultural influences of other processes of enquiry and reasoning.[28] To give a simple example, to decide what constitutes a legitimate form of experimentation, a scientist will not merely engage

[24] Or, at the least, as something to be relied upon, I Koskinen, 'Defending a Risk Account of Scientific Objectivity' (2020) 71 *The British Journal for the Philosophy of Science* 1187, 1192ff.

[25] Lees (n 10).

[26] Fisher (n 3) 750.

[27] See also eg Pascual et al (n 18) 434; Sheila Jasanoff, *Science at the Bar: Law, Science and Technology in America* (Harvard University Press, 1997) 42; and Bruno Latour, *Science In Action* (Harvard University Press, 1987).

[28] Fisher (n 3); Pascual et al (n 18) 436; and Paloniitty and Kotamäki (n 7) 284.

with the question of the most accurate ways in which to uncover the information sought. Rather, they will also engage with ethical and regulatory issues in shaping their experiments and data handling. The 'scientific conclusion' is therefore part scientific method and part ethical and legal duties.[29]

There are also different forms of scientific practice which interact with regulation in different ways – as Fisher identifies – from the identification of an environmental 'problem' or challenge, to being an integral part of regulatory standard-setting and processes.[30] In this book we are focussing on the second of Fisher's categories (regulatory science). Specifically, we consider the subset of regulatory science which operates in relation to individual decisions, which takes on a distinctively different character from the scientific practices engaged in the other two categories thanks to the necessity for specificity.

C. Disciplinary Framework and the Scientific Method

Finally, we may define science categorically. That is, any information which emerges within a particularly disciplinary framework (ie by 'scientists) is 'science'. Thus, information derived from biology as a discipline is scientific. For interdisciplinary subjects, such as geography, it may be near impossible to draw the boundary line between that which emerges scientifically and that which emerges in other ways.

This means that we may have (at least) four approaches to defining what science is: one which looks at information, one which looks at expertise, one which looks at its role in decision-making, and one which looks at discipline. All are often correct, and yet cannot claim to being always right. For this reason, we can consider science as an essentially contested term, open to differential definitions in instant cases and particularly susceptible to those definitions going unarticulated but rather presumed.

However, the label scientific is not value-free. Deciding that information is scientific information has legal consequences – as shown also in the rest of this book. First, it puts that information into a separate category (ie kettling on Fisher's language,[31] even if in practice the black boxing of this information is not clear cut, as the chapters in this book show). Second, it imbues that information with both a stature and normative force, and with the values of the decision-maker who has used their own institutionalised but idiosyncratic value-system to label or treat the information as being 'scientific'. The effect of defining information as science or not is therefore both categorical and expressive of unarticulated values, rendering the relationship this specific regulatory role, and the political/ legitimising role (Fisher's third category) a complex one. As much as 'scientific conclusion' is a

[29] Fisher et al (n 9) 1716; David Kriebel et al, 'The Precautionary Principle in Environmental Science' (2001) 109 *Environmental Health Perspectives* 871.
[30] Fisher et al, *ibid.*
[31] *ibid* 755–60.

product of an inferential process including value choices, recognition and definition of 'science' by decision-makers hinges on certain value-systems too.[32]

D. Essentially Contested

Having examined the potential definitions or approaches to understanding what science is and is not, the only real conclusion to reach is that science is essentially contested. That is that it can never be given a clear and single meaning. Why this matters has already been hinted at – it means that decision-makers import their own ideological pre-conceptions in their approach to defining science even though the process is an ostensibly a-political one. The notion of essentially contested concepts emerges from Gaillie[33] and its importance in the political context is emphasised by Freeden amongst others.[34] This concept helps to explain what the consequences of the fuzzy boundaries around science means for adjudication. One of us, together with Shepherd,[35] have argued elsewhere that analysis recognising the constellations of meaning which can emerge in relation to essentially contested terms, and the ideologies which drive the formation of these constellations, are hugely significant in relation to the operation of law and to judicial practice.[36] Indeed, the ideologies that underpin the judicial role, which are themselves made up of essentially contested ideas, such as separation of powers (a theme which emerges again and again in the chapters of this book) are, on our argument, a central part of what makes up legal culture. Recognising that these concepts shape how courts reason with science is critical to the project of understanding context and contingency in the practice of environmental regulation.[37]

Fisher et al take this argument specifically in respect of climate change, arguing that '[t]he concept of resolving cases "well" will ultimately depend on the constitution and traditions of a particular legal culture and legal order, where such orders and cultures are a complex mass of "essentially contested" concepts'.[38] In discussing these issues there is concern always about ideology as part of political decision-making, for the term itself brings with it connotations of illegitimate action, and of

[32] Wendy Wagner et al, 'Misunderstanding Models in Environmental and Public Health Regulation' (2010) 18 *New York University Environmental Law Journal* 293, 308.

[33] Walter Bryce Gallie, 'Essentially Contested Concepts' (1955/1956) 56 *Proceedings of the Aristotelian Society* 167.

[34] See Michael Freeden, *Ideologies and Political Theory: A Conceptual Approach* (Oxford University Press, 1998); Michael Freeden, 'The Morphological Analysis of Ideology' in M Freeden et al (eds), *The Oxford Handbook of Political Ideologies* (Oxford University Press, 2013) 115–34; and Michael Freeden, *The Political Theory of Political Thinking: The Anatomy of a Practice* (Oxford University Press, 2013).

[35] Emma Lees and Edward Shepherd, 'Morphological Analysis of Legal Ideology: Locating Interpretive Divergence' (2018) 10 *Journal of Property, Planning and Environmental Law* 5.

[36] *ibid* 8ff.

[37] See also, Jeremy Waldron, 'Is the Rule of Law and Essentially Contested Concept (in Florida)' (2002) 21 *Law and Philosophy* 137.

[38] Elizabeth Fisher et al, 'The Legally Disruptive Nature of Climate Change (2017) 80 *MLR* 173, 197, citing Gaillie (n 33).

action beyond the rule of law, but as Lees and Shepherd explain, ideology need not be pejorative in this sense. Instead, 'we theorise ideologies as comprising morphologies of essentially contested concepts, with different ideologies seeking to fix the meanings of these concepts in competing ways to exert control over the terms by which the political is understood'.[39] As an explanation of how science is handled in court, the emphasis on the intimacy of connection between definitions, acknowledgement of uncertainty, politics and power, is key. It is also unavoidable:

> First, ideology can be understood as a ubiquitous form of political thinking which seeks to fix the meanings of essentially contested concepts and whose influence on the legal framework can therefore be systematically analysed by considering variations in how such concepts are interpreted in various legal contexts. Second, ideology in this sense forms an important part, but is distinguishable from, the wider notion of legal culture. Finally, understanding this can help in the analysis of judgments in areas of high levels of administrative discretion, such as planning and environmental law, as it helps us to understand how any particular judge sees the role of the court in its wider political context.[40]

In sum, science can legitimately be understood to mean a range of different things. When a court is required to decide on the scientific evidence provided to them, in order to meet the tests established by the CJEU regarding the probative value of scientific evidence, they will need to first decide which range of evidence before them is properly 'scientific'. In so doing, they will divide power between themselves, administrative authorities, expert consultants and the public at large. In deciding the delineation between the scientific and the political, courts keep in mind explicitly and implicitly a range of constitutional and other values, such as their own conception of separation of powers or rule of law. Thus, in each case, the decision as to what is scientific information, and what is not, and therefore whether uncertainty is scientific, or not, is determined not by some pre-determined and objective standard, but by an on-going and developing dialogue between context, understandings of the judicial role, and constitutional principles in any particular jurisdiction.

E. Uncertainty

Thus far, this section has focussed its attention on scientific information generally. But a focus of this book is how scientific *uncertainty* in particular is handled. Thus, the final element of the argument presented here is this. What constitutes science is contested. As a result, what constitutes uncertainty in that science is also contested. It is contested on two fronts – what is uncertainty; and what is science. Uncertainty, *just as much as science* is a construct which is both extra-legal (where the scientific information or the expert opinion tells us that uncertainty exists) and

[39] Lees and Shepherd (n 35).
[40] *ibid* 14.

legal, whereby a legal forum decides whether the uncertainty which exists is legally significant or not.[41] The role of burden of proof in this is obviously critical, but similarly any uncertainty or absence there will also be utilised in more or less open ways by a court to determine spectrum tests, for example. Thus 'if true' an effect predicted may certainly be significant, but if there is some doubt over its effect, whilst a court may decide that on the balance of probabilities there will certainly be an effect, there is no need to determine the exact probability of scale to take account of the impacts for the purposes of judging significance.

In different chapters of this book, the meaning of uncertainty here is explored and explained in different ways. Significantly, it is also a legal decision which is made by judges in a number of the cases considered here. However, in wrapping up this discussion of the meaning of scientific information, we return briefly to the categories of uncertainty explained by Regen et al.[42] We included this article in the package sent to our authors. This unpacking of the notion of uncertainty therefore helped to form each of our understandings of uncertainty as we considered the case law.[43] In that article, the authors explain that in the context of conservation in particular, uncertainty comes in two main forms: epistemic (ie uncertainties around the knowledge we have) and linguistic (ie uncertainties emerging from the vague notions we use to express ourselves in the context of conservation). These main forms of uncertainty are themselves further divisible. Epistemic uncertainty can emerge though, 'measurement error; systematic error; natural variation; inherent randomness; model uncertainty; and subjective judgement'.[44] Linguistic uncertainty, by contrast, can emerge through 'vagueness, context dependence, ambiguity, indeterminacy of theoretical terms, and underspecificity'.[45] In the context of this book we regularly encounter linguistic uncertainty. The courts themselves will regularly encounter epistemic uncertainty. These different kinds of uncertainty too will impact the way in which courts overcome or operate within the uncertainty.

IV. Conclusions

Taken together, this framework of analysis drives our comparative approach. It seeks to combine what we have discussed here: analysis of the Habitats Directive

[41] Ky (n 8) 213; Preston (n 7) 139–40.

[42] Helen M Regan et al, 'A Taxonomy and Treatment of Uncertainty for Ecology and Conservation Biology' (2002) 12 *Ecological Applications* 618.

[43] Preston in particular explores this taxonomy in detail. See chapter 14 of this volume. This chapter does not repeat that excellent analysis, but rather is designed to provide some context for the chapters which follow in this respect.

[44] Regan et al (n 42) 619.

[45] *ibid* 621.

itself, and understandings of science and scientific uncertainty. In recognising the contextual dependency of the role of science, our first task in putting together this book was to emphasise that variation between countries, to be worthy of exploration, must be examined against a framework which reveals the underlying dynamics which may be pushing that variation. Analysing the difference between the Finnish treatment of the 'significant' test and the UK treatment of the existence or otherwise of 'effects' from the plan or project for the protected sites may not be a fruitful exercise unless we also consider the kind of tests these are, where they fit within the Directive, and how they are shaped by the court's approach to scientific information. Any difference in treatment may be a result of variations in approaches to constitutional and environmental principles, of legal culture and procedural ecosystems more generally, or, more likely, it will be a consequence of the fact that these are different legal tests in terms of what they ask an adjudicator or administrator to decide. Treating the WBD and the HD as a single whole does not work. The role for environmental and constitutional principles in negotiating the existence or otherwise of 'effects' engages a scientific paradigm wholly different from that which judges the significance of those effects.

Let us bring the two planks of this analysis together – that is, the conclusion that science is an essentially contested term thus engaging ideology as a sub-element of legal culture; and the conclusion that the WBD and HD establishes tests which engage people, process, information and scrutiny in different ways, all under the heading of adjudication on the basis of scientific information. In the absence of a recognition of the dynamics within the Directive itself, the framework would have been less revealing in terms of what it means for the role that constitutional and environmental principles may play: in the absence of an understanding of the nature of 'science' and scientific information as part of legal process, and in particular of the consequences of its essentially contested nature, the analysis would have been unable to capture all the avenues through which legal culture can affect legal decision-making.

As a result, this chapter has raised a number of issues with which our country authors will be to a greater or lesser extent contending. First, any decision that information relevant to a decision is 'scientific' is necessarily attributing to that information characteristics determined by the decision-maker's own understanding of what science consists. That understanding will be personal but to an even greater extent it will be institutional, generated, at least in part, by the legal culture operating in that state. Second, the text of the Directive itself does not proceed on the basis of a homogenous understanding of how scientific information and uncertainty may be relevant to the decision-making process at hand. In some cases scientific information appears to be determinative, and in others, it is merely one factor in a decision but because what science *is* also varies, there is a 'double pressure' of variation, which is particularly interesting as a matter of comparative analysis. Finally, it means that when utilising scientific information as generative of a regulatory outcome, the boundary between the regulatory in this sense, and the political becomes very fine.

These conclusions are not only methodologically significant for the analysis carried out in this book, and for emphasising the importance of specificity in such analysis. The conclusions reached here are also substantive. They show not only the potential strength of the impact of prevailing legal culture on how environmental law works in practice – that is, its contingent nature – but going beyond existing arguments in that respect, also shows its pervasive effect on extra-legal considerations when they are filtered through the legal process. The cultural baggage which is associated with the law imbues itself not only into the mode of expression, content and technique used in the extra-legal context, but also in the very understanding of what, in this case, science is.[46] This has enormously significant implications for power structures developed in relation to environmental law, for it must be emphasised that whilst the majority of environmental law may not happen in court, the arbiters of these power structures, of the nature of the legal culture, and of their own and others powers, are the courts,[47] and so it is important when thinking about context and contingency to remember that sometimes this context is not a matter of historical coincidence, but rather of judicial creation.

[46] For discussion of 'cultural baggage' emerging through legal structures, see Lees and Pedersen (n 17).
[47] *ibid.*

2

The European Court of Justice's Approach to Scientific and Factual Matters in the Habitats Directive – Between Uncertainty and Precaution

AGUSTÍN GARCÍA-URETA

I. Introduction

As presented in chapter one, the Habitats Directive (HD) generates several layers of scientific uncertainties, which are for national authorities to assess and for national courts to adjudicate upon. Seized by both national courts in preliminary rulings, and by the European Commission in infringement proceedings, the Court of Justice of the European Union (CJEU or the Court) has delivered a significant volume of decisions in respect of the HD.

Broadly speaking, the CJEU engages with, and indeed demands, robust *certainty* regarding scientific information in national decision-making. This is based on the language of the HD itself, and is further supported by the precautionary principle. As this chapter will show, this certainty-focused jurisprudence has a hugely influential role in constraining and directing national courts (and public authorities) in their interpretation of the HD. Furthermore, in establishing a standard of certainty of knowledge, the CJEU, in effect, precludes judicial discussion about diverse scientific methodologies and practices at Member State level by emphasising the need for consensus. How this plays out in Member State courts is shown in the ensuing chapters. The present chapter discusses the CJEU's case law and how it has handled the HD-related uncertainties.

Three key areas stand out in this landscape: first, the classification-declassification of sites; second, the protection of individual species; and third the environmental assessment requirement in the case of plans or projects affecting Natura 2000 sites. In examining these three areas, it will be shown that the focus of the CJEU is on preserving the objectives of the HD regarding both the protection of Natura 2000 sites and of fauna and flora species. In so doing, the CJEU gives guidance as to what constitutes scientific certainty and how it can be managed within the decision-making systems and processes engendered by the HD.

A. Science Setting the Pace of EU Biodiversity Rules

The HD (together with the Wild Birds Directive (WBD) is one of the pillars of EU biodiversity law and of the so-called Natura 2000 network, the flagship of this normative system.[1] Both Directives have generated a growing number of cases before the CJEU concerning their application and interpretation, more particularly with respect to the designation of sites; the avoidance of alterations or deteriorations; the rules on the assessment of activities affecting Natura 2000 sites; and more recently (and intensively) of those regarding the protection of specific species. In one way or another, the consideration of scientific aspects and factual data has a relevant role in these judgments.[2] The 13-year lapse between the two directives reflects certain differences in their texts and in the approach undertaken by the EU. Whilst the WBD lacks any definitions, the HD includes 14, some of them subdivided into several limbs. Both 'conservation status' and 'favourable conservation status' (FCS), are central to the HD. Second, the WBD contains general mandates, arguably owing to the debate in the 1970s regarding EU environmental purview. However, the CJEU made it clear that the WBD is a provision 'which *does not proclaim a programme orientation* but contains a *mandatory legal rule* to which the legal systems of the Member States must conform' (emphasis added).[3] This applies mutatis mutandis to the HD. This Directive lays down a more elaborated text in terms of principles, but also in relation to the procedural stages involved in classifying protected areas. It sets out key rules on the assessment of plans and projects, firmly based on the precautionary principle, albeit with open-ended grounds that may finally serve to authorise the realisation of such plans and projects despite their significant repercussions on the environment.[4] The protection of species, based on general prohibitions and a limited list of exceptions, remains largely parallel in both Directives. This mechanism too is permeated by the precautionary principle. Thus, the first point to note is that despite the different forms of legal test established by the wording of the HD, as considered in chapter one, the approach to navigating both the individual parts, and the Directive as a whole, is firmly precautionary.

The Directives incorporate legal concepts which are difficult to interpret and apply which have generated a number of cases before the CJEU (and its national

[1] For full details of these Directives, see the Table of Legislation or the Introduction. See Ann Cliquet, 'EU Nature Conservation Law: Fit for Purpose' in Marjan Peeters and Mariolina Eliantonio (eds), *Research Handbook on EU Environmental Law* (Edward Elgar, 2020) 265–79.

[2] C-308/08 *Commission v Spain* [2010] ECR I-04281, ECLI:EU:C:2010:281.

[3] C-507/04 *Commission v Austria* [2007] ECR I-05939, ECLI:EU:C:2007:427 [88].

[4] HD, art 6(4).

counterparts) such as FCS, 'most suitable territories', 'small numbers', 'natural range' or 'appropriate assessment' to name but a few. Hence, science becomes key to unravel their meaning. Science is expressly mentioned in both Directives, for instance in the case of the adaptation of their Annexes or of the calls to scientific knowledge to implement them.[5] The position of science and ecological matters vis-à-vis the other considerations that may be involved in their application is addressed in the Directives. According to art 2 WBD, Member States

> [S]hall take the requisite measures to maintain the population of the species referred to in Art 1 at a level which corresponds in particular to ecological, scientific and cultural requirements, while taking account of economic and recreational requirements, or to adapt the population of these species to that level.

A literal reading would give the impression that science-based matters can be tempered by the others subsequently mentioned in that provision. However, such conclusion is not correct. As the CJEU has held, art 2 WBD does not constitute 'an autonomous derogation'[6] from the system of protection established by the WBD and, consequently, the ecological requirements do not have to be balanced against the other requirements. Although the HD does not include a parallel rule to that laid down in the WBD, a similar conclusion can be reached in view of art 2(3): 'Measures taken pursuant to this Directive shall take account of economic, social and cultural requirements and regional and local characteristics'. In both cases the principle of non-regression, expressly enshrined in art 13 WBD and in the notion of FCS in the HD, reinforces the position of environmental (science-based) requirements vis-à-vis other extraneous considerations. The second key point, then, is that in employing the precautionary principle, the CJEU recognises that this principle guides, or indeed perhaps dictates, decisions, not only about how to interpret and apply the rules, but also about how to interpret the facts and evidence underpinning those decisions.

B. The CJEU's Role: Interpretive Guidance, Setting Criteria and Embedding Precaution

i. *Expounding Complex Rules and Specifying Substantive Criteria*

To commence the examination of the relevant jurisprudence, it must be emphasised, first, that the CJEU delivers judgments based on rules.[7] These rules include numerous science-related notions (eg long-term natural distribution, endangered

[5] HD, arts 4(1), 5(1), 16(3)(a), 18 and 19. WBD, arts 2, 15 and 16.

[6] C-44/95 *The Queen v Secretary of State for the Environment, ex parte Royal Society for the Protection of Birds* [1996] ECR I-03805, ECLI:EU:C:1996:297 [25].

[7] Treaty on European Union [2016] OJ C202/1, art 19.

species' natural range, 'in the wild' and 'adverse effects'). Their interpretation is not, however, trouble-free. In the last few decades the CJEU has deciphered the meaning of different rules and laid down consistent criteria. However, repeated questions submitted to Luxembourg by its national counterparts insist on matters that prima facie could be regarded as unambiguous after such rulings. It appears, therefore, that although the continuous dialogue between national and EU jurisdictions is certainly key for unravelling the complexities of rules, the case law reflects the difficulties faced by the national judiciary. As has happened with other environmental directives (eg the Environmental Impact Assessment Directive), the CJEU's case law both elaborates on, and, in line with a teleological approach to interpretation, 'makes the most of' the relevant provisions. For example, the environmental assessment mechanism in art 6(3) HD has been interpreted widely, and the open-ended nature of certain mandates (eg the duty to avoid deterioration or alterations in art 6(2) HD),[8] the lack of definition of 'natural range' in art 12(1) HD,[9] or the different criteria for the grant of a derogation (eg art 16 HD) have been overcome by reference to, and reliance on, the environmental goals of the HD. In other words, the Court has eluded a formalistic understanding of the relevant rules by filling in possible lacunae in the HD. This stance is consistent with the 'autonomous' nature of EU standards,[10] but of course, in equal measure, challenges traditional national approaches. The broad interpretations of the CJEU are a consequence of the Court's assessment as to its role within the Union and its own approach to interpretation.

Second, the CJEU demands updated, 'rigorous' or the 'best' scientific grounds either to: (a) classify a Natura 2000 site, be it an special protection area (SPA), a site of Community importance (SCI) or a special area of conservation (SAC); (b) conclude that an 'appropriate' environmental assessment has in effect been carried out; (c) justify that certain measures do compensate for biodiversity loss; or (d) that an exception circumventing a ban protecting a species is justified (eg to allow its capture or killing in 'small numbers').[11] Although the CJEU has not explained the difference between 'best' and 'rigorous', such criteria may be regarded as interchangeable and in any case very demanding for those conducting deeds that may affect Natura 2000 areas or species and for national authorities, including the judiciary, who are empowered, as the case may be, to annul the corresponding authorisations owing to a deficient knowledge-based decision. Those tests and criteria essentially run in harmony with the ambitious protection

[8] Directive 2011/92/EU of the European Parliament and of the Council of 13 December 2011 on the assessment of the effects of certain public and private projects on the environment [2012] OJ L26/1. See, for instance, C-504/14 *Commission v Greece*, ECLI:EU:C:2016:847.

[9] C-88/19 *Asociația 'Alianța Pentru Combaterea Abuzurilor' v TM*, ECLI:EU:C:2020:458.

[10] C-900/19 *Association One Voice and Ligue pour la Protection des Oiseaux v Ministre de la Transition Écologique et Solidaire*, ECLI:EU:C:2021:211.

[11] See C-304/05 *Commission v Italy* [2007] ECR I-07495, ECLI:EU:C:2007:532 and C-674/17 *Luonnonsuojeluyhdistys Tapiola Pohjois-Savo – Kainuu ry v Risto Mustonen*, ECLI:EU:C:2019:851.

objectives established by the HD, in particular the attainment of a FCS for habitats and species, or the completion of a 'coherent' network of protected sites. The standards of scientific knowledge established, therefore, sit in line with the teleological approach to the interpretation of normative terms.

ii. The CJEU, Burden of Proof and the Precautionary Principle

A closer look at the CJEU's articulation of such standards manifests that, contrary to criticisms asserting that European judges seem 'quite at ease when manipulating scientific data',[12] the CJEU respects basic burden of proof rules.[13] Insufficient factual or scientific evidence from the Member States can legitimately tip the balance in favour of habitat and species protection because this is precisely the stated objective of the EU as expressly enshrined in the HD. There is no known case of a CJEU's request under the Rules of Procedure of an expert's report to provide a different opinion on the matter.[14] Thus, in assessing whether the burden of proof has been met, the CJEU's standard of review requires checking the reliability and accuracy of the evidence brought forward by the parties,[15] this being apparent in cases regarding deterioration of habitats, environmental assessments under art 6(3) HD, or those involving species protection. Thus, the CJEU delivers its rulings exclusively in view of the evidence submitted to and by the referring court.[16]

However, and notably, the precautionary principle has also been invoked by the CJEU to ease the Commission's burden of proof, particularly regarding the likelihood of adverse effects and the duty to carry out an environmental impact assessment (EIA) under art 6(3) HD, or in cases regarding alterations or deterioration of natural habitats and species in Natura 2000 sites under art 6(2). Therefore, whilst the Commission must demonstrate 'to a sufficient legal standard' that a Member State has not adopted the appropriate protective measures to prevent the operational activities of projects from giving rise to deterioration of habitats, in order to establish an infringement, the Commission does not have to prove a causal relationship between a certain activity and the adverse effects on the integrity of habitats and species. It is enough for it to establish the existence of a 'probability or risk' that that activity may give rise to such an effect.[17] Thus, a similar approach

[12] Eve Truilhé Marengo, 'How to Cope with the Unknown' in Charles-Hubert Born et al (eds), *The Habitats Directive in its EU Environmental Law Context* (Routledge, 2015) 345.

[13] See Agustin García-Ureta, *EU Biodiversity law* (Europa Law Publishing, 2020) 103–106.

[14] Rules of Procedure of the Court of Justice [2012] OJ L 265/1, art 70.

[15] See Mariolina Eliantonio, 'The Impact of EU Law on Access to Scientific Knowledge and the Standard of Review in National Environmental Litigation: A Story of Moving Targets and Vague Guidance' (2018) 27 *European Energy and Environmental Law Review* 115–24.

[16] C-387/15 and C-388/15 *Orleans v Vlaams Gewest* ECLI:EU:C:2016:583 [38] and [55]; and C-441/17 *Commission v Poland* ECLI:EU:C:2018:255 [179].

[17] *Commission v Poland, ibid* [158]; *Commission v Greece* (n 8) [29]; C-141/14 *Commission v Bulgaria*, ECLI:EU:C:2016:8 [58]; and C-461/14 *Commission v Spain*, ECLI:EU:C:2016:895 [77].

must also be applied in national courts in cases where a decision has been alleged to have risks for the environment.

II. The Classification of Natura 2000 Sites

The 'coherence' of the Natura 2000 network largely, albeit not only, depends on the most complete possible designation of SPAs and SACs (formerly SCIs). The approach of the CJEU to this most fundamental of issues markedly underpins the operation of the Directive. This section examines the CJEU's approach to scientific information within the designation process by examining the role of scientific (and other) criteria; the key cases considering this question; and the process of de-classification. As indicated in the ensuing paragraphs, science is critical, and, in many places, scientific uncertainty is overcome by reliance on precaution.

A. Only Scientific Criteria

The case law has made it clear that only scientific data are relevant for both the designation and territorial extent of protected areas. The decision is therefore cast as purely scientific.[18] The requirement that science be the only relevant factor takes precedence over any type of location (eg urban areas),[19] or economic activity (eg ports). In the *Royal Society for the Protection of Birds* case, which concerned the designation of an SPA and its effects on a port, the British Government argued that economic concerns could be considered in selecting a site. The CJEU held that, in the context of art 4 WBD, considered as a whole, economic requirements could not 'on any view' correspond to a general interest 'superior' to that represented by the ecological objective of the WBD.[20] Therefore, it was only the ornithological criteria (number and variety of birds), in conjunction with other natural factors (eg the natural boundaries of wetland ecosystem) that determined the extent of SPAs.[21] Allegations arguing that certain territories were not the most appropriate because of existing disruptions and disturbances have also been rejected in so far as those territories met the conditions of the WBD and because their classification as SPAs guaranteed precisely the conservation of certain species of birds.[22]

[18] C-290/18 *Commission v Portugal*, ECLI:EU:C:2019:669.
C-97/17 *Commission v Bulgaria*, ECLI:EU:C:2018:28 (concerning SPAs).

[19] There are 11,000 Natura 2000 sites within, or partly within, cities, representing 15% of the total area of the Natura 2000 network. European Commission, 'EU Biodiversity Strategy for 2030. Bringing Nature Back into our Lives' (2020) 380 final, 13, fn 52.

[20] *The Queen v Secretary of State for the Environment* (n 6) [30].

[21] C-418/04 *Commission v Ireland* [2007] ECR I-10947, ECLI:EU:C:2007:780 [138].

[22] C-209/04 *Commission v Austria* [2006] ECR I-02755, ECLI:EU:C:2006:195 [41].

A parallel approach has been followed under the HD in the landmark case *First Corporate Shipping*.[23] According to the CJEU, the Commission should have at its disposal a comprehensive inventory of sites which, at national level, have an ecological interest relevant to the objective of conservation of natural habitats and wild fauna and flora pursued by the HD. This is the only possible way to achieve the objective of maintaining or restoring the natural habitat types and species' habitats at an FCS in their natural range. Such a range could, however, be situated on either side of one or more internal EU borders. Therefore, a Member State is not entitled, even if there are economic, social and cultural requirements, or regional and local characteristics, to exclude sites which are of ecological interest at national level relevant to the conservation objective. In other words, the 'coherence' of the Natura 2000 network depends on its completeness and this can only be achieved if all areas complying with the scientific criteria laid down in the WBD and HD are designated.

The basic principles for zone classification are therefore clear. However, their actual application is not untroubled. Instructive here in terms of how scientific evidence is generated is the case of the Inventory of Important Bird Areas in the European Community (IBA). This is used as the main reference for determining the possible existence of SPAs, even though the IBA has no official status in the EU or in the Member States. The CJEU has emphasised that the IBA contains scientific evidence which makes it possible to assess compliance by the Member States. Consequently, the IBA, although not legally binding on the Member States concerned, is used by the CJEU because of its recognised scientific value in the field. The prominent role of the IBAs has been enhanced by the institutions in charge of their drafting (eg universities)[24] and, paradoxically, also by Member States' inability to refute their findings in successive cases before the CJEU.[25]

Unlike the WBD, however, the criteria for the designation of sites under the HD are more complex, as they involve habitats and species of EU importance mentioned in the corresponding annexes to the HD. The approval of the list of SCIs and finally SACs includes a three-stage mechanism, beginning in the Member States (SCIs), continuing in the Commission (definitive list of SCIs) and ending again in the Member States (SACs). To undertake the selection of sites, the Commission published three reference documents: (1) the standardised Natura 2000 data form (which also includes the criteria for site selection); (2) the map of the EU biogeographical regions; and (3) the Interpretation Manual for EU habitat types.[26] Unlike the WBD, there is not a designation guide as represented

[23] C-371/98 *The Queen v Secretary of State for the Environment, Transport and The Regions, ex parte First Corporate Shipping* [2000] ECR I-09235, ECLI:EU:C:2000:600.

[24] C-235/04 *Commission v Spain* [2007] ECR I-05415, ECLI:EU:C:2007:386.

[25] C-355/90 *Commission v Spain* [1993] ECR I-04221, ECLI:EU:C:1993:331 [27].

[26] Commission Decision 97/266 of 18 December 1996, concerning a site information format for proposed Natura 2000 sites. See also Commission Implementing Decision 2011/484/EU, of 11 July 2011, concerning a site information format for Natura 2000 sites.

by the IBA, but the Interpretation Manual already mentioned has provided the Member States with information regarding annex I HD,[27] which concerns priority habitat types requiring the designation of SACs. The Commission has also successfully relied on documents edited by the Member States to show the limited number of proposed SCIs.[28]

B. 'Natural' Evolution of Sites and the CJEU's Approach to their Declassification

More instructive in terms of the ways in which scientific evidence, read with a precautionary mindset, and applied to tests with in-built precautionary standards, is the approach of the CJEU to de-classification. The HD includes a provision whereby the Commission shall periodically review the contribution of Natura 2000 towards achievement of the objectives set out in arts 2 and 3.[29] In this context, a SAC may be considered for declassification where this is warranted by 'natural developments' noted because of the surveillance provided for in the HD.[30] Leaving aside the debatable question of whether this provision does in fact allow for a declassification of a SCI or SAC, this may only happen if, owing to natural causes, the sites have lost the characteristics that motivated their classification. Whilst this may be in principle clear, determining the factual conditions supporting a declassification may not be straightforward. According to the CJEU in the *Cascina* case, where the results of the surveillance give rise to the conclusion that those criteria can irretrievably no longer be met, the Member States 'must of necessity' make a proposal for the adaptation of the list of SCIs seeking to make that list meet those criteria once again.[31]

> Thus, when a site on the list of SCIs is definitively no longer capable of contributing to the achievement of the objectives of the Habitats Directive and, accordingly, it is no longer warranted for the site to remain subject to the provisions of that directive, the Member State concerned is required to propose to the Commission that the site be declassified. If that State were to refrain from proposing its declassification, it could continue to use resources in vain to manage that site which would prove to be of no use to the conservation of natural habitats and species. In addition, keeping sites in the Natura 2000 network which no longer definitively contribute to the achievement of those objectives does not meet the quality requirements of that network.[32]

[27] European Commission, 'Interpretation Manual of European Union Habitats' (April 2013), available at https://ec.europa.eu/environment/nature/legislation/habitatsdirective/docs/Int_Manual_EU28.pdf.

[28] C-71/99 *Commission v Germany* [2001] ECR I-05811, ECLI:EU:C:2001:433 and C-220/99 *Commission v France* [2001] ECR I-05831, ECLI:EU:C:2001:434.

[29] HD, art 9.

[30] *ibid*, art 11.

[31] C-301/12 *Cascina Tre Pini Ss v Ministero dell'Ambiente e della Tutela del Territorio e del Mare*, ECLI:EU:C:2014:214 [27].

[32] *ibid* [28].

The cause that eventually would justify a declassification is the irremediable non-compliance with the HD's criteria. However, there appears to be a gap between, on the one hand, the situation of 'irremediable' non-compliance and, on the other, a 'natural evolution' leading to such a state of affairs, which is the criterion used by the HD. Does it imply that such irretrievable non-compliance can be reached by actions that are not natural (eg a road plan or an airport extension)? This question is pertinent as the land owner in the *Cascina* case requested the declassification of an SCI because he understood that the progressive increase in air traffic from an airport had caused, over time, the progressive environmental degradation of his land. It should be noted that the ruling did not openly contest causes of irremediable deterioration *alien* to a natural evolution. In other words, the ruling would accept other deeds that directly or indirectly could lead to a 'natural' deterioration of a site, albeit the original and efficient cause could not be 'natural'. The judgment is not as clear (and consistent) as the opinion of the Advocate General who indicated that the reference for a preliminary ruling provided two grounds: (1) it was claimed that the operation of the airport had caused environmental degradation on the land in question; and (2) the land was in an area intended for 'commercial and industrial' development, but as she noted neither circumstance was due to natural developments. Therefore, the Advocate General concluded that neither warranted the declassification of the land as part of an SCI.[33]

The CJEU was arguably aware that the criterion of irremediable environmental deterioration required further clarification ('not all degradation of a site on the list of SCIs justifies its declassification').[34] According to the CJEU, it must be a deterioration which should make the site

> *irretrievably* unsuitable to ensure the conservation of natural habitats and of the wild fauna and flora or the setting up of the Natura 2000 network, so that that site can *definitively* no longer contribute to the achievement of the objectives of the directive (emphasis added).[35]

No further elaboration can in principle be found in the judgment. It could be argued that it is not for the CJEU to adopt a complete canon on this matter. However, as it has allowed the declassification of SCIs, an option not expressly envisaged in the HD, it should have required a more elaborated justification. It is true that the CJEU referred to other guarantees that are included in the HD (eg art 6(2) and the duty to avoid alterations) but these do not necessarily clarify the central concern, which is the notion of deterioration making a site irretrievably unsuitable to meet the objectives of the HD. Indeed, the CJEU also held that '[t]he failure of a Member State to fulfil that obligation of protecting a particular site *does not* necessarily justify the declassification of that site' (emphasis added).[36] Admittedly, the case law

[33] *ibid*, Opinion [43]–[44].
[34] *ibid* [31].
[35] *ibid* [30].
[36] *ibid* [32].

could be interpreted as saying that only if such state of irreparable environmental deterioration is reached can a declassification take place. The use of adverbs 'irretrievably' and 'definitively' in a key section of the ruling undoubtedly raises the burden of proof required to activate the mechanism laid down in the HD. In the meantime, recourse to art 9 HD would necessarily remain unavailable. The existence of a relationship between, on the one hand, a degree of deterioration which makes the continuation of a site irremediably unsuitable and, on the other hand, the legal consequence of declassification, is a legal question. Whether a cause is natural or unnatural, could be understood as a scientific question.

III. Species Protection and the Assessment of their Favourable Conservation Status

A. CJEU's Cruising Waters of Contradictory Data

The second pillar of the HD concerns the protection of individual species. Following a standard approach in international law,[37] the HD includes general prohibitions but also a series of limited exceptions that can be invoked by the Member States to bypass them.[38] Most of the cases that are submitted before the CJEU, particularly those initiated by the Commission under the infringement procedure, require careful consideration of facts and of reports supporting alleged breaches of the HD or conversely of compliance with its provisions. This is not a trouble-free undertaking. An illuminating example can be found in the *Doñana case* which concerned the designation of an area as a SCI (Doñana Natural Park)[39] owing to the presence, inter alia, of the Iberian lynx, a highly endangered species. However, during the period ranging from the submission of the site as a proposed SCI to the Commission and its formal designation, the Spanish authorities adopted a project for the upgrading of a country road running alongside the edge of the area and cutting through a section of it. The Commission concluded that the upgrading had been carried out without all necessary measures being taken to prevent a negative impact on the environment and on the Iberian lynx.[40] The CJEU was confronted with a difficult task as different and conflicting reports delivered by public authorities, non-governmental organisations and consultancies supported either the absence of appreciable effects on the species or the existence of such consequences.

[37] Agustin García-Ureta, 'Nature Conservation' in Emma Lees and Jorge E Viñuales (eds), *Oxford Handbook of Comparative Environmental Law* (Oxford University Press, 2019) 460–88.

[38] Hendrik Schouckens and Kees Bastmeijer, 'Species Protection in the European Union: How Strict is Strict?' in Charles-Hubert Born et al (eds), *The Habitats Directive in its EU Environmental Law Context* (Routledge, 2015) 56–70.

[39] This is not to be confused with Doñana National Park, albeit both form Doñana's natural space.

[40] However, it failed to allege the lack of EIA under art 6(3) HD.

Although the CJEU finally concluded that there was no breach of the HD, its ruling contains contradictory statements reflecting its uneasiness in reaching a conclusion in so-called 'technical' cases that may encumber its position as a court of first and final instance in infringement cases and preliminary references. The CJEU noted that the upgrading had led to an increase in traffic, particularly private cars, travelling at higher speeds.[41] It also held that it was common ground that, in general, linear transport infrastructures could constitute a real barrier for certain species referred to in the HD and, by thus fragmenting their natural range, promote endogamy and genetic drift within those species. However, the measures adopted by the Spanish authorities to discourage speeding had brought about a significant reduction in traffic speed on the road at issue. Nevertheless, illustrating the contradictory findings on which the judgment was based, the CJEU also noted that, according to a report, the average speeds recorded on that road exceeded the authorised speed limits.[42] The CJEU also took into consideration other aspects that could be regarded as alien to the subject matter of the case, as it observed that a census report stated that thanks to the capture of 13 specimens and to a breeding in captivity programme, two cubs were born to broodstock originating respectively from two populations that included the Doñana regions. In the CJEU's opinion that represented 'a step forward in the preservation of current genetic variability'.[43] However, this reasoning is not convincing. The fact that a number of cubs were born *in captivity* did not bear any relation to the substance of the case (ie whether the upgrading was affecting or was likely to significantly affect the population of the Iberian lynx *in the wild*). Perhaps being conscious of its bitter conclusions, the CJEU found it necessary to add that although certain elements in the case-file appeared to indicate that the 'overall situation' of the Doñana site might have not been satisfactory in the light of the requirements relating to conservation of the Iberian lynx, in particular, because of the 'relatively high number' of cases in which animals of that species had died due to being struck by a vehicle, the evidence before the CJEU was not sufficient for it to find that the project for upgrading the country road, accompanied by the corrective measures, constituted in itself intervention of a kind which placed the Iberian lynx on the site concerned 'in danger of extinction' and which, accordingly, risked seriously compromising the ecological characteristics of that site.[44]

The judgment illustrates a short-sightedness in the CJEU's approach when dealing with the contested road and arguably a lost opportunity (at that time) to have reinforced the role of the precautionary principle. The protection requirements of a highly endangered species should have required a proper balance of data regarding the killings and their distribution during different years. The case therefore

[41] *Commission v Spain* (n 2) [24].
[42] *ibid* [43]–[44].
[43] *ibid* [35].
[44] *ibid* [52].

provides a relatively rare example of the CJEU addressing different uncertainties in the factual position and attempting to reach its own conclusion on such matters, rather than deciding that since uncertainty was present, the right legal course was dictated by precaution.

B. Species Protection and FCS: CJEU's Approach to Dissecting its Components

i. *General Remarks on Derogations and FCS*

As indicated above, FCS is one of the key notions in the HD.[45] According to art 1(i) HD, 'conservation status' of a species means the sum of the influences acting on the species concerned that may affect the long-term distribution and abundance of their populations within the European territory of the Member States.

FCS contemplates the evolution of a species in the long term. However, it does not provide any conclusive clues as to its meaning. Some precision is derived from the definition in art 1(i) HD in so far as it includes a reference to the '*foreseeable* future'. In other words, there must be a non-faraway possibility of determining what the evolution of a species will be like. Member States are entitled to waive certain prohibitions established to protect species.[46] However, the HD makes the grant of derogations conditional on the maintenance of the FCS of the species concerned.[47] Hence, FCS is a necessary pre-condition.[48] In addition, the HD requires a balance of interests that may be difficult to appraise: on the one hand matters requiring a present or even an immediate solution (eg public health or public safety, serious damage, in particular to crops);[49] and, on the other, the protection of a species population within favourable margins avoiding a likely regression (eg a minimum number of specimens necessary to ensure the long-term viability of the species).

The CJEU has dealt with two cases affecting the same Member State (Finland) and species (wolf) in which the role of FCS has been central.[50] Broadly speaking, the CJEU has closely followed the text of the relevant rules and the conditions they lay down, especially to derogate from the relevant prohibitions. It has also endorsed a stricter approach to the central question of whether the FCS could

[45] FCS depends on three intertwined criteria (art 1(e) HD):

> population dynamics data on the species concerned indicate that it is maintaining itself on a long-term basis as a viable component of its natural habitats, and – the natural range of the species is neither being reduced nor is likely to be reduced for the foreseeable future, and – there is, and will probably continue to be, a sufficiently large habitat to maintain its populations on a long-term basis.

[46] HD, art 12.

[47] *ibid* art 16.

[48] C-508/04 *Commission v Austria* [2007] ECR I-03787, ECLI:EU:C:2007:274 [115].

[49] HD, arts 16(1)(b) and (c) respectively.

[50] See Suvi Borgström, 'Legitimacy Issues in Finnish Wolf Conservation' (2012) 24 *Journal of Environmental Law* 451–76.

be nevertheless achieved despite the application of a derogation. Reviewing these disputes is problematic as they require proper examination of factors such as: (1) the population of the species concerned and its evolution; (2) the area affected by the derogation; and (3) the precautionary principle as the guardian of the whole system of derogations. The CJEU has placed the protection of species above other considerations. While the thresholds it has set are not impossible to comply with, they certainly require substantial scientific basis ('rigorous' and 'best'). Arguably, the most problematic matter is the addition of further notions to those already mentioned in the HD so that instead of assisting in the proper evaluation of a waiver, the additional tests may actually encumber this procedure. It also remains to be seen whether the criteria laid down by the CJEU may be applied to other species with much larger populations in a particular Member State.

ii. FCS and Pre-Emptive Hunting of Species

In the first *Finnish wolves* case the CJEU noted that, according to a report drafted by the Finnish authorities, the number of individuals capable of reproduction was less than 50, which was the threshold below which there was an 'acute danger' of extinction. Finland had at that time 20 breeding pairs.[51] These data were invoked by the CJEU to declare that the conservation status of the wolf in Finland was 'not favourable'.[52] However, it then noted that granting an exception would still be possible provided it was not such as '*to worsen the unfavourable* conservation status of those populations or to prevent their restoration at a favourable conservation status' (emphasis added).[53] This assertion was not made in a vacuum (albeit in view of the existing population it was questionable). Based on the Commission's guidance document on the strict protection of animal species of EU interest,[54] the CJEU concluded that it could not be excluded that the killing of a limited number of individuals would have no impact on the maintenance of the wolf population at an FCS in its natural range. In the CJEU's view, such an exception would be 'neutral' for the species in question.[55] Nevertheless, the CJEU held that permits authorising the hunting of a fixed number of wolves in a well-defined geographical area without: (a) relying on an assessment of the conservation status of the species; (b) providing a clear and sufficient statement of reasons as to the absence of a

[51] Finnish Management Plan for the Wolf Population in Finland (2005). C-342/05 *Commission v Finland* [2007] ECR I-04713, ECLI:EU:C:2007:341, Opinion of the Advocate General, conclusions and [46].

[52] *Commission v Finland, ibid* [27].

[53] *ibid* [29].

[54] European Commission, 'Guidance Document on the Strict Protection of Animal Species of Community Interest under the Habitats Directive 92/43/EEC' (Final version, February 2007), available at https://ec.europa.eu/environment/nature/conservation/species/guidance/pdf/guidance_en.pdf.

[55] *Commission v Finland* (n 51) [29].

satisfactory alternative; and (c) specifically identifying the wolves causing serious damage which could be killed, were contrary to art 16 HD.[56]

Arguably, the CJEU's reasoning was motivated by several matters. First, the definition of 'conservation status' is interpreted as 'the sum of the influences acting on the species concerned that may affect *the long-term distribution* and abundance of its populations' (emphasis added).[57] This long-term perspective could have justified the conclusion that the measures adopted by the Finnish authorities were not such as '*to worsen the unfavourable* conservation status' of those populations. This was reinforced by the very text of art 16(1) HD. Second, the CJEU balanced the capture of a limited number of specimens against a broader issue (ie, a long-term conservation objective). Last, but not least, the CJEU held that the Commission had not adduced enough evidence as required by art 258 Treaty on the Functioning of the European Union.

This decision demonstrates that whilst there was indeed a significant level of uncertainty, that uncertainty was managed by taking a long-term view which appeared, on the facts of the case, to overcome uncertainty. By accepting the frame of reference as the foreseeable future, rather than the immediate present, the Court delineated which uncertainties in the data could engage the precautionary principle and which could be safely managed within the CJEU's assessment of the administrative decision of the Finnish authorities.

iii. Raising the Threshold for the Adoption of a Derogation: A Three-Tier Test Shrouded in the Precautionary Principle

Twelve years later a new case related to wolf-hunting in Finland gave the CJEU the opportunity to set out more stringent criteria.[58] Unlike the first case, wolves were at that time 'seriously endangered' as their populations had declined to approximately 120 specimens.[59] The importance of the case lies in the tests set out by the CJEU regarding: (1) the level of proof required to sustain that a derogation could achieve the objectives pursued; (2) the study of alternatives; (3) the role of FCS; and (4) the safeguard represented by the precautionary principle. These criteria are not watertight compartments but the essentials which, jointly, may justify a derogation from a general ban which includes the killing of certain specially protected specimens. Above all, the judgment provides a more elaborated reasoning in comparison with the first. It also reflects the complexity of the matters underpinning the adoption of a derogation as the above tests incorporate other

[56] *ibid* [29].

[57] HD, art 1(e).

[58] *Luonnonsuojeluyhdistys Tapiola Pohjois-Savo* (n 11). See Jan Darpö, 'The Last Say? Comment on CJEUs Judgement in the *Tapiola* Case (C-674/17)' (2020) 17 *Journal for European Environmental & Planning Law* 117–30.

[59] Lowest level in 2013.

sub-matters which, in conjunction with the precautionary principle, do indeed represent an important hindrance for granting a derogation under art 16 HD.

a. Justification of the Objectives Pursued and 'Rigorous' Data

As regards the test set out to determine the adequacy of the derogations to achieve the objectives pursued by the national authorities, the CJEU has held:

> [I]t is for the national authority to support, on the basis of rigorous scientific data, including, where appropriate, comparative data on the effects of hunting for population management purposes on the conservation status of wolves, the proposition that hunting for population management purposes is actually capable of reducing illegal hunting to such an extent that it would have a net positive effect on the conservation status of the wolf population, whilst taking account of the number of derogation permits envisaged and the most recent estimates of the number of wolves taken illegally.[60]

This test consists of three different intertwined limbs. First, there must be a 'rigorous' scientific foundation. The CJEU did not refer to the 'best' scientific data, but to 'rigorous' data. Although these two adjectives may be interchangeable,[61] the choice of the latter term was arguably conscious as the judgment refers to the 'best' data in a section regarding the existence of alternatives.[62] Given that the aim is to establish the correlation between *specific* measures and the *objectives* pursued, it may not be possible to establish beforehand whether they will actually be achieved, as science may not necessarily be able to provide unambiguous certainty and dispel any possible doubt. Second, such data must support that the hunting of specimens will have a 'net positive effect' on their conservation status. It is interesting that the CJEU did not refer to FCS in this section of the judgment. It rather included a notion that is nowhere mentioned in the HD. However, the CJEU held that FCS was a necessary precondition in art 16.[63] Third, the CJEU requires the national authorities to consider the number of derogation permits envisaged. This is necessary, as the system of derogations under art 16 HD is an exception to general prohibitions. Hence, the particular-general relationship in this provision forces the national authorities to specify a number of specimens to hunt and whether this guarantees the attainment of the objectives pursued.

b. The Study of Alternatives in the Light of the 'Best' Scientific Evidence

The study of alternatives is another matter that must be considered by the national authorities before adopting a derogation.[64] The case law under the WBD has

[60] *Luonnonsuojeluyhdistys Tapiola Pohjois-Savo* (n 11) [45].
[61] See, for instance, *Association One Voice and Ligue pour la Protection des Oiseaux* (n 10) [30].
[62] *Luonnonsuojeluyhdistys Tapiola Pohjois* (n 11) [51].
[63] *ibid* [55].
[64] See C-10/96 *Ligue Royale Belge pour la Protection des Oiseaux ASBL and Société d'Études Ornithologiques AVES ASBL v Région Wallonne* [1996] ECR I-06775, ECLI:EU:C:1996:504.

already made it clear that as long as there are reasonable alternatives, the Member States are not entitled to have recourse to a derogation.[65] The same approach is followed in the HD. Logically, it is not for the CJEU to justify the reasonableness of an alternative but to review whether it is acceptable. Uncertainty in predictive data becomes a significant problem in judging such alternatives. According to the Court, a derogation may only be granted where there is no alternative measure that could achieve the objective pursued in a satisfactory manner, whilst complying with the prohibitions laid down in the HD. This test is stated in the *second Finnish* case in the following terms:

> [I]t is for the competent national authorities, when authorising derogation permits such as those at issue in the main proceedings, to establish, taking account in particular of the best relevant scientific and technical evidence and in the light of the circumstances of the specific situation in question, that there is no satisfactory alternative that can achieve the objective pursued, in compliance with the prohibitions laid down in the Habitats Directive.[66]

Unlike the previous test seen above, the judgment emphasises that the national authorities must consider the 'best' scientific evidence. As in the case of the 'appropriate' assessment, the CJEU demands state-of-the-art knowledge. Second, the authorities are under a duty to contemplate 'any' satisfactory alternative. There is a further matter inextricably linked to the search for alternatives as the CJEU has held that the mere existence of an illegal activity (eg poaching) 'or difficulties associated with its monitoring' cannot be sufficient to exempt a Member State from its obligation to ensure the safeguarding of species protected under annex IV HD. In other words, the grant of a derogation depends, first and foremost, on the effectiveness of the measures adopted by the national authorities to fulfil the general obligations laid down in the HD.[67]

c. FCS, Range of Species and Number of Specimens: Has the CJEU Adopted an Unsurmountable Test?

In both of the cases above, one of the key matters was whether FCS was guaranteed. One of the features derived from the later judgment is the elaboration of various notions related to FCS. This may certainly help to explain the complexities of this term, but paradoxically may add further complexity to the assessment of whether FCS is preserved. By reference to its definition, the CJEU held that a derogation must be based on criteria described in such a manner as to ensure the long-term preservation of the dynamics and social stability of the species in

[65] *ibid.*
[66] *Luonnonsuojeluyhdistys Tapiola Pohjois-Savo* (n 11) [51].
[67] See C-473/19 and C-474/19 *Föreningen Skydda Skogen, Naturskyddsföreningen i Härryda, Göteborgs Ornitologiska Förening v Länsstyrelsen i Västra Götalands län, B.A.B., U.T.B*, ECLI:EU:C:2021:166.

question.[68] Assuming that the CJEU carefully selected its wording, it is noticeable that whilst the first term ('population dynamics') is indeed mentioned in the definition of FCS, social stability is nowhere cited. It could be argued that both are inextricably linked to the notion of long-term basis, social stability being a subdivision of a general term. However, 'population dynamics' also depends on other factors, such as the natural range of a species and in particular the number of specimens that may be hunted. As regards the former aspect, the CJEU did not depart from the definition of FCS and held that the assessment of a derogation on the territory of a local population must 'determine its impact on the conservation status of the population concerned *on a larger scale*'.[69] This finding is logical as the conservation status of a population at national or biogeographical level depends on the cumulative impact of different derogations affecting local areas. In other words, the local-national-biogeographical liaison manifests that such three levels depend on each other. In doing so, the CJEU also seeks to avoid a patchwork of derogations which, in isolation, could have a limited impact on FCS, although this would not be the case if they were considered cumulatively.

However, the analysis of art 16 HD involved a greater degree of complexity, raising the burden of proof to satisfy by the national authorities and correspondingly the standard of review by the judiciary. According to the CJEU, the number of specimens affected by a derogation cannot entail 'the risk of a *significant negative impact* on the structure of the population in question, *even if it is not, in itself, detrimental* to the maintenance of the populations of species concerned' at a FCS in their natural range (emphasis added).[70] Unlike FCS, this criterion, nowhere mentioned in the HD, involves a *likelihood* of effects qualified by a *degree* of detriment. In addition, the judgment avoids laying down the relationship between FCS and this new criterion, albeit it appears that the latter is a pre-condition. It remains to be seen whether it may help to clarify that of FCS or whether FCS is to be substituted by a more general criterion based on risk.

Arguably, the Achilles' heel of the decision adopted by the Finnish authorities, which was turned down by the CJEU, rested on three issues: (1) they had not demonstrated that the 'only way' of achieving the objectives pursued was to authorise a certain level of wolf hunting for population management purposes; (2) they had not provided a clear and sufficient statement of reasons as to the absence of a satisfactory alternative by means of which the objective relied upon could be achieved; and (3) the derogation permits were part of a 'trial' intended to ascertain whether limited authorisation of legal hunting could help reduce poaching. As the CJEU noted, the ability of the derogations to achieve that objective was surrounded by uncertainty.[71] The position of the CJEU cannot be criticised as

[68] *Luonnonsuojeluyhdistys Tapiola Pohjois-Savo* (n 11) [57].
[69] *ibid* [59].
[70] *ibid* [72].
[71] *ibid* [44].

it is based on the HD's own scientific criteria and, ultimately, on the fact that the burden of proof lies with the Member State.

d. The Precautionary Principle as Overseer of Derogations

Unlike the first *Finnish wolves* case, the CJEU stressed the importance of the precautionary principle. Whilst the CJEU maintained the thesis in the second *Finnish wolves* case that it was possible that the killing of a limited number of specimens could have no effect on the objective envisaged in art 16(1) HD, it however held that, in accordance with the precautionary principle, if, after examining the best scientific data available, there remained uncertainty as to whether or not a derogation could be detrimental to the maintenance or restoration of populations of an endangered species at a FCS, the Member State had to refrain from granting or implementing that derogation.[72] Thus, the question for the Court morphs from assessing whether FCS, was, on the balance of probability likely to be maintained, to whether, on the balance of probabilities, there was any uncertainty present in scientific assessments as to the maintenance of FCS.

It is noteworthy that in this shifting emphasis, the reference to the precautionary principle was repeated twice in the ruling, first before recalling what was held in the first *Finnish wolves* case on the possibility of killing a limited number of specimens and maintaining a FCS, and second after the above quotation. In other words, the CJEU wanted to make it clear that this principle pervades the whole mechanism for granting derogations and that any reasonable uncertainty as to achieving FCS requires the turning down of an exception under art 16 HD.

IV. 'Appropriate' Environmental Assessment and Best Available Scientific Knowledge

A. Precautionary Principle Weakened by Conservation Objectives?

The EIA procedure under art 6(3) HD represents one of the major obstacles a plan or project affecting a Natura 2000 site may encounter as it is firmly anchored in the precautionary principle.[73] In addition, art 6(3) HD, as interpreted by the CJEU, imposes a demanding threshold in terms of the content of the 'appropriate' EIA the public authorities must undertake. The requirement for an appropriate

[72] *ibid* [66] and [69].

[73] Agustin García-Ureta, 'Environmental Assessment under the Habitats Directive: Something other than a Procedure?' (2018) 10 *Journal of Property, Planning and Environmental Law* 113–25.

EIA of the implications of a plan or project is conditional on its being likely to have a significant effect on the site. Therefore, the triggering of the EIA protection mechanism does not presume that the plan or project considered definitely has significant effects on the site concerned but follows from 'the mere probability' that such an effect attaches to that plan or project. According to the CJEU, such an interpretation of the condition to which the assessment of the implications of a plan or project for a specific site is subject, which implies that in case of doubt as to the absence of significant effects such an assessment must be carried out, makes it possible to ensure effectively that plans or projects which adversely affect the integrity of the site concerned are not authorised, and thereby contributes to achieving its main aim, namely, ensuring biodiversity through the conservation of natural habitats and of wild fauna and flora.[74]

The precautionary principle also pervades the scope of the environmental analysis as developers (and public authorities) cannot ignore potential impacts by arguing that a project is located far away from a Natura 2000 site. It is for this reason that it was held in the *Moorburg* case that the fact that a project was not situated in Natura 2000 areas, 'but rather at a *considerable distance* from them' (emphasis added),[75] (eg 600 kilometres) in no way precluded the applicability of the requirements laid down in art 6(3) HD. Admittedly, the CJEU conclusion had sound factual and legal basis owing to the existence of a watercourse sustaining, on the one hand, activities depending on water resources (power plant) and, on the other hand, migrating species and protected areas hosting them at such distance. However, the same could be said regarding other types of projects, the key question being a non-merely hypothetical causal link between the implementation of a plan or project and its likely effects on sites or species,[76] the physical distance having an ancillary position. Indeed, the CJEU's finding was consistent with the HD as nowhere does art 6(3) HD refer to a project within or close to the boundaries of a Natura 2000 site as a precondition for the carrying out of an EIA but basically to its upshots on a site.[77]

The expansive force of the precautionary principle is subject to a constraint as the CJEU has observed that art 6(3) HD indicates that the EIA is to be undertaken 'in view of the site's conservation objectives'.[78] Therefore, a plan or project cannot be regarded as likely to have a significant effect on the site concerned if, despite having some impact on it, it nevertheless does not compromise the site's conservation objectives.[79] These objectives are those laid down by the national

[74] C-127/02 *Landelijke Vereniging tot Behoud van de Waddenzee v Staatssecretaris van Landbouw, Natuurbeheer en Visserij* [2004] ECR I-07504, ECLI:EU:C:2004:482 [44].

[75] C-142/16 *Commission v Germany*, ECLI:EU:C:2017:301 [29].

[76] *ibid* [31].

[77] See C-98/03 *Commission v Germany* [2006] ECR I-00053, ECLI:EU:C:2006:3.

[78] Lucile Sthal, 'The Concept of 'Conservation Objectives' in the Habitats Directive: A Need for a Better Definition?' in Charles-Hubert Born et al (eds), *The Habitats Directive in its EU Environmental Law Context* (Routledge, 2015) 56–70.

[79] *Waddenzee* (n 74) [47].

authorities depending on the characteristics of each Natura 2000 site and the HD objectives. In addition, those objectives may be drafted in broad terms. Therefore, there is a risk that the adoption of non-specific conservation objectives may favour (a) greater leeway when analysing the impact of a plan or project; and (b) wider discretion as to 'protection' ('mitigation'); and ultimately 'compensation' measures that may be needed in the light of art 6(3) and (4), respectively. An approach based on the likelihood of effects on the site's objectives, as the primary key for the triggering of the EIA would also contradict the very essence of the HD in so far as it basically protects habitats and species as singular components of designated sites. Arguably, the CJEU has softened the above case law by holding that the assessment of the risk must be made in the light, in particular, of 'the characteristics and specific environmental conditions of the site concerned by such a plan or project'.[80] Therefore, objective consideration of factual circumstances is key in the EIA.

B. Preserving the 'Integrity' of Sites

The CJEU has reiterated that the national authorities cannot agree to the construction of a plan or project until they have ascertained that it could not adversely affect the integrity of the sites concerned.[81] This entails the lasting preservation of the constitutive characteristics of the site, a matter that is to be viewed in the light of FCS. This case law, strictly based on the HD's wording, goes beyond the standard approach in European Union EIA legislation severely limiting Member States' capability to authorise an activity no matter its deleterious effects. According to the CJEU, '[a] less stringent authorisation criterion would not ensure as effectively the fulfilment of the objective of site protection'.[82] Therefore, it could be said that the precautionary principle acts in a genuine form and, naturally, precaution can only respond in one direction to the presence of such uncertainty.

Yet, the crux of the matter also lies in the meaning of some key terms such as 'integrity of the site' or, in particular, 'adverse effects'. In the *Sweetman* case, the CJEU employed the term of a risk bringing about 'the *disappearance* or the *partial and irreparable* destruction' of a priority natural habitat or species (emphasis added).[83] Whilst the threshold for requiring an EIA under art 6(3) (first sentence) HD is fairly (but rightly) low in the light of the precautionary principle, the one precluding the Member States from authorising a plan or project would arguably require a greater degree of evidence as to its effects on habitats and species. However, it should be noted that the CJEU has refrained from employing conclusive terms

[80] C-258/11 *Sweetman v An Bord Pleanála*, ECLI:EU:C:2013:220 [30]; *Orleans v Vlaams Gewest* (n 16) [45]; and *Commission v Poland* (n 16) [112].

[81] C-182/10 *Solvay v Regione Wallone*, ECLI:EU:C:2012:82 [67]. See also *Commission v Austria* (n 22). *Commission v Ireland* (n 21).

[82] C-441/17 *Commission v Poland* (n 16) [118].

[83] *Sweetman v An Bord Pleanála* (n 80) [43].

when referring to the notion of adverse effect. First, it has mentioned the likelihood of a 'risk'. Second, the concept of 'lasting harm' is to understandably be measured on a case-by-case basis in light of the various effects derived from a plan or project (eg those affecting the continuity of a site or its capability to sustain an ecosystem or its functions, or certain species). The expressions of 'disappearance' or 'partial and irreparable destruction' were mentioned in the *Sweetman* case as qualified examples of a risk, but they are not the only circumstances that may turn down an authorisation. The case law does not actually rule out other situations as the *Sweetman* case mentioned those two circumstances 'in particular' ('That would *particularly* so'[84]). In fact, it is doubtful whether only those two benchmarks would prevent the carrying out of a project as there may be a wide range of situations not encompassing the disappearance or a partial destruction of habitats and species but having apparent effects on them owing to their vulnerability or fragility. Nevertheless, the CJEU has confirmed situations of 'partial and irreparable destruction' as happened in a case against Poland regarding the removal of trees purportedly for sanitary reasons.[85] Last but not least, the construction of art 6 HD as a 'coherent whole'[86] would also uphold the conclusion that lasting degradation of habitats and species without entailing actual destruction would also qualify as a constraint for the authorisation of plans and projects. It is for this reason that the CJEU has held that where the conservation status of a natural habitat is unfavourable, the likelihood of authorising activities which may subsequently affect the ecological situation of the sites concerned, seems 'necessarily limited'.[87] In this way, the effects of uncertainty are felt two-fold in the application of precaution: first, precaution drives the interpretation of the relevant terms; and second, it influences the judicial assessment of the evidence at hand.

C. How Complete Should a 'Complete' EIA Be?

i. *Appropriate EIAs and the Lack of Harmonised Scientific Methodologies at EU Level*

Another thorny feature addressed by the CJEU concerns the meaning of 'appropriate' EIA as there is neither a definition nor a reference to Directives 2011/92[88] (EIA of projects) and 2001/42[89] (EIA of plans). Although the EIA is driven by objective

[84] *ibid.*

[85] *Commission v Poland* (n 16) [161]–[164].

[86] *Orleans v Vlaams Gewest* (n 16) [32].

[87] C-293/17 and C-294/17 *Coöperatie Mobilisation for the Environment UA and Vereniging Leefmilieu v College van gedeputeerde staten van Limburg and College van gedeputeerde staten van Gelderland*, ECLI:EU:C:2018:882 [103].

[88] Directive 2011/92/EU of the European Parliament and of the Council of 13 December 2011 on the assessment of the effects of certain public and private projects on the environment [2012] OJ L26/1.

[89] Directive 2001/42/EC of the European Parliament and of the Council of 27 June 2001 on the assessment of the effects of certain plans and programmes on the environment [2001] OJ L197/30.

considerations based on scientific evidence,[90] the HD does not prescribe a methodology (or a variety of methods) for the assessment of an activity (eg checklists, matrices or guidelines). Hence, the lack of harmonised methods would remain under the principle of subsidiarity and Member States' duty to faithfully and effectively transpose the HD.[91] However, disparate scientific approaches may certainly have a bearing on compliance with the very objectives of the HD as different techniques may provide divergent levels of thoroughness and certainty. According to consistent case law, the EIA requires the identification, in light of the best available scientific knowledge, of all aspects of the plan or project which, alone or in combination with other plans or projects, are likely to affect those objectives.[92] This means that the EIA must contain complete, accurate and definitive findings or conclusions so as to remove any reasonable scientific doubt about the effects of the plan or project on the integrity of the site concerned.[93] This obligation is incumbent on the authority designated to carry out the tasks of the HD.[94]

ii. Towards a State-of-the-Art EIA

Whilst the benchmark set out by the CJEU seems to be clear, the question would be how complete an EIA must be to reach such degree of comprehensiveness. The same would apply to the notion of 'definitive finding' and to the dispelling of 'any' doubt. According to the case law, an assessment cannot be regarded as 'appropriate', without up-to-date data concerning the protected habitats and species.[95] Second, given that 'all' aspects that may affect a site's conservation objectives should be identified and that the EIA should contain full findings and conclusions, 'all' habitats and species for which the site is protected should be accounted for.[96] For other habitat types or species, present on the site for which it has not been classified, as well as for habitat types and species outside the site, the HD conservation objective requires that such typical habitats or species should be included in the appropriate EIA if they are necessary for the conservation of the habitat types and species classified with respect to the protected area.[97] Third, the national authorities cannot take a favourable decision on the implementation of a plan or project

[90] Emma Lees, 'Allocation of Decision-Making Power under the Habitats Directive' (2016) 28 *Journal of Environmental Law* 197.

[91] Treaty on the Functioning of the European Union [2016] OJ C202/47, art 288.

[92] *Waddenzee* (n 74) [54].

[93] *ibid* [56] and [59]; C-239/04 *Commission v Portugal* [2006] ECR I-10183, ECLI:EU:C:2006:665 [20]; *Commission v Italy* (n 11) [58] and [59].

[94] C-461/17 *Holohan v An Bord Pleanála*, ECLI:EU:C:2018:883 [44].

[95] C-43/10 *Nomarchiaki Aftodioikisi Aitoloakarnanias v Ipourgos Perivallontos, Chorotaxias kai Dimosion ergon*, ECLI:EU:C:2012:560 [115].

[96] *Holohan v An Bord Pleanála* (n 94) [37]. C-241/08 *Commission v France* [2010] ECR I-01697, ECLI:EU:C:2010:114 [69]; C-404/09 *Commission v Spain* [2011] ECRI-11853, ECLI:EU:C:2011:768 [99]; *Nomarchiaki Aftodioikisi Aitoloakarnanias* (n 95) [112] and [113]; and C-399/14 *Grüne Liga Sachsen v Freistaat Sachsen*, ECLI:EU:C:2016:10 [49].

[97] *Holohan v An Bord Pleanála* (n 94) [38].

if the conclusions of the EIA are negative: 'it is at the time of adoption of the decision authorising implementation of the project that there must be no reasonable scientific doubt remaining as to the absence of adverse effects on the integrity of the site in question'.[98]

As is readily apparent, the CJEU has laid down several essential principles to verify whether an EIA is appropriate. However, as in any scientific analysis there may be a margin of uncertainty regarding various matters (eg the detail of the inventory of habitats or species; their degree of conservation; and, last but not least, the range of likely effects derived from an activity, eg short-term, lasting, serious, moderate, cumulative, isolated or irreversible to name but a few). In addition, dispelling 'any' scientific doubt may be demanding in so far as science is not one-sided. Therefore, there may be discrepancies regarding the data contained in the assessment and the conclusions finally reached. As mentioned above, there is no technical scientific standard at EU level regarding the carrying out of an EIA. Hence, the CJEU has understandably refrained from prescribing any as this would surely go beyond its jurisdiction. However, the reference in its rulings to up-to-date and best knowledge plainly points to a state-of-the-art EIA both in terms of the description of the environment to be likely affected and to the scientific technique(s) employed in assessing possible impacts. From a legal perspective, the key lies in examining (a) the extent to which such an analysis may have been flawed and (b) its bearing on the conclusions reached by a public authority. Failure in the EIA to identify all the relevant habitats and species in a Natura 2000 site would disregard from the outset the above requirements and therefore not be enough to remove any reasonable scientific doubt regarding the absence of adverse effects on the integrity of the protected site.

The case law provides examples of detailed review of weaknesses in the assessments.[99] Case C-304/05, *Commission v Italy*, was arguably the first judgment where the CJEU expressly forbade the carrying out of subsequent studies. In that case the CJEU observed that a first assessment, carried out by an architect, had highlighted itself the summary and selective nature of the examination of the environmental repercussions of the project. The study had also mentioned many matters which had not been considered, recommending additional environmental analyses and a new examination of the impact of the works. In view of these findings, the 'inescapable conclusion' was that the study did not constitute an appropriate assessment on which the national authorities could rely for granting authorisation for the works pursuant to art 6(3) HD.[100] Successive preliminary questions have asked whether it is feasible to postpone until the final stage of a project the carrying out of more comprehensive assessments and studies on its environmental effects. The key for the CJEU is whether they are sufficiently complete to satisfy the threshold of the first sentence of art 6(3) HD. Hence, it

[98] *Solvay v Regione Wallone* (n 81) [67].
[99] See, in particular, *Commission v Poland* (n 16) [128]–[151].
[100] *Commission v Italy* (n 11) [65].

has held in the *WWF Italy* case that such an EIA could not be continued 'validly on the basis of examinations and studies carried out subsequently'. Thus, 'as soon as it is considered necessary *to complete or deepen* it, an assessment of the impact of a plan or project in a special area of conservation cannot be regarded as the assessment provided for in that provision' (emphasis added).[101] The above is the standard threshold of review the CJEU's national counterparts are to carry out.

V. Concluding Remarks

Since the entry into force of the HD, the CJEU has faced the task of deciphering different notions that have a very direct relationship with science. This task is not easy, as it has been shown in several judgments, either on the protection of sites, species or other requirements contained in the HD, in particular the 'appropriate' EIA or the avoidance of deterioration. The CJEU has established demanding tests to be able to conclude that a Member State measure complies with the HD protection standard. There is a constant trend in the CJEU's reasoning which concerns the application, with greater or lesser intensity, of the precautionary principle and a presumption in favour of the protection of species and habitats. Added to this is the inability of the Member States to provide conclusive evidence on the adequacy of their measures in the light of CJEU's case law. The issues addressed by the CJEU are often not straightforward and require special attention to data that may be contradictory.

The precautionary principle pervades the HD, but its application has not been made in an 'indiscriminate' manner. Hence, it is logical (and mandatory) that the CJEU takes it into account when reviewing the rules and actions of Member States' authorities. The evolution of the case law also shows how uncertainty, and its corollary, precaution, have affected the judicial interpretation of terms central to the HD, as is the case of FCS. Here, however, a significant complexity can be observed when it comes to concluding whether a Member State complies with a particular criterion, as this may be divided into other subsidiary criteria the national judiciary cannot disregard in performing the corresponding review. In any case, it cannot be conclusively argued that the CJEU has forced the interpretation of the HD for the protection of habitats and species beyond its text when the EU is ascertaining the constant loss of biodiversity. Overall, the case law examined here shows that, in its approach, the CJEU interprets the HD with the precautionary principle as a guide. In addition to this, the approach to assessing contradictory scientific evidence raises the question of the degree of uncertainty involved. If such uncertainty exists, then precaution becomes a relevant factor in concluding whether a decision complies with the threshold set out in the HD.

[101] C-411/19 *WWF Italia Onlus v Presidenza del Consiglio dei Ministri and Azienda Nazionale Autonoma Strade SpA (ANAS)*, ECLI:EU:C:2020:580 [50].

PART II

Reviewing Science and Law in the Member States' Courts

3

Judicial Review and Enforcement of the Habitats Directive in Ireland

ÁINE RYALL*

> Every aspect of planning applications is now saturated not only with complex domestic regulation and caselaw, but also European law, overlain by a tapestry of jurisprudence from Luxembourg. Every paragraph and maybe every line of a planning decision … now bristles with legal significance. The days when planning decisions were just matters of planning judgement, to be challenged only on an unreasonableness basis, are long over, and they aren't coming back.[1]

I. Introduction

Ireland has a magnificent natural environment and enjoys a considerable 'green' image internationally. The latest data from the Environmental Protection Agency (EPA), however, confirms a worrying trend. Ireland's environment continues to deteriorate, with climate change and biodiversity loss identified as the two most pressing challenges to be addressed.[2] Nature and habitats are being damaged, with 85 per cent of European Union (EU) listed habitats in an unfavourable condition and 46 per cent demonstrating ongoing declines.[3] Wetland species, such as the curlew, are under severe threat as breeding species.[4] Against this stark backdrop, the EPA has called for nature and wild places to be protected as a national priority and to leave a legacy for future generations. Environmental law, including

* This contribution is written in my personal capacity. I thank the editors, together with Tom Flynn SC and Andrew Jackson, for very helpful comments on an earlier draft. David Browne BL's comprehensive new work, *Simons on Planning Law*, 3rd edn (Round Hall / Thomson Reuters, 2021) was an excellent resource when working to finalise this chapter. Any errors or omissions remain my responsibility.

[1] *Clonres CLG v An Bord Pleanála* [2021] IEHC 303, per Humphreys J at [78].

[2] 'Ireland's Environment 2020 – An Assessment' (Environmental Protection Agency, 2020) Ch 1.

[3] *ibid* 153.

[4] *ibid* 134–35.

enforcement of existing nature protection legislation, is identified by the EPA as a key intervention to bend the curve of biodiversity loss.[5]

Ireland has long struggled with the transposition and implementation of EU environmental law.[6] A highly fragmented legislative framework, under-resourced public authorities and a weak enforcement architecture continue to undermine the effectiveness of environmental laws in practice. In the context of land use planning, the obligations created in the Environmental Impact Assessment (EIA) Directive[7] and in the Habitats Directive (HD)[8] are transposed by means of specific provisions in the Planning and Development Act 2000, as amended[9] (PDA), together with detailed regulations made thereunder. Beyond land use planning, the main instrument transposing the HD is the European Communities (Birds and Natural Habitats) Regulations 2011[10] as amended. The EIA and HD Directives have generated, and continue to generate, substantial implementation challenges for the Irish authorities. These Directives are invoked frequently in litigation before the national courts and the jurisprudence continues to evolve at a rapid pace.

There are, unfortunately, many examples of Ireland failing to transpose EU environmental law requirements correctly and on time.[11] Ireland has also been found to be in breach of EU environmental law on numerous occasions by the Court of Justice of the European Union (CJEU).[12] Financial penalties under art 260

[5] *ibid* 152. See further Pádraic Fogarty, *Whittled Away: Ireland's Vanishing Nature* (Collins Press, 2017) in particular Ch 1 (appropriately titled 'Not as Green as we'd Like to Think') and the fascinating, stark account of the destruction of The Gearagh, near Macroom, County Cork in Kevin Corcoran, *Saving Eden: The Gearagh and Irish Nature* (Gearagh Press, 2021).

[6] For a detailed analysis in the specific context of the Environmental Impact Assessment Directive, see Áine Ryall, *Effective Judicial Protection and the Environmental Impact Assessment Directive in Ireland* (Hart Publishing, 2009).

[7] Directive 2011/92/EU on the assessment of the effects of certain public and private projects on the environment [2011] OJ L26/1 as amended by Directive 2014/52/EU – Directive 2014/52/EU of the European Parliament and of the Council of 16 April 2014 amending Directive 2011/92/EU on the assessment of the effects of certain public and private projects on the environment [2014] OJ L124/1.

[8] For full details see Introduction or Table of Legislation.

[9] PDA Part X contains the provisions governing EIA, while PDA Part XAB governs appropriate assessment as regards land use plans and projects requiring development consent.

[10] European Communities (Birds and Natural Habitats) Regulations 2011 (SI No 2011/477).

[11] Transposition of the EIA Directive has proven to be especially problematic, see Ryall (n 6) 3–11 and Áine Ryall 'Challenges and Opportunities for Irish Planning and Environmental Law' (2018) 25 *Irish Planning and Environmental Law Journal* 104.

[12] Selected high profile examples include: C-392/96 *Commission v Ireland* [1999] ECR I-05901, ECLI:EU:C:1999:43 (failure to transpose obligations under the EIA Directive); C-215/06 *Commission v Ireland* [2008] ECR I-04911, ECLI:EU:C:2008:380 (breach of the EIA Directive concerning inter alia provision for retrospective planning permission); C-50/09 *Commission v Ireland* [2011] ECR I-00873, ECLI:EU:C:2011:109 (breach of the EIA Directive as regards the need to ensure assessment of the interaction between factors likely to be directly or indirectly affected by the proposed project); C-418/04 *Commission v Ireland* [2007] ECR I-10947, ECLI:EU:C:2007:780 (breach of the Wild Birds Directive and the Habitats Directive); and C-494/01 *Commission v Ireland* [2005] ECR I-03331, ECLI:EU:C:2005:250 (here, the CJEU found that Ireland had 'generally and persistently' failed to fulfil its obligations under the Waste Framework Directive – Directive 2008/98/EC of the European Parliament and of the Council of 19 November 2008 on waste and repealing certain Directives [2008] OJ L312/3).

Treaty on the Functioning of the European Union (TFEU) have been imposed on Ireland in three cases to date involving serious, ongoing failures to comply with a judgment of the CJEU in the context of environmental law obligations.[13] Two of these cases concern failure to implement the EIA Directive.[14] At the time of writing (August 2021), a daily penalty of €15,000 continues to mount up as regards the failure to carry out an EIA prior to the development of a major windfarm at Derrybrien in County Galway.[15]

In Ireland, judicial review involves the court examining whether the contested decision was taken in accordance with the law: it does not involve the court engaging in a fresh inquiry into the merits of the application for development consent itself. Judicial review is a discretionary remedy in that the High Court may withhold relief from an otherwise successful applicant in certain circumstances.[16] In cases where the court quashes a planning decision, remittal of the matter to the decision-maker is usually the most frequent outcome in practice.[17] The fact that judicial review is concerned with legality, rather than merits review, means that judges are not usually required to engage in their own assessment of the scientific evidence. The issue for the court to determine is usually whether the competent authority had sufficient material before it to support the conclusion reached. The HD, however, creates specific obligations which require the courts to examine how the competent authority addressed ecological concerns during the various stages of the decision-making process.

This chapter introduces the system of judicial review as it applies in the context of enforcement of the HD in Ireland (section II).[18] This is followed by an account of the contemporary jurisprudence to explain the role played by the courts when called upon to enforce the HD (section III). The analysis here confirms a minimum 'hard core' of established principles that anchor this body of jurisprudence. The application of these principles in practice will, of course, depend heavily on the facts of each case. The jurisprudence demonstrates that the Irish courts have

[13] Treaty on the Functioning of the European Union [2016] OJ C202/47. C-374/11 *Commission v Ireland* ECLI:EU:C:2012:827 (failure to comply with the CJEU judgment in C-188/08 *Commission v Ireland* [2009] ECR I-00172, ECLI:EU:C:2009:670 (concerning waste water treatment systems); C-279/11 *Commission v Ireland*, ECLI:EU:C:2012:834 (failure to comply with the CJEU judgment in C-66/06 *Commission v Ireland* [2008] ECR I-00158, ECLI:EU:C:2008:637 concerning the EIA Directive and agriculture and aquaculture projects); and C-261/18 *Commission v Ireland*, ECLI:EU:C:2019:955 (failure to comply with the EIA Directive as regards the Derrybrien windfarm in County Galway).

[14] C-279/11 *Commission v Ireland*, *ibid* and C-261/18 *Commission v Ireland*, *ibid*.

[15] C-261/18 *Commission v Ireland* (n 13).

[16] See David Browne, *Simons on Planning Law*, 3rd edn (Round Hall / Thomson Reuters, 2021) 12-1634–39.

[17] On the High Court's discretion to remit the matter to the decision-maker, see Browne, *ibid* 12-1595–12-1617.

[18] On the HD more generally, see Charles-Hubert Born et al (eds), *The Habitats Directive in its EU Environmental Law Context: European Nature's Best Hope?* (Routledge, 2015); Gregory Jones (ed), *The Habitats Directive: A Developer's Obstacle Course?* (Hart Publishing, 2012); and Andrew LR Jackson, *Conserving Europe's Wildlife: Law and Policy of the Natura 2000 Network of Protected Areas* (Routledge, 2018), especially chs 10 and 11.

gradually come to play a more interventionist role in review of decision-making by public authorities when called upon to enforce the HD. In the specific context of art 6(3) HD, for example, the courts will consider the scientific evidence that was before the decision-maker to determine whether obligations arising under EU and national law have been met. This approach stands in sharp contrast to the EIA jurisprudence, where the orthodox, highly deferential approach to the expertise and judgment of public authorities continues to hold sway. Conclusions are presented in section IV. The analysis of the jurisprudence presented in this chapter confirms that there are still significant tensions between the deeply entrenched principles governing judicial review at national level and the more prescriptive requirements mandated by EU law.

II. Legal Framework Governing Judicial Review of Planning Decisions

The specific focus in this chapter is judicial review of planning decisions taken by *An Bord Pleanála* (the Planning Board). The Board, which has been in existence since 1977, is a specialist quasi-judicial tribunal vested with a range of statutory functions relating to the regulation of land use.[19] Under Irish planning law, the Board determines appeals *de novo* from planning decisions taken at first instance by local planning authorities. These appeals form the greater part of the Board's workload. However, proposed development projects which qualify as being of 'strategic' importance to the economy will by-pass the local decision-making process. The application for planning permission (development consent) for these 'strategic' development projects, which include strategic housing development, is made *directly* to the Board. In such cases the Board is the first-instance decision-maker and not an appellate body. The validity of its decision may only be challenged by way of judicial review. The Board appoints one of its Inspectors (a 'scientific expert')[20] to prepare a report for it as regards the appeal or application for development consent, as the case may be.

The Constitution of Ireland (*Bunreacht na hÉireann*), adopted in 1937, provides for the separation of powers between the executive, legislative and judicial branches of the State. The power of judicial review is exercised by the High Court, with the possibility (subject to the requirement to obtain leave to appeal in certain cases) of an appeal to the Court of Appeal.[21] There is provision for a further appeal to

[19] *An Bord Pleanála* is categorised as an 'environmental tribunal' in George Pring and Catherine Pring, 'Environmental Courts & Tribunals: A Guide for Policy Makers' (United Nations Environment Programme, 2016) 84. For a detailed evaluation of the Board's operations, see Independent Review Group, 'Organisational Review of An Bord Pleanála' (February 2016).

[20] *Rushe v An Bord Pleanála* [2020] IEHC 122 [141] per Barniville J.

[21] PDA, s 50A(7) provides that the determination of the High Court on the application for leave to bring judicial review proceedings, or on the substantive application for judicial review, is final and there

the Supreme Court, subject to obtaining leave to appeal from that court.[22] The Constitution does not mandate a certain level of scrutiny in cases of scientific uncertainty. There is no mention of the precautionary principle in the Constitution. The courts are required to provide remedies sufficient to ensure effective judicial protection in the fields covered by EU law, including environmental law.[23] Ireland is a party to the Aarhus Convention[24] and is bound by the obligations created in that multilateral environmental agreement as a matter of international law. Because the Aarhus Convention is part of the EU legal order, obligations arising under the Convention can be enforced before the Irish courts indirectly by invoking EU law.[25]

The legal framework governing the judicial review process as it relates to decision-making by the Board is set down in ss 50, 50A and 50B of the PDA.[26] This framework establishes the overarching procedure, including the applicable time limits, standing requirements and the rules governing liability for costs.[27] It is notable that this is a specific statutory procedure for planning cases which is more restrictive and more onerous than that governing judicial review generally. Section 50(2) provides that a challenge to a decision taken by the Board may only be brought by way of an application for judicial review under Order 84 of the Rules of the Superior Courts. Judicial review is therefore the only remedy available when seeking to challenge the validity of a decision of the Board.

Judicial review proceedings are brought before the High Court which will usually comprise one judge sitting alone. There are no specialist environmental courts in Ireland, although the current *Programme for Government* commits to the establishment of a new 'Planning and Environmental Law Court' to be managed by 'specialist judges'.[28] In the case of 'strategic' development,[29] however,

is no appeal except with the leave of the High Court. Leave can only be granted where the High Court certifies that its decision involves a point of law of exceptional public importance and it is desirable in the public interest that an appeal should be taken. If leave is granted, the appeal is heard by the Court of Appeal.

[22] There is also the possibility of a so-called 'leap-frog' appeal, directly to the Supreme Court from the High Court.

[23] See Case C-664/15 *Protect Natur-, Arten- und Landschaftsschutz Umweltorganisation v Bezirkshauptmannschaft Gmünd*, ECLI:EU:C:2017:987 [35].

[24] United Nations Economic Commission for Europe (UNECE), *Convention on Access to Information, Public Participation in Decision-making and Access to Justice in Environmental Matters*' 2161 UNTS 447, 25 June 1998 (the Aarhus Convention).

[25] Áine Ryall, 'The Relationship between Irish Law and International Environmental Law: A Study of the Aarhus Convention' (2019) 41 *Dublin University Law Journal* 163.

[26] For a detailed analysis of the statutory scheme, see Browne (n 16) Ch 12.

[27] The detailed rules applicable to judicial review proceedings more generally are found in the Rules of the Superior Courts (RSC), including the rules governing evidence, affidavits, etc.

[28] Programme for Government, 'Our Shared Future' (June 2020) 85. Very little detail is provided in this document on the precise model of a specialist court envisaged by the Government and no further details have emerged to date.

[29] 'Strategic Infrastructure Development' (PDA, s 37A and Seventh Schedule) and 'Strategic Housing Development' (Planning and Development (Housing) and Residential Tenancies Act 2016, pt 2, ch 1). See further Browne (n 16) Ch 7.

there is a specific List in the High Court whereby all such cases are dealt with by the judge assigned to this List. This List also includes planning cases admitted to the Commercial List. This means that, in practice, there is an *ad hoc* element of specialisation in that the judges hearing these cases will build up expertise. A more streamlined process applies to the Commercial Planning and Strategic Infrastructure Development (SID) List, as well as proactive case management by the judge, with a view to determining challenges expeditiously.[30] 'Ordinary' planning judicial review cases will stay in the Judicial Review List, leading to fragmentation in practice.

There are multiple grounds on which a challenge may be brought against a planning decision, including: breach of a statutory and / or procedural requirement; where the decision-maker had regard to an irrelevant consideration or failed to consider a relevant consideration; breach of constitutional justice or fair procedure; failure to state adequate reasons for a decision; breach of constitutional rights and / or rights under the European Convention on Human Rights; and breach of EU law. In practice, alleged breach of EU law (especially the EIA Directive and the HD) and alleged failure to provide adequate reasons for the decision, are important and popular grounds of challenge. However, the merits of a planning decision may only be challenged indirectly on the basis that the contested decision is 'unreasonable' or 'irrational'. The doctrine of unreasonableness (or irrationality) – which is considered below – is a fundamental element of the law of judicial review in Ireland.[31]

In the Irish system, it is the parties to the litigation who present evidence to the court, including expert scientific evidence.[32] In the context of judicial review proceedings, evidence is presented to the court in the form of affidavits (ie sworn written testimony), with relevant documents and reports exhibited. Cross examination of witnesses is very rare in practice. As a general principle in judicial review proceedings, a court cannot consider new evidence that was not before the decision-maker.[33] The rationale here is that judicial review is concerned with whether the contested decision was taken in accordance with the law: it is not an appeal on the merits of the decision taken. The issue for the court to determine is whether the material that was before the decision-maker supports the conclusions reached. Browne has identified 'a possible tension' between this prohibition on

[30] See Practice Direction HC 107 Commercial Planning and SID List, 17 June 2021.

[31] On the doctrine of administrative unreasonableness, see Browne (n 16) 3-220–41.

[32] The Rules of the Superior Courts provide that the court may appoint an 'assessor' (or 'assessors') in a particular case. An assessor is a person with 'skill and experience' in a particular field whose role is to assist the court in understanding or clarifying a matter, or evidence in relation to a matter. Such appointments are very rare in practice and the author is not aware of any planning or environmental case where a court appointed an assessor. See generally RSC, Order 36, rule 41 (as amended); see also RSC, Order 63B, rule 23 and Order 64, rule 43 (as amended), concerning competition proceedings and admiralty proceedings respectively.

[33] See Browne (n 16) 12-543–53.

presenting new evidence on affidavit and the requirement that appropriate assessment must have regard to best scientific knowledge or evidence.[34] The question as to whether the court is constrained only to consider matters that were before the Board or is entitled – or obliged – to have regard to any new or additional evidence remains open at the time of writing.[35] Browne argues that if an applicant was permitted to bring forward expert evidence purporting to be 'best available scientific' knowledge, then:

> [T]his could convert judicial review proceedings into a trial by evidence and the better view is that any such evidence by, for example, an expert ecologist must be brought to the attention of the decision-maker as part of the public consultation process.[36]

This state of affairs reveals a clear and very significant flashpoint between the fundamental principles of judicial review and the more prescriptive approach required under EU law (in particular 'the *Sweetman* test')[37] to ensure that the obligations set down in art 6(3) HD are met.[38] In a recent judgment of the High Court in *An Taisce v An Bord Pleanála*,[39] Humphreys J identified three possible ways in which an applicant could proceed to make a point about scientific doubt, in this specific case with a view to challenging the Natura Impact Statement (NIS): (1) bring forward something raising doubt during the course of the planning process itself; (2) point to something raising doubt that was brought forward by somebody else; or (3) establish evidentially in the judicial review that the developer's material, even if uncontradicted would on its face have created doubt in the mind of a reasonable expert.[40] Section III below considers a selection of recent High Court decisions where it was alleged that the Board had failed to comply with the requirements of art 6(3). The aim is to give an insight into how the High Court

[34] *ibid* 12-549.

[35] This question was among the points of law of exceptional public importance certified by the High Court for appeal to the Court of Appeal in *People Over Wind v An Bord Pleanála* [2015] IEHC 393. However, the Court of Appeal determined that 'it was not strictly necessary to answer this question' (see [53] and [54] of the judgment). Consider also the Court's analysis on the concept of 'best scientific evidence' and 'the *Sweetman* test' at [23]–[56].

[36] Browne (n 16) 12-551. See also *Sliabh Luachra against Ballydesmond Wind Farm Committee v An Bord Pleanála* [2019] IEHC 888, discussed in Browne (n 16) 12.552–53.

[37] C-258/11 *Sweetman v An Bord Pleanála*, ECLI:EU:C:2013:220 [44]. As Hogan J put it when giving judgment for a unanimous Court of Appeal in *People Over Wind v An Bord Pleanála* [2015] IECA 272, the test as per *Sweetman* is: that the Board 'has demonstrated to the necessary degree of certainty that the integrity of the SAC will not be affected by the proposed works'. See also C-127/02 *Landelijke Vereniging tot Behoud van de Waddenzee v Staatssecretaris van Landbouw, Natuurbeheer en Visserij* [2004] ECR I-07504, ECLI:EU:C:2004:482 [36]–[38].

[38] For an insightful analysis of the assessment of impacts, which highlights the importance of 'the dialogue between scientists and decision-makers or judges' in the implementation of the precautionary principle, see Eve Truilhé-Marengo 'How to Cope with the Unknown: A Few Things about Scientific Uncertainty, Precaution and Adaptive Management' in Charles-Hubert Born et al (eds), *The Habitats Directive in its EU Environmental Law Context: European Nature's Best Hope?* (Routledge, 2015) 343–47.

[39] *An Taisce v An Bord Pleanála* [2021] IEHC 422 (judgment on the application for leave to appeal under section 50A(7) PDA).

[40] *ibid* [7].

exercises its supervisory function in this particular context and the extent to which it interrogates the scientific evidence.

A. The *O'Keeffe* Principles

The concept of 'unreasonableness' or 'irrationality' has been interpreted narrowly by the Irish courts. The starting point is Henchy J's analysis in *Keegan*[41] where he described judicial review on the ground of alleged 'unreasonableness' as the court examining:

> whether the conclusion reached in the decision can be said to flow from the premises. If it plainly does not, it stands to be condemned on the less technical and more understandable test of whether it is fundamentally at variance with reason and common sense.[42]

The classic statement of principle is to be found in the judgment of Finlay CJ in *O'Keeffe v An Bord Pleanála*[43] where the Supreme Court confirmed that the circumstances in which a court can intervene on the basis of alleged irrationality 'are limited and rare'.[44] More specifically, a court cannot interfere with an administrative decision on the grounds that the court itself would have raised different inferences or conclusions from the facts, or because it is satisfied that the case against the contested decision was stronger than the case for it.[45]

The justification for this narrow approach is grounded firmly in the expertise of the public authorities who decide applications for development consent.[46] The judges themselves are not expert in specific technical and scientific matters. The courts also justify the approach adopted in *O'Keeffe* by emphasising the fundamental principle of the separation of powers and the fact that under the relevant legislative framework the *Oireachtas* (Parliament) has vested the task of making what are often complex and highly controversial administrative decisions in expert public authorities rather than the courts.[47] The courts are also understandably alert to the practical importance of certainty for developers, particularly in the case of significant infrastructure projects, and the need for finality in the planning process.[48]

O'Keeffe demands that to succeed based on alleged 'irrational' decision-making, the applicant seeking judicial review must prove that the decision-maker had no

[41] *State (Keegan) v Stardust Victims' Compensation Tribunal* [1986] IR 642.
[42] *ibid* 658.
[43] *O'Keeffe v An Bord Pleanála* [1993] 1 IR 39.
[44] *ibid* 71.
[45] *ibid.*
[46] *ibid* 71–72.
[47] *ibid.*
[48] Consider for example the comments of Finlay CJ in *KSK Enterprises v An Bord Pleanála* [1994] 2 IR 128, 135.

relevant material before it to support its decision.[49] This approach sets a very high threshold, which is difficult to meet in practice.[50] It is important to acknowledge, however, that 'unreasonableness' or 'irrationality' is only one of the many grounds on which a planning decision may be challenged and that the High Court's judicial review jurisdiction is not as narrow as a consideration of '*O'Keeffe* irrationality' alone might suggest. As Clarke J (as he then was) explained in *Sweetman v An Bord Pleanála*:

> O'Keeffe irrationality only arises in circumstances where the decision-maker properly considered all of the matters required to be taken into account and did not take into account any matters which should not. The limitations inherent in the irrationality test, therefore, only arise where all, but only, those matters properly considered were taken into account and the decision-maker comes to a judgment based on all those matters. It is in those circumstances that the court, by reason of the doctrine of deference, does not attempt to second guess the judgment of the [decision-maker] provided that there was material for coming to that decision. In particular the court does not attempt to reassess the weight to be attached to relevant factors.[51]

In *Meadows*,[52] Denham J (as she then was) in the Supreme Court confirmed that *O'Keeffe* applied to 'a specialised area of decision making where the decision-maker has special technical or professional skill', such as planning and development, and that a court 'should be slow to intervene in a decision made with special competence in an area of special knowledge'.[53] While the main focus of the jurisprudence is on the doctrine of 'unreasonableness' / 'irrationality', the principle of proportionality will come into play in cases where fundamental rights are engaged.[54]

It is clear from the *Keegan / O'Keeffe* line of authority that where a decision has been taken by an expert public authority, the courts will tend to defer to that authority's expert judgment – so called 'curial deference'.[55] It is very difficult to succeed in having a decision quashed by the courts because of alleged 'unreasonableness' or 'irrationality'. There is no doubt that the threshold for judicial intervention on this ground of challenge is very high indeed. Generally speaking,

[49] *O'Keeffe v An Bord Pleanála* (n 43) 72.

[50] For a (very rare) example of where the applicant succeeded on *O'Keeffe* grounds, see *Halpin v An Bord Pleanála* [2019] IEHC 352 [92]–[99]. Here, the High Court ruled that the Board's determination that a proposed anaerobic digester plant constituted an 'establishment' for the purpose of the Seveso III Directive (Directive 2012/18/EU on the control of major-accident hazards involving dangerous substances [2012] OJ L197/1) was 'unreasonable and irrational in the sense that there was simply no material before the Board capable of justifying its conclusions' ([92]). Note that Simons J stressed 'the very unusual facts' of the case. An application by the Board for leave to appeal to the Court of Appeal on a point of law (concerning the application of the *O'Keeffe* principles) was unsuccessful: *Halpin v An Bord Pleanála* [2020] IEHC 218.

[51] *Sweetman v An Bord Pleanála* [2007] IEHC 153 [6.12]–[6.13].

[52] *Meadows v Minister for Justice, Equality and Law Reform* [2010] 2 IR 701.

[53] *ibid* 738.

[54] In the Irish context, arguments based on fundamental rights can arise under the Constitution, EU law and / or the European Convention on Human Rights.

[55] See *Halpin v An Bord Pleanála* (n 50) [90] per Simons J. See generally Browne (n 16) 13-23–30.

alleged failure to comply with EU environmental law obligations, and/or alleged failure on the part of the public authority to provide adequate reasons to support its decision, tend to be far more fruitful grounds for judicial review in practice.

B. Evolution in the Standard of Review?

In a number of cases to date the Irish courts have been called upon to consider the impact, if any, of the Aarhus Convention and EU environmental law 'access to justice' obligations on the standard of judicial review applied by the national courts in the planning and environmental law field. There is an express requirement in art 9(2) of the Aarhus Convention, which is replicated in art 11 of the EIA Directive, that the review procedure must provide for a challenge to '*the substantive and procedural legality* of any decision, act or omission' falling within the scope of art 6 of the Convention (emphasis added). The question arises as to whether the narrow *O'Keeffe* principles are compatible with this standard?

I have argued elsewhere that limited judicial scrutiny, such as that provided for by *O'Keeffe*, is inappropriate in the context of EIA where the decision-maker's discretion is clearly constrained by the obligations set down in the Directive.[56] Whether a project is likely to have significant effects on the environment, the adequacy of the Environmental Impact Assessment Report and the comprehensiveness of the EIA are all fundamental questions if the objectives of the Directive are to be achieved. These are not matters falling within the discretion of the decision-maker. The deferential *O'Keeffe* test is not sufficient to ensure that the EU law principles governing EIA are applied effectively – which is the standard demanded by the CJEU. A more robust level of scrutiny is required. The difficulty lies in articulating the required standard in precise terms that can be applied with confidence by the courts in practice. The fact that more intensive review will involve the court drilling down into the technical and scientific evidence adds significantly to the arguments in favour of a specialist Planning and Environmental Law Court – or at least a system that facilitates the Court having timely access to independent technical expertise where necessary.

At the time of writing, the jurisprudence from the Irish courts has not determined that a more intensive standard of review is required in cases involving EU environmental law.[57] There are indications in the jurisprudence that if a more intensive standard was to be required, then the common law principles (*O'Keeffe*) are sufficiently flexible to be adapted to meet any heightened requirements prescribed

[56] Áine Ryall, 'Enforcing the Environmental Impact Assessment Directive in Ireland: Evolution of the Standard of Review' (2018) 7 *Transnational Environmental Law* 515. For discussion of whether 'a more interrogative standard of review' is required given the demands of EU law, and consideration of the relevant jurisprudence, see Browne (n 16) 13.311–29 (on the 'manifest error' test) and 14.1064–90 (on the standard of review in the EIA context).

[57] Ryall, *ibid.*

by EU law or by art 9 of the Aarhus Convention.[58] In the particular case of the HD, however, it is clear from the contemporary jurisprudence that the courts must determine whether the requirements of the Directive have been met in a particular case. The fundamental importance of the duty on the competent authority to give adequate reasons to support a particular decision has also emerged in the jurisprudence. Indeed, there are some striking examples from the jurisprudence where the courts did allow what could be described as a 'merits-based' challenge, albeit through the lens of inadequate reasons.[59]

A careful analysis of the contemporary jurisprudence suggests that although the courts consistently refer to, and defend, the *O'Keeffe* test as the standard to be applied, in practice some judges are inclined to engage in a fairly close analysis of the material that was before the decision-maker.[60] It will be recalled that under *O'Keeffe* the court's inquiry is limited to determining whether there was sufficient material to support the conclusions drawn by the decision-maker. The actual degree of judicial scrutiny applied in making this determination – at least in some cases – may be more intensive and less deferential than the courts' persistent invocation of the *O'Keeffe* formula suggests. It remains the case that to bring a greater degree of certainty to this area of the law an authoritative statement of principle from the Supreme Court is necessary.[61]

In the specific context of the prescriptive obligations imposed on the decision-maker under art 6(3) HD, the contemporary jurisprudence confirms a fairly robust level of review to verify whether *An Bord Pleanála* carried out an appropriate assessment in accordance with law. This inquiry involves the court considering the scientific evidence underpinning the appropriate assessment to ensure that there is no gap in the material on which the assessment and determination is based. The adequacy of the reasons provided by the decision-maker in support of its conclusions is another critical factor in these cases. Section III considers the role of the Irish courts in judicial review proceedings alleging breach of obligations arising under the HD and / or the national measures giving effect to that Directive.

[58] *Sweetman v An Bord Pleanála* (n 51) [6.21].

[59] *Kelly v An Bord Pleanála* [2014] IEHC 400 and *Connelly v An Bord Pleanála* [2018] IESC 31. See also *Balz v An Bord Pleanála* [2016] IEHC 134.

[60] Consider, for example, the detailed, insightful analysis of the *O'Keeffe* principles by Simons J in *Halpin v An Bord Pleanála* (n 50) (the principal judgment) and [2020] IEHC 218 (judgment on application for leave to appeal).

[61] In *Carroll v An Bord Pleanála* [2017] IESCDET 15 an application was made to the Supreme Court seeking 'leapfrog' leave to appeal on two points, one of which concerned the appropriate standard of review in relation to planning decisions involving an EIA and/or an appropriate assessment in accordance with art 6(3) HD. The applicants argued that the appropriate standard of review is the 'manifest error' test. The Supreme Court refused leave to appeal. It noted that even if the trial judge was wrong in applying the *O'Keeffe* principles, he had also concluded that even if the 'manifest error' test was applicable that the decision in question did not fail that test. It followed that if the 'manifest error' test was the appropriate test to be applied, the applicants would still have failed and so an appeal to the Supreme Court could not be of any use to them in the circumstances. The applicants therefore failed to meet the constitutional threshold for leave to appeal on this point.

III. The Habitats Directive in Judicial Review Proceedings

The Irish courts have confirmed that the Board does not have jurisdiction to grant development consent unless the appropriate assessment obligations are applied correctly.[62] The decision of Finlay Geoghegan J in *(Éamon 'Ted') Kelly v An Bord Pleanála*[63] articulated in clear terms what is required for a lawful appropriate assessment. The case involved a challenge to decisions of the Board granting planning permission for two proposed wind farm developments in the vicinity of a number of European sites in County Roscommon. It was alleged that the Board had failed to comply with the requirements of national law and EU law in carrying out an EIA and an appropriate assessment. It was also asserted that the Board had failed to record its conclusions or give any adequate statement of its reasons. Having set out and considered the requirements in the relevant legislative framework, Finlay Geoghegan J noted the different effects that EIA and appropriate assessment have on the Board's decision-making process.[64] The outcome of the examination undertaken in an EIA informs rather than determines the planning decision that may be made. The Board has jurisdiction to grant development consent notwithstanding the outcome of the EIA, although the Board must have regard to the results of the EIA in coming to its decision. The situation is very different where an appropriate assessment is required. Here, the Board is obliged 'to make a determination as to whether or not the proposed development would adversely affect the integrity of the relevant European site or sites in view of its conservation objectives'.[65] The Board's conclusion on this issue determines its jurisdiction to make the planning decision. Unless the outcome of the appropriate assessment is that the proposed development will not adversely affect the integrity of any relevant European site, the Board may not proceed to take a decision granting development consent, except where it does so pursuant to the exceptional circumstances provided for in art 6(4) (imperative reasons of overriding public interest).

Finlay Geoghegan J then considered the nature of an appropriate assessment by reference to the relevant CJEU jurisprudence.[66] She summarised what is required for an appropriate assessment that complies with EU law as follows:

> It must be recalled that the appropriate assessment, or a stage two assessment, will only arise where, in the stage one screening process, it has been determined (or it has been implicitly accepted) that the proposed development meets the threshold of being considered likely to have significant effects on a European site. Where that is the position, then … the appropriate assessment to be lawfully conducted in summary:
>
> (i) Must identify, in the light of the best scientific knowledge in the field, all aspects of the development project which can, by itself or in combination with other plans

[62] *Kelly v An Bord Pleanála* (n 59) and *Connelly v An Bord Pleanála* (n 59).
[63] *Kelly v An Bord Pleanála* (n 59).
[64] *ibid* [15]–[34].
[65] *ibid* [34].
[66] *ibid* [35]–[39].

or projects, affect the European site in the light of its conservation objectives. This clearly requires both examination and analysis.

(ii) Must contain complete, precise and definitive findings and conclusions and may not have lacunae or gaps. The requirement for precise and definitive findings and conclusions appears to require analysis, evaluation and decisions. Further, the reference to findings and conclusions in a scientific context requires both findings following analysis and conclusions following an evaluation each in the light of the best scientific knowledge in the field.

(iii) May only include a determination that the proposed development will not adversely affect the integrity of any relevant European site where upon the basis of complete, precise and definitive findings and conclusions made the Board decides that no reasonable scientific doubt remains as to the absence of the identified potential effects.[67]

Applying these principles to the case at hand, Finlay Geoghegan J concluded that the Board had failed to carry out an appropriate assessment that met the requirements of art 6(3) HD and had also failed to provide adequate reasons for its conclusion following that assessment.

The judgment in *Kelly* was considered extensively and approved by the Supreme Court in *Connelly v An Bord Pleanála*.[68] This case concerned proposed wind-farm development in County Clare. Having examined the principles articulated by Finlay Geoghegan J (above), Clarke CJ explained that the 'overall conclusion' which must be reached before the Board will have jurisdiction to grant development consent following an appropriate assessment 'is that all scientific doubt about the potential adverse effects on the sensitive area have been removed'.[69] There was also 'a separate obligation [on the Board] to make specific scientific findings which allow that conclusion to be reached'.[70] Clarke CJ identified 'four distinct requirements' which must be satisfied in order for a valid appropriate assessment determination to be taken:

> First, the [appropriate assessment] must identify, in the light of the best scientific knowledge in the field, all aspects of the development project which can, by itself or in combination with other plans or projects, affect the European site in the light of its conservation objectives. Second, there must be complete, precise and definitive findings and conclusions regarding the previously identified potential effects on any relevant European site. Third, on the basis of those findings and conclusions, the Board must be able to determine that no scientific doubt remains as to the absence of the identified potential effects. Fourth and finally, where the preceding requirements are satisfied, the Board may determine that the proposed development will not adversely affect the integrity of any relevant European site.[71]

[67] *ibid* [40].
[68] *Connelly v An Bord Pleanála* (n 59).
[69] *ibid* [8.5].
[70] *ibid* [8.5].
[71] *ibid* [8.16].

As regards the obligation to give reasons where an appropriate assessment is undertaken, the Supreme Court insisted that the decision-maker is required, not only to provide reasons for reaching the relevant conclusion, but 'to make complete, precise and specific scientific findings' which justify that conclusion.[72] The Court determined that the Board had failed to meet this standard as regards its conclusion in this case that no reasonable scientific doubt remained as to the absence of any identified potential detrimental effects on the protected site.

The principles identified in *Kelly* and *Connelly* are now well-established. With a view to elaborating on how the courts approach enforcement of the obligations arising under the HD in practice, it is helpful to examine particular aspects of three recent High Court decisions: *(Eoin) Kelly v An Bord Pleanála*,[73] *Rushe v An Bord Pleanála*[74] and *Highlands Residents Association v An Bord Pleanála*.[75] This analysis also demonstrates how the general principles of judicial review, including the *O'Keeffe* principles (see section II above), intersect with the specific legal test that applies under the HD as per *Kelly* and *Connelly*.

In *(Eoin) Kelly v An Bord Pleanála*, it was alleged inter alia that the Board had failed to apply the correct test for screening for appropriate assessment and further alleged that there were gaps or lacunae in the screening process. This case involved the proposed development of a discount foodstore in Laytown, County Meath. Having reviewed the relevant authorities and identified the applicable principles,[76] Barniville J explained that the,

> [S]creening obligation will be complied with where it is clear from the substance of the reports [in this case the screening report prepared by the developer and the Board Inspector's report] that the risk of the development having a significant effect on the European site concerned can be excluded on the basis of objective information.[77]

Barniville J worked through the detailed content of the screening report in the course of his judgment.[78] He then examined the manner in which the Inspector had considered the screening report in her report to the Board.[79] Barniville J concluded that the substance of the screening report and its conclusion 'amply' supported a finding that the risk of any significant effect on any of the relevant European sites could be excluded on the basis of objective information.[80] Moreover, it is primarily a matter for the Board and its Inspector to determine whether it has sufficient information before it in order to carry out the stage one screening.[81] Barniville J

[72] *ibid* [13.11].
[73] *(Eoin) Kelly v An Bord Pleanála* [2019] IEHC 84.
[74] *Rushe v An Bord Pleanála* (n 20).
[75] *Highlands Residents Association v An Bord Pleanála* [2020] IEHC 622.
[76] *(Eoin) Kelly v An Bord Pleanála* (n 73) [38]–[69].
[77] *ibid* [104].
[78] *ibid* [71]–[87].
[79] *ibid* [89]–[92].
[80] *ibid* [107].
[81] *ibid* [109]. This was particularly so in this case in light of the fact that neither the applicant seeking judicial review nor the National Parks and Wildlife Service (one of the relevant prescribed bodies

was also satisfied that the Inspector's conclusion that the proposed development would not be 'likely to have a significant effect' on any of the European sites described in the screening report, and that a stage two appropriate assessment was therefore not required, was a conclusion that she was entitled to draw on the basis of the evidence before her, and in particular, in light of the screening report.[82]

As regards the further argument that there were particular gaps or lacunae in the screening report (specifically, an alleged failure to consider properly the consequences of the use of concrete and of sediment run-off from the site during the construction phase), Barniville J recalled that it is primarily a matter for the Board to determine whether it has sufficient information to undertake the stage one screening.[83] He was convinced, on the basis of the evidence that was before the Inspector, that she was entitled to conclude that there was indeed sufficient information in this regard. The conclusion that the Inspector has adequate information to issue a screening determination is one which can be challenged on the grounds set out in *O'Keeffe* (see above section II).[84] Barniville J explained that it would therefore be open to an applicant to point to 'obvious deficiencies' in the information before the Board in mounting a challenge on *O'Keeffe* grounds.[85] In this case, however, the judge concluded that there were no such deficiencies. He was satisfied, having reviewed the screening report and the conclusions it set out, that there were no gaps or lacunae in the report in relation to the screening of the proposed development.[86] The applicant had failed to discharge the onus of proof in this regard.[87] These issues 'were adequately considered' in the screening report prepared by the developer and in the screening for appropriate assessment carried out by the Board and its Inspector.[88]

Rushe v An Bord Pleanála[89] concerned proposed windfarm development in County Galway. It was alleged inter alia that the Board had failed to carry out an appropriate assessment in accordance with the provisions of art 6(3) HD and the relevant provisions of Irish law.[90] EIA grounds were also pursued, but the main thrust of the challenge was in relation to the stage two appropriate assessment undertaken by the Board and its Inspector. The High Court was required to consider whether this appropriate assessment was valid by reference to the now well-established legal test identified in the jurisprudence of the CJEU and the Irish courts as per *Kelly* and *Connelly*.

in the process) had raised any environmental or ecological concerns in the course of the planning process. The Board had not been provided with any evidence to contradict the evidence and information presented in the screening report ([105]).

[82] *ibid* [111].
[83] *ibid* [116].
[84] *ibid.*
[85] *ibid* [116].
[86] *ibid* [117].
[87] *ibid* [122].
[88] *ibid* [234].
[89] *Rushe v An Bord Pleanála* (n 20).
[90] PDA, s 177V.

For the purpose of exposition, the analysis here focuses exclusively on how the High Court approached the applicants' assertion that there were lacunae or deficiencies in the information provided by the developer for the purposes of the appropriate assessment, in particular as regards the potential impacts on golden plover (*feadóg bhuí* – a protected species in a number of the European sites in the vicinity of the proposed development). In a detailed, 91-page report prepared for the Board, the Inspector, having considered the NIS submitted by the developer, expressed a number of concerns. One significant concern focused on the impact of the operation of the wind farm on golden plover. The Inspector considered that there was a 'serious weakness' here and that the authors of the NIS had failed to prove that there would not be an adverse effect on golden plover, known to occur in three of the European sites situated within 15 km of the development site.[91] Having regard to the assessment of the impacts likely to occur (specifically the risk of collision with the turbine blades), the Inspector did not consider that adequate information had been provided to establish 'beyond reasonable scientific doubt' that the wind farm would not impact on the natural flight lines of the golden plover and would not have an adverse impact on the integrity of the relevant European sites.[92] The Inspector therefore concluded that the Board should refuse development consent on that basis.

The Board considered the Inspector's report and requested further information from the developer, including, specifically, a revised NIS addressing the concerns raised by the Inspector in relation to golden plover.[93] A revised NIS was submitted which included, by way of an attachment, a document entitled 'Response to request for further information on golden plover' ('the golden plover report').[94]

Barniville J recalled the relevant legislative provisions[95] and the necessary requirements for a valid appropriate assessment as per *Kelly* and *Connelly*.[96] At an earlier point in his judgment he had considered the Inspector's report in detail.[97] The judge regarded the ground of challenge relating to the potential impacts on golden plover as 'the high point' of the applicants' case. Specifically, the applicants maintained that the Board had failed to comply with the substantive requirements for an appropriate assessment in that it had failed to address properly the lacunae identified by the Inspector concerning the potential adverse impacts on this species. They argued that the Board was not in possession of any new additional relevant material following the request for further information which would have enabled it to carry out a valid appropriate assessment and reach a different conclusion to its Inspector. Barniville J disagreed.

[91] *Rushe v An Bord Pleanála* (n 20) [32].
[92] *ibid* [34].
[93] This further information was requested pursuant to PDA, s 132.
[94] *Rushe v An Bord Pleanála* (n 20).
[95] *ibid* [119]–[126].
[96] *ibid* [127]–[134].
[97] *ibid* [19]–[35].

Following a detailed examination of the revised NIS, and the golden plover report, Barniville J was satisfied that 'both documents provided significant further and additional information'.[98] The judgment includes a detailed account of the content of the golden plover report.[99] This report was 'an entirely new document' which was not before the Inspector and which contained information which had not been provided to her. There was also significant additional information in the revised NIS, supported by academic and scientific papers which were not available to the Inspector. The relevant sections of the NIS and the golden plover report provided 'detailed discussion' on the potential impact of the operation of the wind farm on golden plover. Barniville J concluded that the applicants were wrong in their assertion that there was no new relevant additional information before the Board which had not been considered previously by the Inspector.[100] In reaching this conclusion the Court was answering a specific, narrow question (ie whether there was any relevant additional information before the Board), rather than engaging in its own analysis of the new material with a view to determining whether the new material resolved the concerns raised by the Inspector.

On receipt of the revised NIS and the golden plover report, the Board had invited submissions and observations from interested parties and observers, including the applicants in the proceedings. Barniville J noted that it was 'certainly the case' that no expert evidence was submitted to the Board in any submissions or observations 'to contradict or question' what was set out in the revised NIS and the golden plover report in relation to the impact on the golden plover or on the relevant European sites as regards that particular species.[101] The Board considered the revised NIS, the golden plover report and the submissions and observations received. It was satisfied that the information contained in the revised NIS and the further information provided to it was 'comprehensive, through and robust and had employed the best available scientific expertise in relation to research, the collection of survey data and the analysis of same'.[102] The Board accepted the findings and conclusions set out in the revised NIS. Having done so, it determined that it was satisfied beyond reasonable scientific doubt that the proposed development would not adversely affect the integrity of the site.[103] Here, too, the Court does not engage in an inquiry of its own as to whether there was the necessary degree of certainty. Rather the question to be determined is the narrow issue of whether the Court is satisfied that there was sufficient material before the Board to support its conclusions.

Barniville J determined that the appropriate assessment carried out by the Board did indeed comply with the substantive requirements for a valid assessment

[98] *ibid* [169].
[99] *ibid* [170]–[175].
[100] *ibid* [176].
[101] *ibid* [177].
[102] *ibid* [178].
[103] *ibid*.

under EU law as per the principles confirmed by the Supreme Court in *Connelly*.[104] He was satisfied that the Board had complied with its obligations under the HD and had correctly identified and applied the test for a valid appropriate assessment. He found that the appropriate assessment did indeed,

> [I]dentify, in light of the best scientific knowledge in the field, the aspects of the development which could, by itself or in combination with other plans or projects, affect the golden plover and the relevant European sites in light of their conservation objectives.[105]

On the basis of those findings and conclusions, the Board was able to determine that no scientific doubt remained as to the absence of the identified potential effects on the golden plover and the relevant sites.[106] Barniville J concluded that it was open to the Board to make such a determination.[107] In a further confirmation of the deference the courts continue to demonstrate towards the Board's expertise, Barniville J explained that, 'it was a matter for the Board, being familiar with and applying the required test for appropriate assessment under EU law, to form its view as to whether the test had been complied with on the evidence before it …'.[108]

This conclusion confirms, yet again, that although the High Court will consider carefully the evidence that was before the competent authority, it is a matter for the expert decision-maker itself to determine whether it has sufficient material to carry out its functions for the purposes of art 6(3) and to determine whether the test for appropriate assessment has been met. These determinations are only open to challenge on the traditional *O'Keeffe* principles. The High Court's role is to ensure that the competent authority applied the correct test and recorded its conclusions appropriately. *Sweetman v An Bord Pleanála*[109] (Killaloe By-Pass) was cited in this context. In *Sweetman*, McDermott J had stressed that the issue for the High Court is 'the legality of the decision not its correctness'. Following *O'Keeffe*, the Board's assessment and decision 'is an exercise by it of its specialist planning expertise'.[110]

In *Rushe*, Barniville J took the opportunity to explain why he had reached a different conclusion on the facts here when compared with the outcome in the Supreme Court in *Connelly* – a case with somewhat similar facts. The 'real difference' between the two cases 'is the manner in which the Board reached its determination on appropriate assessment and recorded that determination in its decision'.[111] There was no separate section in the Board's decision in *Connelly* dealing with the appropriate assessment. Also, in that case, unlike *Rushe*, the Board

[104] *ibid* [179]–[180].
[105] *ibid* [180].
[106] *ibid* [181].
[107] *ibid.*
[108] *ibid.*
[109] *Sweetman v An Bord Pleanála* [2016] IEHC 277.
[110] *ibid* [95].
[111] *ibid* [186].

did not set out the scientific findings underpinning its conclusion on appropriate assessment. The *(Éamon 'Ted') Kelly* case was also distinguished on the basis that, in that case, the appropriate assessment purportedly undertaken by the Board 'consisted of a couple of sentences with some uncertainty as to how much of the Inspector's report was accepted by the Board'.[112]

In *Highlands Residents Association v An Bord Pleanála*,[113] the High Court was called on to determine inter alia whether the Board, in carrying out the stage one screening, failed to exclude the possibility of significant effects on the surrounding Natura 2000 sites by reference to best scientific knowledge. More specifically, it was alleged that in the absence of appropriate bird surveys, the Board could not lawfully exclude *ex situ* effects on avi-fauna from the proposed development. This case involved a proposed housing development comprising 509 houses, 152 apartments, as well as a crèche, a shop and a café, with two Special Protection Areas (SPAs) for birds in proximity to the site. Although the High Court quashed the planning permission on the ground that the land in question was not zoned for residential purposes at the time the Board made its decision, McDonald J proceeded to consider a number of the additional grounds advanced by the applicants in relation to the HD. For the purpose of exposition, the analysis of this case presented here focuses exclusively on the allegation concerning *ex situ* effects.

McDonald J considered in detail the *Boyne Estuary Special Protection Area: Conservation Objectives – Supporting Document* (December 2012) prepared by the National Parks and Wildlife Service (NPWS).[114] This document provided guidance as regards the potential use of surrounding lands as *ex situ* habitats of bird species for which the SPAs are designated. However, there was nothing in the Environmental Impact Assessment Report (EIAR), the screening report or the NIS to indicate that a survey was carried out specifically with a view to identifying whether any part of the subject lands were used from time to time by the bird species for which the SPAs were designated.[115]

McDonald J agreed with the observation made by Barniville J in *(Eoin) Kelly* that it is primarily a matter for the Board to determine whether it has sufficient information before it to undertake its functions in relation to a stage one screening exercise.[116] Where the Board has made such a determination, the High Court will not intervene:

> [U]nless it is clear, either on the basis of the evidence placed before the court by the applicant in the proceedings or on the basis of some objective material, that there is a gap or lacunae in the information before the Board.[117]

[112] *ibid* [187].
[113] *Highlands Residents Association v An Bord Pleanála* (n 75).
[114] *ibid* [49]–[53].
[115] *ibid* [54] and [57].
[116] *ibid* [68].
[117] *ibid* [68].

The applicants in the proceedings had not placed any evidence of their own or of an expert before the High Court. Nevertheless, McDonald J was satisfied that there was 'objective material' before the Court which was not addressed in the Inspector's report and which had not been addressed sufficiently in the EIAR or the NIS.[118] This concerned the information contained in the NPWS *Supporting Document*, referred to above. This document, according to McDonald J, 'very clearly' identified that in the case of a number of the designated species that normally forage across the tidal flats, including lapwing and golden plover, many will move to nearby fields to feed when the tidal flats are covered at high water. The NPWS had therefore recommended that assessments should examine factors that have the potential to impact on the achievement of the SPA's conservation objectives and should also consider the use of *ex situ* habitats. The SPA is 4.4 or 4.5 km from the development site. McDonald J could find nothing in the Inspector's report or in the material submitted by the developer to establish that this distance is sufficient to support a conclusion at the screening stage that the site is not used on an *ex situ* basis by any of these species.[119] McDonald J determined that, in the present case, 'there is an obvious lacuna in the information before the Board in relation to bird surveys'.[120] There was 'no information' available in the materials before the Court to establish whether the surveys and inspections which had been done took place during the high tide period. On this basis, McDonald J concluded that it could not be said that there was objective material which could be assessed by reference to 'the best scientific information standard' to support the Board's conclusion that *ex situ* impacts could be properly excluded at the screening stage.[121] McDonald J also identified 'an obvious error' in the EIAR and the Inspector's report whereby they purported to exclude *ex situ* impacts due to the fact that the development site does not contain habitats that could support any of the species which are the subject of the conservation objectives of the SPAs.[122] On the basis of the information presented in the NPWS *Supporting Document*, this conclusion is 'plainly erroneous'.[123] The screening exercise therefore had not involved the application of the best scientific information. This conclusion was based on the Court's own assessment of the information that was before the Board – and, in particular, the Court's finding that there was an 'obvious lacuna' in this information as regards the bird surveys. It followed that the screening exercise carried out by the Board did not comply with the requirements of the PDA and that the Board's decision must also be quashed on that ground.

Highlands Residents Association provides a good example of a case where the Court identified an obvious lacuna in the scientific evidence that was before the

[118] *ibid* [69].
[119] *ibid.*
[120] *ibid* [73].
[121] *ibid.*
[122] *ibid* [74].
[123] *ibid.*

Board. It is notable that McDonald J engaged closely with the relevant material, and in particular with the NPWS *Supporting Document*. While the general approach remains one of deference to the expertise of the decision-maker, the court must always be satisfied that there is no gap in the material before the Board that prevents it from carrying out a lawful appropriate assessment.

IV. Conclusion

Over the past ten years or so, the Irish courts have become more inclined to engage with arguments based on EU environmental law and to make references for preliminary rulings to the CJEU. In fact, a significant number of the recent CJEU judgments concerning the HD have their origin in references from the Irish courts.[124] New questions concerning the interpretation of art 6(3) continue to arise, leading to further references.[125]

The classic, narrow approach to judicial review set down by the Supreme Court in *O'Keeffe v An Bord Pleanála* remains the mainstream standard as regards the intensity of review undertaken by the Irish courts. The judges are not experts in technical and scientific matters and they tend to defer to the expert judgment of the relevant public authority. In the context of the EIA jurisprudence, it remains to be seen whether the impact of the 'access to justice' obligations in the Aarhus Convention (art 9) and the EIA Directive (art 11) will ultimately lead to a more intense level of review. The jurisprudence of the Irish courts to date suggests that if a more intensive standard of review was to be required at some point in the future, then the common law principles are flexible enough to accommodate this. The difficulty lies in identifying the precise adjustments necessary and articulating a clear standard that is workable in practice.

As regards the prescriptive requirements set down in the HD, the contemporary jurisprudence confirms that the courts now play a more interventionist role in review of decision-making by public authorities where art 6(3) is in play. The decisions in *Kelly* and *Connelly* also confirm the strong interconnection between rationality and reasons. The High Court must ensure that the decision-maker applied the correct test and recorded its conclusions appropriately. It remains the case, however, that the *O'Keeffe* principles continue to dictate the extent to which the courts carry out their supervisory function. This is clear from *(Eoin) Kelly*, *Rushe* and *Highlands Residents Association* where the High Court confirmed that it is for the Board to determine whether it has sufficient material to carry out

[124] *Sweetman v An Bord Pleanála* (n 37); C-164/17 *Grace and Sweetman v An Bord Pleanála*, ECLI:EU:C:2018:593; C-323/17 *People Over Wind and Sweetman v Coillte Teo*, ECLI:EU:C:2018:244; C-461/17 *Holohan v An Bord Pleanála*, ECLI:EU:C:2018:883; and C-254/19 *Friends of the Irish Environment v An Bord Pleanála*, ECLI:EU:C:2020:680.

[125] In *Eco Advocacy CLG v An Bord Pleanála* [2021] IEHC 265, the High Court decided to refer two questions to the CJEU concerning the level of reasons required for a negative AA screening decision.

its functions under art 6(3) and that such determinations are only open to challenge on the basis of the *O'Keeffe* principles.

It remains to be seen how the jurisprudence will evolve. There is an obvious tension between the deferential *O'Keeffe* standard and the principle of effective judicial protection. This tension is particularly stark in the context of the prescriptive requirements set down in art 6(3) of the HD as interpreted by the CJEU. The standard of review has proven to be remarkably resilient to the influence of EU law to date. It is understandable that the courts are reluctant to move away from the *O'Keeffe* standard in complex, technical fields such as planning and environmental law. This reluctance highlights the value of judicial specialisation and timely access to independent expertise where necessary. A definitive ruling from the Supreme Court is required to resolve the standard of review conundrum and to provide certainty on this fundamental point.

4

The Boundaries of Administrative Judicial Review in Lithuania in Natura 2000 Cases

JURGITA PAUŽAITĖ-KULVINSKIENĖ AND INDRĖ ŽVAIGŽDINIENĖ

I. Introduction

Transformational processes of political and legal systems in Europe at the end of the twentieth century affected a number of Eastern and Central European countries, including Lithuania, which renewed its constitutional foundations in 1992 by adopting the Constitution of the Republic of Lithuania through a referendum.[1]

Article 111(2) of the Constitution provides that 'specialized courts may be set up to hear administrative, employment, family and other categories of cases'. Specialised environmental courts have not been established and environmental disputes currently fall under the jurisdiction of the administrative courts. These latter exercise judicial review of the activities of administrative authorities and help to preserve legality in the activities of administrative authorities.[2] It should be noted that administrative courts have de facto been operating only since 1999, when art 111(2) of the Constitution was implemented and a special law on establishment of administrative courts was adopted, following criticism from international institutions for the lack of legal standards for the protection of individuals from public administration and the requirement to strengthen the capacity of the judiciary.[3]

Administrative cases belong to the jurisdiction of the courts of first instance (two regional administrative courts since 2018) and one appeal instance (the Supreme

[1] The Constitution of the Republic of Lithuania, Lietuvos aidas, 1992-11-10, No 220-0. For the original language versions of constitutional and legislative provisions, see Table of Legislation.

[2] There is also an opinion that the concept of 'public government' is broader than 'public administration'. See Arvydas Andruškevičius, *Administracinės Teisės Principai ir Normų Ribos* (Teisines Informacijos Centras, 2004) 42–45.

[3] Jurgita Paužaitė-Kulvinskienė, *Administracinė Justicija: Teorija ir Praktika* (Justitia, 2005) 51.

Administrative Court of Lithuania since 2001). The Supreme Administrative Court (*Lietuvos vyriausiasis administracinis teismas*) (LT) investigates both the legal and factual aspects of the case. Currently environmental disputes account for about two per cent of all cases received by this Court.[4]

Judicial proceedings before the administrative courts are regulated by the Law on Administrative Proceedings (hereinafter the Law on Administrative Proceedings or LAP), adopted in 1999 by adapting the Code of Civil Procedure to include administrative litigation.[5] This has the status of a general procedural code[6] for the settlement of all kinds of administrative disputes. In some cases, it is still possible to use the Code of Civil Procedure or special procedural norms as *lex specialis*. In particular, in environmental, tax and migration cases, special rules are applicable if the procedural norms of special legislation are different from the LAP or in cases of lack of norms in the LAP.

Following an examination of the general scope and depth of review of Lithuanian courts, as well as the applicable procedural provisions concerning expert knowledge, this chapter analyses how Lithuanian administrative courts control administrative discretion when examining environmental cases, paying special attention to Natura 2000-related cases. After assessing the relevant jurisprudence, the chapter concludes that scientific uncertainty is not an issue often dealt with by the administrative courts, as the courts limit themselves to evaluating the legality and reasonableness of the decisions taken by the administrative authorities.

II. General Approach Towards the Scope and Intensity of Judicial Review of Lithuanian Administrative Courts

A. Legality Review and Limited Control of Administrative Discretion

Administrative courts in Lithuania generally carry out a legality review. According to art 88 (2)–(5) of the LAP, the administrative courts can annul the contested administrative act (or a part thereof) or oblige the competent administrative

[4] 'Overview of the Activities of the Supreme Administrative Court of Lithuania in 2019' (*LVAT*, 2020) 33, available at https://lvat.lt/data/public/uploads/2020/03/metinis-pranesimas_2019_final.pdf.

[5] Republic of Lithuania Law on Administrative Proceedings, Valstybės žinios, 1999-02-03, No 13-308. Code of Civil Procedure of the Republic of Lithuania, Valstybės žinios, 2002-04-06, No 36-1340.

[6] Jurgita Paužaitė-Kulvinskienė, 'Administracinio Proceso Modelio Paieškos Lietuvos Teisės Moksle' in *Ketvirtis Amžiaus Tiriant ir Reformuojant Lietuvos Teisinę Sistemą. Recenzuotų Mokslinių Straipsnių Rinkinys* (VŠĮ Akademinė Leidyba, 2016) 354–56.

authority to remedy the committed violation or carry out other orders of the court; can oblige the competent entities of the municipal administration to implement a law, governmental resolution or other legal act; can award damages caused by unlawful acts or omissions of administrative authorities; or may settle the dispute in any other manner provided for by law. In cases relating to omissions by administrative authorities, the administrative court may adopt a decision obliging the competent administrative authority to adopt a decision or comply with any other court order within the prescribed time limits.

The LAP limits the control of the administrative court to the review of the legality of the administrative action, namely to the control of whether the act being challenged was adopted ultra vires or whether procedural principles were violated. It should be noted that the LAP neither contains a list of grounds of annulment nor a list of remedies which can be sought before the administrative courts.

Within the system of legality review, Lithuanian administrative courts recognise areas which are reserved to the exercise of discretionary powers by administrative authorities.[7] Judicial control in these areas is limited to controlling whether the administration acted objectively and impartially, and whether it took all relevant circumstances into consideration while exercising its discretionary powers. For example, in a case concerning the assessment of air pollution in the living environment, at stake was a provision concerning the control of odour in the ambient air of residential buildings.[8] The persons who had provided information on these odours did not consent to checks and controls being carried out in their living quarters. Therefore, the Court had to assess whether the relevant public authority had discretion in terms of methods by which the air pollution in the ambient air was assessed, and in particular whether it was obliged to assess the air both in the building premises and in their surroundings. The Court ruled that the public administration has discretion to choose the location where the air pollution was to be assessed.

However, this limited control of administrative discretion does not prevent the courts from controlling administrative action from the standpoint of the respect of human rights and other legal principles, such as the environmental principles. While there is no provision in Lithuania requiring a specific scope or intensity of review, Lithuanian administrative courts do control the compatibility of the administrative action with the principles of subsidiarity, proportionality, objectivity and other principles of good administration, as they are set down in the Law on

[7] Eg the discretionary power of the head of state authority to decide whether a specific need exists to move a state servant from one post to another; the discretionary power of the municipal authority to set an expiry date of the licence to provide transport services; or the discretionary power of the Communications Regulatory Authority to impose obligations on an operator having significant market power on the relevant market, etc.

[8] Supreme Administrative Court of Lithuania case eA-2422-822/2019 (2019).

Public Administration[9] and developed in the jurisprudence of the Court of Justice of the European Union.

The courts assess administrative decisions and the evidence collected on the basis of their internal belief, based on a full, thorough and objective examination of the circumstances of the case as a whole, in accordance with the law and the criteria of fairness and reasonableness. Thus, the existence or absence of a fact can be established only on the basis of all the evidence gathered in the case and not on the basis of individual pieces of evidence. When determining the legally significant circumstances, the sufficiency of the collected evidence; its consistency; possible contradictions; logic; the circumstances in which the relevant data has been provided; and the reliability of the sources of evidence must all be assessed. It also follows from art 56(7) of the LAP that the assessment of evidence as a process of establishing objective truth is based on a subjective factor – internal belief. Internal belief is, however, not a preconceived notion or an intuition, but an evidence-based conclusion that is drawn from the evidence gathered. When significant facts are examined, and possible versions of them are raised and investigated, each piece of evidence is assessed individually as well as together.

B. The Active Role of the Judge in the Evidence-Gathering Phase

The administrative court may not go beyond the scope of the complaint, unless the public interest so requires it, or the limits of the complaint would significantly infringe the rights of a municipality and individuals and their interests protected by law (art 80(1) LAP).

However, within the scope of the complaint, the guiding principle is that of the 'active role of the judge' in administrative judicial proceedings.[10] Together with a number of provisions of the LAP (arts 10(1) and 56(4)), the principle of the 'active role of the judge' in administrative judicial proceedings requires that the judge actively participates in the examination of evidence, and, if necessary, at the request of the parties to the proceedings or on its own initiative, requests the bringing of evidence. If the case before the administrative court can be examined fairly by carefully and comprehensively assessing the evidence already gathered in the case, or if the court is able to gather certain additional data or evidence without disproportionate effort and with suitable methods available,[11] it is the duty of the court itself to do so.[12] This means that when, in a particular case, it becomes

[9] Republic of Lithuania Law on Public Administration, Valstybės žinios, 1999-07-09, No 60-1945.
[10] Supreme Administrative Court of Lithuanua case eA-370-822/2018 (2018).
[11] Supreme Administrative Court of Lithuania case A502-2277/2011 (2011).
[12] Supreme Administrative Court of Lithuania case A438-95/2012 (2012).

apparent that additional evidence must be adduced in order to establish all the relevant circumstances of the case allowing a comprehensive, objective examination thereof, the court may take certain procedural steps in order for the necessary documents to be provided, witnesses to be called, examinations to be ordered, and experts to be invited (arts 56(4), 67(1), 79(1) and 80(1) LAP).

It should be noted that the provisions of the principle of the 'active role of the judge' does not mean that the court has a duty to satisfy all the requests of the participants in the proceedings regarding the submission of evidence, the appointment of an expert examination, or the examination of witnesses. The court must, in each case, consider the requests of the participants to the proceedings and resolve them accordingly – ie grant or reject them – with a reasoned opinion.[13] Furthermore, it is important to note that the principle of expediency of proceedings cannot question the principle of fairness, and the right to be heard must be ensured.

Practice shows that the implementation of the principle of the 'active role of the judge' differs at first instance and on appeal. The case law clearly establishes this obligation in absolute terms for the court of first instance, whereas if the Supreme Administrative Court finds that there has been a clear lack of fact-finding in the case in the lower instance, it does not itself request or investigate new evidence but, as a rule, remits the case to the court of first instance.[14]

Next to the principle of the 'active role of the judge', the LAP also establishes the principle of free assessment of evidence, which means that no evidence has a pre-determined weight for the court, and the court assesses evidence according to its internal conviction based on a full examination of the circumstances of the case, the law and the criteria of justice and reasonableness (art 56 LAP). The interpretation of evidence provided by any party to the proceedings is not binding on the court.

C. The Role and Position of Expert Witnesses

In Lithuania, it is widely accepted that the main function of a court is to administer justice and a judge is not required to know or understand specific scientific or technical issues. The LAP does not specify the circumstances in which expert witnesses are required. However, if the court does not have the necessary knowledge to assess the evidence, and nevertheless assesses the evidence without the use of experts with the necessary knowledge, the rules of evidence assessment may be violated.

Generally, two types of evidence are used to acquire what can be regarded as scientific knowledge: specialist explanations and expert conclusions. It should

[13] Supreme Administrative Court of Lithuania case A-796-146/2016 (2016).
[14] Supreme Administrative Court of Lithuania case A756-1124/2011 (2011).

be noted that the assessment of specialist explanations or experts' conclusions as evidence in administrative judicial proceedings are especially influenced by the case law of the Court of Cassation (the highest court of general jurisdiction). As a result, the case law of the SACL is often consistent with the established case law in civil cases.

The essence of the 'specialist explanation' is detailed in art 60 of the LAP, which states that a specialist in a certain field may be invited in cases when the examination of an administrative case requires specialist knowledge to examine and evaluate documents, objects or actions. Specialist explanations may be submitted orally or in writing. The case law confirms that a specialist is usually needed when the data collected in a case or provided by the parties is contradictory[15] and it is necessary to assess evidence that has already been gathered using expertise that the court does not have.[16] Specialists are most often used for medical documents, or land management and spatial planning documents. A specialist may thus be regarded as an impartial court assistant in dealing with issues that require specialist knowledge. It should be noted, however, that, unlike experts, there is no unified list of specialists.

The second type of evidence is the conclusion of a forensic expert – a person who has the qualification of a forensic expert and is entered in the list of forensic experts of the Republic of Lithuania. Article 61 of the LAP establishes the notion of expert conclusion. It provides that, if an administrative case raises questions requiring specialist knowledge in the field of science, art, technology or craft, the court or judge shall appoint an expert or instruct an expert body to carry out an expert examination. The LAP does not provide the circumstances in which an expert examination is required, but the case law of the administrative courts confirms that it is not possible to use experts for issues of interpretation and application of the law, as the court is considered to 'know the law' (*iura novit curia*). An expert examination is usually ordered by the court at the request of the persons involved in the case, but the LAP does not provide that the consent of the parties is required for the appointment of an expert examination. The court may also order an expert examination on its own initiative, taking the opinion of the persons involved in the case into account (art 61(2) LAP).

In case the expert report is insufficiently clear or is incomplete, the court may order additional expertise or re-examination.[17] The expert's report is not binding on the court. The court assesses the expert's opinion on the basis of the judge's

[15] For example, the case contains two property valuation reports. As this is evidence obtained through the use of specialist knowledge, the court must invite a person with accounting knowledge to assess it, and cannot do so himself. Supreme Administrative Court of Lithuania case A438-3362/2010 (2010).

[16] Supreme Administrative Court of Lithuania case A442-203/2011 (2011).

[17] Supreme Administrative Court of Lithuanua case A438-190/2008 (2008).

internal conviction, based on a comprehensive, thorough and objective examination of the evidence in the case. Factual data obtained in an expert's examination may be rejected as evidence (or critically assessed) by the judge, if they are considered to be unsubstantiated, unreliable or otherwise deficient.[18] However, in all cases the court's disagreement with the expert's opinion must be motivated in the final court ruling.

It should be noted that the expert's report has a particular weight in the proceedings. The case law recognises that the data contained in an expert's opinion is generally more reliable and objective than data from other sources of evidence, given the process through which it was obtained. The expert's opinion can thus not be equated with other written evidence, eg documents that record the research performed by persons with specialist knowledge and their conclusions. In case an expert opinion is delivered by persons who have not been appointed by the court as experts in the case, the expert opinion is considered equivalent to any other written evidence. However, the right of a court to order an expert examination in no way restricts the right of the persons involved in the case to submit documents to the court that record the research performed by persons with special knowledge and their conclusions. There may also be situations in which the court refuses to appoint an expert. In such case, the applicant still retains the right and is given the additional opportunity to defend their interests by seeking private expertise and obtaining an expert opinion. However, the conclusion of a private expert is, in such cases, considered as ordinary written evidence.

III. The Issue of Scientific Uncertainty in the Case Law on the Habitats, Birds and EIA Directives

A. Transposition of the Habitats, Birds and EIA Directives in Lithuania

The Habitats Directive (HD) and Wild Birds Directive (WBD) have been implemented by two legal acts in Lithuania: the Law on the Protected Species of Fauna, Flora and Fungi[19] and the Law on Protected Areas.[20]

The Environmental Impact Assessment (EIA) Directive is implemented in Lithuania by the Law on Environmental Impact Assessment of the Planned Economic

[18] Supreme Court of Lithuania case e3K-3-9-421/2021 (2021).

[19] For full details of these Directives, see the Table of Legislation or the Introduction. Republic of Lithuania Law on the Protected Species of Fauna, Flora and Fungi, Valstybės žinios, 1997-11-28, No 108-2727.

[20] Republic of Lithuania Law on Protected Areas, Valstybės žinios, 1993-11-24, No 63-1188.

Activity (hereinafter – EIA Law[21]). The said law distinguishes two independent processes, which are detailed by the 'Description of the Procedure for Screening of a Planned Economic Activity for Environmental Impact Assessment' and the 'Description of the Procedure for Environmental Impact Assessment of Planned Economic Activity' contained in two orders of the Minister of the Environment.[22] These measures combine all the rules concerning the content and preparation requirements of the mandatory documents, the implementation of both the screening for the EIA and EIA procedures, and the relations between their participants. The responsible authority in both the screening for the EIA and the EIA process itself is the Environmental Protection Agency (*Aplinkos apsaugos agentūra*) (LT) (an authority under the responsibility of the Ministry of Environment).

The significance of the possible impact of a planned economic activity, plan or programme on Natura 2000 sites is determined according to another procedure, approved by the Minister of Environment,[23] considering the objectives of the protection of the areas, the size and extent of the impact of the planned economic activity, the probability and nature, magnitude, duration, frequency, reversibility of the impact and the possibilities to avoid and reduce the impact. The effect on the Natura 2000 sites is considered significant in those cases in which, in accordance with the provisions of the Law on Environmental Protection[24] (ie the framework law regulating the data used to determine the significance of adverse effects, inter alia, on protected species and their habitats) and having regard to objectives of the protection of specific areas, the planned economic activity may have significant adverse impact on protected species and natural habitats and/or the integrity of Natura 2000. The State Service for Protected Areas under the Ministry of Environment (*Valstybinė saugomų teritorijų tarnyba prie Aplinkos ministerija*) takes the decision on the significance of the impact on the Natura 2000 site – and at the same time on the necessity to carry out an EIA (as an EIA is mandatory when the effects are considered significant and the decision of the State Service for Protected Areas is binding on the Environmental Protection Agency in this case).

[21] Republic of Lithuania Law on Environmental Impact Assessment of the Planned Economic Activity, Valstybės žinios, 1996-08-30, No 82-1965.

[22] Order of the Minister of the Environment of the Republic of Lithuania No D1-845 of 16 October 2017 'On the Approval of the Description of the Procedure for Screening of Planned Economic Activity for Environmental Impact Assessment' and Order of the Minister of the Environment of the Republic of Lithuania No D1-885 of 31 October 2017, TAR, 2017-11-02, No 17241, 'On the Approval of the Description of the Procedure for Environmental Impact Assessment of Planned Economic Activity'.

[23] Order of the Minister of the Environment of the Republic of Lithuania No D1-255 of 22 May 2006, Valstybės žinios, 2006-05-31, No 61-2214 'On the Approval of the Procedure for Determining the Significance of the Impact of the Plans or Programmes and the Implementation of the Planned Economic Activities on the Designated or Potential Natura 2000 Sites'.

[24] Republic of Lithuania Law on Environmental Protection, Lietuvos aidas, 1992-01-30, No 20-0.

B. The Issue of Scientific Uncertainty in the Assessment of the Legality of Administrative Decisions

The Environmental Protection Agency (making decisions in the screening for EIA and EIA processes) or State Service for Protected Areas (deciding on the significance of the impact on the Natura 2000 site), while taking the above-mentioned decisions, are the first to face the question of possible scientific uncertainty, if any arises in a particular situation. These administrative decisions are taken on the basis of the information supplied by the operator of the planned economic activity or the consultants, hired by the operator. Administrative authorities might request additional information from the operator if necessary (that is, if matters remain unclear), as well as use consultants, when the administrative authority lacks expertise on specific questions. According to the case law of the Supreme Administrative Court of Lithuania, when assessing the legality of such decisions:

> account must be taken of the legislation which governs the specific legal relationship, i.e. it is necessary to assess whether and to what extent there are legally significant facts and what specific substantive legal norms may create appropriate preconditions and conditions for a person to create, revoke or change a person's subjective rights in certain legal relations.[25]

All factual aspects of the individual situation must also be considered.

A decision of the Vilnius Regional Administrative Court serves to illustrate the approach of the Lithuanian courts when dealing with scientific uncertainty in Natura 2000 cases.[26] In this case, the Court assessed the lawfulness of a decision of the State Service for Protected Areas under the Ministry of Environment to refuse to change the boundaries of a protected area by removing the applicants' plots of land from it. As the Court itself defined, the subject-matter of the current administrative proceedings was the legality and reasonableness of the decision of the State Service for Protected Areas. The Court examined whether, in the particular case, there had been a breach of the law or of another legal act; whether the Service had not exceeded its powers; and whether the act was in conformity with the aims and objectives for which the institution had been set up and for which it had been given the relevant powers. In order to determine the validity of the applicant's claim for annulment of the contested decision, it was first necessary to assess the conformity of the contested decision with the requirements laid down in the Law on Public Administration[27] that an individual administrative act must be based on objective facts and legal rules.

[25] Eg Supreme Administrative Court of Lithuania case A438-774/2010 (2010); case A438-1744/2012 (2012); and case A756-856/2014 (2014).

[26] Vilnius Regional Administrative Court case eI-293-643/2019 (2019).

[27] Republic of Lithuania Law on Public Administration, Valstybės žinios, 1999, No 60-1945.

In examining this case, the Court assessed both the legal (in terms of compliance with the applicable legal framework and the limits of the institution's competence) and the factual lawfulness of such a decision. In assessing the factual validity of the decision, the data on the presence of protected environmental elements in the respective territory, on the methods of determining presence of these values in that territory, and their reliability and time were analysed. First, the Court analysed the data received from the Central Data Bank of the Real Estate Register. The Court also assessed the historical information provided by the State Service for Protected Areas, which indicated that the protected area in the disputed area was established as early as 1974. The State Service for Protected Areas also provided information that in the framework of the project 'Inventory of natural habitats of European Community importance, establishment of criteria for favourable conservation status and development of a monitoring system', implemented by the Ministry of the Environment in the period from 2011 to 2015, Lithuania had inventoried natural habitats of European Community importance. The Service indicated that through this inventory, it was found that the natural habitats of Community importance were present in the protected area on the land plots of the applicants.

On the basis of the considerations set out above, the Court concluded that the contested decision provided the applicants with sufficient information, in relation to which the applicants did not provide any rebuttal evidence, and that there were therefore no legal grounds to oblige the Service to re-examine the applicants' application. This case shows that usually the evidence is provided by the parties of the case; however the right of the administrative court to take evidence on its own initiative (granted by law) can and must be exercised by the court in cases where it becomes apparent that, in order to establish all the circumstances relevant to the case in question and to examine them fully and objectively, it is necessary to adduce additional evidence.[28] The active role of the court in administrative proceedings implies that not only the circumstances of the case put forward by the parties to the proceedings, but also the circumstances which the court deems relevant, may be investigated and evaluated.[29] If necessary, the court may invite the persons involved in the case to submit additional evidence, to obtain the necessary documents from those persons or on its own initiative, or to request explanations from officials.

In the context of this chapter, seeking to evaluate the approach of Lithuanian courts towards scientific uncertainty, the case law on EIA is also to be considered. First, there is very little case law relating solely to appropriate assessment under the HD. Second, the EIA is the main instrument used in Lithuania to evaluate

[28] The Practice of the Supreme Administrative Court of Lithuania on application of the provisions of the Law on Administrative Proceedings. Administrative Jurisprudence: Bulletin of the Supreme Administrative Court of Lithuania, 23, 588.

[29] Supreme Administrative Court of Lithuania case A575-88/2012 (2012).

possible effects on Natura 2000 sites and species, to avoid negative impacts, and to choose the necessary mitigation measures. When analysing the case law on EIA, it is possible to observe that screening conclusions and final EIA decisions are challenged most often.

In their case law, the administrative courts have established certain (uniform) criteria to be borne in mind when assessing the legality of decisions in the EIA process. During the screening stage, it is sufficient to assess whether the planned economic activity is likely to have an impact, without deciding at this stage on the specific extent of the potential impact, ie at this stage it is not necessary to resolve completely any scientific uncertainty, if such exists. According to the EIA Law, the competent authority (Environmental Protection Agency) shall perform a screening for the EIA by assessing the screening information prepared by the organiser (developer) of the planned economic activity, or the drafter of the EIA documents, in compliance with the Screening Methodological Instructions as submitted thereto. However, as duly stated in the case law, though the EIA Law stipulates what must be taken into account by the competent authority when adopting a screening conclusion, it does not detail the grounds on which the competent authority must accept a conclusion to carry out an EIA or not to carry it out.[30] Thus, the final decision is left to the discretion of the competent authority.[31]

However, the Supreme Administrative Court is keen on clarifying that the competent authority does not have unlimited discretion to decide on the necessity of the EIA and must assess all the circumstances specified in the EIA Law when adopting its final conclusion.[32] When adopting the final screening conclusion, the criteria set out in the EIA Law must be assessed and at least a general statement must be made as to which specific environmental factors (fauna, flora, soil, water, etc) are likely to be adversely affected. In addition, each public authority is bound by constitutional and other legal principles (such as the rule of law, the principles of equality and of proportionality) as well as the principles of good administration (namely legality, objectivity, non-abuse of power, transparency and accountability). This means that the competent authority, when deciding on the final screening conclusion, must duly justify its decision.[33] According to the Supreme Administrative Court the assessment of the lawfulness of the final screening conclusion must also take the evaluation of the opinion of the public concerned and the local authorities into account: it is not sufficient for the Environmental Protection Agency to state in the final screening conclusion that certain comments have been received, but it is necessary to assess them and to indicate what circumstances refute the doubts raised in the comments and proposals.[34] The case law on

[30] Supreme Administrative Court of Lithuania case A261-1078/2007 (2007).

[31] Supreme Administrative Court of Lithuania case A492-2371/2011 (2011).

[32] Case law of the Supreme Administrative Court of Lithuania in the field of environmental protection. Bulletin of the Supreme Administrative Court of Lithuania No 28 (2015).

[33] Supreme Administrative Court of Lithuania case A 602-621/2014 (2014).

[34] Supreme Administrative Court of Lithuania case A556-1424/2014 (2014).

environmental matters of the Supreme Administrative Court constantly emphasises that the legality of an administrative act must be assessed by reference to the basic principles of the rule of law and legal certainty, according to which, in carrying out the activities assigned to them by law, national authorities must act only in accordance with the law.[35] The control of the courts is thus largely conducted through the application of legal principles and the courts will strike down decisions where they are not adequately motivated or where the authority did not clearly indicate why certain data or circumstances were not taken into account in the final decision.

With respect to the EIA report, it should also be noted that, as a rule, an EIA report, prepared by specialists, contains statements, modulations and calculations performed using specially designed programs. According to the Lithuanian case law, a party seeking to challenge or refute the said data, or the results of calculations, must base her claim not on abstract statements, but on specific evidence, data, calculations, and research that would allow the court to objectively question the data in the report.[36] The report is prepared by specialists in the relevant fields, therefore statements based on subjective beliefs about technical violations of environmental requirements cannot usually be sufficient to question the conclusions of the specialists.[37] On this basis, it can be concluded that the general rule concerning the distribution of the burden of proof (ie that each party has to prove the circumstances on which her claims and rebuttals are based, unless circumstances which do not need to be proved are relied on) applies when challenging a decision on the possibilities of a proposed economic activity.[38] However, as mentioned above, the court's active role in the proceedings is also important in the collection and examination of evidence. The court should cooperate with the parties at all stages of the evidentiary process: it should draw the parties' attention to any inaccuracies or incompleteness in their submissions and invite them to clarify them; it should indicate which admissible means of proof are to be used to prove a particular matter; it should offer to adduce additional evidence if the parties' submissions appear to the court to be inadequate; and it should gather evidence on its own initiative, if necessary.[39] Although the administrative court must be active, assisting in the exercise of the procedural rights of the parties to the proceedings, and in the full and objective examination of the case, its activity and powers cannot be unlimited. The court shall not be entitled to change the cause of action or the subject-matter of the claim on its own initiative and may not, as a general rule, go

[35] Supreme Administrative Court of Lithuania case A556-383/2009 (2009).

[36] Concerning this aspect, see, eg, Supreme Administrative Court of Lithuania case A525-1745/2013 (2013).

[37] Supreme Administrative Court of Lithuania case A492-1890/2013 (2014).

[38] Supreme Administrative Court of Lithuania case (n 36).

[39] Rimvydas Norkus, 'Įrodymai ir Įrodinėjimas Administraciniame Procese. Lietuvos Vyriausiojo Administracinio Teismo Siuletenis Nr. 2(12)' (Lietuvos Vyriausiasis Administracinis Teismas, 2007) 162.

beyond the limits of the claim in the course of the proceedings.[40] It should also be mentioned that where there is insufficient evidence to support the facts alleged by either the applicant or the defendant, the decision shall be given against the party who bears the burden of proving the unproven facts.[41]

The same principles are applied in Natura 2000-related cases. A good example of this approach is a decision of the Supreme Administrative Court concerning an EIA decision adopted by the Environmental Protection Agency, which prohibited the extraction of peat due to the possible negative impact of such activities on protected species.[42] The dispute in the present case arose from the fact that the EIA report submitted by the operator did not, in the opinion of the Environmental Protection Agency, resolve the doubts as to the possible negative impact of the planned activity on the environment in a particular area. Although the operator had requested it, neither the Environmental Protection Agency nor the court ordered any additional expertise to analyse the possible negative environmental impact. From the description of the planned activity (felling of forest and shrubs, grubbing and removal of stumps, construction of access roads, construction of a production site, excavation of drainage and drainage ditches, etc), the Court concluded that the planned activity could not be described as minimal interference with the natural environment without adverse effects on the status of the site and habitat of the marsh satire included in the List of Protected Species of Protected Animals, Plants and Fungi,[43] as well as the status of the sites and habitats of eight other bird species and three mammal species. The panel of judges concluded that according to the EIA Law, persons who planned to carry out economic activities had to submit such descriptions and arguments of the planned activities in the EIA report that would have allowed the Environmental Protection Agency to decide that the planned activities would not have a negative impact on the environment.

In this specific case, the persons planning to carry out economic activities sought to take the issue of environmental impact assessment to Court and asked the Court to order an expert examination. However, the Court found that the persons who planned to carry out economic activities failed to prove on the basis of objective evidence that the planned activities would not cause violations of the relevant legal provisions. Nor had they proved that they would not have a negative impact on the environment. On the contrary, the negative impact on the protected habitats was obvious. Other arguments – that the acquisition of a peat deposit would create new jobs and that various taxes would be paid to the state

[40] Supreme Administrative Court of Lithuania case AS403-80/2007 (2007).

[41] Supreme Administrative Court of Lithuania cases A556-963/2009 (2009) and A556-862/2010 (2010).

[42] Supreme Administrative Court of Lithuania case eA-289-822/2019.

[43] The List of Protected Species of Protected Animals, Plants and Fungi protection by the Republic of Lithuania, approved by the Order of the Minister of the Environment of the Republic of Lithuania No 504 of 13 October 2003, Valstybės žinios, 2003-10-24, No 100-4506 (with subsequent amendments).

were seen as satisfying private interests, seeking personal gain, and therefore, irrelevant. The Court also stated that, in accordance with the EIA Law, the competent authorities, if necessary, may use consultants when deciding on the admissibility of the planned activity. However, the Environmental Protection Agency was not required to exercise that right, nor was it necessary in the present case, since it was clear from the nature and scale of the proposed activity that most of the protected habitats registered in the area would be destroyed. The Court found that the planned activities, which would destroy the natural cover of the wetland, use noise-causing equipment, mobile machinery and workers – were likely to radically change both habitats and living conditions of protected species, which was going to have a significant negative impact on the survival of protected species. As a consequence, the Court upheld the negative EIA decision of the Environmental Protection Agency.[44]

The case law examined above shows that, when faced with complex scientific questions, Lithuanian courts usually do not question the administration's assessment, provided that it is well reasoned and based on facts and legal provisions. The Supreme Administrative Court has consistently held that, where the institutions are granted a relatively wide margin of discretion in implementing certain legal norms or in pursuing a policy in a certain area (which is the situation in environmental cases), the courts examine only whether, in exercising its discretion, the public administrative body has made a manifest error (in the assessment of the circumstances and in the application of the law); whether it has abused its powers; whether it has manifestly exceeded the limits of its discretion; whether it has complied with the applicable procedural rules; whether the facts on which the disputed choice is based are accurate; and whether the act/action is consistent with the aims and objectives for which the institution was established and the powers conferred on it.[45]

In assessing whether the authority, when exercising its administrative discretion, has not acted ultra vires, the court must determine whether the exceedance of the limits of competence is manifest and clearly contrary to the mandatory provisions of the law defining the competences of the public authority. In assessing whether there has been a breach of essential procedures, the focus is on breaches of the procedures laid down in the law. Formal procedural irregularities which do not affect the adoption of the decision are not considered to be essential. In assessing whether there has been a material error of assessment of the facts, the court must assess whether an administrative decision of a discretionary nature is based on established facts, irrespective of the specific (economic, social or other) nature of those facts. The assessment of the correctness of the determination of those facts is not to be equated with an assessment of economic or political expediency.

[44] Supreme Administrative Court of Lithuania case eA-289-822/2019 (n 42).

[45] Eg Supreme Administrative Court of Lithuania cases: A415-2203/2006 (2006); A261-2286/2012 (2012); A525-2952/2012 (2012); and A492-435/2014 (2014).

The control of the correctness of the essential facts and of errors in their legal assessment involves an identification of: (1) whether the facts which form the basis of the administrative decision are real; (2) whether the institution has assessed these facts in accordance with the procedural rules and requirements, inter alia, including the adequacy of the assessment, the relevance of the assessment to the object of the analysis, its characteristics, the statutory objectives of such analysis and others; (3) the legal test of the allocation of the burden of proof; and (4) whether the facts have been sufficiently and exhaustively investigated and (5) whether the discretionary decision taken is sufficiently motivated by them.

The principle of discretionary powers requires that the environmental authorities which have adopted a contested administrative act would be able to prove before a court that the act was adopted in the effective exercise of their powers (in accordance with the totality of the rights and obligations conferred on them), and that they were able to take into account all the data and circumstances relevant to the situation in question. At the very least, the administrative authorities must be able to state in a clear and unambiguous manner the essential elements which were taken into account in the justification of the act, and on which the exercise of their discretion was dependent. The legal limits of the administrative discretion are also referred to as the external limits of discretion and are determined by assessing whether the institution has complied with the principles of law in its action, how it has gathered all the relevant facts for the decision, and how it has qualified the particular situation. All these actions of the administrative authority are subject to judicial review. In contrast, the internal aspects of the exercise of administrative discretion (sociological, psychological, political, etc) are outside the scope of the legal review of administrative discretion and are also not subject to evaluation and review by the courts.

One of the most effective instruments for delimiting and controlling administrative discretion is the obligation to justify and give reasons for administrative decisions, as implied by the principle of sound administration.[46] Discretion cannot be interpreted as excluding the duty of a public administrative authority to provide reasons for its decisions. According to the Supreme Administrative Court, subjects exercising the right of discretion are constrained by the general requirements and criteria of the principle of legality. In exercising their discretionary powers, public administrative authorities must, inter alia, not abuse the powers conferred on them, respect the principles of objectivity and impartiality, equality before the law and proportionality. The exercise of discretion must not undermine the essential requirements of the rule of law, of the constitutional principle of public authorities serving the people, and of good and responsible administration (legitimacy, objectivity, non-abuse of power, participation of the individual in the relevant

[46] The practice of the Supreme Administrative Court of Lithuania in applying the norms of the Law on Public Administration of the Republic of Lithuania. Administrative Jurisprudence: Bulletin of the Supreme Administrative Court of Lithuania, 30, 549.

decisions, transparency, etc). Compliance with these requirements is shaped by the need to comply with the principles of legal certainty, clarity and the right to a fair hearing.[47] An improper exercise of administrative discretion may constitute grounds for the annulment of the administrative act adopted, for ordering the public administration entity to carry out certain actions, to remedy the infringement, or for compensation for the damage caused by the unlawful exercise of discretion.

At the same time, in order for the court to find a violation of the duty to give reasons, an active engagement of the applicant is necessary. If the latter wants to challenge the administrative assessment, she must provide proof for her arguments (eg alternative expertise, etc). It is not sufficient for the applicant to set out the allegations (in a general manner) which call into question the legality and reasonableness of the decision, but it is necessary for the applicant to set out the circumstances and to provide arguments and evidence in support of the doubts raised.[48] The Supreme Administrative Court in its case law also emphasises that the mere fact that the applicant is defending a public interest in the field of environmental protection does not confer an exceptional position in the proceedings and does not change the content of the burden of proof.[49] Moreover, the Court emphasises that shifting the burden of proof exclusively to participants of the EIA process would be disproportionate, would deny the right to a fair trial and would create grounds for abuse of process.[50] However, as it was already mentioned, the principle of the active judge means that the judge has a duty to actively participate in the examination of evidence, and, if necessary, at the request of the parties to the proceedings or on its own initiative, to demand evidence. If the court concludes that the administrative decision is not substantiated enough by the facts, or is in violation of legal provisions, the court may annul the contested decision/act (or part of it) or order the administrative entity concerned to remedy the infringement or comply with any other court order.

IV. Conclusions

Administrative courts in Lithuania are generally tasked with a legality review of administrative decisions. The scope and intensity of control by administrative courts depends on the nature of the case. Administrative decisions in the field of environmental protection, where specific environmental knowledge is relied upon and used, should be regarded as administrative discretionary decisions. In that

[47] Supreme Administrative Court of Lithuania case A502-1668/2012 (2012).
[48] Supreme Administrative Court of Lithuania case A525-1745/2013 (n 36).
[49] Supreme Administrative Court of Lithuania case A492-1890/2013 (n 37).
[50] *ibid.*

case, they are subject to the standard of judicial review of discretionary decisions as developed by the case law. The main idea of this standard is that the assessment of the lawfulness and reasonableness of such an administrative decision is based on balancing between the discretion conferred on public administrative authorities and the discretion of review granted to the courts.

Within this system of legality review, in order to assess and understand the relevant facts, two types of evidence are used to aid the courts in technically or scientifically complex fields: specialist explanations and expert conclusions. The law does not provide the circumstances for which an expert examination is required, but the practice of the administrative courts confirms that it is most often ordered in the context of truly complex and specific cases, where the expert's conclusion becomes simply necessary evidence.[51] However, in most cases, administrative judges rely on the scientific assessments collected and presented by administrative agencies in environmental cases. They do not attempt to contradict them by engaging additional formal expertise. As regards specialists' explanation, it should be noted that case law confirms that a specialist is usually needed when the data collected in a case are contradictory and when it is necessary to assess evidence that has already been gathered by means of specialised knowledge that is not available to the court.[52]

When assessing the decisions of administrative authorities in the field of designation and protection of Natura 2000 sites, as well as in the EIA process, the case law of the Supreme Administrative Court consistently emphasises that it is necessary to assess all aspects relevant to the case: both legal and factual. An individual administrative act which does not set out in sufficient detail the facts and legal provisions on which the act is based, is not in accordance with the principle of sound public administration. However, where authorities are granted a wide margin of discretion, the courts exercised very restrained control of the administrative action, by limiting their scrutiny to an examination of whether the authority has made a manifest error in the assessment of the facts or in the application of the law; whether it has abused its powers or manifestly exceeded the limits of its discretion; whether it has complied with the applicable procedural rules; whether the facts on which the disputed decision is based are accurate; and whether the act is consistent with the aims and objectives for which the institution was established and the powers conferred on it. This provides for limited control of scientific uncertainty, a matter which largely still remains in the hands of the administrative authorities.

[51] The Practice of the Supreme Administrative Court of Lithuania on application of the provisions of the Law on Administrative Proceedings (n 28) 23, 761.

[52] *ibid* 763.

5

The Scrutiny of Scientific Evidence by UK Courts in Environmental Decisions: Legality, the Fact-Law Distinction, and (Sometimes) Self-Limiting Review

CATHERINE CAINE AND RICHARD BROADBENT

I. Introduction

In the UK, claims regarding obligations generated by the Habitats Directive (HD) are usually dealt with by challenging the legality of a decision through judicial review and statutory appeal. Whilst such claims allow for the legality of a decision to be assessed, the courts are not willing to assess the substance of a decision or to re-make a lawfully made decision of a public body. In other 'routes' of challenge, they may be so-willing, but this is rare. This is guided by the approach the courts take to the separation of powers. However, whilst judicial review helps to hold governments, local authorities and public bodies to account,[1] the reliance on a system which only allows for decisions to be challenged on legal grounds to settle often controversial environmental law cases involving scientific uncertainty can lead to concerns that environmental decision-making lacks a substantive, merits-based examination by the court. Rather, the courts are expressly conscious of the rule of separation of powers in the UK and will not assess the substance of the original decision made by the decision-maker. This is often referred to by judges in the UK as the refusal to comment on the 'merits' of the underlying case.[2]

[1] Lucinda Platt and Maurice Sunkin, 'Why Judicial Review is Valuable to Society's Most Vulnerable' (*The Conversation*, 6 November 2015), available at https://theconversation.com/why-judicial-review-is-valuable-to-societys-most-vulnerable-49781.

[2] See, eg, *R (Save Warsash and the Western Wards) v Fareham Borough Council* [2021] EWHC 1435 (Admin) [48].

This approach has been the subject of challenge brought against the UK before the Aarhus Convention Compliance Committee (ACCC),[3] which argues that the UK's use of judicial review in environmental decision-making is in breach of arts 9(2), 9(3) and 9(4) of the Aarhus Convention.[4]

Other avenues of redress in environmental law cases are available in the UK in specific circumstances and many of these do accord a greater degree of intensity of review to the adjudicator. One example is the tribunal system which scrutinises regulatory action taken in accordance with the Regulatory Enforcement and Sanctions Act 2008 (RESA 2008). Due to the constitutional underpinning of the tribunal system, tribunals are able to take a much more proactive approach to environmental decision-making whereby they are effectively required to 'stand in the shoes' of the decision-maker when assessing the decision that has been made, thus allowing for the merits of a decision to be challenged in a judicial (or quasi-judicial) setting.

This chapter will analyse the extent to which scientific uncertainty in decision-making is assessed by the courts and tribunals in the UK with respect to cases which relate to the application of the Wild Birds Directive (WBD) and HD.[5] The chapter will begin by outlining the way in which these Directives have been implemented in the UK. This will be followed by an overview of the main avenues for challenging decisions relating to the WBD and HD. The chapter will then move on to analyse relevant case law from both judicial review and the tribunal system to determine how scientific uncertainty is assessed. This case law analysis will include: a focus on the extent to which the cross-examination of witnesses is allowed in judicial review and statutory appeal cases; the way in which judicial review decisions focus on only assessing the legality of decisions; an assessment of how the courts deal with uncertainty in judicial review and statutory appeals; and finally how the tribunal system takes somewhat of a contrasting approach in the context of RESA 2008 decision-making. The chapter will then conclude with an analysis of the extent to which the current approach to assessing environmental case law in the UK allows for full scrutiny of scientific evidence. The chapter will also provide a review of the extent to which the approach in the UK conforms with constitutional norms and the extent to which the ACCC has determined the UK's compliance with the requirements of the Aarhus Convention.

[3] United Nations Economic Commission for Europe (UNECE), 'Version 13 February 2015' (ACCC), available at www.unece.org/fileadmin/DAM/env/pp/compliance/C2018-156/Communication_UK_RSPB_07.12.2017.pdf.

[4] UNECE, *Convention on Access to Information, Public Participation in Decision-making and Access to Justice in Environmental Matters*, 2161 UNTS 447, 25 June 1998 (the Aarhus Convention).

[5] For full details, see the Table of Legislation and Introduction.

II. The National Implementation of the WBD and HD in the UK

The WBD was transposed into the law of England and Wales by Pt 1 of the Wildlife and Countryside Act 1981 (WCA 1981). Under the WCA 1981 it is an offence to kill, take or injure all wild birds, with stricter requirements for species listed in the schedules of the Act.[6] The requirements under the WCA 1981 have subsequently been amended and supplemented by the Countryside and Rights of Way Act 2000 (CROWA) and the Natural Environment and Rural Communities Act 2006 (NERCA). The requirements of the HD are transposed in England and Wales through the Conservation of Habitats and Species Regulations 2017, with corresponding legislation in Scotland and Northern Ireland.[7] For offshore areas beyond the territorial boundaries of 12 nautical miles, the same legislation applies to all devolved administrations of the UK – that is the Offshore Marine Habitats and Species Regulations 2017.[8] Due to the devolved status of the UK, a variety of bodies are responsible for taking regulatory action or giving statutory advice to decision-makers in respect of the above-mentioned legislation in each nation. For the WBD and HD, each nation has its own non-departmental public body and statutory adviser dedicated to nature conservation.[9] These are: Natural England; Natural Resources Wales; NatureScot (previously known as Scottish Natural Heritage); and the Northern Ireland Environment Agency. However, it is important to emphasise that the legal systems (relevant particularly to questions of judicial precedent) of the devolved nations are organised differently: Scotland has a separate legal system, as does Northern Ireland. The primary focus in this chapter will be on judicial treatment of the HD in the English and Welsh context.

III. Avenues for Challenging Decisions Relating to the WBD and HD in the UK

The main route for challenging decisions made with respect to the WBD and HD in the UK is through judicial review or by a statutory appeal to a planning permission

[6] Wildlife and Countryside Act 1981, pt 1.

[7] Conservation of Habitats and Species Regulations 2017 (SI 2017/1012). Conservation (Natural Habitats &c) Regulations 1994 (SI 1994/2716) in Scotland, and Conservation (Natural Habitats etc) Regulations (Northern Ireland) 1995 (as amended), Northern Ireland Statutory Rules 1995/380 in Northern Ireland.

[8] The Conservation of Offshore Marine Habitats and Species Regulations 2017 (SI 2017/1013). These Regulations replaced the Offshore Marine Conservation (Natural Habitats &c) Regulations 2007 (SI 2007/1842).

[9] A non-departmental body is 'a body which has a role in the processes of national government but is not a government department or part of one, and which accordingly operates to a greater or lesser extent at arm's length from ministers'. 'Public Bodies' (*GOV.UK*, 19 February 2013), available at www.gov.uk/guidance/public-bodies-reform.

decision (which is, in effect, a statutory authorisation for a court to carry out an exercise akin to judicial review in the context of town and country planning).[10] In addition to this, in the specialist arena of civil sanctions, which are now available for a number of habitats and species offences, the tribunal system also has a role in adjudicating decisions in accordance with RESA 2008. Therefore, this section will outline both systems, considering the procedural rules on evidence and the use of scientific knowledge for both.

A. Judicial Review, Statutory Review and Statutory Appeal in the UK

Judicial review is a legality challenge. A case for judicial review can only be brought under three grounds: illegality, procedural impropriety and irrationality.[11] Challenging a decision based on illegality ensures that 'the decision-maker must understand correctly the law that regulates his decision-making power and must give effect to it'.[12] In order to succeed on the ground of procedural impropriety, the claimant must show that the decision made has infringed either 'the rule against bias' or 'the right to be heard'. In addition to this, the right to be given reasons for a decision also falls under the ground of procedural impropriety. Finally for irrationality or unreasonableness, the decision from the public authority must be found to be 'so outrageous in its defiance of logic or accepted moral standards that no sensible person who had applied his mind to the question to be decided could have arrived at it'.[13] This last test is that of *Wednesbury* unreasonableness, the idea that a decision is so unreasonable that no reasonable decision-maker could have made it. All claims made for judicial review in England are brought before the general Administrative Court, with the exception of planning-related statutory appeals which are to be brought before a special division of the King's Bench, the Planning Court as explained below. Claims for judicial review must be brought promptly and cannot be brought later than three months after the grounds to make the claim first arose – this timeframe is reduced to six weeks for statutory appeals of planning decisions.[14]

Appeals relating to planning matters are dealt with in England in the Planning Court. These appeals are classed as either a statutory review or a statutory planning appeal. Statutory review and statutory planning appeal apply to a discrete

[10] This chapter focuses on the environmental decision-making approach of the courts and tribunal for judicial review and civil sanctions and not statutory appeals to the Secretary of State acting in a quasi-judicial role such as under the WCA 1981, s 28F. Please note that these decisions can be challenged using judicial review.

[11] *Council of Civil Service Unions v Minister for the Civil Service* [1985] AC 374 (HL) 410.

[12] *ibid.*

[13] *ibid.*

[14] Civil Procedure Rules (CPR) 54.5, A1 (1) (b), A1 (5).

number of actions in planning law and are governed by specific legislation.[15] For both statutory review and statutory planning appeals, the general principles of judicial review apply, for example, the grounds of appeal are the same as outlined above,[16] however the constitutional underpinning of each form of statutory review available is dictated by the relevant legislation under which the review is being brought. Matters which will be brought before the Planning Court are outlined in the Civil Procedure Rules (CPR).[17]

An important distinction between the Planning Court and Administrative Court is that the Planning Court is made up of judges that have specialist knowledge in planning law matters, whereas a case of judicial review on environmental matters that comes before the Administrative Court will not be reviewed by a specialist judge. The reason for the introduction of specialist judges in the Planning Court was to speed up the time in which these decisions can be taken.[18] However, despite having a specialist judge present in the Planning Court, this does not mean that specialist evidence will be scrutinised differently than in the Administrative Court, as the grounds for judicial review, statutory review and statutory appeal govern the ways that decisions are reviewed. In other words, whilst the identity of the decision-maker, and the way in which power has been conferred upon them to decide, is different in these two contexts, the underpinning standard of review is the same. Whether in practice the approach is the same is less clear.

It should also be emphasised at this point that the meeting of EU law standards, as defined and articulated by the Court of Justice of the European Union (CJEU), is a question of legality, *not* reasonableness. Thus, a claim that an administrative authority has breached the HD by failing to conduct an appropriate assessment is judged according to the legality of that failure, rather than the reasonableness of the failure. However, we can add into this the complexity engendered by the law/fact distinction in this context. Questions of law, susceptible to definitive 'right or wrong' determination by a court, are reviewed under the legality standard. Questions of fact are questions which are reviewed on a reasonableness basis. To give an example, the meaning of 'appropriate' for the purposes of the HD is a question of law (determined, as we would expect, by the interplay between national courts and the CJEU). However, the question, as a matter of fact, as to whether the

[15] Statutory review can be pursued using the following provisions: Town and Country Planning Act 1990, s 287–88; Planning (Listed Buildings and Conservation Areas) Act 1990, s 63; Planning (Hazardous Substances) Act 1990, s 22; Planning and Compulsory Purchase Act 2004, s 113. Statutory planning appeal can be pursued under Town and Country Planning Act 1990, s 289 and Planning (Listed Buildings and Conservation Areas) Act 1990, s 65.

[16] This was summarised in the cases of *Seddon Properties v Secretary of State for the Environment* [1978] 2 EGLR 148 (QBD) and *Centre 21 Ltd v Secretary of State for the Environment* (1986) 280 EGLR 889 (CA).

[17] CPR 54.

[18] 'Planning Court' (*Courts and Tribunals Judiciary*), available at www.judiciary.uk/you-and-the-judiciary/going-to-court/high-court/queens-bench-division/courts-of-the-queens-bench-division/planning-court/.

assessment *in the particular case* was appropriate (judged against the correct legal benchmark) is a question of fact. The meaning of the term is a question of law: its application to the particular case, a question of fact.[19] Thus, just as important as the decision 'substance' or 'legality' review in the UK context is the question as to whether the alleged breach discloses an incorrect interpretation of the legal standard applicable to the case, or whether it discloses an unreasonable assessment of that correctly-interpreted legal standard as it applies to the facts before a decision-maker. A very great deal of normative complexity, therefore, is packaged into the seemingly simple fact/ law distinction and that complexity is particularly pertinent to the context of scientific uncertainty.

B. Environmental Civil Sanctions under the RESA 2008

Environmental civil sanctions were introduced in England and Wales in 2008 through the RESA 2008. This provides environmental regulators with the power to issue a civil sanction for a number of offences in place of criminal sanction (or ahead of criminal sanctions being used as a last resort). Such sanctions include fixed monetary penalties, remediation notices, stop notices and enforcement undertakings. For example, Natural England has been able to use civil sanctions from January 2012 as an alternative to prosecution for a number of offences, including those relating to the habitats and nature conservation provisions from the Environmental Liability Directive 2004.[20]

Under RESA 2008, s 54 an appeal can be made against a civil sanction on the grounds that it was based on an error of law or fact or unfair or unreasonable for any reason. An appeal is heard under the First-tier Tribunal as opposed to the court and must be made within 28 days of receiving the decision from the regulator.[21] Such appeals are generally heard by specialists who are trained to hear specific appeals and usually comprise of the tribunal judge and up to two other expert members who have been appointed by the Lord Chancellor. Witnesses can be (and often routinely are) called in First-tier Tribunal appeals and can be anyone who has first-hand knowledge of the matter.[22] Witnesses are questioned in the form of cross-examination whereby the appellant will usually call and question a witness first, followed by an opportunity for the other parties and tribunal to

[19] The distinction between questions of law and fact is considered in Elisabeth Fisher, 'EU Environmental Law and Legal Imagination' in Paul Craig and Gráinne de Búrca (eds), *The Evoluation of EU Law*, 3rd edn (Oxford University Press, 2021) 851–54.

[20] Directive 2004/35/EC of the European Parliament and of the Council of 21 April 2004 on environmental liability with regard to the prevention and remedying of environmental damage [2004] OJ L143/56.

[21] The First-tier Tribunal was established by the Tribunals, Courts and Enforcement Act 2007, s 3.

[22] Tribunal Procedure (First-tier Tribunal) (General Regulatory Chamber) Rules 2009 (SI 2009/1976) (as amended), r 16.

pose questions to the witness. In such cases, as we shall see, there is a good deal of scrutiny of scientific uncertainties, methods and advisors, something which is as a matter of procedure if nothing else, conspicuous by its absence in relation to judicial review and statutory appeals in respect of planning.

An appeal against the First-tier Tribunal decision can be made to the Upper Tribunal, but the grounds for such an appeal are on points of law only. So, for example, if the First-tier Tribunal: did not apply the law correctly, did not follow the correct procedures, did not have enough or any evidence to support its decision, or did not give adequate reasons for its decision. Permission to appeal must be sought within 28 days of receiving the decision from the First-tier Tribunal. Appeals in the Upper Tribunal can take place without an oral hearing, and no new evidence will be considered.[23] Appeals from the Upper Tribunal go to the ordinary courts (Court of Appeal).

IV. An Analysis of the Use of Scientific Evidence in the UK Legal System

A. Procedural Rules on Evidence and Use of Scientific Knowledge in Judicial Review and Statutory Appeal

The processes of judicial review and statutory appeal are governed by the CPR.[24] These rules apply to all judicial review cases, and there are no specific rules that apply to judicial review cases that have been brought under an environmental heading (subject to Aarhus Convention rules). There are three relevant questions here in terms of scientific uncertainties and judicial engagement with them. First, can (and will) the court allow cross-examination of witnesses from the decision-making authority to examine their assessment of scientific information? Second, can (and will) the court receive (in writing) and/ or hear (in cross-examination) evidence from experts regarding the scientific information relevant to the case (ie not experts consulted in the original decision, but experts appointed by the parties as part of the process of challenge)? Third, can the court request of its own volition or require from parties expert testimony to assist the court? These questions are answered by a combination of the rules in the CPR and their interpretation in case law.

First, in judicial review cases, in the vast majority of cases, the evidence analysed comes in the form of written witness statements.[25] There is an in-person hearing,

[23] Tribunal Procedure (Upper Tribunal) Rules 2008 (SI 2008/2698), r 15.

[24] CPR 54.

[25] 'The Administrative Court Judicial Review Guide 2020' (*Courts and Tribunals Judiciary*, October 2022) 49, available at https://assets.publishing.service.gov.uk/government/uploads/system/uploads/attachment_data/file/913526/HMCTS_Admin_Court_JRG_2020_Final_Web.pdf.

but this is conducted between the judge and counsel. Witnesses are not required to give evidence in person. However, it is possible for the judge to order the cross-examination of witnesses if they are 'satisfied that there are reasonable grounds to consider that the statement in the report of substance of the instructions is inaccurate or incomplete'.[26] Whilst cross-examination of witnesses is an option available to the courts, this rarely happens precisely because on questions of fact, the standard is that of reasonableness.[27] The Court of Appeal has recently reaffirmed the position that considering 'live evidence' and cross-examining witnesses in cases of judicial review should only be needed in 'exceptional cases'.[28]

A rare example where permission for the cross-examination of a witness was allowed is the case of *R (Jedwell) v Denbighshire CC*[29] which concerned an application for the construction of two wind turbines and ancillary works in Denbighshire, Wales. The case concerned the reasons behind a negative Environmental Impact Assessment (EIA) screening opinion that had been provided, and the Court considered whether it was appropriate to cross-examine the Council employee who had made the decision for a negative EIA screening opinion. Foskett J initially determined that it was not appropriate to cross-examine the witness, however both Lewison LJ in the Court of Appeal and Mr Justice Hickinbottom in the High Court of Justice later disagreed with this and found that cross-examination of the witness was appropriate. Lewison LJ held that the question of fact in this case related to whether Mrs Shaw's written statement had been a justification of the negative screening opinion or a true account of her reasoning at the time of making the statement. He held that this was not a matter for the planning authority to decide but was a question for the Court, and the only way to answer this question was to cross-examine Mrs Shaw.[30] In other words, the Court became directly concerned with the basis for the negative screening opinion because it was relevant to the legality of the authority's decision under EU law.

The rarity of this step however has consequences for the degree to which a court will unpack uncertainties in the scientific basis underpinning an administrative decision. Instead, the question will become whether the decision-maker was *reasonable* in reaching the decision they did in light of the evidence before them. If the administrative decision 'black boxes' (or in Fisher's words, 'kettles'[31]) scientific uncertainty that is unlikely to be revealed in a paper-based examination with the probing of cross-examination.

[26] CPR 35.10.

[27] *O'Reilly v Mackman* [1983] 2 AC 237 (HL) 282.

[28] Hallett LJ in *R (Talpada) v Secretary of State for the Home Department* [2018] EWCA Civ 841 [54].

[29] *R (Jedwell) v Denbighshire CC* [2015] EWCA Civ 1232, [2016] Env LR 17 and *R (Jedwell) v Denbighshire CC* [2016] EWHC 458 (Admin), [2016] 2 CMLR 49.

[30] *R (Jedwell) v Denbighshire CC* (EWCA) (n 29) [56].

[31] Elizabeth Fisher, 'Sciences, Environmental Laws and Legal Cultures: Fostering Collective Epistemic Responsibility' in Emma Lees and Jorge E Viñuales, *The Oxford Handbook of Comparative Environmental Law* (Oxford University Press, 2019) 749, 755–60.

Second, can (and will) the court receive (in writing) and/ or hear (in cross-examination) evidence from experts regarding the scientific information relevant to the case (ie not experts consulted in the original decision, but experts appointed by the parties as part of the process of challenge)? The rules regarding expert evidence can be found in Part 35 of the CPR and are restricted to 'that which is reasonably required to resolve the proceedings'.[32] The general requirement for expert evidence is in writing unless the court dictates otherwise.[33] In 2016, it was confirmed in a non-environmental case that this provision does apply to judicial review proceedings,[34] however in practice the calling of experts to enable a judge to decide on judicial review proceedings is a rare occurrence as the courts have frequently argued that it is not their place to assess the merits of the decision of which judicial review is sought.[35] This matter was revisited in 2021 by Justice Holgate in the case of *R (Transport Action Network Ltd) v Secretary of State for Transport*.[36] Here, it was confirmed that 'where a court needs to understand technical matters to be able to appreciate the basis for a decision challenged for irrationality, expert evidence may be admissible to explain those matters'.[37] When that approach was applied by Justice Holgate to a challenge against a bat species licence issued by Natural England under the Habitats Regulations in the case of *R (Kier) v Natural England*, he noted that although the expert evidence provided by the claimant was '... proffered ... in order to help the court understand technical matters ... in fact those documents were largely directed at challenging the merits of the judgments reached by NE and advancing alternative expert opinions'.[38] Rather, 'where there is room for reasonable differences of opinion, including those of the decision-maker, a rationality challenge cannot succeed'.[39]

Finally, with regards expert evidence the court can request of its own volition or require from the parties expert testimony to assist it with its deliberations. Under Part 32.1 CPR, the court has the power to determine which issues it requires evidence on, the nature of the evidence that is required and the way in which such evidence is presented to the court.[40] However, from the experience of the authors, it is rare, but not unheard of, for a court to request expert evidence of its own volition.

[32] CPR 35.1.

[33] CPR 35.5.

[34] *R (K) v Secretary of State for the Home Department* [2016] EWHC 1394 (Admin), [2016] 1 WLR 4243.

[35] *R (Law Society) v Lord Chancellor* [2018] EWHC 2094 (Admin), [2019] 1 WLR 1649 [36].

[36] *R (Transport Action Network Ltd) v Secretary of State for Transport* [2021] EWHC 568 (Admin).

[37] *ibid* [81].

[38] *R (Keir) v Natural England* [2021] EWHC 1059 (Admin), [2022] Env LR 3 [44].

[39] *ibid* [44].

[40] CPR 32.1.

B. The Limitations of Decision-Making in Judicial Review and Statutory Appeal: Assessing the Legality of Decisions Instead of the Merits

As outlined above, decision-making in judicial review and statutory appeals under s 288 (although not all statutory appeals) is restricted based on the grounds under which the case can be brought before the court – namely through the lens of legality. This approach is demonstrated in *Plan B Earth v Secretary of State for Transport*.[41] In this case, the High Court of Justice concluded that the appropriate standard of review, when considering whether there had been a breach of the requirements of arts 6(3) and (4) HD in the conclusion as to the significance of impact, etc, is *Wednesbury* irrationality, as long as the terms used in the Directive had been interpreted correctly as a matter of law. In coming to this conclusion, it was stated that 'the court should not adopt a more intensive standard or effectively re-make the decision itself'.[42] This position was re-emphasised in the Court of Appeal judgment where Lindblom LJ stated that 'the Court's reviewing role does not stretch to determining disputed issues of technical expert evidence'.[43] The assessment of the merits of a decision was referred to as 'forbidden territory':

> It seems to us that the court should still bear in mind that Parliament has not altered the fundamental relationship between the courts and the executive. In particular, courts should still be cautious about straying, even subconsciously, into the forbidden territory of assessing the merits of a public decision under challenge by way of judicial review. If there has been an error of law, for example in the approach the executive has taken to its decision-making process, it will often be difficult or impossible for a court to conclude that it is "highly likely" that the outcome would not have been "substantially different" if the executive had gone about the decision-making process in accordance with the law. Courts should also not lose sight of their fundamental function, which is to maintain the rule of law.[44]

The standard of review, and the balance of decision-making authority, was also discussed at some length in the case of *Smyth v Secretary of State for Local Community and Government*[45] by Sales LJ. Here, it was recognised that whilst the test under art 6(3) HD is a 'demanding one, requiring a strict precautionary approach to be followed',[46] the assessment is 'primarily one for the relevant competent authority to carry out'.[47] When responding to the submission that art 6(3) HD

[41] *R (Plan B Earth Ltd) v Secretary of State for Transport* [2019] EWHC 1070 (Admin), [2019] JPL 1163; *Plan B Earth v Secretary of State for Transport* [2020] EWCA Civ 214, [2020] JPL 1005.

[42] *R (Plan B Earth Ltd) v Secretary of State for Transport, ibid* [350].

[43] *Plan B Earth v Secretary of State for Transport* (n 41).

[44] *ibid* [273].

[45] *Smyth v Secretary of State for Local Community and Government* [2015] EWCA Civ 174, [2016] Env LR 7.

[46] *ibid* [78].

[47] *ibid.*

carries a more intensive standard of assessment from the Court, Sales LJ disagreed by stating:

> There is no material difference in the planning context in which both instruments fall to be applied. There is no sound reason to think that there should be any difference as regards the relevant standard of review to be applied by a national court in reviewing the lawfulness of what the relevant competent authority has done in both contexts.[48]

Lees notes how the way in which the Court is limited to the role of 'overseer, rather than allowing for a full merits review' contrasts to the approach taken by the CJEU where the robustness of scientific evidence is expressed as a matter of legality, rather than as a question of discretionary judgment.[49] However, despite these observed differences in approaches between the UK courts and the CJEU, the UK courts have strongly maintained this stance in the case of *Savage v Mansfield DC*.[50] This Court of Appeal case concerned a potential Special Protection Area and the advice that Natural England had provided to the Council with respect to this. When considering these arguments surrounding the weight that the Council should have provided to Natural England's advice, it was held that 'an attack based on an allegation that the Council gave too little weight to advice received from one particular source is almost bound to fail'.[51] This observation provides a clear confirmation of the fact that the Court is not willing to involve itself in questions of how much weight decision-makers attribute to expert advice.[52]

Even in instances where a judge appears personally to find the justification for the decision unconvincing, they will not intervene in the decision as long as they are satisfied that the decision-maker has acted rationally to the *Wednesbury* standard. In *The Royal Society for the Protection of Birds v The Secretary of State for Environment Food And Rural Affairs & Ors*,[53] the Court did not overrule the Secretary of State's assessment of facts despite being unconvinced: 'If this was an appeal on the merits I would have said that they are unconvincing, but I am unable to conclude that they are irrational'.[54]

When the court does intervene in cases on grounds of irrational decision-making it will do so only when, on its face, the decision reached appears to be inexplicable. An example of this is *Wealden DCl v Secretary of State for Communities and Local Government & Ors*,[55] a case concerned with whether to quash part of

[48] *ibid* [80].

[49] Emma Lees, 'Allocation of Decision-Making Power under the Habitats Directive' (2016) 28 *Journal of Environmental Law* 191, 206.

[50] *Savage v Mansfield DC* [2015] EWCA Civ 4.

[51] *ibid* [41].

[52] For another example of where the Court engaged with the discussion of extent to which advisors have technical expertise, see *R (McMorn) v Natural England & Anor* [2015] EWHC 3297 (Admin), [2016] Env LR 14 [144]–[146].

[53] *The Royal Society for the Protection of Birds v The Secretary of State for Environment Food and Rural Affairs & Ors* [2015] EWCA Civ 227, [2015] Env LR 24.

[54] *ibid* [34].

[55] *Wealden DCl v Secretary of State for Communities and Local Government & Ors* [2017] EWHC 351 (Admin), [2017] Env LR 31.

the Lewes District Local Plan. The environmental area at threat was the Ashdown Forest Special Area of Conservation (SAC) which is designated for its extensive areas of lowland heath (amongst other reasons) which is vulnerable to nitrogen dioxide pollution from motor vehicles. One of the grounds addressed in the case focused upon advice that Natural England had provided to say that the planning development was not likely to have a significant impact on the SAC in consequence of increased traffic flows. Natural England concluded that increased traffic would not have a significant impact on the site as long as the increase in traffic was less than 1,000 cars per day. However, the increase in housing provision in the local plan ultimately took the increase in traffic to a level that exceeded 1,000 cars per day. Despite this, the same conclusion was drawn that there would not be a significant impact on the site from this traffic.

Clearly, determining the correct threshold for when vehicle emissions will have a significant impact on an SAC is a question for scientific experts. This was recognised by Mr Justice Jay in his judgment:

> I appreciate that this is a specialist area and that the court must avoid delving into the minutiae of expert opinion evidence which is beyond its competence. The court should be doubly slow to criticise expert opinion where there is no contrary evidence being advanced by WDC. Even so, these self-denying ordinances, although salutary, are by no means absolute.[56]

However, whilst Mr Justice Jay was reluctant to question expert evidence, he nevertheless found that the conclusion arrived at by Natural England was not rational as, in effect, it contradicted the 1,000-car threshold that they had set.[57] Therefore, whilst the courts will not interfere with the scientific reasoning behind decisions taken, it does not preclude judges from quashing decisions which, on their face, appear to be irrational. In short, the courts handle questions of the robustness of scientific evidence not as a matter of right or wrong legality, but as a question of the application of discretion. This has significant implications for how *uncertainty* in the science features in judicial reasoning.

C. Dealing with Uncertainty in Judicial Review and Statutory Appeal

Since scientific uncertainty necessitates the application of judgement – weighing up the evidence, options, and risks – the UK courts have shown that they both grant discretion in assessing what the prevailing scientific opinion *is*, and in assessing what this means for the legal steps required of the decision-maker. This is evidenced by the *Plan B Earth* case explained above.[58] The assessment on the

[56] *ibid* [90].
[57] *ibid* [108].
[58] *Plan B Earth v Secretary of State for Transport* (n 41).

likelihood of harm is based on the soundness of the evidence underpinning the decision. The *Wealdon*[59] case above provides an example of the court assessing the soundness of evidence. However, whilst the court does consider the soundness of evidence, it will not second guess the decision-maker's view as to how much weight should be given to that evidence. In *R (Wyatt) v Fareham District Council and others and Natural England*,[60] this was asserted by Mr Justice Jay who stated that:

> [I]t is necessary to underscore the distinction between the degree of rigour the local planning authority must apply to the consideration of its HRAs and the approach this court must take as the reviewing body: the two processes must be kept distinct'.[61]

The case law in this section demonstrates that the court will only assess how rational the decision-maker's assessment of risk and uncertainty is. Thus, separation of powers is maintained as the judicial branch defers to the executive branch.

One area where uncertainty in cases arising under the WBD and HD has the potential to be problematic for the courts is assessing the way in which the precautionary principle has been applied under art 6(3) HD. The courts in the UK do apply the precautionary principle when making their assessment. However, this does not mean that in applying the precautionary principle the court will go beyond determining whether the decision-maker has acted rationally and reasonably.[62] Since their question is whether the decision-maker has made a reasonable decision in reaching a judgement on the scientific position, and in reaching judgement on the legal outcome premised on that scientific position, the precautionary principle can only mediate on the question of reasonableness. Thus, scientific uncertainty is viewed through the prism of *Wednesbury* rationality as per the *Plan B* case.[63]

Where there is scientific uncertainty, the court will require some evidence that the alleged risks associated with that uncertainty are tangible. This is important when considering whether the precautionary principle has been properly applied as the court will not find it sufficient for a claimant to simply posit hypothetical risks which the decision-maker ought to have considered. Rather the *Wednesbury* test requires decision-makers to consider *relevant* information and that means the court will need to take a view on what is or is not relevant when sifting through those factors which make a decision uncertain. A useful survey of the courts' approach to this is set out in the Lydd Airport case.[64] Here the Court had

[59] *Wealden DCl* (n 55).

[60] *R (Wyatt) v Fareham District Council and others and Natural England* [2021] EWHC 1434 (Admin), [2022] Env LR 7.

[61] *ibid* [29].

[62] *Smyth v Secretary of State for Local Community and Government* (n 45) [78]–[81].

[63] A good example of this is *R (Akester & Anor) (On Behalf of the Lymington River Association) v Department for Environment, Food and Rural Affairs and Wightlink* [2010] EWHC 232 (Admin), [2010] Env LR 33 [75] where the Court grapples with and applies environmental principles drawn from CJEU case law and European Commission guidance.

[64] *The Royal Society for the Protection of Birds and Lydd Airport Action Group v Secretary of State for Communities and Local Government* [2014] EWHC 1523 (Admin), [2014] Env LR 30.

to consider whether the appropriate assessment accompanying the Secretary of State's decision contained any lacunae. In determining this, the Court reviewed common law precedent relating to when an appropriate assessment is required and noted the role that it plays in deciding whether some risks are real or simply hypothetical. It was noted that 'merely expressing doubt without providing reasonable objective evidence for doing so is not sufficient'[65] and that 'there must be "credible evidence" of a "real, rather than a hypothetical risk"'.[66] Moving beyond hypothetical risks, the claimant in this case argued that an appropriate assessment would have provided further information about specific gaps in the evidence. In considering this the Judge stated:

> I accept Mr Mould's argument that an appropriate assessment might have provided further information [about specific risks to SPA birds] … But I do not accept this as supporting a case that the Inspector was bound to conclude that a reasonable scientific doubt existed, nor do I accept that any or all of those studies would have been a necessary part of a proper appropriate assessment … On an issue of this sort, the amount of study and research which experts can suggest might yield possibly useful information and the need for yet further research seems to me to be probably limitless. The Inspector was not merely the person best placed to judge the sufficiency of what he had; I am not persuaded that the possibility of further research shows that his judgment on the sufficiency of what he had is irrational.

This response shows the court's position when it comes to encroaching upon the powers of the decision-maker (the Inspector in this instance). It also demonstrates an air of realism from the Judge with respect to the comment about the potential for limitless research even into potential 'actual' gaps in the evidence as opposed to merely 'hypothetical' ones. By acknowledging this, the court is not only acknowledging that it is not best placed to determine where the line is drawn, but is also discretely recognising the vastness of scientific uncertainty.

Similarly, the court will also give further deference or 'margin of appreciation' to bodies which have recognised expertise in a technical field relevant to the environmental decision. This approach can be seen in a number of cases covered in the remainder of this section. For example, in *R (Akester & Anor) (On Behalf of the Lymington River Association) v Department for Environment, Food and Rural Affairs and Wightlink*[67] Mr Justice Owen found that a decision-maker is bound to give 'considerable weight' to Natural England's advice on ecological issues and there had to be 'cogent and compelling reasons for departing from it',[68] thus demonstrating that democratically accountable decision-makers must not ignore the expert scientific advice when making decisions.

> It is submitted on behalf of the claimants that Wightlink could not reasonably have concluded that no doubt remained as to adverse effects given the formal advice given by

[65] *R (Hart DC) v SSCLG [2008]* EWHC 1204 (Admin), [2008] 2 P & CR 16 [81].
[66] *The Royal Society for the Protection of Birds and Lydd Airport Action Group* (n 64) [22].
[67] *R (Akester & Anor)* (n 63).
[68] *ibid* [112].

> Natural England. The fact that Natural England had given contrary advice does not of itself render the decision Wednesbury unreasonable. In making its appropriate assessment Wightlink was not obliged to follow the advice given by Natural England; its duty was to have regard to it. But given Natural England's role as the appropriate national conservation body, Wightlink was in my judgment bound to accord considerable weight to its advice, and there had to be cogent and compelling reasons for departing from it. Unless Wightlink was to come to the conclusion that the conclusion at which Natural England had arrived was simply wrong, it is difficult to see how it could come to the conclusion that no doubt remained as to whether there would be significant adverse effects on the protected sites.[69]

Similarly, in the context of protected species licensing, the Court in *Wild Justice v Natural Resources Wales*[70] recognised Lord Justice Beatson's approach in *R (on the application of Mott) v Environment Agency*[71] as being the correct approach to follow. This is that:

> The very helpful submissions from both parties showed that it was common ground that in principle the court should afford a decision-maker an enhanced margin of appreciation in cases, such as the present, involving scientific, technical and predictive assessments.[72]

Furthermore, in terms of assessments as to the strengths and weaknesses of the evidence underpinning a licensing decision, this is ultimately a matter of judgment for the authority issuing the species licence:

> These assessments were a matter for NRW in the context identified by Mr Corner. Accepting for present purposes that the precautionary principle applies, I am not persuaded that it has been shown that the NRW's judgment on the evidence, either in respect of risk, or other satisfactory solutions, is irrational.[73]

This approach was also followed in *R (BACI) v Environment Agency*[74] in the context of a permission to allow a large waste facility. In that case Lindblom LJ said:

> There may be disagreement over the appropriateness of the intended operating techniques, or on the likely effectiveness of measures proposed for the prevention or acceptable mitigation of polluting emissions. Objectors may suggest other measures … But these are in the end matters for the Environment Agency to resolve.[75]

In conclusion, the courts in this area have been consistently careful to ensure that they do not put themselves in the shoes of the decision-maker and try to re-make decisions which have been taken using scientific evidence. When it comes to

[69] *ibid.*
[70] *Wild Justice v Natural Resources Wales* [2021] EWHC 35 (Admin), [2021] Env LR 24 [30].
[71] *R (Mott) v Environment Agency* [2016] EWCA Civ 564, [2016] 1 WLR 4338.
[72] *ibid* [69].
[73] *Wild Justice v Natural Resources Wales* (n 70) [66].
[74] *R (BACI) v Environment Agency* [2019] EWCA Civ 1962, [2020] Env LR 16.
[75] *ibid* [98].

assessing scientific uncertainty, the court adamantly draws the line that it will only consider matters of scientific uncertainty if, in doing so, this demonstrates that the decision-maker acted unreasonably in making their decision. As the court does not possess the scientific understanding or expertise needed to understand the intricate details of scientific uncertainty, it must instead rely on seeking out any inconsistencies within the decision-maker's use of scientific evidence.

D. An Alternative Approach in the Tribunal System

Turning now to how the Tribunal has approached environmental decision-making under RESA 2008, we can see a glimpse of how the judiciary could take a more proactive role in environmental decision-making. As McKenna J has said:

> In this context the general approach in regulatory appeals to this Chamber is that, unless the legislation indicates otherwise, the appeal is *de novo* i.e. it requires the Tribunal to stand in the shoes of the regulator and to take a fresh decision on the evidence, giving appropriate weight to the original decision-maker's decision.[76]

Two cases concerning stop notices issued by Natural England help to illustrate the Tribunal's *de novo* approach together with the limitations to this. The first case, *Forager Ltd v Natural England (Environment)*,[77] concerned several reports between 2013 and 2014 to Natural England from members of the public who spotted individuals harvesting wild sea kale on the beach at Dungeness. Natural England issued a stop notice to prevent this harmful activity and succeeded at the First-tier Tribunal in defending its actions. The hearing was presided over by a Judge and an expert member due to the technical nature of the submissions. The stop notice was successfully appealed to the Upper Tribunal on several grounds – the successful one being that the notice failed to contain the steps that could be taken to comply with the stop notice.[78] As the activity of harvesting here was directly harmful of the Site of Special Scientific Interest (SSSI) feature, this portion of the stop notice was left blank. In light of submissions that this omission rendered the stop notice invalid, and in order to avoid the time and expense of a further hearing in the First-tier Tribunal, Natural England requested that the Upper Tribunal exercise its powers to correct the stop notice by inserting into it a series of steps which could be taken. The Judge refused to do this,[79] and accordingly, the matter was referred back to the First-tier Tribunal to specify the steps to be taken under the stop notice. The Upper Tribunal was reluctant, therefore, to exert its authority, even at the invitation of the regulator, preferring instead for further evidence to be heard by a judge and an expert member.

[76] *Warren v Natural England* [2018] UKFTT NV_2018_0006 (GRC) [9].
[77] *Forager Ltd v Natural England (Environment)* [2015] UKFTT NV_2015_0002 (GRC).
[78] *Forager Ltd v Natural England* [2017] UKUT 148 (AAC).
[79] *ibid* [32].

The second case, *Warren v Natural England*[80] concerned a stop notice served by Natural England on a commercial shoot on a Suffolk estate adjacent to Minsmere-Walberswick Heaths and Marshes SSSI causing ecological harm. The stop notice issued by Natural England prevented the release of gamebirds to levels which it considered ecologically sustainable. On appeal, the First-tier Tribunal exercised its *de novo* powers to substantially vary the stop notice to levels which it felt, after hearing detailed witness evidence, were 'proportionate'. In reaching this conclusion, the First-tier Tribunal went so far as deciding that it was not 'bound by the Habitats Regulations'[81] because it did not feel bound by principles which apply to a decision-maker in an appeal. The First-tier Tribunal also questioned the status and expertise of Natural England's 'unsatisfactory' witnesses, giving their evidence less weight than the Appellant's witnesses.

The conclusions of the First-tier Tribunal were later successfully appealed by Natural England. In allowing the appeal, the Upper Tribunal scrutinised the First-tier Tribunal's approach to core issues such as the relevance of the Habitats Regulations and the application of the precautionary principle in light of scientific uncertainty as well as the weight to be given to Natural England's expert advice. With regards the relevance of the Habitats Regulations, whilst the Tribunal concluded that it was not a competent authority for the purposes of the Habitats Regulations, nevertheless 'the tribunal was bound to act consistently with the precautionary principle because the duties on Member States under Article 6(2) are binding on all authorities of a Member State including the courts'.[82] With regards the application of the precautionary principle, the Upper Tribunal concluded that because the Tribunal 'stood in the shoes' of Natural England it was: '… bound to apply the principles that governed Natural England's decisions … these included giving effect to the Habitats and Birds Directive (and therefore to the precautionary principle) in exercising its functions in serving the stop notice'.[83]

With regards the status of Natural England's expert evidence, the Upper Tribunal found that the First-tier Tribunal was incorrect to conclude that Natural England's witnesses could not be regarded as expert witnesses because they were employed by Natural England.[84] As far as witness impartiality is concerned, the Upper Tribunal concluded that as long as any employment links of witnesses are declared, then this will not impede on the Tribunal's ability to hear the evidence.[85] This approach by the Upper-tier Tribunal is realistic as it recognises the fact that often expert witnesses can be called from the same organisation as the defendant.

The *Warren* case is therefore an interesting example of the Tribunal exercising its powers to re-make environmental decisions, provided this is done within the

[80] *Warren v Natural England* (n 76).
[81] *ibid* [98].
[82] *Natural England v Warren* [2019] UKUT 300 (AAC) [88].
[83] *ibid* [89].
[84] *ibid* [103].
[85] *ibid* [103]–[104].

proper legal parameters. Where the First-tier Tribunal failed to do this, the Upper Tribunal provided the appropriate corrective. This dynamic provides an insight into how the court system might operate if it was to have more expansive powers scrutinising the merits of environmental decisions.

V. Conclusion: Assessing Conformity with Constitutional Norms

By comparing the approach of the tribunals in RESA 2008 appeals with the approach of the courts in judicial review and statutory appeal, it is clear to see that the former has been granted with the constitutional power to 'put themselves in the shoes of the decision-maker' when assessing environmental decisions, whereas the latter is limited by the grounds of judicial review to the strict tests of *Wednesbury* unreasonableness and whether the law has been interpreted correctly (*ultra vires*). In the UK, the courts defer assessment of how robust the scientific evidence is to the decision-maker. This is because the separation of powers limits the scope of judicial review in this way and because the courts acknowledge that they are not best equipped to pass judgment on whether scientific evidence has been used correctly by the decision-maker. This message has consistently shone through in the judgments from the court outlined in this chapter where in judicial review and statutory appeal, the sustained message is that it is not the court's place to pass judgment on the scientific reasoning and uncertainty that has been used by the decision-maker[86] – even in instances where the judge may not feel personally convinced by the decision that has been made.[87] The court will only assess the use of scientific evidence/uncertainty through the lens of *Wednesbury* unreasonableness, as was the case in *Wealden DCl*[88] where the decision-maker had contradicted its own guidance when it came to imposing a threshold. In this case, the Court did not attempt to assess the scientific evidence present, but simply recognised that the decision-maker had contradicted itself.

The assertion that the courts in judicial review and statutory appeal are bound to assess cases through the lens of legality, as opposed to reviewing the substantive merits of the decisions that have been made, is further evidenced by the limited way in which the courts are able to review evidence from both witnesses and experts. As demonstrated above, the courts have wide-ranging powers from the CPR when it comes to being able to hear evidence from both witnesses, from experts who can comment on scientific information relevant to the case and even from experts who the court has requested to hear from of its own volition. However, despite having

[86] *Plan B Earth v Secretary of State for Transport* (n 41) [350].
[87] *The Royal Society for the Protection of Birds* (n 53) [34].
[88] *Wealden DCl* (n 55) [108].

these powers available, a common law precedent has developed which states that it is rare to examine evidence from witnesses,[89] and even rarer to examine expert evidence on scientific matters.[90] Where witness and expert evidence is used by the courts, it is restricted to being used to help the court understand the basis for the decision which is being challenged.[91] This has not happened by mere happenstance but is rather the product of a view that,

> [T]he facts … can seldom be a matter of relevant dispute under an application for judicial review, since the tribunal or authority's findings of fact, as distinguished from the legal consequences of the facts that they have found, are not open to review by the court.[92]

Indeed, as Lord Diplock has observed, 'to allow cross-examination presents the court with a temptation, not always easily resisted, to substitute its own view of the facts for that of the decision-making body upon whom the exclusive jurisdiction to determine facts has been conferred by Parliament'.[93] The sum total of this is that the scope for reviewing the merits of scientific evidence is limited as the judiciary do not see this as its proper role, in the context of judicial review. Rather, as stated in the abovementioned case *Mott*, the court will afford a decision-maker 'an enhanced margin of appreciation' in cases 'involving scientific, technical and predictive assessments'.[94]

The approach of the UK courts to judicial review has recently and historically led to compliance challenges being made before the ACCC which asserts that the UK's strict judicial review criteria mean that it is in breach of arts 9(2), 9(3) and 9(4) of the Convention. Specifically, the allegations related to the lack of substantive review in procedures for judicial review; the prohibitively expensive costs of judicial proceedings; the lack of rights of action against private individuals for breaches of environmental law; and the restrictive time limits for judicial review. In 2008, the ACCC found that the UK was compliant with the Convention's requirements, however noted that the *Wednesbury* test of unreasonableness provided for a 'very high threshold for review'.[95] Another challenge was raised again in 2017.[96] In this instance the UK continued to argue that the complainants failed to provide any evidence or overview to suggest that access

[89] *O'Reilly v Mackman* (n 27) [282].
[90] *R (Law Society) v Lord Chancellor* (n 35) [36].
[91] *R (Transport Action Network Ltd) v Secretary of State for Transport* (n 36) [81].
[92] *O'Reilly v Mackman* (n 27) [282].
[93] *ibid* [282].
[94] *R (Mott) v Environment Agency* (n 71) [69].
[95] United Nations Economic Commission for Europe, 'Findings and Recommendations of the Aarhus Convention Compliance Committee with Regard to Communication ACCC/C/2008/33 Concerning Compliance by the United Kingdom' (ACCC) [125], available at www.unece.org/fileadmin/DAM/env/pp/compliance/C2008-33/Findings/C33_Findings.pdf.
[96] United Nations Economic Commission for Europe, 'Version 13 February 2015' (ACCC), available at www.unece.org/fileadmin/DAM/env/pp/compliance/C2018-156/Communication_UK_RSPB_07.12.2017.pdf.

to justice would be improved if the process of judicial review were to be changed so as to incorporate a different standard of review.[97] At the time of writing, the results of the proceedings have not yet been released. The Office of Environmental Protection (OEP)[98] may, when it gets underway, choose to look into this in future. The OEP is the body created under the Environment Act 2021 to fill the governance role in the UK to scrutinise compliance with environmental law previously occupied by the European Commission.[99] Indeed, the OEP's statutory powers of Environmental Review under the Environment Act 2021 may open the door to a more merits-based scrutiny of environmental decisions. However, it will not be possible to predict this until the OEP is fully operational.

In somewhat of a contrast to the approach in judicial review and statutory appeal, an analysis of the tribunal system under RESA 2008 shows that not all decision-making in the UK is limited to assessment on legal grounds only. The constitutional underpinnings of the tribunal system allow for the judge to put themselves 'in the shoes' of the decision-maker when it comes to scrutinising the decision. The *Warren* and *Forager*[100] decisions outlined above show how the tribunal is willing to exercise this discretion.

Whilst some may argue that the grounds of judicial review and statutory appeal should be widened so as to allow judges to grapple with the merits of environmental decisions, it is contended that the current degree of scrutiny allowed is compliant with constitutional norms (ie the grounds of judicial review and compliance with the separation of powers). As outlined above in section III, the grounds for judicial review are stricter than those under the tribunal system. Therefore, any suggested change to the status quo would require a constitutional overhaul of the judicial review and statutory appeal system in order to allow for merits-based decision-making. Whilst the benefits of such an overhaul could lead to greater accountability of decision-makers, the arguments on the other hand are that such a move would dilute the separation of powers and could result in requiring courts who are not well-equipped in terms of scientific expertise to pass judgment on complicated scientific matters.

Environmental decision-making does not only concern technical questions, but questions that are based on political, moral, cultural and even religious

[97] United Nations Economic Commission for Europe, 'Re Communication ACCC/C/2017/156 Observations on behalf of the United Kingdom' (ACCC) [6], available at www.unece.org/fileadmin/DAM/env/pp/compliance/C2018-156/Correspondence_with_the_Party_concerned/Party_s_response/C156_UK_Party_s_response_21.08.2018.pdf. These arguments were furthered in the oral presentation by Charles Banner to the Committee: United Nations Economic Commission for Europe, 'Re Communication ACCC/C/2017/156 Note of the Oral Presentation by Charles Banner to the Committee on the 5 November 2019 on behalf of the Government of the United Kingdom' (ACCC), available at www.unece.org/fileadmin/DAM/env/pp/compliance/C2018-156/Correspondence_with_the_Party_concerned/frPartyC156_05.11.2019.pdf.

[98] 'Office for Environmental Protection' (OEP), available at www.theoep.org.uk/office-environmental-protection.

[99] Environment Act 2021, ch 2.

[100] *Warren v Natural England* (n 76) and *Forager Ltd v Natural England (Environment)* (n 77).

values.[101] Even if we were to introduce a court with specialist judges who have scientific expertise, there is much more to environmental decision-making than deciding upon scientific uncertainty alone. Whilst the court may be viewed as a neutral and objective arbiter of scientifically uncertain environmental law cases, perhaps what is needed here is not a reform of the law or the courts, but a reinvestment in our politics. As former Supreme Court Judge, Lord Sumption has stated, whilst judges may hold higher levels of public confidence than politicians, this perception is neither justified nor conducive to achieving better decision-making:

> … the latest Hansard Report on political engagement suggests that judges are somewhere near the top of the list of public confidence and politicians pretty close to the bottom. I don't think that that reputation is really justified. We need to realise, perhaps more acutely than we do, what the political process can contribute to reconciling our differences.[102]

[101] Jane Holder and Maria Lee, *Environmental Protection, Law and Policy: Text and Materials*, 2nd edn (Cambridge University Press, 2007) 11.

[102] A transcript of this lecture is available at: 'The Reith Lectures 2019: Law and the Decline of Politics' (*BBC*, 21 May 2019), available at http://downloads.bbc.co.uk/radio4/reith2019/Reith_2019_Sumption_lecture_1.pdf.

6

Judicial Review of the Application of Art 6(3) Habitats Directive: How the Dutch Council of State Integrates Science, Expertise and Scientific Uncertainty

FLOOR FLEURKE

I. Introduction

The Habitats Directive (HD) is a very frequent protagonist in national judicial proceedings in the Netherlands, as species and ecosystems struggle to cope with severe human pressures in heavily fragmented landscapes extending across a large number of comparatively small Special Areas of Conservation and Special Protection Areas (Natura 2000 sites).

The Netherlands has 166 designated Natura 2000 sites. Efforts to connect all sites into a single network have been dragging on for years. Only 25 per cent of the species and four per cent of protected Natura 2000 sites have a favourable conservation status.[1] This makes the conservation of biodiversity a challenging enterprise, and the need for management particularly great. In particular, the application of art 6(3) HD, and the underlying appropriate assessment, has led to extensive case law.[2] A big proportion of these cases resolves around the problem of excessive nitrogen deposits caused mainly by agricultural activities.[3]

[1] Planbureau voor de Leefomgeving, 'Natura 2000 in Nederland. Juridische ruimte, natuurdoelen en beheerplanprocessen' (*The Hague*, 2011) available at www.pbl.nl/sites/default/files/downloads/Natura_2000_WEB.pdf.

[2] This chapter aims to provide an overview of how science, expertise and scientific uncertainty in the context of the Habitats Directive are integrated in judicial review by the Dutch courts, with a focus on the main administrative court, the Judicial Division of the Council of State. Given the sheer amount of case law, a systematic review of the case law is beyond the scope of this chapter. See, for a very useful yearly overview of case law concerning nature protection law in the Netherlands, *Kroniek Natuurbeschermingsrecht*. For example Marjan Kaajan and Fleur Onrust, *Kroniek Natuurbeschermingsrecht – Gebiedsbescherming* [2021] 72 *BR*.

This chapter begins by briefly setting the Dutch legal context in which the HD operates. Before examining the way that the courts deal with (contested) science, it is essential to address the conditions under which non-governmental organisations (NGOs) and interested parties have access to the courts. This is especially so since the Dutch courts have increasingly narrowed standing rights in recent years and have recently been critically scrutinised by the Court of Justice of the European Union (CJEU) in light of the Aarhus Convention.[4]

Judicial protection, especially before the administrative courts, requires an understanding of the complex technical and scientific environmental issues at hand. The process of integrating expert knowledge into the judicial process, and of reviewing the legality of decisions with a scientific underpinning as required by art 9(2) Aarhus Convention, is considered in this chapter. Finally, we will zoom in on some controversial case law of the Dutch administrative courts regarding the application of art 6(3) and 6(4) HD, highlighting the shift in the Dutch case law caused by the interpretation of art 6 by the CJEU.

II. Legal Context

The national Government has developed general conservation targets at the national level and for designated Natura 2000 sites specifically.[5] The provisions of the Wild Birds Directive (WBD) and HD are fully transposed by the Nature Protection Act.[6] The provinces are responsible for the management of sites; the realisation of conservation objectives; and assessments regarding the art 6 HD authorisation regime. Central Government, however, remains responsible for the overall implementation of EU and international nature law.

The Nature Protection Act includes a duty of care provision, but the precautionary principle is omitted. This principle is however included in the Environmental Act (Omgevingswet).[7] This law will come into effect on 1st January 2023 and the intention is that the Nature Protection Act will be an integral part of the Environmental Act.

[3] See European Environment Agency, 'Critical Load Exceedance for Nitrogen' (2010), available at www.eea.europa.eu/data-and-maps/indicators/critical-load-exceedance-for-nitrogen (no longer updated, accessed 27.06.2022). See also Helle Tegner Anker et al, 'Natura 2000 and the Regulation of Agricultural Ammonia Emissions' (2019) 16 *Journal for European Environmental and Planning Law* 340–71.

[4] United Nations Economic Commission for Europe (UNECE), *Convention on Access to Information, Public Participation in Decision-making and Access to Justice in Environmental Matters*, 2161 UNTS 447, 25 June 1998 (the Aarhus Convention).

[5] Nature Protection Act, Staatsblad 2016, 34. For original language version information, please see the Table of Legislation. The Act replaces three other laws: the Nature Protection Act 1998, Staatsblad 1998, 403; the Flora and Fauna Act, Staatsblad 1998, 402; and the Forestry Act, Staatsblad 1961, 256. For full details of the Directives, see the Table of Legislation or Introduction.

[6] http://wetten.overheid.nl/BWBR0037552/2017-03-01.

[7] Environmental Act, Staatsblad 2016, 156, art 3.3.

A. Judicial Review

The Judicial Division of the Council of State (*De Afdeling bestuursrechtspraak van de Raad van State*, hereafter: the Council) is the main administrative court, as well as the highest court for bringing environmental disputes, in the Netherlands. Since the entering into force of the Nature Protection Act 2017, in certain situations, a case can now also be lodged at the lower courts.

The Council has a dual role. On the one hand, it provides Government and Parliament with advice (including 'legislative advice'). On the other hand, as a 'special court', it articulates the law in disputes between the Government and citizens. These Divisions are formally separated but it is possible that both Divisions will be involved in the same case – one to advise the Government in decision-making, and the other to review that decision.[8] Recently, in a controversy regarding child support benefits that led to the resignation of the Cabinet, which was not caught by the Judicial Division of the Council, the debate about the separation of powers has flared up again.[9] It is questioned whether the Judicial Division of the Council is too close in proximity to the Government.[10] This discussion that illustrates the legal culture is also relevant for the cases that are discussed in this chapter.

Although the Netherlands in general has one of the highest proportion of courts referring cases to the CJEU on the basis of art 267 Treaty on the Functioning of the European Union (TFEU), there is a reluctance among the highest administrative court judges (compared to other high courts) to refer cases due to a desire to resolve disputes.[11] So far, four cases concerning the HD have been referred to the CJEU and two regarding the WBD.[12] All the requested answers of the CJEU in these cases are followed by the referring court. As Krommendijk states, the Dutch courts thus remain 'loyal interlocutors' of the CJEU that are willing to implement CJEU judgments fully and automatically.[13]

[8] In the case concerning the Betuwe route construction decision, the European Court of Human Rights reluctantly decided that the Netherlands was not in violation of art 6 European Convention on Human Rights – *Convention for the Protection of Human Rights and Fundamental Freedoms*, Council of Europe Treaty Series 005 (1950). Cases 39343/98, 39651/98, 43147/98 and 46664/99 *Kleyn* (6.5.2005).

[9] See, eg, Afdeling bestuursrechtspraak van Raad van State, 'Verslag van de Werkgroep Juridische Reflectie' Ten behoeve van de reflectie van de Afdeling bestuursrechtspraak van de Raad van State over de kinderopvangtoeslagzaken (November 2020).

[10] See on the judicial role of the Council ABRvS 11 July 2018, ECLI:NL:RVS:2018:2339.

[11] Jasper Krommendijk, 'The Highest Dutch Courts and the Preliminary Ruling Procedure: Critically Obedient Interlocutors of the Court of Justice' (2019) *European Law Journal* 394, 408.

[12] Concerning the HD: ABRvS 7 November 2012, ECLI:NL:RVS:2012:BY2504; ABRvS 18 May 2016, ECLI:NL:RVS:2016:1351; ABRvS 17 May 2017, ECLI:NL:RVS:2017:1259; and ABRvS 17 May 2017, ECLI:NL:RVS:2017:1259. Concerning the WBD: ABRvS 17 May 2017, ECLI:NL:RVS:2017:1259; and ABRvS 18 May 2016, ECLI:NL:RVS:2016:1351.

[13] Krommendijk (n 11) 408.

B. Access to Justice

According to art 8(1) General Administrative Law Act[14] (Awb), an action before an administrative court against administrative decisions can be brought by interested parties only. Under art 1(2) of the Awb, 'interested parties' are those 'whose interests are directly affected by a decision'. For NGOs to be considered an interested party, public interest should be part of their statutory aims and it should be sufficiently established that they carry out specific activities to that end.[15] For members of the public, arts 8(1) and 8(69a) Awb state that there should be a specific interest. This implies that the so-called 'opera' criteria must be met: there must be an objectively measurable, personal, and current interest that becomes direct through a decision. The courts have interpreted this as meaning that the applicant needs to live in the vicinity of the contested project for which a decision is made.[16]

In recent years the Council has interpreted the requirement of having a specific interest increasingly narrowly. The test as carried out by the Council comes down to determining the distance between the Natura 2000 area concerned and the residence location of the person invoking the Nature Protection Act.[17]

For the adoption of an environmental permit concerning activities of construction and modifications of facilities for the purposes of art 2(1)(1)(a) and (e) of the General Provisions for Environmental Law Act (Wabo),[18] art 3(4) Awb, relating to the 'uniform public preparatory procedure' ('the preparatory procedure') is applicable. In the context of that procedure, art 3(12) Wabo provides that anyone can submit observations on the draft decision.

Under art 6(13) Awb, only interested parties that have submitted observations during the preparatory procedure may bring an action against the decision adopted as a result of that procedure, unless they cannot reasonably be criticised for not having intervened. In addition, only complaints directed against the same aspects of the contested decision as those criticised during its adoption procedure are admissible.

Recently, the CJEU held, in a preliminary ruling, that this legislation regarding access to justice did not conform to art 9(2) Aarhus Convention. The admissibility

[14] General Administrative Law Act, Staatsblad 1992, 315.

[15] See also Jan H Jans and Albert T Marseille, 'The Role of NGOs in Environmental Litigation against Public Authorities: Some Observations on Judicial Review and Access to Court in the Netherlands' (2010) 22 *Journal of Environmental Law* 373. See also C-115/09 *Bund für Umwelt und Naturschutz Deutschland, Landesverband Nordrhein-Westfalen eV v Bezirksregierung Arnsberg* [2011] ECR I-03673.

[16] See, eg, ABRvS 16 April 2014 ECLI:NL:RVS:2014:1308; ABRvS 16 March 2016, ECLI:NL:RVS:2016:737; ABRvS 11 July 2018, ECLI:NL:RVS:2018:2314.

[17] ABRvS 25 April 2018, ECLI:NL:RVS:2018:1337; ABRvS 21 April 2017, ECLI:NL:RVS:2017:1110. A similar test is carried out if an appeal has been lodged by an organisation that bundles individual interests, see, eg, ABRvS 21 February 2018, ECLI:NL:RVS:2018:616; ABRvS 6 February 2019, ECLI:NL:RVS:2019:325.

[18] General Provisions for Environmental Law Act, Staatsblad 2010, 231.

of a court action brought by an NGO cannot be made conditional on the role it may or may not have played during the participatory phase of the decision-making procedure.[19]

III. Expert Knowledge in the Courts

Access to expertise and scientific and technical knowledge can be organised in different ways. In most Member States courts can appoint experts on a case-by-case basis.[20] In the Netherlands there exists no specialised environmental courts, but scientific and technical specialised knowledge can be obtained from a specialised institution, the Foundation of Independent Court Experts in Environmental and Planning Law (*Stichting Advisering Bestuursrechtspraak voor Milieu en Ruimtelijke Ordening*, hereafter: STAB) which was founded 25 years ago.[21] The objective of this agency is to provide technical and scientific expertise needed by administrative judges to scrutinise environmental and planning law cases submitted to them. By providing a third opinion, the STAB enables courts to assess the merits of the often technically complicated questions brought before them and to scrutinise fairly extensively and in detail whether the requirements of European and national environmental and planning law have been met, without having to rely on information brought (and paid for) by one of the parties.

The legal basis and independence of the STAB is laid down in the three main acts dealing with environmental and planning law.[22] In addition, the STAB has adopted its own code of conduct for the purpose of providing independent and impartial advice.[23] It is stated that experts will always act independently and impartially in the performance of the assignment.[24] In the performance of their task, the expert must always meet the requirements of care, professional competence and integrity. The experts of the STAB are specially trained as judicial experts and are registered with the National Register of Judicial Experts.

[19] Tiina Paloniitty and Mariolina Eliantonio, 'Scientific Knowledge in Environmental Judicial Review: Safeguarding Effective Judicial Protection in the EU Member States?' (2018) 27 *European Energy and Environmental Law Review* 108–14.

[20] See the special issue in (2018) 27 *European Energy and Environmental Law Review* on scientific knowledge in environmental litigation in several Member States.

[21] See www.STAB.nl. For an extensive analysis of this institution, see Chris W Backes, 'Organizing Technical Knowledge in Environmental and Planning Law Disputes in the Netherlands – the Foundation of Independent Court Experts in Environmental and Planning Law' (2018) 27 *European Energy and Environmental Law Review* 143.

[22] Environmental Management Act, Staatsblad 1993, 650; Planning Act, Staatsblad 2006, 566; and General Provisions for Environmental Law Act, Staatsblad 2010, 231. In the future, its legal basis is expected to be found in art 17(1) of the Environmental Act.

[23] The Code of Conduct (*Gedragscode*) can be found (in Dutch) at https://stab.nl/expertise-en-producten/gedragscode/.

[24] The STAB is funded by a subsidy from the Ministry of Justice and Security; this is laid down in art 50 of the Justice Subsidies Act, Staatsblad 2021, 138.

The STAB only works on behalf of courts and the Council of State as a guarantee to provide independent advice. Administrative courts may ask the STAB to provide advice on a scientific or technical issue arising from any case pending before them.[25] No procedural rules on the functioning of the STAB or on the use of the expertise of the STAB in judicial proceedings are provided; Article 8:34 Awb only states that an expert who has accepted his appointment is obliged to fulfil his assignment impartially and to the best of his knowledge. All parties are legally obliged to cooperate in the STAB investigation.

Usually, courts will make a request for advice within the written part of the proceedings. The STAB conducts an investigation on the basis of the question asked by the judge. This can be a broad question or a question on a specific part – the latter has become more common. The concern has been raised that the parties do not have opportunity for input on the questions put forward to the STAB, whereas the framing of the questions is of fundamental importance for the outcome of the case.[26]

The STAB talks to all parties individually and gives everyone the opportunity to provide information, and visits the relevant location or installation. There is however no opportunity to comment on the draft report of the STAB before it is delivered to the court. The STAB's final comprehensive report is sent in to the judge or court, which is responsible for dissemination to all parties.[27] The parties can respond to the findings within four weeks after having received it.[28] This can contribute to the equality of arms between the parties, especially for parties without large budgets, and can have the effect of bringing the dispute to the fundamental differences of opinion before the hearing.[29] The report is however not made public and cannot therefore be requested. It is questionable whether this is in line with the Aarhus provisions on access to information. Consequently, it is not directly visible or traceable if and how scientific uncertainties are assessed and taken into account in the report.

The questions that are referred to the STAB concern a great variety of issues, including assessments regarding the application of the HD. The work often involves calculation models; the STAB assesses which model should (have been) be applied and checks the input data. The STAB has experts and expertise in almost all the technical fields that are relevant in environmental and planning law cases. The experts work in teams and provide an integrated report. As Backes observes, it can also function as a 'knowledge broker'.[30] The courts mostly rely

[25] The STAB can also be involved in other proceedings such as interim relief, accelerated proceedings and mediation processes promoted by the court.

[26] See Andy Stirling, 'Precaution in the Governance of Technology (2016), available at SSRN: https://ssrn.com/abstract=2815579 or http://dx.doi.org/10.2139/ssrn.2815579.

[27] See Code of Conduct (n 23).

[28] Art 8(47)(5) Awb.

[29] See Backes (n 21).

[30] *ibid*; see also Brian J Preston, 'Characteristics of Successful Environmental Courts and Tribunals' (2014) 26 *Journal of Environmental Law* 365, 377–78. See also chapter 15 of this book.

on the reports of the STAB, but also take other scientific reports provided by the parties into account.[31]

The STAB is valued for its input; due to its rich experience and specialisation it can help structure and contextualise the factual part in the judicial process, and streamline the process.[32] In recent years however more concerns, particularly relating to transparency, have been voiced.[33]

A. Quality, Impartiality and Independence of Research Standards

Both in the context of species protection (eg exemption from prohibitions on species protection) and in the context of area protection (eg zoning plans and environmental permits), reports and studies of experts are being challenged in courts.

Over the years it has become standard practice to have an ecological report underpinning a decision. The Council requires that, for example, the conclusion that no mitigation plan is needed has to be based on a full report; an oral ecological consultation is not enough.[34] The Council does often allow supplemental information at the hearing to explain further the conducted research.[35] Nevertheless, the Council often concludes that the conducted assessment is insufficient as gaps revealed in that first assessment were not followed up with further research.[36] At least in environmental impact assessment procedures, additional information is often required, and the lack of available knowledge is a concern. However, in other cases the Council seems to be more flexible. For example, it may consider an assessment sufficient even in cases where the appropriate assessment itself explicitly noted that further investigation might be required.[37]

Often the quality of the evidence or the independence of the experts at issue is contested. The Council considers that such a claim requires concrete indications of partiality. The fact that the research consultancy has been cooperating with the administrative body is insufficient to conclude that the conducted

[31] Backes (n 21) 150 referring to Annelies Freriks and Jan Robbe, *Vijf jaar STAB; een onderzoek naar de kwaliteit van de deskundigenadvisering door de Stichting Advisering Bestuursrechtspraak voor Milieu en Ruimtelijke Ordening Gedurende de eerste vijf jaar van haar bestaan* (Boom Juridische Uitgevers, 2001) 104.

[32] Backes (n 21). See also evaluation report 'STAB: Meerwaarde door Verbinding 2016' by Rebelgroep, available at https://stab.nl/wp-content/uploads/2020/01/Rebelgroup.pdf.

[33] See 2020 annual report, available at https://stab.nl/wp-content/uploads/2021/07/STAB-Jaarverslag-2020.pdf.

[34] See, eg, ABRvS 28 June 2017, ECLI:NL:RVS:2017:1717.

[35] *ibid.*

[36] See, eg, ABRvS 19 December 2018, ECLI:NL:RVS:2018:4197; ABRvS 17 April 2019, ECLI:NL:RVS:2019:1264.

[37] ABRvS 4 April 2018, ECLI:NL:RVS:2018:1102.

research is not independent.[38] The starting point of the Council is to rely upon expert advice; this is only different if there are concrete indications for doubts about the quality or completeness of the findings or the independence of the experts. The conclusion that the investigation conducted is incomplete or flawed does not imply that experts should be disqualified. The Council does however check the credentials of the experts.[39] In a case concerning alleged damage to the foraging area of a badger by a planned extension, the Court did question the independence and impartiality of an expert due to an affiliation with third parties.[40] It was accepted that the competent authority had not carried out the assessment itself, but that this had been conducted by the initiator that sought permission.[41]

A counter assessment is, for obvious reasons, not submitted very often. Highly specialised knowledge is required and specialised agencies are not cheap. A related problem that often occurs is that complaints about the ecological reports or assessments are expressed without precise indication of the alleged flaws. If the appellants in those proceedings do not substantiate their claims, the Council will reject them; according to established case law the appellant who states the assessment is flawed must also substantiate this, preferably with an expert counter-expertise.[42] This burden of proof is high: the appellant must 'demonstrate such flaws in nature research that it could not be assumed'.[43]

Sometimes it is claimed by appellants that the reports on which the decision is made are outdated. Regarding environmental decisions in general, the Decree Environmental Law Act states that when it concerns the establishment of a zoning plan, research should not be older than two years.[44] Even if the research is older than two years, it is settled case law, and the data may still be used if no developments have occurred after the research was established to such an extent that the research is outdated; even an ecological report dating from five years ago has been accepted.[45] Again, it is up to the appellants to show that the research is outdated. For example, regarding a quickscan, the Council considers that the

[38] ABRvS 6 March 2019, ECLI:NL:RVS:2019:728.

[39] See, eg, ABRvS 27 December 2018, ECLI:NL:RVS:2018:4269.

[40] Rb. Overijssel 13 March 2019, ECLI:NL:RBOVE:2019:860.

[41] See, eg, Rb. Midden-Nederland 2 March 2018, ECLI:NL:RBMNE:2018:834.

[42] See, eg, ABRvS 6 December 2017, ECLI:NL:RVS:2017:3343; ABRvS 20 December 2017, ECLI:NL:RVS:2017:3503; ABRvS 19 September 2018, ECLI:NL:RVS:2018:3051; ABRvS 25 July 2018, ECLI:NL:RVS:2018:2505; ABRvS 30 April 2019, ECLI:NL:RVS:2019:1399.

[43] See, eg, ABRvS 13 September 2017, ECLI:NL:RVS:2017:2455; Rb. Midden-Nederland 10 August 2017, ECLI:NL:RBMNE:2017:4147.

[44] Art 3(1)(1)(a) Decree Environmental Law Act, Stb. 2010, 143.

[45] See, eg, ABRvS 6 December 2017, ECLI:NL:RVS:2017:3345; ABRvS 6 March 2019, ECLI:NL:RVS:2019:687; ABRvS 11 July 2018, ECLI:NL:RVS:2018:2315; and ABRvS, March 4th 2020, ECLI:NL:RVS:2020:682. Rapport Natuur voor MER Windpark Zeewolde opgesteld door Bureau Waardenburg, available at www.planviewer.nl/imro/files/NL.IMRO.0000.EZip16WZEEWOLDE-3004/b_NL.IMRO.0000.EZip16WZEEWOLDE-3004_tb5.pdf.

appellant 'has not made plausible that the quickscan has become so outdated, or developments in the plan area have taken place after the research report has been drawn up'.[46]

One interesting process is the development of Citizen Science – scientific observations undertaken by members of the general public often in collaboration with or under the direction of professional scientists and scientific institutions – by camera traps, etc. So far, the Council has not accepted observations or pictures from citizens even though some of the research findings made by commercial consultancy agencies are based on observations of citizens.[47] This is also due to the fact that the Council has found it insufficient for intervention if it only showed that a protected species uses the location around, for example, the planning area. The Council requires that it should be established that the area can be considered a permanent resting place.[48]

B. Methodology and Models

If the methodology of the conducted research is challenged, the Council will verify – often assisted by the STAB – whether standardised research protocols have been used (such as bat protocol 2017 and Sovon counting guidelines).[49] In general, the Council accepts the use of models for calculating the effects on protected species and habitats. For example, the so-called 'Flux-Collision-Model' – a widely used model to determine the number of collision victims of a wind farm among certain bird species – has been accepted.[50] Arguments made by NGOs that the actual number of victims can differ greatly from the predicted number have been systematically rejected by pointing to the expert report of the STAB that refers to the inclusion of correction factors.[51]

Regarding mortality of protected birds, the Council follows the ORNIS criterium.[52] In the *Windpark Fryslan* case, the appellant NGO argued that in

[46] See, eg, ABRvS 15 February 2017, ECLI:NL:RVS:2017:437; ABRvS 8 November 2017, ECLI:NL:RVS:2017:3001; ABRvS 11 July 2018, ECLI:NL:RVS:2018:2339.

[47] ABRvS 8 April 2019, ECLI:NL:RVS:2019:1082; ABRvS 23 January 2019, ECLI:NL:RVS:2019:189.

[48] ABRvS 30 August 2017, ECLI:NL:RVS:2017:2365; ABRvS 24 October 2018, ECLI:NL:RVS:2018:3491; ABRvS 20 May 2019, ECLI:NL:RVS:2019:1605.

[49] See, eg, ABRvS 1 July 2015, ECLI:NL:RVS:2015:2081; ABRvS 6 March 2019, ECLI:NL:RVS:2019:728. Sovon Bird Research Netherlands is a non-profit organisation that tracks the occurrence and development of Dutch birds in the Netherlands. Sovon looks at the progress or decline of birds, and has developed guidelines for this.

[50] See, eg, ABRvS 8 February 2012, ECLI:NL:RVS:2012:BV3215; ABRvS 11 July 2018, ECLI:NL:RVS:2018:2339; ABRvS, 19 December 2018, ECLI:NL:RVS:2018:4198.

[51] ABRvS, 19 December 2018, ECLI:NL:RVS:2018:4198 [24.1].

[52] See, eg, ABRvS 11 July 2018, ECLI:NL:RVS:2018:2339; C-79/03 *Commission v Spain* [2004] ECR I-11619 [36] and [41] According to this criterium, any number of less than 1% of the total annual mortality of the population concerned (mean values) may be hunted, as long as this is no more than 1% of the species number. It is also applied to other species, such as bats, See ABRvS 18 February 2015, ECLI:NL:RVS:2015:438.

the appropriate assessment it should not have been assumed that with a natural mortality of less than one per cent, there is no chance of significant adverse consequences, especially considering that the species in question had already been found not to have a favourable conservation status.[53] The argument referred to a research report by the University of Wageningen that concluded that the one per cent criterion has no general applicability and should be used with caution for bird populations. Researchers consider the measure 'Population Persistence Index' (PPI) to be more useful for these bird populations, although uncertainties also remain in this model.[54] The Council however, considers that 'in the absence of another scientifically substantiated criterion', the ORNIS criterion can be used as a starting point to determine whether the expected numbers of bird victims from the wind turbines will affect the natural features of the area concerned or may have a disruptive effect on the conservation objectives of the species for which the area has been designated.[55] The Council also states that the CJEU has accepted the ORNIS criterium.[56] However, this interpretation is contextual since the case referred to revolved around the means of *hunting* of large populations of thrushes.[57] It also stated that it does not follow the CJEU case law that the one per cent criterion cannot be applied to species that are already in an unfavourable conservation status or if it concerns a small population.[58]

Specific 'Species Standards' have been drawn up for listed and endangered plant and animal species for which an exemption is often requested. These species standards contain a number of characteristic ecological aspects of the species concerned, and a set of basic or standard measures to be taken if a spatial intervention takes place. In the species standards documents, it is stated that deviations from those basic set of measures are only possible if the local situation or population so requires. However, the Council does not follow that strictly: in several cases it has accepted that the specific species standard was not adhered to.[59] The competent authority can deviate from an obtained expert advice but in doing so it must clearly motivate the reasons.[60] The Council has also been lenient if an investigation based on the species standard is still in process.[61]

Effects of nitrogen deposits are calculated by the use of the model AERIUS Calculator – which was until the PAS cases concerning the Dutch integrated approach to Nitrogen (*Programmatische Aanpak Stikstof*) (see below) – required by law. Ever since, it has been permitted to base a decision on the

[53] ABRvS 11 July 2018, ECLI:NL:RVS:2018:2339.
[54] *ibid* [24]. Ralph Buij et al, 'Do Assessment Thresholds Underestimate the Mortality Impact of Wind Farms on Bird Populations?' (2017) *Wageningen Environmental Research Report* 2788.
[55] *ibid* [25.1].
[56] *ibid* [25.3].
[57] C-557/15 *Commission v Republic of Malta* ECLI:EU:C:2018:477.
[58] See similar ABRvS 1 April 2009, ECLI:NL:RVS:2009:BH9250.
[59] See, eg, ABRvS 20 January 2021, ECLI:NL:RVS:2021:105 [69.5].
[60] Rb. Overijssel 20 April 2018, ECLI:NL:RBOVE:2018:1318.
[61] ABRvS 29 May 2019, ECLI:NL:RVS:2019:1740.

AERIUS Calculator.[62] Recently, a fixed distance limit of 25 kilometers has been adopted to calculate nitrogen precipitation, which is necessary for applying for a nature permit. Before the introduction of this norm there were no distance limits for housing, agriculture and industry/energy, while nitrogen precipitation up to five kilometers from the road is taken into account for infrastructure projects. The distinction between different sources was deemed arbitrary by the Council in a case concerning a road project.[63] The Council refers to the CJEU when it states:

> The assessment carried out under art 6(3) HD cannot have lacunae and must contain complete, precise and definitive findings and conclusions capable of removing all reasonable scientific doubt as to the effects of the works proposed on the protected site concerned.[64]

For third parties it is however very difficult to verify whether the results are correct and which input data was used.[65] The concern here is that this might be incompatible with the required access to information provisions laid down in the Aarhus Convention. In this regard, the Council has considered that the competent authorities are required to disclose on their own initiative in an appropriate manner the choices, data and assumptions made underpinning the calculation.[66] This requirement obviously applies to any decision based on any given research model.[67]

It can be concluded that the assessment and research reports that support the decision-making of the competent authorities are frequently challenged, but such challenges are almost never successful. There is a strong reliance on calculation methods and models, whereas a more qualitative assessment of scientific uncertainties is omitted.

IV. Key Points in Judicial Review of the Application of Art 6(3)

An environmental impact assessment study is a key aspect of the operation of art 6 HD. A permit can only be granted if it can be demonstrated that there is no adverse effect on the integrity of the site. Since the *Waddenzee* case, any plan or project can only be adopted if – taking into account the precautionary

[62] ABRvS 4 August 2021, ECLI:NL:RVS:2021:1760; ABRvS 22 April 2020, ECLI:NL:RVS:2020:1110.

[63] ABRvS 20 January 2021, ECLI:NL:RVS:2021:105; art 2(1) Decree Nature Protection Act, Stb. 2016, 383.

[64] ABRvS 20 January 2021, ECLI:NL:RVS:2021:105, *ibid* [69.2].

[65] Tiina Paloniitty and Niina Kotamäki, 'Scientific and Legal Mechanisms for Addressing Model Uncertainties: Negotiating the Right Balance in Finnish Judicial Review?' (2021) 33 *Journal of Environmental Law* 283.

[66] ABRvS 17 May 2017, ECLI: NL: RVS: 2017: 1259. See, eg, ABRvS 18 July 2018, ECLI: NL: RVS: 2018: 2454.

[67] See, eg, ABRvS 18 July 2018, ECLI: NL: RVS: 2018: 2454.

principle – significant negative effects cannot be ruled out.[68] In light of scientific uncertainty this implies that in almost all cases an appropriate assessment, at the very least, is required.[69] In a set of cases the Council, however, seems to have replaced this strict precautionary test for a reasonableness test.[70] It considers whether the competent authorities could reasonably have taken the position that, without ecological research, the developments made possible by any particular plan were certain not to affect Natura 2000 sites.[71]

It is practice that, first, a so-called quickscan is conducted to determine whether an appropriate assessment is necessary.[72] If, on the basis of this quickscan, it is concluded that significant negative effects can be excluded, no permit is requested for projects or other activities. The legality of this can then only be raised if enforcement action is subsequently taken against the project or the other act which is unlikely to happen.[73] If it concerns a plan, usually the quickscan and the appropriate assessment are similar, but for projects cumulative effects only have to be taken into account in the appropriate assessment.[74] The standard line in case law is that when assessing cumulative effects, account must be taken of permitted but not yet implemented projects and plans that could lead to adverse effects.[75] Both the quickscan and the appropriate assessment are usually conducted by specialised commercial consultancies. Due to the lack of legal requirements though, each agency draws up its own assessment framework.

A. Mitigating Measures

Since 2008 the Council has held that *mitigating measures* – a concept that does not exist in the HD – could be included in the appropriate assessment of

[68] Case C-127/02 *Landelijke Vereniging tot Behoud van de Waddenzee v Staatssecretaris van Landbouw, Natuurbeheer en Visserij* [2004] ECR I-07504, ECLI:EU:C:2004:482. In that case, an environmental impact assessment was also required, see art 7(2a)[1] Environmental Management Act.

[69] Emma Lees, 'Allocation of Decision-Making Power under the Habitats Directive' [2016] 28(2) *Journal of Environmental Law*, 191–219.

[70] See, eg, ABRvS 26 September 2018, ECLI:NL:RVS:2018:3116; ABRvS 22 May 2019, ECLI:NL:RVS:2019:1663; and ABRvS 6 February 2019, ECLI:NL:RVS:2019:325.

[71] ABRvS 22 May 2019, ECLI:NL:RVS:2019:1663 [7.6].

[72] ABRvS 20 February 2019, ECLI:NL:RVS:2019:547 referring to C-461/17 *Holohan v An Bord Pleanála*, ECLI:EU:C:2018:883.

[73] This is different for (zoning) plans since the assessment of the legality of the zoning plan includes the effects on a Natura 2000 site.

[74] ABRvS 11 April, ECLI: NL: RVS: 201835 in which the Council concluded that no significant negative effects would affect the relevant Natura 2000 site by only taking into account the distance between the intended activity and the site.

[75] See, eg, ABRvS April 16, 2014, ECLI: NL: RVS: 2014: 1312; ABRvS 18 July 2018, ECLI:NL:RVS:2018:2454. See also Sanne Akerboom, Chris Backes, Ralph Buij and Sander Lagerveld, *Wind Energy Development and Protection of Vulnerable Species: An Interdisciplinary Study of Ecological Effects and Legal Instruments in the Netherlands* [2021] SSRN. https://doi.org/10.2139/ssrn.3839332.

art 6 (3) HD.[76] In the highly criticised *IJburg* case concerning the effects of a construction project near a Natura 2000 area for protected birds, the Council held that the construction of mussel beds could qualify as a mitigating measure and should not be regarded as a compensatory measure even though it was established that the construction project could lead to a reduction in the foraging opportunities for tufted duck, pochard, goldeneye, topper and coot, for which the *IJmeer* Natura 2000 area had been designated.[77] The construction of mussel beds served to overcome the adverse effects on the foraging possibilities of these birds. The Council stated that: '[t]he appropriate assessment shows that the timely construction and proper functioning of the mussel beds are *expected* to overcome these effects'.[78]

This line of reasoning was affirmed in other cases, such as *Windpark Urk*.[79] Here it was also not in dispute that the construction of a windmill park is a 'plan' as referred to in art 6(3) and 6(4) HD and that the plan may have significant consequences for the species for which the Natura 2000 area of IJsselmeer has been designated.[80] However, as in the previous case, the Council concluded that 'the appropriate assessment shows that early construction of the facility and its proper ecological functioning are expected to mitigate the negative effects of the wind farm'.[81]

Similar to other cases, it was concluded that conservation measures could count as mitigating measures 'because these measures are intended to prevent possible negative impacts of the project from being mitigated'.[82] In so far as the applicants argued that source measures should have been taken instead of effect measures, the Council considered that neither the applicable Nature Protection Act 1998 nor the HD results in an obligation to give priority to (more far-reaching) source measures over other measures in the context of mitigation, if possible.[83] In this line of cases the Council ignored the scientific uncertainty of the effectiveness of these so-called mitigation measures and instead relied on their 'expected' success.

[76] See also Hendrik Schoukens, 'Habitats Restoration Measures as Facilitators for Economic Development within the Context of EU Habitats Directive: Balancing No Net Loss with the Preventive Approach?' (2017) 29(1) *Journal of Environmental Law* 47–73; Nicholas De Sadeleer, 'Assessment and Authorization of Plans and Projects Having a Significant Impact on Natura 2000 Sites' in B Vanheusden and L Squintani (eds), *EU Environmental and Planning Law Aspects of Large-Scale Projects* (Intersentia, 2016) 281–320; Ralph Frins, *Mitigatie, Compensatie en Saldering in het Omgevingsrecht* (dissertation, Stichting Instituut voor Bouwrecht Nijmegen, 2016); Ralph Frins, *Mitigatie, Compensatie en Saldering in het Omgevingsrecht* (Den Haag: Stichting Instituut voor Bouwrecht, 2016).

[77] ABRvS 21 July 2010, ECLI:RVS:2010:BN1933 [2.5.3].

[78] ABRvS 7 May 2008, ECLI:NL:RVS:2008:BD1090; ABRvS 27 August 2014, ECLI:NL:RVS:2014:3217.

[79] ABRvS 2 February 2012, ECLI:NL:RVS:2012:BV3215.

[80] *ibid* [2.46.1].

[81] *ibid*. For a similar reasoning and outcome, see ABRvS 29 May 2013, ECLI:NL:RVS:2013:CA1362.

[82] *ibid* [18.8].

[83] *ibid* [18.14].

B. A Break in the Case Law: *Briels*

Even though the above interpretation of art 6 (3) HD was the topic of critical debate, only in 2012 did the Council seek clarification on the criteria for determining whether the integrity of the site concerned is affected, and more specifically on division between mitigating and compensatory measures in light of the appropriate assessment of art 6(3) HD.[84] The *Briels* case concerned a Dutch Motorway project affecting a Natura 2000 site designated for the protection of Molinia meadows.[85] It was proposed to create new Molinia meadows elsewhere within the site as a mitigating measure. The Minister stated that this would allow for the development of a larger area of Molinia meadows of higher quality, thereby ensuring that the conservation objectives for this habitat type are maintained through the creation of new Molinia meadows. Briels and others argued that the development of new Molinia meadows on the site could not be taken into account in the determination of whether the site's integrity was affected.

The Court ruled that the provision of new habitat was not aimed at avoiding or reducing the significant adverse effects and therefore deemed it a compensatory measure as it tended to 'compensate after the fact for those effects'.[86] The CJEU emphasised the importance of the precautionary principle and observed the assessment required by art 6(3) should contain 'complete, precise and definitive findings capable of removing all reasonable scientific doubt as to the effects of the works proposed on the protected site'.[87] It considered that:

> any positive effects (…) aimed at compensating for the loss of the area (…) are highly difficult to forecast with any degree of certainty and, in any effect, will be visible only several years into the future (…). Consequently, they cannot be taken into account at the procedural stage provided for in article 6(3) HD.[88]

The provision of new habitat should therefore be assessed within the meaning of art 6(4) HD, taking the specific conditions laid down into account. This line of reasoning has been confirmed in subsequent case law.[89]

Interesting, and also concerning, is that in this specific case, the Minister ignored the path to art 6(4) HD set by the Court by ordering a new appropriate

[84] Case C-258/11 *Peter Sweetman and Others v An Bord PleanaÂla* [2013] ECLI:EU:C:2013:220 and Joined Cases C-387/15 and 388/15 *Hilde Orleans and Others v Vlaams Gewest* [2016] ECLI:EU:C:2016:583 are also relevant for the distinction between compensation and mitigation but will not be further discussed here. See Lorenzo Squintani and Jacqueline Zijlmans, 'Stel Gerust een Prejudiciële Vraag! Toepassing van de CILFIT-doctrine in Geval van Mitigerende (en Compenserende) Maatregelen' [2018] *NBR Tijdschrift Natuurbeschermingsrecht* 40, 51.

[85] C-521/12 *Briels v Minister van Infrastructuur en Milieu* ECLI:EU:C:2014:330. See Floor M Fleurke, 'Het arrest Briels: Begrippen Mitigatie en Compensatie Habitatrichtlijn Nader Verklaard' [2014] *Nederlands tijdschrift voor Europees Recht* 275.

[86] *Briels v Minister van Infrastructuur en Milieu, ibid* [31].

[87] *ibid* [27].

[88] *ibid* [32].

[89] C-387/15 and C-388/15 *Orleans v Vlaams Gewest* ECLI:EU:C:2016:583 and C-142/16 *European Commission v Federal Republic of Germany* [2017] EU:C:2017:301.

assessment in the context of art 6(3) HD. It may be less surprising that the new conclusion of the additional appropriate assessment carried out reads as follows: 'the natural features of the site in the light of the conservation objectives will not be affected by the project'.[90] Earlier, it was established that the A2 route project did have negative consequences for the existing acreage and for the quality of the protected natural habitat type 'blue grasslands' due to the drying out and acidification of the soil due to nitrogen deposits.

The additional appropriate assessment states, among other things, that the nitrogen deposits due to total road traffic at the habitat types is structurally lower in both the reference year and planned years. The nitrogen deposits as a result of the road widening would also be structurally lower. The lower nitrogen deposit levels is explained by the application of the latest version of the calculation model – the use of which is accepted in the case law of the Council – but again is difficult to challenge and does not include a more qualitative assessment of scientific uncertainties.[91]

The Court's clarification, therefore, did not affect the outcome of the procedure in which the questions had been raised. However, it did impact subsequent cases held before the Council – some of which were put on hold pending the preliminary ruling procedure. After *Briels* the Council is stricter in assessing the certainty of the effectiveness of measures.

In a 2016 case regarding the extension of a piggery, the Council required that management measures could only account as mitigating measures if there is insight into whether the management measures concerned will sufficiently prevent the negative effects of the activities to be assessed and therefore whether it is ensured that the natural features of the Natura 2000 area will not be affected.[92] Hence, there has to be a direct link between the management measures, the intended project and the location of the project. In a case concerning the construction of a golf course, the Council reached a similar conclusion: the harmful consequences were a direct result of the removal of 1.8 ha protected dunes while those effects were not removed by the proposed measures. The Council followed *Briels* and concluded that the measures were thus aimed at developing a new area of habitat type at a new location.[93]

[90] Additional appropriate assessment A2 's-Hertogenbosch – Eindhoven17 juni 2014, definitief rapport AD1208-105-100. Opgesteld in opdracht van Rijkswaterstaat Zuid-Holland provided by the consultancy agency Royal Haskoning DHV.

[91] Aanvulling Passende Beoordeling A2's-Hertogenbosch – Eindhoven ABRvS 17 juni 2014 ECLI:NL:RVS:2016:2017, 46.

[92] ABRvS 20 July 2016, ECLI:NL:RVS:2016:2017 [5.7]. The Council explicitly took into account the fact that according to the assessment report, the critical deposition values were still being exceeded. Any increase in nitrogen deposition could therefore have consequences for the achievement of the conservation objectives. See also ABRvS 15 July 2015, ECLI:NL:RVS:2015:2224; ABRvS 11 March 2015, ECLI:NL:RVS:2015:706.

[93] ABRvS 24 December 2014, ECLI:NL:RVS:2014:4630. See also ABRvS 24 December 2014, ECLI:NL:RVS:2014:4632 [8.6]. See also ABRvS 12 October 2016, ECLI:NL:RVS:2016:2683; ABRvS 11 February 2015, ECLI:NL:RVS:2015:345 [32.4]; ABRvS 6 May 2020, ECLI:NL:RVS:2020:1184.

For cases concerning species protection (birds), the Council seemed to accept more flexibility. In these cases the creation of new foraging outside the protected area due to the loss of the existing foraging area is regarded by the Council as mitigating measures not affecting the natural characteristics of the designated area.[94] The Council did take other (scientific) factors into account, such as that the new area was already developed, and therefore presumably effective, the (temporal) increased winter mortality, and the loss of a relatively small area. Particularly relevant here was that the project was carried out outside the Natura 2000 area and had no consequences for the size of the habitat or for the possibilities of improving the quality of the habitat in the designated area. The Council therefore took the position that the natural characteristics were not affected by 'temporary' consequences and that therefore no mitigating measures were needed. In another series of cases, the Council also accepted a decrease in a protected population or a habitat type if the size of the population/habitat did not fall below the size stated in the conservation objectives, concluding that there was in these cases no intervention affecting the natural features of the site.[95] Squintani and Zijlmans rightly point out that this however does not conform to the CJEU case law (*Briels*) and is contrary to the certainty criterium.[96] They also point out that in the latter cases the Council ignores the fact that the intended project will affect the habitat of the protected species and thus the question of whether mitigating measures can prevent or reduce this damage.[97]

In several rulings the Council has confirmed that conservation measures and management measures under art 6(1) and 6(2) HD may be taken into account in an appropriate assessment.[98] It was however contested whether conservation measures that are implemented in the future and of which the effects are not yet visible could not be included in an appropriate assessment. The same line of reasoning was followed for autonomous developments. The Council held that if it is 'sufficiently certain' that the autonomous development will occur, it may be taken into account in the appropriate assessment.[99] The question here as well was whether 'sufficiently certain' complies with the precautionary approach taken by the CJEU in its case law where this is interpreted as meaning without scientific reasonable doubt. In general, it can be concluded that when dealing with the scientific uncertainties the Council almost applies a reversed precaution: projects and activities are allowed according to a 'reasonable' test.

[94] ABRvS 29 October 2014, ECLI:NL:RVS:2014:3884.

[95] ABRvS 12 November 2014, ECLI:NL:RVS:2014:4074; ABRvS 29 October 2014, ECLI:NL:RVS:2014:3884; ABRvS 11 March 2015, ECLI:NL:RVS:2015:735; ABRvS 29 March 2017, ECLI:NL:RVS:2017:847.

[96] Squintani and Zijlmans (n 84) 51.

[97] *ibid* 52.

[98] ABRvS 30 October 2013, ECLI:NL:RVS:2013:1694; ABRvS 10 December 2014, ECLI:NL:RVS:2014:4431; ABRvS 11 February 2015, ECLI:NL:RVS:2015:345; ABRvS 27 January 2016, ECLI:NL:RVS:2016:170.

[99] ABRvS 31 October 2012, ECLI:NL:RVS:2012:BY1743; ABRvS 1 April 2015, ECLI:NL:RVS:2015:992.

As we will see hereafter these questions have been addressed in the preliminary ruling regarding the PAS case.

C. The Overturning of the Programmatic Approach to Tackling Nitrogen Deposits

Before 2015, the Council of State was strict on addressing additional nitrogen deposits in Natura 2000 areas. Any additional deposits caused by a plan or project leading to an excess of the critical loads in a protected area needed to undergo an appropriate assessment as required by art 6(3) HD. The courts did not accept any threshold to establish significant effect, leading to a huge blockage of projects.

As a response, a programmatic approach has been drawn up by the Netherlands in order to tackle the problem of excessive nitrogen deposits in natural sites: The programmatic approach to tackling nitrogen deposition 2015–2021 (*Programma Aanpak Stikstof 2015–2021*, hereafter 'the PAS'), came into force on 1 July 2015. The objective of this programme was reduction of nitrogen deposits and restoration measures so that the conservation objectives for the areas will be achieved in the long term, while flexibility for further economic development remained possible. The PAS therefore continuously anticipated future consequences of measures for protected nature areas and thereby provided 'prior' permission to new activities.

The assessment of art 6(3) HD was performed at a 'programmatic' level. For each Natura 2000 site an assessment of the current status was conducted including permitted activities, general reduction trends and additional restoration measures. The Dutch programmatic approach implied that management and conservation measures, as well as the autonomous development of the deposit levels as a whole, were considered in an art 6(3) HD assessment. Projects were hence authorised through the PAS programme, and only new projects with ammonia emissions resulting in an additional calculated deposit above one mol N/ha/year still needed a Natura 2000 appropriate assessment in accordance with the Nature Protection Act 2017. The compatibility with the requirements of art 6(3) HD of this scheme was, from the start, highly disputed but it took until 17 May 2017 before the Council of State requested a preliminary ruling from the CJEU on the interpretation of art 6 HD in two joined cases concerning ten authorisations under the PAS.[100]

[100] ABRvS 25 July 2018, ECLI:EU:C:2018:622; C-293/17 and C-294/17 *Coöperatie Mobilisation for the Environment UA and Vereniging Leefmilieu v College van gedeputeerde staten van Limburg and College van gedeputeerde staten van Gelderland*, ECLI:EU:C:2018:882. See also Lorenzo Squintani, 'Balancing Nature and Economic Interests in the European Union: On the Concept of Mitigation under the Habitats Directive' (2020) 29 *Review of European Community and International Environmental*

The Court of Justice acknowledged the relevance of a programmatic approach, including its potential to 'examine better the cumulative effects of various projects' at a programmatic level.[101] However, the Court observed that 'in circumstances … where the conservation status of a habitat is unfavourable, the possibility of authorising activities which may subsequently affect the ecological situation of the sites seems necessarily limited'.[102] A programmatic approach must therefore meet the same requirements as individual project assessments, in so far as,

> [a] thorough and in-depth examination of the scientific soundness of that assessment makes it possible to ensure that there is no reasonable scientific doubt as to the absence of adverse effects of each plan or project on the integrity of the site concerned.[103]

The Court accepted that thresholds could be used to exclude projects from individual permit requirements, but emphasised again that there should be no reasonable scientific doubt as to the lack of adverse effects of those plans or projects on the integrity of the sites concerned.[104]

In line with previous rulings, the Court rejected taking into account (active) management measures or other (autonomous) measures which do not have the effect of preventing extra deposits and consequential negative effects on the relevant habitat, but which will improve the habitat or otherwise have positive effects on the habitat. Such measures may be taken into consideration as compensatory measures and may also play a role when examining the conservation status, but may not be taken into account when assessing the effects of plans and projects on the basis of art 6(3) HD.[105]

The Council of State has followed the strict interpretation and ruled that the PAS was not in accordance with the requirements of art 6 HD.[106] In its very long judgment, the Council extensively considers the different types of measures within the meaning of the HD and their different role, and subsequently, assesses the PAS measures.[107] If a project causes any additional deposit, even if this is less than 0,1 mol, on a site in which the critical nitrogen loads are exceeded, an appropriate assessment is needed. It has to then be proven that the additional deposits, in combination with the existing deposits, will not have any detrimental effect on the conservation objectives of the site. The Council also ruled – breaking with the previous line of reasoning – that the effects of measures necessary under

Law 129 and Anker et al (n 2); Chris Backes and Tonny Nijmeijer, Het PAS-arrest van het Hof van Justitie: hoe nu verder? [2019] 2/3 *Milieu en Recht*, 103; Marjan Kaajan, 'Het PAS-arrest; en nu?' [2019] 2/3 *Milieu en Recht* 105.

[101] *Coöperatie Mobilisation for the Environment*, *ibid* [97].

[102] *ibid* [103].

[103] *ibid* [104].

[104] *ibid* [112].

[105] *ibid* [123]–[125].

[106] ABRvS 29 May 2019, ECLI:NL:RVS:2019:1603.

[107] *ibid*.

art 6(1) and 6(2) HD can no longer be taken into account to outbalance negative effects of plans or projects, even if the positive effects of such measures are certain.[108] The only measures which can be taken into account when assessing the effects of plans and programmes are measures which intend to reduce the negative effect of such plans and projects.[109]

In establishing that the appropriate PAS assessment was insufficient, the Council considered in detail that measures were included in the assessment that had not yet been carried out at the time of the appropriate assessment and their effects were therefore to some degree uncertain. Some measures had been implemented but here also the expected benefits were by no means certain or did not take into account any potential adverse effects. As stated before, mitigating measures may be considered only if it is sufficiently certain that they will effectively contribute to avoiding harm to the integrity of the site concerned, 'by guaranteeing beyond all reasonable doubt that the plan or project at issue will not adversely affect the integrity of that site'.[110] The Council concluded that many of the mitigating measures of the PAS did not meet this requirement.[111]

In subsequent case law however, the Council only undertook a light test for assessing whether mitigation measures were correctly presented in the assessment. In a case concerning the effects of a road enlargement plan, the Council rejected the argument that a general measure limiting speed on the highway should be regarded as a management measure and thus accepted this measure as a mitigating measure in the appropriate assessment.[112]

The Council is overall now considerably stricter and more meticulous than in previous case law.[113] The implications of the PAS cases are enormous, and difficult to overestimate.[114] However, the Council still grants competent authorities considerable leeway that is in contradiction with the certainty criterium of the CJEU. An example of this is that small extra nitrogen depositions from new projects are allowed when, according to an appropriate assessment, the ecological effects of this extra deposition are not 'measurable'.[115] The Council has also approved the practice of so-called 'external netting'.[116]

[108] *ibid* [11.5]

[109] *ibid* [11.6].

[110] *ibid* [112].

[111] *ibid* [19.6].

[112] See, eg, ABRvS 20 January 2021, ECLI:NL:RVS:2021:105 [72.2]; ABRVS 30 September 2020, ECLI:NL:RVS: 2020: 2318.

[113] For example in a recent case concerning a windmill park, the Council considered that mere reference to the 'significant effect' framework and the threshold values included therein of neighbouring country was insufficient and therefor the Flemish method for assessing nitrogen deposition was rejected. See ABRvS20 October 2021, ECLI:NL:RVS:2021:2304.

[114] One of the most severe consequences is that, under the PAS programme, activities with a nitrogen deposition of less than 0.05 mol / ha / year, or which concern the development of main roads and waterways at a distance greater than 3 to 5 km to a Natura 2000 site were not subject to a permit requirement. See art 2(12) of the Decree Nature Protection Act.

[115] See, eg, ABRvS 24 February 2016, ECLI:NL:RVS: 2016: 497.

[116] See, eg, ABRvS 30 September 2020, ECLI:NL:RVS:2020:2318.

This means that the nitrogen emissions of installations that terminate their activities are taken over. The Council states that reduction of deposit is not a requirement to use external netting as mitigating measures in an appropriate assessment.[117] It would however be interesting to learn if the CJEU agrees with this interpretation of art 6 HD.

Similarly, only a limited cumulation test is required. It is not necessary, for example, to look at activities that have been licensed in the past and have already been or are being carried out.[118] This marginal review is also applied to the procedure of art 6(4) HD where the Council again relies on the research report provided by the competent authorities for the assessment of alternatives and the effectiveness of the compensatory measures.[119] According to settled case law, it is not required that the areas in which compensatory measures are taken must be in a favourable state of conservation before the project or plan is conducted.[120]

V. Conclusion

In a densely populated and multifunctional landscape where species and habitats need to be protected across a large number of comparatively small Natura 2000 areas or sites, governmental authorities have struggled with the practical implementation of, and compliance with, the HD.

Concretely, the application of art 6(3) HD, and the underlying appropriate assessment, has led to extensive case law as NGOs in the Netherlands have relatively easy access to courts and can build on a legal culture of public interest litigation. A big proportion of these cases revolves around the problem of excessive nitrogen deposits, caused mainly by agricultural activities, and the disputes often have a particular focus on scientific evidence and scientific uncertainty.

This case law is very rich and context dependent, and it has become clear from the analysis above that it is not easy to discern clear lines about how, and to what extent the courts (mainly the Council) take account of scientific uncertainty. However, the following observations stand out.

First, the case law of the Dutch administrative courts shows a preference for a *quantitative* test (distance, reduction area, population size, mortality) regarding the application of the obligations of the HD. However, due to clarification through the case law of the CJEU this has necessarily developed into a more *qualitative* standard (certainty criterium).

[117] *ibid* [4.1]; ABRvS 24 November 2021, ECLI:NL:RVS:2021:2627; ABRvS 20 January 2021, ECLI:NL:RVS:2021:71. See however Rb. Midden Nederland, 22 September 2021, ECLI:NL:RBMNE:2021:4519.

[118] ABRvS March 4th 2020, ECLI:NL:RVS:2020:682 [18.7]; ABRvS 20 January 2021, ECLI:NL:RVS:2021:71 [9.8].

[119] ABRvS 24 July 2019, ECLI:NL:RVS:2019:2560; ABRvS 4 March 2020, ECLI:NL:RVS:2020:682.

[120] ABRvS 18 July 2018, ECLI:NL:RVS:2018:2454; ABRvS 24 July 2019, ECLI:NL:RVS:2019:2560.

Second, Dutch administrative judges tend to follow the case law of the CJEU – leading to significant turns in the case law of the Council – but it has been noticed that administrative courts remain reluctant to send preliminary questions to Luxembourg on the interpretation of contentious issues regarding the provisions of the HD, even if they are under an obligation to do so. If the CJEU has not clarified certain aspects of the HD, the Council tends to be permissive (not siding on precaution) towards decision-making of public authorities.

Third, with respect to the scientific basis of challenged decisions the appropriate assessment is the central focus in legal disputes. There are however no legal requirements for the compilation of this report, and the report is usually composed by a commercial agency according to their own procedures.

Fourth, appellants challenging the content of the appropriate assessment are confronted by the burden of proof to provide counter evidence preferably with an expert counter-expertise. It is doubtful if this apportion of the burden of proof is in line with the precautionary principle as explained by the CJEU.

Fifth, the courts do review scientific reports, and are assisted in this task by the STAB. This unique independent expert body harbours expertise on a wide range of environmental technical and scientific issues and is often asked to provide concrete advice on a particular matter that is before the court. The STAB's final comprehensive report is sent to the judge or court to be distributed to all parties for comment. This contributes to the equality of arms between the parties; the report is however not made public and cannot therefore be requested and it is therefore difficult to assess how scientific uncertainties are taken into account. This lack of transparency is arguably at odds with the Aarhus provisions on access to information.

Finally, in reviewing the scientific basis of decision-making, scientific uncertainties are considered but this rarely leads to the explicit application of the precautionary principle. The Council takes a rather 'legal reality' approach instead of an 'ecological approach' emphasising a procedural approach.

For instance, competent authorities have continuously sought flexibility in the interpretation of art 6(3) HD to avoid the strict test of art 6(4) HD (which is not used very often). The case law discussed shows that in many cases the Council has allowed this flexible approach, and is continuing to do so even after the highly anticipated guidance of the CJEU is the PAS case.

The Council often bases its rulings on administrative decisions on a lack of motivation, and then subsequently gives the competent authorities a time limit to take a new decision and procedurally repair the decision. It can be concluded that scientific assessment and research reports that support the decision-making of the competent authorities are frequently challenged, but such challengers are ultimately not often successful.

7

Of Ostensible Self-Restraint, Explicit Environmental Protection, and a Missing Link: The Appropriate Assessment in Italy

ROBERTO CARANTA

I. Introduction

A number of difficulties have to be surmounted when analysing judicial review by Italian courts. Judgments tend to be highly 'doctrinal'. Theories as to the appropriate standard of judicial review are expounded at length. Precedents are referred to not to highlight the similarity/dissimilarity in the factual circumstances of the different cases but to reaffirm points of doctrine. The present Italian doctrines require a rather hands-off approach to the judicial review of administrative decisions. This is particularly true when the law leaves a margin of factual or policy appreciation to the decision-maker. Actual judgments do not, however, necessarily reflect this repeated doctrine, which are to be rather read as obiter. This leaves the problem of finding the actual ratio decidendi of each case or – most modestly – to gauge the real trends in judicial review. It is therefore necessary to delve into the case law.

The present chapter will first set the ground of the investigation by shortly describing how the Habitats Directive (HD) and Wild Birds Directive (WBD) were implemented in Italy (section II). The illustration of both the doctrines of judicial restraint and of the limited tools administrative courts have to assess the facts of the case will then follow (section III). A number of cases will be analysed. However, the sharp dichotomy between facts and law is a poor guide to understanding judicial review in Italy. What are relevant, more often than not, are margins of assessment, discretion and policy. As will be shown, the doctrines calling for judicial self-restraint are no obstacle for what is often a searching scrutiny of the fact-finding tools used by the decision-maker, as well as of the reasons given by it. Nevertheless, complex factual decisions are not directly assessed by Italian courts, which only exceptionally have recourse to expert witnesses (section IV). A short conclusion summarising the main findings will close this chapter (section V).

II. The Italian Implementation of the HD and WBD: A Paper Tiger?

In Italy, the (central) State has exclusive legislative competence over the 'protection of the environment, the ecosystem and cultural heritage',[1] while the regions and local authorities are called to enforce national and EU environmental legislation.[2]

Italy's and the regions' implementation record is far from spotless. The Evidence Gathering Questionnaire for the Fitness Check of the Nature Directives[3] prepared in view of what became the 2016 Evaluation study to support the Fitness Check of the Birds and Habitats Directives[4] highlighted many shortcomings.[5]

A notorious example is represented by annual plans for the hunting season. Many regions consistently adopt plans breaching international, EU and national law which are routinely challenged by environmental non-governmental organisations. A formal agreement (*intesa*) between the State and the regions foreseeing that those plans had to be preceded by an assessment of the implications of plans or projects on special areas of conservation (*valutazione di incidenza – VINCA*)[6] as provided by the national measures implementing art 6(3) HD was not enough to prevent such breaches.[7]

Currently, environmental legislation in Italy is codified in the so-called 'Environmental Code' (*codice dell'ambiente*).[8] Article 3 *quinquies* specifies the subsidiarity principle and that of loyal cooperation between the different territorial levels. Other generally relevant provisions include art 3 *ter*, titled 'principle of environmental action', which refers to the precautionary principle and the

[1] The situation predating the 2001 Constitutional reform was illustrated by Salvatore Patti, 'Environmental Protection in Italy: The Emerging Concept of a Right to a Healthful Environment' (1984) 24 *Natural Resources Journal* 535.

[2] Article 117(2) letters of the Italian Constitution. For full details of the Directives and original language versions of legislation, see the Table of Legislation. See on this Barbara Pozzo and Mauro Renna (eds), *L'Ambiente nel Nuovo Titolo 5. della Costituzione* (Giuffrè, 2004).

[3] European Commission, 'Evidence Gathering Questionnaire for the Fitness Check of the Nature Directives', available at https://ec.europa.eu/environment/nature/legislation/fitness_check/evidence_gathering/docs/Member%20State%20Stakeholders/Non-Govermental%20Organisations/IT/MS%20-%20IT%20-%20NGO%20-%20EGQ.pdf.

[4] European Commission, 'Evaluation Study to Support the Fitness Check of the Birds Habitats Directives' (Final Report, March 2016), available at https://ec.europa.eu/environment/nature/legislation/fitness_check/docs/study_evaluation_support_fitness_check_nature_directives.pdf.

[5] *ibid* 8.

[6] See the text (in Italian) at www.gazzettaufficiale.it/eli/id/2019/12/28/19A07968/SG (published 28 November 2019); the EU Pilot 6730/14/ENV is expressly referred to in the 'recitals'.

[7] eg T.A.R. Liguria, Sez. II, 7 Aug 2020, n. 570, *LIPU*.

[8] Enacted with Legislative Decree of 3 Apr 2006, No 152, GU No 88 of 14 April 2006.

'polluter pays' principle (referring specifically to then art 174 TEU[9]). Article 3 *quater* is dedicated to the 'principle of sustainable development' and provides that every activity relevant under the Code must conform with the principle of sustainable development to ensure that today's needs are not satisfied at the expense of future generations. The second indent of the latter provision specifically articulates the principle of sustainable development, providing that administrative action must aim at implementing that principle, so that, when weighing competing public and private interests in the exercise of discretion, protection of the environment and of cultural heritage must be given more weight.

Immediately after laying down the general principles of environmental legislation, the Code in its second part (arts 4 to 52) transposes the Strategic Environmental Assessment (SEA), Environmental Impact Assessment (EIA) and Integrated Pollution Prevention and Control (IPPC) EU Directives.[10]

Article 5(1)(c) defines 'environmental impact' as significant effect on a number of aspects, including biodiversity. To this end, the species and habitats protected by both the WBD and the HD are covered. Moreover, under art 6(2)(b), all plans and projects potentially impacting on Special Protection Areas (SPAs) under the WBD and Sites of Community Importance (SCIs) must undergo assessment.

The Code does not, however, encompass all environmental legislation in Italy. More specifically, the WBD was enacted very late by Law of 11 February 1992, No 157, later amended by the Decree of the President of the Republic (*Decreto del Presidente della Repubblica*) of 8 September 1997, No 357, as in turn amended. The HD is still implemented by a secondary source, namely the *Decreto del Presidente della Repubblica* of 8 September 1997, No 357, as modified by the *Decreto del Presidente della Repubblica* of 12 March 2003, No 120.[11] Article 6 of the latter text

[9] See, considering illegal a positive EIA adopted notwithstanding the scientific opinion given by the regional environmental agency was negative, Cass. civ., Sez. Un., 31 October 2019, n. 28094.

[10] These provisions have been amended from time to time to implement changes at EU level. Commission Staff Working Document, 'The EU Environmental Implementation Review 2019 Country Report – ITALY', SWD(2019) 123 final, 41. Directive 2008/1/EC of the European Parliament and of the Council of 15 January 2008 concerning integrated pollution prevention and control [2008] OJ L24/8; Directive 2011/92/EU of the European Parliament and of the Council of 13 December 2011 on the assessment of the effects of certain public and private projects on the environment [2012] OJ L26/1; and Directive 2001/42/EC of the European Parliament and of the Council of 27 June 2001 on the assessment of the effects of certain plans and programmes on the environment [2001] OJ L197/30.

[11] Law of 11 February 1992, No 157, Rule concerning the protection of warm-blooded fauna and hunting authorisations, GU No 46 of 25 February 1992; Decree of the President of the Republic of 8 September 1997, No 357, Regulation transposing Directive 92/43/EEC of 21 May 1992 on the conservation of natural and semi-natural habitats and of wild fauna and flora, GU No 248 of 23 October 1997; Decree of the President of the Republic of 12 March 2003, No 120, Regulation amending and supplementing Decree of the President of the Republic of 8 September 1997, No 357, Regulation transposing Directive 92/43/EEC of 21 May 1992 on the conservation of natural and semi-natural habitats and of wild fauna and flora, GU No 124 of 30 May 2003. See also Decree of the President of the Republic of 5 July 2019, No 102, Regulation containing further amendments to Article 12 of Decree of the President of the Republic of 8 September 1997, No 357, Regulation transposing Directive 92/43/EEC of 21 May 1992 on the conservation of natural and semi-natural habitats and of wild fauna and flora, GU No 208 of 5 September 2019.

implements art 6 HD, including art 6(3) concerning the *VINCA* (ie the appropriate assessment under the HD). Under art 6(1)(b) of the Environmental Code, the *VINCA* may also take place as part of a SEA.

While the relevant EU Directives were duly – albeit late – transposed, the actual designation of Natura 2000 areas was significantly delayed, so much so that the Commission launched a successful infringement procedure against Italy.[12] As will be shown, the necessity to comply with this judgment has opened the way to the classification of a number of Natura 2000 sites which has fed much of the litigation before the administrative courts.

III. The Intensity of Review and the Rules on Evidence before Italian Administrative Courts: Of Hands-Off Doctrines and Limited Access to the Facts of the Case

Article 24(1) of the Italian Constitution provides that 'Anyone may bring cases before a court of law in order to protect its rights and legitimate interests under civil and administrative law'. Article 113(1) affirms that rule with specific regard to administrative action providing that the judicial protection of those holding rights or legitimate interests is always granted against administrative decisions. These provisions have, since the 1990s, been seen as enshrining the principle of effective judicial protection in the Italian legal order.

The Constitution does not however provide any indication as to the standard of review. As a consequence, it is seen as having perpetuated the approach embodied in legislation since the unification of the country in the nineteenth century. According to this traditional approach, the review performed by the administrative courts is a legality review, the courts only exceptionally having been given the power to substitute the decision challenged with one of their own – in the so-called 'merits control' (*giurisdizione di merito*) (eg when the administration fails to give effects to a previous judgment).

Since the second half of the nineteenth century, legality review has covered three grounds: (a) lack of competence; (b) breach of a specific legal rule or a general principle binding the decision-maker (both procedural and more rarely substantive rules); and (c) *eccesso di potere* (see now art 21 *octies* of the Law of 7 August 1990, No 241). The latter has traditionally been the door – or rather the window – allowing Italian courts to look at the substance of the decision taken when the administration must assess complex factual situations and/or enjoys discretion or makes policy decisions. *Eccesso di potere* is spelled out in a long series of instances or occurrences, such as insufficient reasons given, or unreasonableness (see below section III, A).

[12] C-378/01 *Commission v Italy* [2003] ECR I-02857, ECLI:EU:C:2003:176 [18]; and C-3/96 *Commission v Netherlands* [1998] ECR I-03031, ECLI:EU:C:1998:238 [68]–[70].

A. Approach to Scope and Intensity of Review in Environmental Matters in General

The distinction between legality and merits is of course fraught with difficulties in Italy as elsewhere. Basically, Italian courts embraced a wide notion of discretion which covers both policy decisions about conflicting public and private interests, and decisions concerning complex factual assessments (the latter being referred to as *discrezionalità tecnica*).[13] Moreover, Italian courts are most ready to read complex decisions as involving both policy choices and complex factual assessments. Traditionally, these decisions and assessments were reviewable only in so far as they were close to irrational. Judicial review was limited to questions of procedure and on the reasons given by the decision-maker, with administrative courts being generally deferential to the choices made by the administration.[14] Full review has, instead, always been performed concerning simple facts, such as for instance measuring noise emissions.[15]

In the past 20 years or so, there has been both a reconsideration of the appropriate level of deference to the decision-maker and a change in the applicable procedural rules.[16] Under pressure from scholars and taking stock of the evolving case law on effective judicial protection developed by the European courts (both the Court of Justice of the European Union (CJEU) and the European Court of Human Rights (ECtHR)), the administrative courts reconsidered their approach to judicial review.[17] In particular, the *Consiglio di Stato* expressly disavowed marginal, peripheral or extrinsic (*estrinseco*) judicial review of complex technical assessments or discretionary and policy choices, and instead embraced a direct appraisal of the decision-making process (so-called *controllo intrinseco*).[18] The courts still considered themselves forbidden from taking the decision in the place of the administration (substitutive review), but were willing to fully and directly review whether the right factual investigation process was chosen by the decision-maker and whether the relevant scientific and technical rules had been respected.[19]

[13] Roberto Caranta, 'On Discretion' in Sacha Prechal and Bert van Roermund (eds), *The Coherence of EU Law* (Cambridge University Press, 2008) 191 ff.

[14] Mariolina Eliantonio, *Europeanisation of Administrative Justice?* (Europa Law Publishing, 2008) 185.

[15] eg T.A.R. Sicilia, Palermo Sez. I, 12 Dec 2011, n. 2333.

[16] See also Eliantonio (n 14) 181 ff.

[17] This influence is analysed by *ibid* 190 ff. See Cons. Stato, Sez. VI, 9 Apr 1999, n. 601 and Cons. Stato, Sez. VI, 23 Apr 2002, n. 2199, in *Foro amm. CdS*, 2002, 1007, with note by Nicoletta Rangone 'Intese nel Mercato Assicurativo e Sindacabilità dei Provvedimenti Antitrust', e in *Giur. comm.* 2003, II, 170, with note by Roberto Caranta 'I Limiti del Sindacato del Giudice Amministrativo sui Provvedimenti dell'Autorità Garante della Concorrenza e del Mercato'.

[18] Eliantonio (n 14) 190 f.

[19] For further discussion, see Eliantonio (n 14) 190 ff.; Roberto Caranta and Barbara Marchetti, 'Judicial Review of Regulatory Decisions in Italy; Changing the Formula and Keeping the Substance?' in Oda Essens, Anna Gerbrandy and Saskia Lavrijssen (eds), *National Courts and the Standard of Review in Competition Law and Economic Regulation* (Europa Law Publishing, 2009) 150 ff.

Through this case law, *Consiglio di Stato* has been trying to strike an uneasy balance between the effectiveness of judicial protection on the one hand, and what it perceives as the impossibility for a court to decide on the merits of an administrative case on the other hand. In a case concerning sanctions for abuse of dominant position, the highest administrative court held that judicial review covers both the rationality and proportionality of the decision taken and the reasons given for it. It also extends to check whether accepted scientific procedures were adhered to. However, given what is assumed to be the uncertainty of scientific knowledge (*relatività delle valutazioni scientitiche*), judicial review must stop short of second guessing the substance of the administrative decision.[20]

Hard(er) look doctrines are often expounded with reference to the review of decisions which would have most probably not withstood judicial scrutiny even under a hands-off approach. This is the case with a decision ordering immediate remedial action to avoid groundwater contamination. The Court found that the public administration had failed to consider whether the measures imposed were actually needed and whether there were any less detrimental alternatives on the facts of the case. Whatever the power of factual evaluation given to the decision-maker, its actual use was labelled as 'arbitrary'.[21]

In easy cases, reference to a doctrine expounding marginal review may actually hide the fact that the judges – or rather the member of the panel tasked with presenting the case to his/her colleagues – had instead peered into the file and were satisfied with the substantive outcome achieved by the decision-maker. This is believed to have been the case when a first instance Court upheld a decision not to leave un-sanctioned breaches of rules concerned with the protection of cultural heritage by a landowner who had built some shanties or shacks, constructed from a mismatch of materials, in an area along the shores of Lake Garda characterised by olive groves. After having recalled precedents advocating restraint in reviewing discretion, the Court basically concluded that the pictures in the file showed that the local authority was justified in coming to the conclusion that the huts were nothing less than an eyesore which could only be remedied by levelling them.[22]

B. Procedural Rules on Evidence and Use of Scientific Knowledge in Court

Procedural rules for judicial review laid down in the Royal Decree of 17 August 1907 No 642[23] gave indications as to the evidence allowed and they were fully in line

[20] Cons. Stato, Sez. VI, 13 Sept 2012, n. 4873; Cons. Stato, Sez. VI, 7 Nov 2005, n. 6152.

[21] T.A.R. Toscana, Sez. II, 19 May 2010, n. 1524.

[22] T.A.R. Lombardia, Brescia Sez. II, 18 March 2011, n. 440; see also T.A.R. Lombardia, Brescia Sez. II, 2 Feb 2011, n. 224.

[23] Royal Decree of 17 August 1907 n. 642 for the consolidation of the rules concerning the institutions competent for administrative justice, GU No. 227 of 25 September 1907.

with the paper-based procedure which was briefly described above. The administrative courts had full access to the facts of the case, including through recourse to outside expertise in those exceptional situations in which their jurisdiction extended to cover the merits of a decision. When their jurisdiction was limited to legality review, the administrative courts had to rely on the documents in the administrative file. At most it could ask the decision-maker for clarification (*schiarimenti*) or additional factual investigation (*verificazioni*).[24] Recourse to expert witnesses was not an option. As Mariolina Eliantonio has remarked,

> Since the choices of the administration involving technical aspects could not be reviewed by the courts, there was no point in giving the courts themselves the power to entrust an independent expert with the task of analysing and reporting on these choices.[25]

A series of changes in the law culminated in the 2010 Code of Judicial Administrative Procedure (*codice del processo amministrativo*), which has widened the means of proof available in legality review proceedings. The starting point is to be found in arts 63 and 64 of the Code, which has reaffirmed the traditional approach to the burden of proof. Since it is the public administration which conducted the investigation, the parties are asked to provide what evidence they have. The courts have wide powers as to how to find evidence, including by asking of their own motion the administration, the parties or third parties for documents and information.[26]

Generally speaking, Italian administrative courts seem to have become somewhat more confident in having recourse to outside help in order to collect information on facts which are not too complex and (importantly) are not interlinked with policy considerations. In one case, some farmers were refused an ex post authorisation to build a small shelter near their blueberry orchard because the Cuneo municipality considered it to be too close to a canal. The applicable rules related to minimum building distances contained different standards for canals with concrete banking and those without. The documents in the administrative file mentioned two canal names. There was some uncertainty as to whether this was two canals, or just one, and whether there were concrete banks. Showing some scepticism in respect of the accuracy of the municipality's information, the Court commissioned an expert investigation.[27]

Notwithstanding these examples, recourse to experts is rare (see also below section IV, E).

[24] See also Eliantonio (n 14) 183 f.

[25] *ibid* 186.

[26] See generally Paola Chirulli, 'Istruttoria' in Roberto Caranta (ed), *Il Nuovo Processo Amministrativo* (Zanichelli, 2011) 521–72.

[27] T.A.R. Piemonte, Sez. II, 17 Apr 2017, n. 611; see also, concerning the measurement of noise levels, T.A.R. Sicilia, Palermo Sez. I (n 15).

IV. Case Law in the Fields of the HD and WBD

This section considers 11 judgments or opinions delivered by the higher administrative courts concerning the application of the HD and WBD. Most are from 2020, a few somewhat older. Three especially significant first instance judgments were also added. In some cases, the Appropriate Assessment (AA) had been absorbed in an environmental impact assessment (EIA), but that is immaterial, since the same approach to judicial review is applied to EIA generally, whether or not the WBD and HD are applicable, and to *VINCA*.

Table 1 Cases Analysed in this Chapter

Case/s	**Shorthand**	**Action brought by developer (DEV)/ civil society (CIV)**	**Upheld/ Quashed**
Cons. Stato, Sez. II, 24 November 2020, n. 2661	Paludi Manfredonia	DEV	Q
Cons. Stato, Sez. IV, 30 August 2020, n. 4889	Civitas	DEV	U
Cons. Stato, Sez. I, 30 June 2020, n. 252	Pineta Grosseto	CIV	Q
Cons. Giust. Amm. Reg. Sic., 7 April 2020, n. 107	Buzzi Unicem	DEV	Q
Cons. Stato, Sez. II, 6 April 2020, n. 2248	Marangoni Tyre	DEV	U
Cons. Stato, Sez. IV, 13 February 2020, nn. 1166 and 1167	Florence airport	CIV	Q
Cons. Stato, Sez. II, 22 January 2020, n. 537	Gonnesa	DEV	U
Cons. Stato, Sez. IV, 29 November 2018, n. 6773	Parco del Pollino	CIV	U
Cons. Stato, Sez. III, 5 November 2018, n. 6240	Torbiere del Sebino	DEV	U
Cons. Stato, Sez. IV, 13 Septmeber 2017, n. 4327	WWF Matera	CIV	Q
TA.R. Liguria, Sez. II, 7 August 2020, n. 570	Lipu	CIV	Q
T.A.R. Puglia, Lecce. Sez. I, 21 November 2019, n. 1838	Kentish plover	DEV	U
TA.R. Lombardia, Brescia Sez. II, 9 April 2010, n. 1532	Alpine region	CIV	Q

A. Distinguishing Questions of Fact, Questions of Law and Questions of Policy and/or Discretion

The relevant distinction in the Italian case law is not so much between factual/technical assessments on the one hand, and 'purely' legal questions of interpretation on the other hand. The distinction is rather between (a) simple factual/technical assessments, (b) complex technical assessments (entailing *discrezionalità tecnica*), and (c) administrative discretion/or policy decisions. Reasoning in terms of policy tends to trigger a self-restraining reflex on courts. Moreover, in practice the case law often sees a mix of all of these elements, considering the inextricable links between the technical and the policy aspects. This is very relevant here, since decisions taken under the WBD and HD (as much as decisions taken under the SEA or EIA Directives) are considered as involving a mix of factual and discretionary/policy decisions. This also leaves limited space to (d) 'pure' legal questions of interpretation that fully and squarely fall under the remit of administrative courts.[28]

While the grounds for challenging (a) and (d) are breach of a specific legal rule or a general principle binding the decision-maker or, more rarely, lack of competence, recourse to *eccesso di potere* will be referred to in actions brought to review (b) and (c) or of a mix of the latter two.

B. (More or Less) Straightforward Cases Focusing on Legal Issues

Cases concerning breaches of a legal rule binding the decision-maker are often rather straightforward (if the legal question is framed correctly). In one case, Buzzi Unicem, the largest cement maker in Italy, challenged a decision denying the extension of a quarrying permit and imposing a duty to restore the natural condition of the area concerned. The decision was grounded on a blanket prohibition to renew such permits in an SCI area enacted by a regulation of the regional Government to stop habitat loss in the implementation of both the WBD and HD and to avoid possible infringement procedures by the Commission.[29] In its advice, the Sicilian correspondent of the *Consiglio di Stato* concluded for the unlawfulness of the negative decision in that it was not preceded by a *VINCA* specific for the area concerned by the proposed quarry expansion, as required by the national legislation having transposed the HD.[30]

This judgment may be contrasted with the one in the *Civitas* case concerning the withdrawal of an authorisation for an energy production plant using vegetal biomass that was to be built in an important bird and biodiversity area (IBA) which

[28] eg Cons. Giust. Amm. Reg. Sic., 25 Feb 2020, n. 107, *Buzzi Unicem*.
[29] *ibid* [3].
[30] *ibid* [9.1].

was not, however, also a special protection area under the WBD.[31] The withdrawal was based on regional legislation which, availing itself of the leeway given by the Italian measures implementing Directive 2001/77/EC on the promotion of electricity produced from renewable energy sources,[32] had forbidden the building of such plants not only in SCIs or other areas protected under EU law, but also in relation to IBAs. The case did not involve any factual investigation as the developer challenged the withdrawal, arguing that the prohibition breached the HD in going beyond what the Directive required, and also that there was a breach of the proportionality principle. The *Consiglio di Stato* first recalled that the CJEU had already held that Directive 2001/77/EC does not preclude legislation which prohibits the location of wind turbines on sites forming part of the Natura 2000 European Ecological Network, without any requirement for a prior assessment of the environmental impact of the project on the site specifically concerned, on condition that the principles of non-discrimination and proportionality are respected.[33]

The *Consiglio di Stato* was easily satisfied that the principle of non-discrimination had been respected, since a rule had been enacted covering all renewable energy plants.[34] Concerning proportionality, the Court first considered that the provision aimed at safeguarding specific habitats characterised by a precarious environmental balance that could be easily altered by emissions from the plant or other forms of pollution coming therefrom.[35] It is noteworthy that the Court did not feel the need to refer to any evidence about these potential effects, implicitly treating them as self-evident. Finally, the *Consiglio di Stato* found that the prohibition was fully in line with the precautionary principle enacted in art 191 TFEU.[36]

Clearly, the two Courts had different takes on what is allowed under EU law, and only the *Consiglio di Stato* applied the correct standard set by the case law of the CJEU.

C. The Standard Approach to Situations Characterised by a Mix of Factual and Discretionary/Policy Decisions

A negative EIA relating to a request to build and exploit a dump for industrial waste in the territory of the Gonnesa municipality in Sardinia was challenged,

[31] The differences and overlaps are clarified in European Commission, 'Science for Environment Policy' (February 2017), available at https://ec.europa.eu/environment/integration/research/newsalert/pdf/important_bird_biodiversity_areas_natura_2000_europe_potential_to_extend_network_483na4_en.pdf.

[32] Directive 2001/77/EC of the European Parliament and of the Council of 27 September 2001 on the promotion of electricity produced from renewable energy sources in the internal electricity market [2001] OJ L283/33.

[33] Cons. Stato, Sez, IV, 3 Aug 2020, n. 4889, *Civitas srl*, § 3.7., referring to C-2/10 *Azienda Agro-Zootecnica Franchini sarl and Eolica di Altamura Srl v Regione Puglia* [2011] ECR I-06561, ECLI:EU:C:2011:502.

[34] Cons. Stato, Sez, IV, 3 Aug 2020, n. 4889, *Civitas srl*, *ibid* [3.7.1].

[35] *ibid* [3.7.2].

[36] *ibid* [3.7.3].

arguing that it was based on considerations not pertaining to human health or the environment, especially when taking account of the fact that the relevant area made much less than one per cent of the total area for the proposed SCI. The action was rejected in 2011 and the first instance judgment was appealed to the *Consiglio di Stato*, which gave its ruling at the beginning of 2020.

The *Consiglio di Stato* restated the case law on the review of EIA before addressing the grounds of review.[37] It first recalled that the EIA process is characterised by a wide discretion in respect of factual assessments made by the administration. As such it may be challenged only for: (a) insufficient fact-finding (*difetto di istruttoria*); (b) lack of reasons or totally illogical reasons (*totale carenza o assoluta illogicità della motivazione*); (c) factual mistake (*erroneità dei presupposti di fatto*); or (d) manifest incoherence in the assessment (*manifesta incoerenza valutativa*). This is because such discretionary decisions often belong to the merits of administrative action, and as such fall outside the scope of legality review. Discretionary decisions may only be challenged for: (e) being manifestly arbitrary (*manifestamente arbitrario*); (f) irrational (*irrazionale*); (g) illogical (*illogico*); or (h) based on a manifest misunderstanding of the facts (*evidente travisamento dei fatti*), which is up to the applicant to demonstrate.[38]

This litany, which is often repeated word for word like a kind of cut and paste obiter, lists some of the usual red flags – traditionally referred to as 'symptoms' – pointing to an *eccesso di potere*. Actually those listed under (b) – first part – and (c) would be more correctly classified as cases of breaches of legal rules, but what is important is not the articulated incantation, but which symptom is actually relevant in any given case. Also, the burden of proof is not really on the applicant, who is simply asked to raise the flag and bring some argument to sustain it.

The decision concerning the EIA for the Gonnesa case is analysed as one characterised as widely discretionary, since it is based on and justified by the highest values in the legal order.[39] The EIA is not a simple factual assessment (*mero giudizio tecnico*) based on objective criteria for measurement, so that in the end it can be reviewed only in case of manifest (*rilevabile ictu oculi*) illegality.

On this basis, the *Consiglio di Stato* considered that EIA covers not only environmental aspects, but also involves a balancing of such aspects with the social and economic elements of a case. This can as a result lead to no possible development options, when, as in the case at hand, even an arguably modest environmental impact is not compensated by any socio-economic benefits as another dump was not needed in the area. Concerning the proposed SCI, the Court considered it evident that, even if the area covered by the proposed works is limited, the effect linked to pollution and anthropic activities will be felt more widely on the local ecosystem.[40]

[37] Cons. Stato, Sez. II, 22 Jan 2020, n. 537, *Ekosarda*. The same restatement may be found word for word in other judgments, such as Cons. Stato, Sez. II, 6 Apr 2020, n. 2248.

[38] *ibid* [3.4.2].

[39] *ibid*. C-142/07 *Ecologistas en Acción-CODA v Ayuntamiento de Madrid* [2008] ECR I-06097, ECLI:EU:C:2008:445 is referred to.

[40] *ibid*.

A few takeaways are notable from this discussion. First, the review is on its face somewhat peripheral and superficial. Second, and because of this, the Court does not feel the need to refer to experts. As the passages on the proposed SCI make clear, the Court assessed for itself what the evident effects were on the environment. Finally, the somewhat peripheral character of the initial review did not necessarily lead to harm to the environment. In this case the developers had to bear their losses.

The review performed by Italian administrative courts does bite even in cases concerning large infrastructure projects. Two major recent cases concerned the strategic plan for the development of the airport of Florence, including by building a new runway over a plain which included SCIs and special protection areas. The plan was annulled at first instance and the judgments were upheld on appeal, even if for partly different reasons.[41] Based on a careful dissection of the relevant case law of the Court of Justice, the *Consiglio di Stato* first held that, as a matter of EU law, the EIA must be based on projects that are sufficiently developed for the competent authority to fully grasp and evaluate all the relevant environmental aspects and so to allow the Court to assess the reasonableness of the decision taken.[42] On this basis, the Court held that the positive EIA had been taken on inadequate fact-finding and was manifestly unreasonable because, besides not having been preceded by a lawful SEA,[43] it was based on studies that had failed to develop the bird strike risk analysis and mitigation and plans to change the course of some waterways and compensate the loss of habitat.[44]

D. Of Certainty and Uncertainty

Paradoxically, the specific approach to the judicial review of administrative decisions in Italy does not leave much room for a discrete notion of uncertainty. The starting point is that complex factual assessments, discretionary and policy decisions all usually entail wide margins of appreciation since there is no red line setting correct decisions apart from wrong ones. On this basis, a decision will be upheld if, besides being exempt from procedural and formal illegalities which are not relevant in this context, it is neither illogical nor irrational (along the vagaries of *eccesso di potere* listed above in section IV, C).

A rare case expressly discussing scientific uncertainty is represented by the most recent (to date) challenge to the annual hunting plan of the Liguria region which had not been preceded by a *VINCA* and had departed on many aspects from the advice given by the High Institute for the Protection and Research over the Environment (ISPRA). Before assessing one by one the instances in which

[41] Cons. Stato, Sez. IV, 13 Feb 2020, nn. 1166 and 1167, *Toscana Aeroporti*.
[42] *ibid* [16].
[43] *ibid* [17]; the SEA was quashed in a separate proceeding.
[44] *ibid* [18].

the hunting plan had departed from the advice of ISPRA, the first instance Court observed that the advice in question is not binding, but an adequate statement of reasons is needed to justify a departure from that advice. More specifically, the advice can only be disregarded as a result of 'univocal, specific and up to date data'. This is also because, in situations where scientific certainty is absent ('*in mancanza di certezza scientifica*') the precautionary principle requires that protective measures are taken.[45] On this basis, all but one of the provisions in the plan that, departing from the advice, had extended the hunt to more species and/or for a longer period were annulled because they were based on data that predated those used in the advice. Basically, the Court translated the uncertainty into a matter of chronology. Only one measure in the plan, which was based on more recent data on the status of the bird species concerned, escaped annulment.[46]

Generally speaking, the Italian administrative courts very much translate what could be otherwise perceived as a question of uncertainty into a duty placed on the decision-maker to investigate the relevant facts reinforced by a duty to give reasons imposed on the decision-maker. One good example is provided by the positive EIA for a new heating gas generator to be built a few kilometres from a special area of conservation. The first instance Court and the *Consiglio di Stato* on appeal upheld the challenge brought by the local chapter of the World Wide Fund for Nature (WWF).[47] Referring rather generically to the case law of the CJEU and of the national courts, the *Consiglio di Stato* held that art 6(2) HD applies to plans and projects concerning areas both within and outside the borders of special areas of conservation, in the latter case provided that their effect may spill into the protected areas.[48] Based on this, the authorisation was annulled because it simply stated that the proposed project fell outside of protected areas and was based on insufficient fact-finding, especially concerning potential effects on those areas.[49]

A more complex case concerned the creation of a SPA encompassing some marshland adjacent to the Gulf of Manfredonia.[50] The owners challenged the measure arguing that their lands were kept artificially wet by pumping water so that the area could be used for hunting. Both the first instance Court and the *Consiglio di Stato* preferred not to engage with the interpretative question of whether artificial wetlands could be classified under the WBD and HD. Instead, it focused on the fact that the regional government had simply rubber-stamped the findings on the IBA list without any investigation of fact to assess what the actual conditions of the wetland concerned were and without hearing from the owners.[51]

[45] T.A.R. Liguria, Sez. II, 7 Aug 2020 (n 7) [10]. C-78/16 and C-79/16 *Pesce and others v Presidenza del Consiglio dei Ministri* ECLI:EU:C:2016:428, is referred to.

[46] T.A.R. Liguria, Sez. II, 7 Aug 2020, *ibid* [11] ff.

[47] Cons. Stato, Sez. IV, 13 Sep 2017, n. 4327, *Lucana Ambiente*.

[48] *ibid* [7.2.2].

[49] *ibid* [7.2.3].

[50] Cons. Stato, Sez. II, 24 Nov 2020, n. 2661, *Regione Puglia*.

[51] *ibid* [12] f.

Occasionally, administrative courts can resort to hindsight to rebut arguments calling into question a *VINCA*. This was the case with some hunting huts in and on the shores of a moorland (*torbiere del Sebino*) near to the Iseo lake.[52] The huts had been in the area for decades, before parts of the moorland were classified as a Natura 2000 site. They were located just a few hundred meters from the classified parts of the moorland. In 2012 their use was authorised again for an additional period based on a regional statute providing for automatic renewal. The authorisations were then withdrawn and granted again in 2014 following a cursory AA based on studies submitted by one hunter's association, together with the owners of the huts. Following the launch of the EU Pilot 6730/14/ENVI, the Italian Government put pressure on the Lombardy Region to make sure that measures were taken to address the EU Commission's concerns, including by evaluating the cumulative impact of the hunting huts. A technical analysis of human interference was commissioned by the *Gruppo Ricerche Aviofauna*, a bird watching association. On the basis of this analysis, all the authorisations were again withdrawn, with the indication that the hunting huts on land had to be moved so they were situated at least one kilometre from the boundaries of the Natura 2000 site. These measures were challenged by the owners of the huts who appealed the unfavourable first instance judgment. The *Consiglio di Stato* very much insisted that a full AA concerning the cumulative impact of the huts was required by the EU Commission[53] and is required by the case law of the Court of Justice.[54] Concerning the AA itself, the Court found it to be neither manifestly illogical nor contradictory or wrong, as it highlighted the impact of hunting following a thorough investigation (*attenta istruttoria*).[55] Moreover, those findings have been confirmed by bird count reports for 2017 and 2018 (the first added to the file during the first instance and the second in appeal) showing remarkable growth in both the species and the number of individuals after the hunting huts were closed or removed from the protected site.[56]

E. Reviewing Factual/Technical Assessments

The party challenging an administrative decision bears the burden of specifically raising what it considers to be insufficient fact-finding, lacking or insufficient reasons, etc (section III, A). As already indicated, most situations relevant here are understood as involving a mix of factual assessment and discretion/policy.

[52] Cons. Stato, Sez. III, 5 Nov 2018, n. 6240, *Bosio*.

[53] eg *ibid* [10.8] and [13.4].

[54] C-127/02 *Landelijke Vereniging tot Behoud van de Waddenzee v Staatssecretaris van Landbouw, Natuurbeheer en Visserij* [2004] ECR I-07504, ECLI:EU:C:2004:482 [13.7].

[55] *ibid* [14.3]; see also [21.2].

[56] *ibid* [16].

In practice, the administrative courts first ascertain whether the grounds of review brought against the challenged decision in fact require the court to probe the merits of the decision, in which case they are rejected as inadmissible. If this is not so, in most cases, the facts will be assessed by the court itself on the basis of its own appreciation.[57] Exceptionally, the administrative court may have recourse to expert witnesses (section IV, F).

A prominent recent case shows once more that the administrative courts tend to rely on their appreciation of manifest factual mistakes. The case concerned the authorisation for fire prevention works in the large Natura 2000 littoral pine forest in the South of Tuscany (*Pineta di Grosseto*).[58] The work-plan outlined the felling of 70 per cent of the trees and 80 per cent of the bushes in a section (about 15 per cent) of the forest. Additionally, 'controlled fire' was to be used for the management of the forest. The work-plan was preceded by a very short and upbeat *VINCA*. The *Consiglio di Stato* considered that the authorising authority was content with ticking boxes in a template provided together with the applicable rules, without any real consideration of the overall effects of the proposed plan. While stating that it could not go into the merits of the decision, the Court considered the *VINCA* not to be sufficiently reasoned. While the idea that many of the different protected habitats would have benefitted from measures to prevent forest fire could in principle be entertained, the challenged decision should have been clarified as to how this could still hold true when most vegetation is razed and/or intentionally burned down.[59] Also, the management measures foreseen were no more detailed than basic forestry practices.[60]

Once more, the Administrative Court focused on whether the reasons given are sufficient instead of lacking when checked against the common sense understanding of natural phenomena. This approach is coherent with the doctrine limiting legality review to manifest errors. The fact that even judges not trained in natural sciences may spot them attests to their manifest character.

F. Recourse to Expert Witnesses

The somewhat restrained approach to judicial review explains the limited recourse Italian administrative courts have to expert witnesses.

One of the most interesting cases concerning access to scientific knowledge on environmental matters involved a series of provincial hunting plans of the Bergamo province in the Lombardy Region. The judgment is significant both for clarifying the possibilities open under the current legislation, including having recourse

[57] See also Cons. Stato, Sez. II, 22 Jan 2020 (n 37).
[58] Cons. Stato, Sez. I, 24 Jan 2020, n. 1233, *Italia Nostra*.
[59] *ibid* [12.2] f.
[60] *ibid* [12.3.3].

to expert witnesses, and for the limits that administrative courts place on their review.[61] In 2006 WWF Italy challenged the provincial hunting plan. The latter was amended in 2008 to remedy the fact that the EIA had followed the adoption of the plan, instead of preceding it, and that the EIA document was largely cut and pasted from one that had been drafted by another province. The WWF challenged the new plan as well. The analysis by the first instance Court started by recalling the boundaries of its review power. The Court held that the case fell under the scope of the legality review, meaning that it could not go into the merits of the case, substituting its own decision with the one taken by the administration.[62] In this framework, reports by expert witnesses might only be used to assess whether the choices made by the decision-maker were logically coherent, taking as the standard the scientific knowledge relevant to those choices.[63]

Two of the main pleas raised by the WWF were held to be well-grounded. The first concerned the proper delimitation of the 'alpine region'. This is relevant because the national legislation provides a lower rate of protected territories for sanctuary and reproduction for the alpine region. The expert witness named by the Court clarified that two conflicting theories may be used to delimit the alpine region. The first is 'natural' in that it only relies on the presence of specific fauna found exclusively in mountain areas. The second is 'cultural' and also takes into consideration the traditions of the local populations and how they interact with the environment. All the experts, including those named by the parties, agreed that both approaches are acceptable, meaning that there is no consensus in the science. However, the Bergamo province did not adhere to either of the two theories. According to the expert witness chosen by the Court, the province had simply copied the cartography already used 20 years before (if not earlier). This made the plan adopted by the province illegal for both breach of the duty to give reasons and irrationality. The plan did not explain the methodology chosen and in any case, given the changes in the environment which may be expected after 20 years, the 1997 cartography could not but be considered obsolete.[64]

The first instance Court also held that the methodology applied to define set aside areas was unlawful. The province, acting on a literal interpretation of the regional legislation, included all areas in which hunting is forbidden to make up the tally of areas set aside for sanctuary. Therefore, areas along roads or railways and close to houses were so considered. Interpreting the legislation in light of its purpose, ie to allow enough areas for the fauna to find shelter and reproduce, the Court found such areas unfit for purpose. Therefore, they should have not been factored among the areas set aside for conservation in compliance with the national

[61] TA.R. Lombardia, Brescia Sez. II, 9 Apr 2010, n. 1532, *WWF*.
[62] *ibid* [3].
[63] *ibid* [4].
[64] *ibid* [12] f.

law, which on this matter acts as a framework for the regional one. Here the Court was mainly concerned with law rather than with facts. The expert witness was however relied upon to find that indeed a sizeable part of the areas ostensibly set aside as sanctuary could not answer the needs of the fauna.[65]

This judgment shows that (some) administrative courts are at least ready to have recourse to expert witnesses to check the accuracy of some uncomplicated facts on which policy decisions are based.

Still, this is a rare occurrence. An obiter dictum in a recent judgment of the *Consiglio di Stato* can be taken as an example of the reticence of the administrative courts to have recourse to expert advice. The case concerned the production of energy from burning car fluff.[66] To challenge the negative assessments of all public administrations taking part in the EIA, the developer requested that the expert witness should be named. The Court bluntly turned the request down, holding that the assessments came from a well-qualified administrative agency, having all the necessary technical and scientific expertise. These could be challenged only if clearly illogical, and with this not being the case, they could not be substituted by an expert's opinion. Arguably, the original challenge was really far-fetched since the applicant had not provided all the required scientific evidence and the evidence provided raised more concerns than it assuaged, so that the technical assessment clearly grounded the decision taken.

G. The Precautionary Principle

The *Consiglio di Stato* treats the precautionary principle as a pillar of EU environmental law which requires preventing risks with the aim of achieving a high level of protection.[67]

While the judicial reasoning of the Italian administrative courts cannot easily be structured along the line between factual/technical questions and legal questions, in the specific environmental context, the precautionary principle may either (a) require an additional motivational effort from the decision-maker making a decision which is potentially harmful to the environment, or (b) reduce the burden on the decision-maker to give reasons when taking measures to protect the environment.

An example of reference to the precautionary principle to lessen the burden of giving reasons when protecting the environment is provided by the Kentish plover case. The concessionaire of a beach in a Natura 2000 area wanted to equip it with permanent structures – bars, showers – and challenged the decision of the municipality of Palagiano which required the structures to be set up no earlier than

[65] TA.R. Lombardia, Brescia Sez. II, 9 Apr 2010 (n 61) [14] ff, and especially [20] concerning the information derived from the report established by the expert witness.

[66] Cons. Stato, Sez. II, 6 Apr 2020 (n 37).

[67] Cons. Stato, Sez, IV, 3 Aug 2020 (n 33) [3.7.3].

1 June and dismantled no later than 15 October. The *VINCA* indicated that those prescriptions were needed to limit disturbance and loss of habitats for nesting species like the *Charandrius alexandrinus* (Kentish plover). The local Administrative Court drew on the relevant case law to reiterate that the *VINCA* is characterised by wide *discrezionalità tecnica*. Therefore, a short statement of grounds will be sufficient for a decision based on the *VINCA* if it adheres to environmental assessment and if, based on the precautionary principle, the protection of the environment takes precedence over economic interests.[68]

An example of the need of a strengthened motivation to impinge on protected areas is provided by the case concerning the positive EIA for a new heating gas generator to be built a few kilometres from a special area of conservation (see above section IV, D). Here, the *Consiglio di Stato* applied the precautionary principle to hold that a significant effect is considered to be present any time that this cannot be ruled out based on 'objective elements'.[69]

In the case concerning the production of energy (and of dioxine and of a number of other harmful substances) from the burning of car fluff, the *Consiglio di Stato* upheld the position of the many public authorities involved in the EIA that had recalled the precautionary principle to reinforce their negative opinion. The case is of particular interest because it lists the precautionary principle among the 'community' law principles that are treated as general principles of Italian administrative law under art 1 of l. 7 August 1990, No 241.[70]

One final remark is that in most cases the one based on the precautionary principle is just one of many lines of argumentation – but often the final – allowing the administrative court to dispose of the case.

H. Imperative Reasons of Overriding Public Interest

One relevant case concerning 'imperative reasons of overriding public interest' concerned the review of a decision taken by the Council of Ministers in a situation where competent and other relevant authorities, including at regional and local level, could not agree. Under the general administrative procedural rules enacted in art 14(3) l. 7 August 1990, No 241, when a plurality of public interests is involved in a decision-making process, all the public administrations charged with their safeguarding must meet to decide together. Decisions are taken by majority voting, but the authorities competent for some overriding public interests, including the environment, have veto power. If the competent authorities failed to reach a majority or veto was used, the Council of Ministers may take the decision, including by overriding vetoes.

[68] T.A.R. Puglia, Lecce, Sez. I, 21 Nov 2019, n. 1838, *Lido L'Oasi di Lecce Beniamino*

[69] Cons. Stato, Sez. IV, 13 Sept 2017 [7.2.2].

[70] Law of 7 August 1990, No 241, New rules concerning administrative decision-making proceedings and right of access to administrative documents GU No. 192 of 18 August 1990. Cons. Stato, Sez. II, 6 Apr 2020 (n 37).

This procedure was followed concerning the authorisation to restart a power plant in the Pollino national park. The plant had not been operational for many years, and ENEL, the largest energy producer in Italy and a former monopolist, asked to restart production after retrofitting the plant to use biomass. The *Consiglio di Stato* qualified the decision by the Council of Ministers as an *atto di alta amministrazione*.[71] This is a decision taken at the highest administrative level possible, just short of a political decision which is not reviewable. Article 14(3) of Law of 7 August 1990, No 241 is seen as a consequence of the constitutional principle of unity of the Republic (art 1 of the Constitution).[72] As such, the decision by the Council of Ministers is characterised by very wide discretion to assess conflicting interests, including by deciding that some public interest will not be satisfied. Therefore, judicial review is limited to checking whether the challenged decision is illogical or irrational or lacks sufficient reasons. Moreover, coming after a regular, if not concluded, proceeding, the reasons for the decision do not need to cover each and every aspect that were debated in the earlier phases. What is sufficient is that those reasons explain the considerations having led to override the veto.[73]

On the facts of the case, the only ground of appeal the *Consiglio di Stato* examined in some detail concerned the possible breach of art 6 HD. Generally recalling the case law of the CJEU and the national courts, the *Consiglio di Stato* held that art 6(4) HD – contrary to the appellants' contentions – does not totally prohibit any developments having a negative effect on protected areas.[74]

What is remarkable is that at no point in the case were the scientific evaluations performed during the *VINCA* discussed and even less so challenged. In all the cases leading up to the last judgment of the *Consiglio di Stato* the contention was about the interpretation of the relevant provisions, foremost among them art 6(4) HD.

I. The Constitutional Framework: National, EU and International Law

As already recalled (section III, A), art 24(1) of the Italian Constitution lays down a rule which is read as requiring effectiveness of judicial review. The standard, however, is not very detailed, and so far has not been called up to challenge the standards of judicial review as evolved about 20 years ago. The entry into force of the EU Charter of Fundamental Rights caused no wrinkles in this understanding

[71] See Gabriele Pepe, 'Il Principio di Effettività della Tutela Giurisdizionale tra Atti Politici, Atti di Alta Amministrazione e Leggi-Provvedimento', available at www.federalismi.it/nv14/articolo-documento.cfm?Artid=35191.

[72] Cons. Stato, 29 Nov 2018, n. 6773 [3.2].

[73] *ibid.*

[74] *ibid* [4.2].

of the principle of effective judicial protection in so far as the standard of review is concerned. Also no further adaptation of the national procedural rules have been considered as necessitated by the Aarhus Convention.[75]

The judgment concerning a decision of the Council of Ministers discussed above (section IV, G) may well be read as a particular instance concerning the distribution of powers between the executive and the judiciary.

The status quo concerning the bounds of legality review has not been called into question with reference to EU law either. As far as it was possible to ascertain with a full text search of the case law of the administrative courts, *Kraaijeveld*[76] was referred to only once, in a case concerning limitation to vehicle traffic to limit pollution.[77] The first instance Administrative Court in Sicily referred to the judgment of the CJEU to argue that the national authorities enjoy discretion in weighing the relevant conflicting public interest, but this does not allow them to remain inactive.[78]

One member of the *Consiglio di Stato* has extrajudicially remarked that a limitation to the wide discretion ostensibly given to the decision-maker descends from *Janecek* and each time EU law set some threshold in subsequent cases, such as for instance concerning water or air pollution.[79]

The European Convention on Human Rights principle of effective judicial protection, together with the above-mentioned provisions in the Italian Constitution, has instead been utilised to justify giving prospective effects only to the judgment concerning the fire prevention works in the Grosseto pine forest.[80]

Finally concerning the possibility of raising questions of breaches of EU law of the court's own motion, this is excluded generally by the Italian case law, and no case specific to the WBD and HD has been found.

V. Conclusion

The difficulty in reading Italian judgments is finding the actual decision and its ratio behind the haze of the declamations stressing the bounds on the review of administrative courts and the discretion enjoyed by the administration.

[75] See critically Giovanni Tulumello, 'Il diritto dell'UE e la Disciplina del Processo Amministrativo: l'Accesso alla Giustizia e l'Estensione del Sindacato di Legittimità degli Atti Amministrativi nella Materia della Tutela Ambientale', available at www.giustizia-amministrativa.it, especially 7ff.

[76] C-72/95 *Aannemersbedrijf P.K. Kraaijeveld BV e.a. v. Gedeputeerde Staten van Zuid-Holland* [1996] ECR I-05403, ECLI:EU:C:1996:404.

[77] T.A.R. Sicilia, Palermo, Sez. I, 28 Feb 2013, n. 458.

[78] *ibid* [3.1.2.1].

[79] Tulumello (n 75) 29 ff, with analysis of C-237/07 *Janecek v Freistaat Bayern* [2008] ECR I-06221, ECLI:EU:C:2008:447; C-752/18 *Deutsche Umwelthilfe eV v Freistaat Bayern* ECLI:EU:C:2019:1114; and C-197/18 *Wasserleitungsverband Nördliches Burgenland and Others* ECLI:EU:C:2019:824.

[80] Cons. Stato, Sez. I, 30 Jun 2020, n. 252, *Italia Nostra* [16.2].

Table 2 Outcomes of the Cases Analysed in this Chapter

Shorthand	Action brought by developer (DEV)/ civil society (CIV)	Decision Upheld/ Quashed
Paludi Manfredonia	DEV	Q
Civitas	DEV	U
Pineta Grosseto	CIV	Q
Buzzi Unicem	DEV	Q
Marangoni Tyre	DEV	U
Florence airport	CIV	Q
Gonnesa	DEV	U
Parco del Pollino	CIV	U
Torbiere del Sebino	DEV	U
WWF Matera	CIV	Q
Lipu	CIV	Q
Kentish plower	DEV	U
Alpine region	CIV	Q

In all but one case discussed in this chapter, civil society managed to have decisions perceived as harmful for the environment quashed. They only failed when they challenged a decision by the national Government overcoming the veto of the Pollino Park administration. Recourse to experts was had only once, in the Alpine region case. In all other cases, different variants of *eccesso di potere*, such as insufficient reasons, insufficient investigation, unreasonableness or factual mistakes, were directly established by the administrative courts.

By contrast, in only two cases developers were successful in their attempts to overturn decisions protecting the environment. The cases in which a 'protective' decision did not withstand judicial scrutiny concerned situations in which the competent administration had acted quite mechanically following the pressure on Italy to increase the number and extension of Nature 2000 areas.[81] In three out of five cases in which developers were unsuccessful, the precautionary principle was enlisted to defend the choices of the administration.

A larger sample of cases will most probably confirm this picture of a judicial review mechanism whose roots deeply push into tradition but still produce outcomes protective of the environment in the vast majority of cases.

Still, it is not a transparent mechanism, as it entrusts factual decisions to the wisdom of judges only trained in law, thus hiding the complexity of many factual situations and the uncertainties in the sciences.

[81] Eg Cons. Stato, Sez. II, 24 Nov 2020 (n 50) [3] and [12].

8

Legal Approaches to Scientific Uncertainty in Germany – The Case of EU Nature Conservation Law

WOLFGANG KÖCK AND TILL MARKUS

I. Introduction

Social sciences have made lawyers aware that one distinctive feature of modern societies is their conscious and systematic approach to uncertainty. For example, they have interpreted the establishment of private and public insurance systems as early responses to uncertainty.[1] Along these lines, they described the development of the welfare state as a means to cope with risks of poverty looming large in developing industrial societies.[2]

In the area of environmental law, the early development of technical safety standards has played an important role in addressing uncertainty. In Germany, environmental standards emerged during industrialisation in the nineteenth century. Standards were developed and used, for example, by the so-called Steam Boiler Associations (*Dampfkesselvereinigungen*) which were founded in Prussia to improve the safety of technical installations. These standards were widely accepted as 'generally recognised rules on technology', or 'standards based on the present state of technology', or the 'best available technology', and have subsequently become legal technical safety standards, used in administrative or judicial decision-making or simply integrated into legislative acts.[3] The effort to systematically approach technological risks, however, has not only been interpreted as an attempt to reduce uncertainty and increase safety, but also as a strategy to address unintended side-effects. Ulrich Beck, in particular, in his famous study on the 'risk society'[4] has drawn attention to what he referred to

[1] François Ewald, *Der Vorsorgestaat* (Suhrkamp, 1986).
[2] Adalbert Evers and Helga Novotny, *Über den Umgang mit Unsicherheit* (Suhrkamp, 1987).
[3] Rainer Wolf, *Der Stand der Technik* (Springer, 1986).
[4] Ulrich Beck, *Risikogesellschaft* (Suhrkamp, 1986).

as 'blind spots in risk management'. He developed his thoughts in view of the Chernobyl Disaster, aptly describing certain approaches to risk management as 'organised irresponsibility'.[5] Anthony Giddens has similarly pointed towards the consequences of modernity, using the image of the famous juggernaut wagon, pointing out that technological inventions and accelerating social processes can be extremely difficult to control.[6]

Targeting uncertainty in general should be distinguished from addressing scientific uncertainty in particular, the latter being of great importance in the area of environmental law. Since the 1970s, uncertainty is no longer a mere scientific problem, but rather is increasingly a governance challenge for law-making as well as for administrative and judicial decision-making. In Germany, uncertainty and knowledge problems have played a major role in several areas of environmental law, particularly in respect of planning and permitting industrial and nuclear plants or genetic engineering. Both the German Atomic Energy Act (AtomG)[7] and the Genetic Engineering Act (GenTG)[8] (the latter being strongly influenced by EU law) have defined levels of protection by explicitly referring to the 'state of science and technology' or the 'state of the art in science' and thus have made the available scientific knowledge the yardstick for granting different kinds of permits.[9] In the national legal discourse, related questions have been discussed under the term 'risk administration' or 'risk management law'.[10] Both terms (or headlines) try to capture how the administration, courts, and the legislature systematically call for the generation and evaluation of risk-relevant knowledge and systematically address remaining uncertainties regarding possible damage by applying the precautionary principle. In the international social science discussion, the term 'regulatory science'[11] has also become prominent in this regard. The terms 'risk management' and 'regulatory science' indicate and highlight that science is increasingly important in the

[5] *ibid* and Ulrich Beck, *Gegengifte* (Suhrkamp, 1988).

[6] Anthony Giddens, *The Consequences of Modernity* (Polity Press, 1990).

[7] Atomic Energy Act (BGBl. I S. 1565). For original language information, see Table of Legislation.

[8] Genetic Engineering Act (BGBl. I S. 2066).

[9] See s 7 I No. 3 Atomic Energy Act; s 11 I No. 4 and s 16 I No. 2 Genetic Engineering Act. In Directive 2001/18/EC of the European Parliament and of the Council of 12 March 2001 on the deliberate release into the environment of genetically modified organisms and repealing Council Directive 90/220/EEC [2001] OJ L106/1 reference is made at various points to scientific findings and the precautionary principle; see, eg, art 4(1) annex II, pt B.

[10] Udo Di Fabio, *Risikoentscheidungen im Rechtsstaat* (J.C.B. Mohr, 1994); Gotthard Bechmann, *Risiko und Gesellschaft Society* (Westdeutscher Verlag, 1993); Arno Scherzberg, 'Risiko als Rechtsproblem' (1993) 84 *Verwaltungsarchiv* 484; Arno Scherzberg, 'Risikosteuerung durch Verwaltungsrecht' (2004) 64 *Veröffentlichungen der Vereinigung Deutscher Staatsrechtslehrer* 214; Wolfgang Köck, 'Risikoverwaltung und Risikoverwaltungsrecht – Das Beispiel des Arzneimittelrechts' [2003] *UFZ-Diskussionspapiere* 1; Wolfgang Köck, 'Rationale Risikosteuerung als Aufgabe des Rechts' in Erik Gawel (ed), *Effizienz im Umweltrecht* (Nomos, 2001).

[11] Sheila Jasanoff, *The Fifth Branch: Science Advisers as Policy Makers* (Harvard University Press, 1990); Sheila Jasanoff, 'What is the Regulatory Science? Concept and History in United States and in Japan' (2011) 39 *Clinical Evaluation* 167.

context of regulation, eg particularly with a view to generating knowledge about environmental and health risks; identifying adequate levels of protection; and for supporting procedures of acquiring and processing risk knowledge for practical decision-making.[12]

German courts have proved to be important drivers in the development of risk-related administrative law, especially in the area of emission control and nuclear safety. Since the 1970s, courts have been repeatedly and continuously confronted with knowledge issues regarding reactor safety and radiation protection;[13] regarding air quality and health impacts; and – increasingly since the 1990s – with safety issues concerning genetic engineering. In response, they have developed concepts for addressing emerging knowledge issues, for example, the 'practical reason formula' provided by the Federal Constitutional Court in its jurisdiction on nuclear power plants.[14]

In Germany, specific knowledge standards regarding habitat and species conservation, however, fell under the judicial gaze more recently, mainly in connection with nature conservation law regulating interferences with nature (the so-called *Naturschutzrechtliche Eingriffsregelung*[15]). In this regard, German courts were strongly influenced by the Court of Justice of the European Union (CJEU), making clear that the state of science or the best available scientific knowledge is of paramount importance for governing species and habitat conservation.[16] Since then, questions regarding the adequate level of protection in nature conservation have increasingly been subject to court proceedings, culminating in a decision by the Federal Constitutional Court in 2018 regarding the killing of protected species.[17] The Court addressed the question of how to handle scientific uncertainty regarding the effects of wind energy projects on specific animals. The decision had a strong impact on the German legal scientific discourse. According to the Court, scientific uncertainty must not prevent the decision-maker from taking decisions and that they must not wait in such cases until 'better' or 'full knowledge' is available. According to the Court, however, the administration is instead required to provide for directions that address existing uncertainties, including the adoption of binding standards.[18]

The following considers the German approach to such questions in more detail. The chapter is structured as follows: first, we will explain how

[12] Ivo Appel, 'Methodik des Umgangs mit Ungewissheit' in Wolfgang Hoffmann-Riem and Eberhard Schmidt-Aßmann (eds), *Methoden der Verwaltungsrechtswissenschaft* (Nomos, 2004).

[13] BVerwG (1 C 102/76) *Coal-fired power plant Voerde*, BVerwGE [1978] 55, 250.

[14] *ibid*.

[15] See Federal Nature Protection Act (BGBl. I S. 2542).

[16] C-127/02 *Landelijke Vereniging tot Behoud van de Waddenzee y Nederlandse Vereniging tot Bescherming van Vogels v Staatssecretaris van Landbouw, Natuurbeheer en Visserij* [2004] ECR I-07405, ECLI:EU:C:2004:482 and C-674/17 *Luonnonsuojeluyhdistys Tapiola Pohjois-Savo – Kainuu ry v Risto Mustonen* ECLI:EU:C:2019:851.

[17] BVerfG (1 BvR 2523/13) *Red Kite*, BVerfGE [2018] 149, 407.

[18] *ibid* [24].

environmental and technology law deal with knowledge problems and how decisions regarding conservation requirements have been linked to the best available knowledge (section II). In particular, the chapter considers how courts have developed different doctrinal approaches to connect them (section II, A). The second section then provides some general information about the German judiciary, explaining the courts' margin of control over administrative decision-making, and introduces the courts' tasks in identifying scientifically unresolved issues that matter for the decision-making process (section II, B). The third section is dedicated to nature conservation law (section III). Here, information about the CJEU's case law on knowledge requirements is provided (section III, A). Subsequently, the German case law on habitat and species protection is analysed (section III, B). Special attention will be paid to the seminal ruling of the Federal Constitutional Court (section III, C). We then draw some conclusions in section IV.

II. Environmental and Technology Law, Scientific Uncertainty, and the Role of the Courts

Courts in Germany were initially confronted with questions concerning the state of the art in science and how to handle scientific uncertainty in areas where the protection of humans from technical risks was at stake. Permit applications for industrial and nuclear plants were particularly important in this regard.

Laws aiming to guarantee the safety of industrial and nuclear plants emerged from laws regulating regular industrial activities (the *Gewerberecht*) or public order (*Polizeirecht*). In the 1970s, it transformed into what is nowadays referred to as Emission Control Law (*Immissionsschutzrecht*). All of these laws shared the aim to control or prevent hazards.[19] In German law, a hazard is understood as a situation in which damage to a legally protected good seems not only possible, but is reasonably likely (*hinreichend wahrscheinlich*). While laws governing traditional industrial activities or relating to public order[20] based their assessments regarding the imminence of hazards on the police's day-to-day experience,[21] the newly emerging special law branches drew on 'expert knowledge' and based their assessments regarding state of the art in respect of scientific and technical knowledge.[22]

[19] Wolfgang Martens, 'Immissionsschutzrecht und Polizeirecht' (1981) 96 *Deutsches Verwaltungsblatt* 597, 609.

[20] Bill Drews et al, *Gefahrenabwehr* (Heymanns, 1986).

[21] Karl-Heinz Ladeur, 'Risiko und Recht. Von der Rezeption der Erfahrung zum Prozess der Modellierung' in Gotthard Bechmann (ed), *Risiko und Gesellschaft* (Westdeutscher Verlag, 1993).

[22] Martens (n 19) 609; Wolfgang Köck, 'Grundzüge des Risikomanagements im Umweltrecht' in Alfons Bora (ed), *Rechtliches Risikomanagement. Form, Funktion und Leistungsfähigkeit des Rechts in der Risikogesellschaft* (Duncker and Humblot, 1999).

A. Defining Conservation Requirements in Accordance with the Scientific State of the Art and the Precautionary Principle

i. Scientific State of the Art in the Laws Governing Industrial Plants

Legal requirements regarding levels of protection are often worded vaguely. One illustrative example is the German law regulating industrial plant safety (s 4 ff *Bundes-Immissionsschutzgesetz* (BImSchG)).[23] For approval, industrial plants must not inflict any harmful effects on the environment, avoiding inter alia negative effects on the 'public' or the 'neighbourhood' (s 5 I No 1 BImSchG). In this regard, the Federal Administrative Court (*Bundesverwaltungsgericht* (BVerwG)) stated in an early landmark decision that the required level of protection should be based on 'general life experience, in particular on the state of the art in science' and that the application of the law must ensure 'risks identified on the basis of the state of the art in science' are avoided with 'sufficient probability' as well as 'in accordance with the principle of proportionality'.[24] Initially, risks were only those for which it could be reasonably assumed that they would result in damages.[25] Here, the law ties in with the older concept of hazard as explained above. Scientific uncertainties, however, had to be taken into consideration, irrespective of any known risks, by requiring the industrial plant operator to take preventive measures in accordance with the state of the art, in order to keep pollutant emissions as low as possible (s 5 I No 2 BImSchG).

ii. Scientific State of the Art in the Laws Governing Nuclear Plants

The AtomG defined the level of protection in Germany for nuclear power plants. Compared to laws regulating regular industrial plants, the requirements were much more stringent. Permits for building and operating nuclear plants could only be granted if 'necessary measures' were adopted to prevent damage. Whether measures were necessary was determined on the basis of the 'state of the art in science and technology' (s 7 II No. 3 AtomG). In its famous decision on the *Kalkar Nuclear Power Plant*, the Federal Constitutional Court (BVerfG) ruled that:

> by referring to the state of the art in science, the legislator exerts an even stronger constraint to ensure that the legal regulation is in conformity with the latest scientific and technical developments. Measures deemed necessary in accordance with the latest scientific knowledge must be taken to prevent damages. Where preventing damages is not yet technically feasible, permissions may not be granted; what is deemed necessary thus does not equal what is currently technically feasible. This formula, however, raises

[23] Federal Emission Control Act (BGBl. I S. 1274; 2021 I S. 123).
[24] *Coal-fired Power Plant Voerde* (n 13) [254].
[25] *ibid.* BVerwG (7 C 19/02) *Nanopowder*, BVerwGE [2003] 119, 329 [329].

> even more problems for the authorities than the referring to the 'state of the art'. In case expert opinions are contradictory, authorities may have no choice but to take a position on the dispute over science.[26]

The Court then continues:

> As far as damages to life, health and property are concerned, the legislator has established a standard in the Atomic Energy Act which only permits granting a licence if a damaging event appears *practically impossible, i.e.* according to the state of science and technology (…). Remaining uncertainties which lie beyond this threshold of practical reason flow from the limits of human cognitive capacities; they are inevitable and insofar to be accepted and borne by all citizens as socially adequate burdens.[27]

What this means was further explained by the Federal Administrative Court in its 1985 decision on the *Wyhl Nuclear Power Plant*:

> Where the necessary measures within the meaning of Section 7 II No. 3 Atomic Energy Act are taken, risks must practically be rendered impossible; the decision required in this regard must be based on the 'state of the art in science and technology'. Uncertainties with a view to the identification and assessment of risks must be considered in light of the damage potential, particularly by making sufficiently conservative assumptions (…) in doing so, the authority responsible for granting permission must not rely on the 'prevailing opinion' in science, but must consider all reasonably justifiable scientific findings.[28]

In the same decision the Court elaborated generally on the relationship between the legislature, judiciary and executive with a view to taking risk-decisions. The Court held that the executive is particularly well equipped institutionally to identify and assess risks, including its capacities for consulting with the scientific community. Accordingly, the judiciary is restricted in reviewing its decisions in this regard.[29] The following subsection will draw some general conclusions.

iii. Interim Conclusions: Increased Importance of Administrative Risk Management

Against this background, it may be concluded that the way the German legal system has approached scientific uncertainty has depended on the requirements regarding a specific level of protection. Law governing the development and operation of regular industrial plants refers to the 'state of the art technology' with a view to preventing damages and to the 'state of the art of scientific knowledge' when there is confirmed knowledge about likely damage (ie the standard aiming at hazard prevention). The remaining uncertainties are addressed by an obligation

[26] BVerfG (2 BvL 8/77) *Kalkar Nuclear Power Plant*, BVerfGE [1978] 49, 89 [136].
[27] *ibid* [143] (emphasis added).
[28] BVerwG (7 C 65/82) *Nuclear Power Plant Wyhl*, BVerwGE [1985] 72, 300 [316].
[29] *ibid.*

to use the 'best available technology' (ie as a standard of extended risk prevention). By contrast, laws governing the development and operation of nuclear plants or genetic engineering refer to the 'state of science and technology' and oblige addressees to make sufficiently conservative assumptions, ie apply further safety factors or make 'worst case assumptions' in order to provide for safety. In this case, the application of the precautionary principle is an integral part of the protection standard.

At the same time, the courts have emphasised the executive's competence regarding risk assessments, particularly their margin of discretion. Accordingly, courts will respect administrations' discretion and not replace it with their own considerations. The courts justify their limited will to review administrative discretion by arguing that the executive is much better equipped to organise and draw up expertise. Courts, instead, should concentrate on controlling whether the best available knowledge has been taken into consideration and processed without arbitrariness. Courts have also emphasised that the effectiveness of judicial review can be increased by laying down procedural requirements that determine the process of administrative knowledge generation and processing.

Referring to 'practical reason', courts have made clear that some risks may simply have to be accepted in a modern, technology-driven society. There is no 'zero risk', especially when applying the precautionary principle. What level of (residual) risk has to be accepted may vary with a view to different activities. Regarding the operation of nuclear plants, the obligation to take preventive measures ends where a risk can no longer be recognised, ie at the limits of what humans can possibly know.[30] With a view to permitting regular industrial plants or managing hazardous substances, things are different. Where substances are of very high concern (which is the case when a complete risk control is not deemed possible), permission depends on whether the substance's socio-economic benefits outweigh the risks and whether lower-risk alternatives are available (art 60(4) REACH Regulation[31]). Against this backdrop it becomes clear that both the legislative design and application of the precautionary principle varies greatly from sector to sector.

iv. The Concept of 'Normative Concretisation'

In order to relieve the burden for administrative authorities in specifying protection requirements in accordance with the scientific state of the art for each individual case, legislatures often empower governments to adopt generally applicable directives. For example, the German Government has issued the so-called Technical Instructions on Air Quality (*Technische Anleitung Luft*).[32]

[30] *Kalkar Nuclear Power Plant* (n 26) [143].

[31] Regulation (EC) No 1907/2006 of the European Parliament and of the Council on the Registration, Evaluation, Authorisation and Restriction of Chemicals (REACH) [2006] OJ L396/49.

[32] See Administrative Regulation for Air Pollution Control (GMBl. 2021, Nr. 48–54, S. 1050–1192).

Doctrinally these Technical Instructions constitute an administrative regulation. This regulation contains both general emission limits as well as specific requirements regarding emissions.[33] Several landmark decisions by the Federal Administrative Court have characterised this set of rules as 'anticipated expert opinions'[34] and later as administrative rules that bind the administration.[35] Such administrative rules can be reviewed by the courts only to a certain extent to control: a) whether the Government has considered scientific and technical knowledge indiscriminately; b) whether the state of knowledge has developed since the adoption; and c) whether the case in question has special features that require the application of different standards.[36] To the authors' knowledge, the concept of 'normative concretisation' by the Government or administrations is probably still one of the special characteristics of German environmental law.[37] In essence, the approach emphasises executive competence to evaluate the state of the art in science and technology and to develop specific requirements that allow for a uniform application of openly worded environmental laws. The courts have both co-developed and accepted this approach.

v. Procedural Requirements: Organisation of Scientific Expertise in Risk Management

To this day, courts in Germany have not developed detailed procedural requirements to ensure that the executive bases its decisions on the scientific state of the art. Many environmental and technical laws, however, provide rules that demand the involvement or establishment of expert bodies as well as obligations to consult specialised expert councils or governmental agencies that can hold expert knowledge. For example, the Federal Emission Control Act requires the establishment of a 'Commission for Plant Safety' (s 51a BImSchG), which is required to identify options for improving plant safety at regular intervals or on special occasions. The GenTG contains a similar provision that requires the establishment of a 'Commission for Biological Safety' (s 4 GenTG). The latter's main function is to advise the federal Government on safety-related issues and to provide advice on specific permission procedures under the Genetic Engineering Act (s 10 VII GenTG). The GenTG is an illustrative example of a law that requires the involvement of expert bodies in permission or licensing procedures. For example, decisions over the release of genetically modified organisms are taken by a

[33] Wolfgang Köck, 'Grenzwerte im Umweltrecht' (2020) 31 *Zeitschrift für Umweltrecht* 131.

[34] *Coal-Fired Power Plant Voerde* (n 13) [256].

[35] *Nuclear Power Plant Wyhl* (n 28) [315].

[36] Reinhard Hendler, 'Umweltrechtliche Grenzwerte in der Gerichts- und Verwaltungspraxis' [1998] *Die Öffentliche Verwaltung* 48.

[37] See also Olaf Dilling and Wolfgang Köck, 'Environmental Law – Country Report Germany' in Emma Lees and Jorge E Viñuales (eds), *Oxford Handbook of Comparative Environmental Law* (Oxford University Press, 2019).

federal authority which must involve three additional expert bodies, ie the Federal Agency for Nature Conservation, the Robert Koch Institute (a typical regulatory science authority), and the Federal Institute for Risk Assessment (s 16 IV GenTG). This illustrates how the legislator has responded to knowledge problems as well as the difficulties in assessing and identifying the state of science by establishing expert authorities and by involving external expertise.

vi. The Role of Courts

German administrative courts themselves have defined their own function regarding the control of administrative decision-making in the face of uncertainty as follows. They ensure that a) science has to be consulted, and b) knowledge about risks needs to be based on the existing state of the art. They have refrained from laying down specific procedural requirements in this regard. They have made clear, however, that the Government and administrations cannot base their decisions about what should be done on the 'prevailing opinion in science' alone, but must form their own judgments, especially in cases where a sound and well established knowledge-base is lacking, ie 'at the limits of knowledge'. This holds particularly true for those areas of the law which are guided by the precautionary principle. This requirement is based on the idea that at the very limits of knowledge a) legitimacy must be generated through political and not expert decision, and b) applying laws and rules is a normative process, which cannot draw conclusion from sciences alone, if natural fallacies should be avoided.[38]

vii. Result: Renaissance of Legislation? On the Importance of Procedural Law-Making

Decision-making at the limits of knowledge thus requires normative legitimacy. This, in turn, calls for both the executive taking responsibility as well as the legislator providing guidance through legislation and public participation.[39] The recent Corona pandemic has indeed made clear that taking important political decisions in the face of uncertainty must not be left to experts alone, but requires democratic political discourse and public support.[40]

[38] Olaf Dilling and Till Markus, 'Ex Rerum Natura Ius? Sachzwang und Problemwahrnehmung im Umweltrecht' in Olaf Dilling and Till Markus, *Ex Rerum Natura Ius? – Sachzwang und Problemwahrnehmung* (Nomos, 2014).

[39] Laura Münkler, *Expertokratie* (Mohr Siebeck, 2020); Erhard Denninger, *Verfassungsrechtliche Anforderungen an die Normsetzung im Umwelt- und Technikrecht* (Nomos, 1990); Rudolf Steinberg, *Der Ökologische Verfassungsstaat* (Suhrkamp, 1998); Till Markus, 'Changing the Base: Legal Implications of Scientific Criteria and Methodological Standards on What Constitutes Good Marine Environmental Status' (2013) 4 *Transnational Environmental Law* 145.

[40] Anika Klafki, 'Mehr Parlament Wagen? Die Entdeckung des Art. 80 IV GG in der Corona-Pandemie' (2020) 39 *Neue Zeitschrift für Verwaltungsrecht* 1718.

Irrespective of whether and to what extent Parliament engages risk management, there is and will be a demand for legislative guidance for the executive in its approaches to scientific uncertainty. The legislator has to consider carefully how precisely it needs to direct the executive's own regulation and decision-making through law, both with a view to the levels of protection and procedures. With regards to procedural requirements the parliamentary legislator needs to ensure that the law generates clarity about: a) what we know for sure, ie what is soundly proven or evident; b) what currently remains not fully understood (eg concerns exist due to first scientific assessments); c) whether existing knowledge gaps may be closed in the near future through systematic research; d) on which additional criteria and arguments decisions are to be based; and e) what kind of assessments and evaluations need to be carried out to revisit decisions and adapt them in accordance with updated and improved knowledge.[41] Different aspects of these ideas were discussed in the early 1990s during the course of the effort to codify environmental law in a unified environmental act (*Umweltgesetzbuch*). The codification effort failed, however, due to lack of a political majority. Nevertheless, discussions have been revitalised by the German Constitutional Court's Decision of 23 October 2018, which may place some of the suggestion made here back onto the political agenda (see section III, C).

B. Dealing with Scientific Uncertainty in Judicial Proceedings

i. *The Organisation of the Judiciary in Germany*

The judicial system in Germany comprises the ordinary courts (responsible for civil and for criminal cases) and the specialised courts (responsible for administrative, social welfare, fiscal and labour law cases). In addition, constitutional courts exist at the federal and state levels which are responsible for disputes between state organs as well as for individual claims regarding violations of fundamental rights (including cases relating to state obligations resulting from fundamental rights to protect the environment). Repeatedly over the last decades, the Federal Constitutional Court had to decide cases in which it had to evaluate compliance of environmental legislation or administrative acts with fundamental rights, most recently issuing its spectacular ruling on the fundamental right to climate protection in March 2021.[42]

[41] Wolfgang Köck, 'Grenzwerte im Umweltrecht' [2020] *Zeitschrift für Umweltrecht* 131.

[42] BVerfG (1 BvR 2656/18, 1 BvR 96/20, 1 BvR 78/20, 1 BvR 288/20, 1 BvR 96/20, 1 BvR 78/20) *Klimaschutz*, BVerfGE [2021] 157, 30; see Gerd Winter, 'The Intergenerational Effect of Fundamental Rights: A Contribution of the German Federal Constitutional Court to Climate Protection' (2022) 34 *Journal of Environmental Law* 1.

German environmental law is largely regulated in different administrative codes which address specific environmental issues such as, for example, nature protection, waste treatment, emission control and renewable energy. Administrative decisions based on these codes are mostly subject to the jurisdiction of administrative courts. Regular administrative courts are at the lowest level, higher administrative courts are placed at the middle ground (level of the federal states), and the Federal Administrative Court is at the top level. The Federal Administrative Court was originally conceived as a court of appeals, ie to merely review the interpretation of the law by the lower courts with no power to investigate facts. In an effort to accelerate judicial procedures after the German reunification in 1989, however, the Federal Administrative Court has gained additional adjudicative powers in some specific areas, now also being responsible for investigating facts in all major infrastructure projects. Another judicial reform was adopted in the interest of accelerating the transformation of the German energy sector. In the course of this reform the higher administrative courts were assigned the responsibility to act as courts of first instance in certain emission control cases, which include, for example, cases concerning the permission of wind turbines (Investment Acceleration Act 2020[43]). The purpose was to accelerate judicial procedures to ramp up climate protection through the development of renewable energies.

Within the system of specialised courts in Germany, a system of specialised judges has evolved. At the Federal Administrative Court, for example, special panels (senates) are responsible for environmental disputes. These *environmental senates*, however, consist exclusively of lawyers and thus do not follow the model of so-called 'environmental courts', which have been introduced in a number of other countries (such as Sweden or New Zealand) to establish scientific and technical expertise within the court structures.[44] To this day, there has not yet been a political discussion in Germany on whether specific environmental courts could improve the judicial process. In principle, however, the German judicial system knows of specialised courts including non-legal experts on the bench. For example, patent courts, trade courts, and courts deciding social welfare cases include judges or honorary judges who are not lawyers but acknowledged experts in the respective field.[45]

To date, however, non-legal-experts have not been included in administrative courts. Accordingly, environmental law proceedings rely strongly on

[43] Investment Acceleration Act (BGBl. S. 2694).

[44] George Pring and Catherine Pring, 'Environmental Courts & Tribunals. A Guide for Policy Makers' (UN Environment, 2016); Ria Guidone and Holly Jonas, 'A Review of Environmental Courts and Tribunals' in Christina Voigt and Zen Makuch (eds), *Courts and the Environment* (Edward Elgar, 2018); Don C Smith, 'Environmental Courts and Tribunals: Changing Environmental and Natural Resources Law around the Globe' (2018) 36 *Journal of Energy and Natural Resources Law* 137–40.

[45] Linda Schönfelder, 'Umweltgerichte – eine Mögliche und Gebotene Institution in der Deutschen Gerichtsbarkeit?' (2021) 19 *Europäisches Umwelt- und Planungsrecht* 302.

external expertise in cases in which difficult scientific or technical questions are involved. Of particular importance are experts appointed by the courts. Expert opinions drawn up and funded by the parties or expert opinions from third parties submitted by the parties (official reports, etc) are treated differently. Courts need to consider them and particularly assess whether they are based on correct assumptions and if they are comprehensible and coherent. Both judges and parties have the right to question experts.[46] Some senates at the Federal Administrative Court are exclusively responsible for environmental law proceedings. Accordingly, judges serving on these chambers have acquired substantial experience in dealing with external non-legal experts. Nevertheless, the relationship between legal and extra-legal knowledge remains precarious.[47] Currently, there is a discussion about improving the quality of experts by means of qualification and certification processes. It was suggested that the Government should establish an agency for this purpose.[48] All this is important to facilitate the functioning of the courts.

ii. Judicial Legal Protection

Article 19 IV of Germany's Constitution (Basic Law – *Grundgesetz*) states 'Should any person's rights be violated by public authority, he may have recourse to the courts'. The right to judicial protection is thus based in constitutional law and is deemed to have the legal status of a fundamental right.

Public authorities include, in particular, the executive (government and administration). Their actions are subject to review by administrative courts. In principle, access to courts is only granted to those who can claim that their rights have been violated by decisions of the executive. Since the executive bases all its decisions on (environmental) laws, what matters in this regard is whether a legal norm grants rights to individuals (particularly whether a specific norm aims to protect specific persons, ie in accordance with the so-called *Schutznormtheorie*) and whether the respective norm has been applied correctly or not.

If an authority addresses a legally binding decision directly at a specific person (for example, when granting a permit or issuing a prohibition), access to courts will always be granted, based on the so-called Addressee Theory (*Adressatentheorie*). In these cases it is irrelevant whether the relevant norm aims to protect the plaintiff (ie in accordance with the abovementioned *Schutznormtheorie*). Addressees of administrative decisions, for example persons who want to carry out a construction project, can therefore have all administrative decisions reviewed by a court.

[46] Annette Guckelberger, 'Erschließung extrajuridischen Wissens durch die Verwaltungsgerichte' (2017) 108 *Verwaltungsarchiv* 143.

[47] Horst Sendler, 'Richter und Sachverständige' (1986) 39 *Neue Juristische Wochenschrift* 2907.

[48] Klaus Rennert, 'Funktionswandel der Verwaltungsgerichtsbarkeit unter dem Einfluss des Unionsrecht?' (2016) 71 *Deutscher Juristentag* 1.

In case an administrative decision affects third parties or the environment, legal standing before courts depends on whether claimants can base their arguments on rules that have been adopted also to protect their specific individual interests (for example, their interests as neighbours), but not solely on rules which aim to direct administrative decision-making in pursuing general public objectives. For example, a specific individual interest has been confirmed by courts with regards to laws that set limits for certain air pollutants but was denied, however, with regards to general provisions protecting habitats or species. In her opinion in the *Bund* case, AG Sharpston described the German administrative judicial system as a 'Ferrari with closed doors'.[49] While the review and control are deep and thorough ('Ferrari'), getting access to courts can be difficult, particularly for third parties ('closed doors').

EU legislation implementing the Aarhus Convention[50] has brought about substantial change to the German judicial review system. Several strategic lawsuits before the CJEU have also contributed to clarifying the law on access to justice in environmental cases.[51] As a result, the German Environmental Remedies Act[52] had been amended several times – and has extended non-governmental environmental organisations' access to courts with a view to having administrative decisions in environmental matters reviewed.[53] In addition, recent CJEU decisions have also made clear that individual plaintiffs can file cases even where laws were not meant to protect them or where there were no individual effects emerging from an administrative decision.[54]

iii. Dealing with Scientific Uncertainty: Standards of Control and Recognition of Administration's Margin of Discretions

In Germany, judicial review of administrative decisions is comparatively thorough. In principle, all administrative decisions can be fully reviewed by the

[49] C-115/09 *Bund für Umwelt und Naturschutz Deutschland, Landesverband Nordrhein-Westfalen eV v Bezirksregierung Arnsberg* [2011] ECR I-3676, ECLI:EU:C:2011:289, Opinion of AG Sharpston [77].

[50] Directive 2003/35/EC of the European Parliament and of the Council of 26 May 2003 providing for public participation in respect of the drawing up of certain plans and programmes relating to the environment and amending with regard to public participation and access to justice [2003] OJ L156/46.

[51] C-237/07 *Dieter Janecek v Freistaat Bayern* [2008] ECR I-6223m ECLI:EU:C:2008:447 and *Bund für Umwelt und Naturschutz Deutschland* (n 49).

[52] Environmental Remedies Act (BGBl. I S. 3290).

[53] Bernhard Wegener, 'Der Braunbär Lernt Schwimmen' [2018] *Zeitschrift für Umweltrecht* 217; Annette Guckelberger, 'Die Ausgestaltung der Umweltrechtsbehelfe für Verbände seit der UmwRG-Novelle 2017' (2020) 42 *Natur und Recht* 505.

[54] Wolfgang Köck and Elisabeth V Henn, 'Die Rechte der Wasserversorger bei der Grundwasserressourcenbewirtschaftung – am Beispiel der PFC-Grundwasserbelastungen in Mittelbaden' (2020) 39 *Neue Zeitschrift für Verwaltungsrecht* 5041; C-674/17 *Luonnonsuojeluyhdistys Tapiola Pohjois-Savo* (n 16).

courts. Restrictions only exist where the law grants administrative discretion to a) determine the content of a norm or b) decide on its legal consequences.[55] This decision-making power has been acknowledged by the courts, inter alia, with regards to laws governing the operation of nuclear plants as well as in cases in which the Government has been authorised to concretise the law through ministerial decrees (see section II). Recently, the Federal Constitutional Court has indicated that in the face of substantial scientific uncertainty it does not matter to what extent the legislator has entitled the executive to specify existing legislation. With a view to their legal review, courts are allowed to follow the executive's assessment at the limits of knowledge. According to the Federal Constitutional Court, the limits of knowledge constitute the limits of judicial review and control.[56] This will be explained in greater depth in section III.

iv. Fact Finding: The Role of Expert Opinions in German Administrative Courts

Proceedings before German administrative courts are guided by the so-called 'inquisitorial principle' (*Untersuchungsgrundsatz*). The principle manifests in s 86[1] of the Code of Administrative Court Procedure which provides that '(t)he court investigates the facts ex officio (…). It is not bound by the submissions of and requests for evidence by the parties'.[57] In accordance with this principle, the courts must 'make all reasonable efforts' to investigate the facts of the case and are required to make use of all possibly relevant sources of evidence, including expert opinions.[58] Courts are only obliged to call in experts if they are not confident that they themselves have sufficient expertise. Where experts are relied on, their task is to provide courts with specialist knowledge and enable the judges to fully assess the facts. From a legal point of view, the experts remain 'assistants to the court', ie it is upon the courts to eventually determine which facts are relevant and how they are to be assessed from a legal point of view. Judges are particularly required to resolve contradictions that may arise from the submitted facts and – where relevant – different expert opinions.[59] The following section will elaborate on how these principles are implemented by courts with regards to existing scientific uncertainty in the application of EU nature conservation law.

[55] Marielle Schuster, *Beurteilungsspielräume der Verwaltung im Naturschutzrecht* (Duncker and Humblot, 2020); BVerwG (9 A 22/11), BVerwGE [2013] 146, 145.
[56] *Red Kite* (n 17) [23].
[57] Code of Administrative Court Procedure (BGBl. I S. 686).
[58] Stephan Rixen in Helge Sodan and Jan Ziekow (ed), *Verwaltungsgerichtsordnung* (Nomos, 2018) s 86 [48].
[59] Heinrich Lang in Sodan and Ziekow, *ibid* s 96 [41].

III. Scientific Uncertainty in EU Nature Conservation

Uncertainty had been a prominent issue in German nature conservation law, even before the latter was significantly influenced by EU legislation. Since the 1970s German nature conservation law's central legal instrument was the so-called Interference with Nature Regulation[60] (*Eingriffsregelung* in s 14 *Bundesnaturschutzgesetz* (BNatSchG)). This Regulation requires those who would like to take actions that may have a significant impact on protected habitats or species to minimise the effects and to provide for compensation, primarily through taking measures that promote nature conservation (ss 13–18 BNatSchG). To some extent the Interference Regulation bears a resemblance to two other important environmental law instruments, ie the environmental impact assessment and the requirement to compensate for environmental damage. Scholars have also classified the Interference Regulation as a 'soft version' of the 'non-deterioration-obligation' as well as a specific approach to implement the 'polluter pays' principle.[61]

Both methods and criteria to assess the impacts on habitats and species as well as compensation measures were left unregulated and, accordingly, subject to legal conflicts. The courts responded by granting administrations a prerogative to assess nature conservation issues.[62] The courts would only go and check whether the impact assessments and the compensation concepts were based on suitable methods and whether the official assessment was 'plausible'.[63]

This early approach developed by the courts was of limited use, however, with a view to reviewing the implementation of the increasingly important EU nature conservation law, particularly with a view to the formalised assessment approach in the area of habitats-protection. Courts became quickly aware that investigation requirements are comparatively high under the EU law and that their own control requirements would have to mirror and live up to them. These requirements, however, would seem somewhat less demanding in the context of compensation pursuant to art 6(4) of the Habitats Directive (HD)[64] and in the context of species protection law (art 12 and art 16 HD) (see section III, B). Before going into greater detail, the CJEU's case law on the HD knowledge requirements for site and species protection will be briefly outlined.

[60] See Federal Nature Protection Act, s 14.
[61] Andreas Voßkuhle *Das Kompensationsprinzip* (J.C.B. Mohr, 1999).
[62] BVerwG (9 A 11/03) *New Construction of Federal Road B 2*, BVerwGE [2004] 121, 72.
[63] *ibid* 72.
[64] For full details of the Directive, please see the Table of Legislation or Introduction.

A. CJEU Case Law Concerning Knowledge Requirements for Site and Species Protection under the HD – The Impact on German Case Law

The CJEU case law is discussed in detail in chapter two of this book. Here some specific rulings in three important CJEU decisions will briefly be highlighted in order to explain the Court's influence on German case law.

In its case law on the HD, the CJEU has laid down knowledge requirements both with regard to site and species protection. It also provided guidance on how to deal with scientific uncertainty.

In *Waddenzee*,[65] the Court dealt with the protection of Natura 2000 sites, particularly with the assessment of the implications of certain projects for protected sites. Among other things, the Court had to decide when an assessment pursuant to art 6(3) HD has to be carried out and under which conditions projects affecting protected areas can be approved. The CJEU concluded that art 6(3) HD requires the application of the precautionary principle.[66] In addition, the Court decided that

> Any plan or project not directly connected with or necessary to the management of the site is to be subject to an appropriate assessment of its implications for the site in view of the site's conservation objectives if it cannot be excluded, on the basis of objective information, that it will have a significant effect on that site, either individually or in combination with other plans or projects.[67]

The degree of certainty required by the Court appears relatively high. After completing a screening process, it must be clear – with reasonable certainty – that there will be no adverse effects. If uncertainties remain in this respect, precautionary measures are required.

In its ruling in *Coöperatie Mobilisation for the Environment*,[68] the CJEU exempted certain agricultural fertilising practices from art 6(3) HD assessments if they did not exceed a certain threshold value or a certain limit value in terms of nitrogen deposits (see the discussion in chapter six of this volume for more detail on this programmatic approach in the Netherlands). National courts, however, have to be satisfied that the 'appropriate assessment' within the meaning of that provision, carried out in advance, ensures that there is no reasonable scientific doubt as to the lack of adverse effects of those plans or projects on the integrity

[65] *Waddenzee* (n 16).
[66] *ibid* [58].
[67] *ibid* [45].
[68] C-293/17 and C-294/17 *Coöperatie Mobilisation for the Environment UA and Vereniging Leefmilieu v College van gedeputeerde staten van Limburg and College van gedeputeerde staten van Gelderland* ECLI:EU:C:2018:882.

of the site concerned.[69] The CJEU also made clear that national courts need to be satisfied in respect of all Natura 2000 sites.[70]

In practice, however, it is most likely to be very difficult for courts to be satisfied in this respect. Affected sites can be very diverse and average thresholds may not provide sufficient evidence.[71] Accordingly, both a) projects within protected areas and b) projects outside these areas impacting them will have to undergo an assessment which considers their cumulative effects.

The CJEU has repeatedly and consistently argued that the fact that the appropriate assessment of a plan's or project's implications for a specific site that must be carried out pursuant to art 6(3) HD implies that 'all the aspects of the plan or project which … either individually or in combination with other plans or projects … must be identified in the light of the best scientific knowledge in the field'.[72] The CJEU emphasises that there must be no reasonable scientific doubt that the project will not have a significant effect on the protected site.[73] It follows from this that all aspects of the project that may lead to adverse effects, either individually or in combination with other plans or projects, must be identified.[74] In addition, assessments 'may not have lacunae and must contain complete, precise and definitive findings and conclusions capable of dispelling reasonable scientific doubt as to the effects of the proposed work on the protected area concerned'.[75] However, the required level of certainty ('capable of dispelling reasonable doubt') does not require authorities to consider every existing expert opinion. Nevertheless, the authority empowered to take a decision must give a detailed statement of reasons why it rejected the finding of a scientific expert opinion.[76] This suggests that the authorities are granted a certain margin of discretion.

If an assessment indicates that significant adverse effects of a plan or project cannot be ruled out, protective measures aimed at avoiding or reducing any direct adverse effects may be taken into account. The effectiveness of the protective measures, however, must be confirmed. According to the CJEU, confirmation of their effectiveness at the level of 'beyond all reasonable doubt' cannot be achieved by merely conducting monitoring activities.[77] In case a significant adverse impact cannot be ruled out with certainty, the project may be approved only subject to the conditions laid down in art 6(4) HD. Exceptions, in turn, require compensatory

[69] *ibid* [112].
[70] *ibid* [120].
[71] Stefan Möckel 'Natura 2000 Impact Assessment – Neue Entscheidungen des EuGH' (2019) 41 *Natur und Recht* 152.
[72] C-399/14 *Grüne Liga Sachsen v Freistaat Sachsen* ECLI:EU:C:2016:10 [49].
[73] *Waddenzee* (n 16) [59].
[74] *Grüne Liga Sachsen* (n 72) [49].
[75] C-461/17 *Holohan v An Bord Pleanála* ECLI:EU:C:2018:883 [49].
[76] *ibid* [52].
[77] C-142/16 *European Commission v Federal Republic of Germany* ECLI:EU:C:2017:301 [34]–[38].

measures necessary to ensure the overall coherence of the Natura 2000 network. To this day, however, the CJEU has not required the same certainty standards it applies to protection measures under art 6(3) to the question of effectiveness of compensation measures in art 6(4).

The CJEU has also not decided yet whether the same certainty requirements apply to species protection provisions. Notably, however, the Court has never referred to the precautionary principle in determining whether the species protection prohibitions have been complied with. It has also not used the formula 'best scientific knowledge'.

Against this background, the German Federal Administrative Court has concluded that habitat protection standards cannot be applied 1:1 to species protection.[78] In contrast, the European Commission's 2007 Guidance Document on Species Protection has referred to the precautionary principle with a view to the provisions on species protection, namely with regard to the protection of resting places and the concept of preserving the ecological functionality of a site. According to the Commission, there must be a high degree of certainty that the measures are sufficient to avoid any deterioration or destruction in order to meet the requirements of species protection.[79] The Commission's opinion does not contradict with the rulings of the Federal Administrative Court (BVerwG), ie that a strict certainty requirement only applies to the effectiveness of protective measures that aim to counter known damage risks.

However, in *Tapiola* the CJEU explicitly applied the precautionary principle to art 16(1) HD. It states:

> It must also be noted that, in accordance with the precautionary principle enshrined in Article 191(2) TFEU, if, after examining the best scientific data available, there remains uncertainty as to whether or not a derogation will be detrimental to the maintenance or restoration of populations of an endangered species at a favourable conservation status, the Member State must refrain from granting or implementing that derogation.[80]

The decision concerned wolf hunting in Finland (see also chapters two and ten of this volume), which was to be permitted on the basis of a population management plan by the Finnish Government. Since European wolf populations are considered to be seriously threatened, the CJEU imposed a strict ruling.[81] Whether the CJEU will apply this standard to all Annex IV species or even to all European bird species is not yet clear.

[78] BVerwG (9 A 3/06) *Highway A 44 (Hessisch Lichtenau)*, BVerwGE [2008] 130, 299 [56 et seq]; Red Kite (n 17) [123].

[79] European Commission, 'Guidance Document on the Strict Protection of Animal Species of Community Interest under the Habitats Directive 92/43/EEC' (Final version, February 2007) [48] and [76].

[80] *Luonnonsuojeluyhdistys Tapiola Pohjois-Savo* (n 16) [66].

[81] Christoph Sobotta, 'Zur Rechtsprechung: Neues vom Vorsorgeprinzip – jeder Zweifel ausgeschlossen?' (2020) 41 *Natur und Recht* 453.

In summary, the case law provides:

- With a view to assessing the impacts of projects on site-protection, the precautionary principle must be applied in case uncertainties exist. This also applies to the so-called 'programmatic approach', which seeks to avoid project-specific assessments through the adoption of threshold standards (ie the nitrogen issue described above). Here, too, the precautionary principle requires that no reasonable scientific doubt remains.
- The CJEU also requires that an assessment has to be based on the 'best scientific knowledge'. Plans or projects may only be approved if there is no reasonable doubt that they will not have any significant adverse effect on the protected site. Expert opinions that may give rise to doubts must not be ignored. Instead, the responsible decision-making body has to address submitted arguments and provide nature conservation-specific reasons why they are not being followed.
- Regarding species protection, the CJEU does not require the application of the precautionary principle in cases of scientific uncertainty. This is different, however, if exceptions under art 16 HD are under consideration. In these cases, it must be ensured that the affected species remain in or can achieve a favourable conservation status. In this regard, too, no reasonable doubt must remain, and assessments must be based on the best available scientific knowledge.

B. Case Law of German Courts

The following sections investigate how German courts deal with knowledge requirements and scientific uncertainties in the areas of site and species protection.

i. Site Protection

The national case law on appropriate assessments under art 6(3) HD has established substantive, procedural and methodological requirements. The leading case was the Federal Administrative Court's ruling of 17 January 2007 on the further development of a motorway near the city of Halle.[82] In this decision, the Court decided that the relevant assessment should not aim at a 'zero risk'. Accordingly, mere theoretical concerns should be deemed irrelevant. Concerns about possibly significant adverse effects must at least be based on some sort of actual indication or evidence.[83]

[82] BVerwG (9 A 20/05) *West Bypass Halle*, BVerwGE [2007] 128, 1.
[83] *ibid* [60].

If the screening of a project, however, gives rise to serious concerns about possible adverse impacts 'this concern can only be dispelled by a conclusive scientific argumentation (including nature conservation expertise) that proves existing concerns wrong'.[84]

The Court then proceeds:

> Proving concerns about a project's damaging potentials fails in two cases: First, if risk analyses, predictions and assessments do not consider the best available scientific knowledge. Second, if reasonable doubts regarding significant adverse effects cannot 'objectively' be ruled out on the ground of existing scientific knowledge. Remaining scientific uncertainties about cause-effect relations, however, may be compensated through by an effective risk management approach (…). In addition, it is permissible to work with basing forecasts on probabilities and estimations; these, however, have to be made explicit and transparent (…). One example of a legitimate methods is drawing conclusions by analogy. Where scientific standards are being met, this method can be used to bridge existing knowledge gaps. (…). In addition, to assess and estimate the impact of a project on conservation objectives regarding a specific site, so-called key indicators can be used (…). Another common approach to make estimates is to develop 'worst-cases' in which the project will create long-lasting negative effects (…). This approach basically equals a widely accepted conservative risk assessment. However, this method must provide results that are scientifically sound and unequivocal ('on the safe side') with regards to the issue in question.[85]

With a view to applying the precautionary principle, the Court expresses the following Opinion[86] (referring several times to AG Kokott's Opinion in *Waddenzee*):

> The precautionary principle requires that existing scientific uncertainties are minimized.[87] This requires exhausting all scientific means and sources (…), but does not require that new research is to be carried out (by tendering new research contracts) to fill existing knowledge gaps and remedying methodological uncertainties in the assessment. Rather, Art. 6.3 Habitats Directive only requires the use of the 'best available scientific means'. This includes identifying knowledge gaps that cannot be closed within a reasonable time and assessing their relevance to the findings (…). This kind of risk assessment can contribute to developing proposals for an effective risk management within the framework of the assessment, particularly to determining which measures are appropriate and necessary to prevent the risk from materialising.[88]
>
> In the view of the Court it is also clear that Art. 6.3 Habitats Directive does not only lay down a control standard, but also a requirement for the administrative approval or permit procedure: The core requirement regarding the procedure is to obtain expert scientific advice for the risk analysis, prognosis and evaluation. No other type of evidence is admitted. Notably, no special method is required for carrying out the

[84] *ibid* [62].
[85] *West Bypass Halle* (n 82) [64].
[86] Referring several times to General Kokott's Opinion in *Waddenzee* (n 16).
[87] See opinion of General Kokott in *Waddenzee* (n 16) [100].
[88] *West Bypass Halle* (n 82) [66].

> assessment (…). The available scientific findings, however, must not remain abstract. They must become the basis for investigations making 'specific observations (…). In order to prove the project to be harmless, the assessment must compare all the adverse effects arising from the plan or project. To that end, both the adverse effects and the conservation objectives must be identified.'[89] It follows that, in principle, the resulting scientific findings must be documented (…). Particularly in complex or controversial cases, documentation is the only means by which an assessment can prove that it was based on the best available scientific standard.[90]

In a later decision, the Federal Administrative Court made it clear that species-specific studies must be carried out in case potentially affected species have different behavioural patterns (the case concerned the construction of energy grids and potentially negative effects on different bird species with different flight behaviour).[91]

Today in Germany, a significant number of nature conservation guidelines have been developed that attempt to standardise conservation requirements.[92] The Federal Administrative Court has accepted some of these guidelines, confirming that they have been developed on the basis of the best available scientific knowledge. The executive, however, has so far not integrated the respective guidelines into an administrative regulation or issued a decree granting them binding status (despite having the legal authority to do so – see s 54 XI BNatSchG). Overall, the Federal Administrative Court has[93] only recognised a rather small margin of discretion for administrations in terms of their own assessments regarding nature conservation, ie only with a view to qualifying habitat types.[94] Nevertheless, in principle, administrations may develop their own expert forecasts and estimates, as long as they develop their arguments in a transparent and accessible manner.

Despite the CJEU's ruling in *Coöperatie Mobilisation for the Environment*[95] in which it assessed the programmatic approach to nitrogen management in the Netherlands, the German Federal Administrative Court continues to argue that the method to assume critical loads and to cut-off an additional load of 0.3 kg/ha*a reflects the best scientific knowledge available for determining allowable nitrogen deposits in Natura 2000 sites.[96] The Court obviously assumes that this approach complies with EU law requirements.

[89] *Waddenzee* (n 16) [97].
[90] *West Bypass Halle* (n 82) [68] and [70].
[91] BVerwG (4 A 5/14) *Uckermarkleitung*, BVerwGE [2016] 154, 73 [78].
[92] See Katrin Wulfert et al, 'Standardisierungspotenzial im Bereich der Arten- und Gebietsschutzrechtlichen Prüfung' in Bundesamt für Naturschutz (ed), *FuE- Vorhaben im Rahmen des Umweltforschungsplanes des Bundesministeriums für Umwelt, Naturschutz und Reaktorsicherheit im Auftrag des Bundesamtes für Naturschutz – FKZ 3512 82 2100* (2015).
[93] In contrast to voices in the literature, see Kurt Fassbender and Anne-Christin Gläß, 'Schutz der Natura 2000-Gebiete' in Herbert Posser and Kurt Faßbender (eds), *Praxishandbuch Netzplanung und Netzausbau* (De Gruyter, 2013).
[94] *Highway A 44* (Hessisch Lichtenau) (n 78) [74].
[95] *Coöperatie Mobilisation for the Environment* (n 68).
[96] *Red Kite* (n 17) [76] et seq.

With a view to ensuring that compensation measures do not impair the coherence of Natura 2000 sites (within the exception regime in art 6(4) HD), the Federal Administrative Court does not require the absence of all doubts regarding their effectiveness. The Court states:

> Assessment requirements are less stringent compared to those regarding the damage avoidance and mitigation [i.e. within the assessment pursuant to Art. 6.3]. While the latter requires full proof of effectiveness, because only then the necessary certainty about the compatibility of a plan or project with the law can be obtained (…), it is sufficient to ascertain a high probability (based on best available scientific knowledge, of coherence measures). Unlike damage prevention and mitigation, creating coherence typically involves restoring or redeveloping habitats or habitat types. Imponderables usually occur throughout this process. Accordingly, the success of the measure cannot be predicted with certainty ex ante, but only be prognostically estimated. Requiring certainty would render impossible a positive decision, because the coherence requirement would prevent any balancing under Art. 6.4 Habitats Directive. In essence, this would contradict the regulatory purpose of Art. 6.4 Habitats Directive.[97]

Finally, German courts' reviews of administrative decision-making is limited in this area. The German Federal Administrative Court grants the authorities the prerogative to assess nature conservation issues. According to its rulings, courts will only check whether administrations' assessments of impacts and compensation is transparent and comprehensible.[98]

ii. Species Protection

The leading case in the field of species protection is the Federal Administrative Court's ruling of 9 July 2008.[99] This decision addresses different legal questions regarding a road construction project (federal motorway bypassing the city of Bad Oeynhausen). In this decision, the Court stated that the precautionary principle has to be taken into account, not only with a view to assessing habitats protection, but in the area of species protection as well.[100] It pointed out, however, that normative differences exist between these two issues. It highlighted that the assessment requirements in art 6(3) HD are directed at very specific protected areas and at clearly defined objectives regarding their protection. Accordingly, requirements regarding the depth of investigation in this area can be very high. Regarding species protection law, the object of investigation has not been defined as clearly, and a formalised assessment procedure is not required. Against this background, species protection law requires a court to consider – from the outset – not only the precautionary principle, but also the principle of proportionality, 'The latter

[97] *Highway A 44* (Hessisch Lichtenau) (n 78) [201].
[98] *ibid* [202].
[99] BVerwG (9 A 14/07) *Highway North Bypass Bad Oeynhausen*, BVerwGE [2008a] 131, 274.
[100] *ibid* [57].

determining significantly the investigation effort'.[101] In other words, regarding the protection of Natura 2000 sites, the law structures normative decisions relatively clearly and the review procedure merely addresses cognitive questions of how to deal with uncertainty. In contrast, the investigation requirements are less clearly contoured with a view to species protection, so that the investigation requirements are also co-determined by the principle of proportionality.

The Court states:

> The principle of proportionality is failed where requirements were imposed with regards to species assessment that would not promise any significant gain in knowledge for the approval decision of a (important infrastructure) project and were out of any reasonable proportion with a view to the benefits for nature and the environment. Accordingly, an assessment has to be carried out in accordance with a standard of practical reason.[102]

The same decision continues:

> The species conservation assessment must be exclusively based on scientific criteria, both with regards to finding and evaluating possible impacts. The relevant legal questions, e.g. whether a species is 'significantly disturbed' and whether a population remains in a 'favourable conservation status', require ecological assessments and evaluations for which more detailed standards are lacking. In contrast to other areas of environmental law (…), the legislator has so far not even come close to establishing sufficient guidelines for applying the laws governing species conservation, i.e. neither by issuing such guidelines by himself nor by involving or commissioning expert committees. Accordingly, those who have to apply the law depend on the extra-legal expertise of ecological science and practice. This ecological expertise, however, in many areas is not yet sufficiently developed enough to provide applicants with reliable answers (…). In many cases with regards to numerous questions, different scientific assessment may justifiably contradict each other, and a sound and well established body of scientific knowledge is missing.[103]
>
> This finding has significance for all levels of the nature conservation assessment, which (can also) include normative assessments, i.e. both in the ecological investigations and in the assessment of the findings, namely in the quantification of possible impacts and in evaluation of their population-related effects. It is obvious that the results of the assessment, which is an indispensable legal requirement, may vary depending on the methodological approach and the criteria and standards applied. If and as long as ecological science does not prove to be a clear source of knowledge in this respect, the courts lack the authority (which would have to be based on better knowledge), to object the administration's as 'wrong' and 'not legal'. Accordingly, their assumptions are only subject to limited judicial review. They are to be accepted by the court as long as they are justified from a nature conservation point of view and not based on an assessment procedure that proves to be a method that is to be regarded as inadequate or unsuitable

[101] *ibid.*
[102] *ibid* [57].
[103] *ibid* [64].

> to meet the legal requirements. In this respect, the approving authority has a prerogative to assess nature conservation issues, which has already been recognised by the Federal Administrative Court for various comparable issues.[104]

And with regards whether an expert opinion is justified, the Federal Administrative Court states:

> A nature conservation expert opinion is not superior or preferable to another one simply because it deems more extensive or more elaborate investigations or 'stricter' requirements to be correct. This is only the case when such an investigation has become the generally accepted state of the art and the contrary opinion can no longer be maintained (anymore). The provision governing species protection do not require the project sponsoring party or the permit approving authority in cases of scientific uncertainty or conflict to award research assignments (…) or to conduct studies that would require a similar amount of effort. If they take a scientifically justifiable position which is in accordance with the current state of knowledge, it would not be objectionable.[105]

As is often the case with the law governing environmental and risk management (see section II), the Court grants authorities a real margin of discretion to decide in the face of existing scientific uncertainty. It does not require a 'worst-case assessment' and it does not call for keeping the standard of 'leaving no reasonable doubt' as it does with a view to defining the required certainty standard regarding the conservation of sites.

The killing prohibition laid down in art 12(1)(a) HD has become particularly significant in the context of both road construction (roadkill) and wind energy projects (bird and bat species). This is mainly due to two factors. First, the killing prohibition applies to individual animals. Second, the CJEU has adopted a broad interpretation of the concept of intention, ie killing an animal in the sense of art 12 HD does not only involve deliberate killing, but also accepting its death.[106] According to the case law of the Federal Administrative Court, the killing prohibition in art 12(1)(a) HD only applies if a project significantly increases the risk of killing a species protected under EU law (significance criterion).[107] To establish whether this is the case, the following steps are taken:

- determine a baseline risk for the protected species in the project-relevant area;
- determine the risk for killing induced by the project;
- compare the baseline risk and the project-induced risks;
- assess the risk's significance based on
  - species-specific behavioural patterns;
  - criteria related to the specific biology of the species concerned; and
  - other nature conservation criteria.

[104] *ibid* [65].
[105] *ibid* [66].
[106] C-103/00 *Commission v Greece* [2002] ECR I-1163, ECLI:EU:C:2002:60 [36] and [39]; C-221/04 *Commission v Spain* [2006] ECR I-4537, ECLI:EU:C:2006:329 [69].
[107] *Highway North Bypass Bad Oeynhausen* (n 99) [91].

Of great practical importance for the construction and operation of wind turbines are measures that require projects to keep a specific distance from certain areas and to avoid certain aspects in the design of projects. All these measures aim to keep the risk of killing below the significance threshold.[108]

As with habitats protection, there is a growing number of concepts for species conservation.[109] Since the German *Länder* (ie German federal states) are responsible for implementing the nature protection law, recommendation differs quite significantly between the regions.

Since courts have generally accepted the administrations' assessment prerogative,[110] their main responsibility is to reject and sort out scientifically and technically unsuitable concepts and methods. With a view to the remaining issues, courts restrict themselves to reviewing only whether the administrative decisions' overall results are compatible and justified under the existing law. In principle, courts accept uncertainties and do not require keeping a strict standard of certainty. They will intervene where a decision contradicts views that clearly prevail in science ('generally accepted state of science') and which render opposing views unjustified.[111] Accordingly, the courts' current review standard cannot ensure the uniform implementation of species conservation law in Germany. As a result, the call for uniform federal guidelines for implementation has become louder in recent years.

C. The Constitutional Court's Decision on Uncertainty in Species Protection Law

Questions regarding scientific uncertainty in nature conservation law led to a sensational decision by the Federal Constitutional Court at the end of 2018. The decision was prompted by the complaint of a project developer who felt that his right to effective legal protection enshrined in art 19 IV Basic Law had been violated. He claimed that he was illegally denied a permit for the development of a wind turbine. The claimant criticised in particular the way the competent authority had determined a 'significantly increased risk of killing' for the protected species (red kite). The Federal Administrative Court had previously confirmed the authority's decision. The claimant asked the Federal Constitutional Court whether the administration's approach was in compliance with German constitutional law.

[108] Sanna Akerboom et al, 'Wind Energy Projects and Species Protection Law: a Comparative Analysis of the Application of EU Law in Five Member States' (2019) 28 *European Energy and Environmental Law Review* 144–58.

[109] Wolfgang Köck and Jana Bovet, 'Die Anwendung des EU-Artenschutzrechts bei der Zulassung von Erneuerbare Energien-Projekten' [2018] *Zeitschrift für Umweltrecht* 579.

[110] *Highway North Bypass Bad Oeynhausen* (n 99) [65].

[111] BVerwG (9 A 9/15) *Northwest Bypass Hamburg*, BVerwGE [2016a] 155, 91 [144].

Although eventually the Federal Constitutional Court denied the claimant access to court, it made several far-reaching decisions. First, it confirmed that courts' judicial review ends where they, after the greatest possible effort, reach the limits of the knowledge currently provided by nature conservation science and practice. In such a situation, the right to effective legal protection does not compel the respective court to

> [C]onduct further investigations, but allows it to base its decision on the authority's plausible assessment of the relevant question. The limits to judicial control do not flow from the administration's assessment prerogative and it does not require specific legislator authorisation.[112]

The Court pointed out, however, that

> [The legislature] may not permanently transfer decisions to implementing authorities where those decisions are relevant to fundamental rights and where there is a 'knowledge vacuum' that neither the executive nor the judiciary are able to fill (…). Depending on how severely fundamental rights are affected, the legislature may assume in the short term that knowledge gaps will be closed by advances in professional circles and science. In the longer term, however, the legislature must not stand idly by, mainly because it would evade its decision-making responsibility, open up uncontrolled and far-reaching influence on state decision-making to private expertise, and fail to guarantee a uniform application of the law. Where scientific and technical aspects remain unclear, the legislature must at least provide for the establishment of standards which can be applied uniformly by administrations, for example by setting up expert committees that determine uniform standards and methods, or by prescribing more precise rules for choosing between several scientifically justified opinions.[113]

The Federal Constitutional Court has obviously relied on the principles governing risk administration and risk management law that were developed in different court decisions relating to nuclear power plants during the 1970s and 1980s (see section II, A). At that time, particularly the Federal Administrative Court had based decisions on the argument that the executive is better suited to prepare and guide normative decisions in face of high levels of scientific uncertainty, ie at the 'limits of knowledge'.[114] However, the executive actually needs to take that action, either by developing administrative standards that specify the laws or by means of adopting delegated legislative acts.[115]

[112] *Red Kite* (n 17) [23].
[113] *Red Kite* (n 17) [24].
[114] *Nucelar Power Plant Wyhl* (n 28).
[115] See Klaus-Peter Dolde, 'Naturschutzfachliche Einschätzungsprärogative – Normkonkretisierung tut not!' (2019) 38 *Neue Zeitschrift für Verwaltungsrecht* 1567; Wolfgang Köck, 'Grenzwerte im Umweltrecht' [2020] *Zeitschrift für Umweltrecht* 131.

IV. Conclusions

The legal approach to scientific uncertainty in environmental law is largely influenced and determined by the desired level of protection. Where the level of protection should be high, any concern or reasonable doubt will be sufficient to assume that a legally protected good will be impaired. If the level of protection is less high, indications regarding an impairment must be significantly clearer. In German environmental law, the concepts of hazard (it is sufficiently likely that damage will occur) and risk (legitimate concerns regarding a damage exist) are pertinent. Where the executive implements the law, it will have to specify abstract rules in this regard. The judiciary monitors whether the executive's actions comply with the law.

Regarding the EU's habitat and species conservation law, no binding Union-wide standards exist to specify different levels of protection. To this day, the EU Commission's guidelines have remained incomprehensive and non-binding. In Germany, too, there are no binding standards at the Federal level, but these are only non-legal scientific and technical recommendations. At the State level, however, there are some administrative regulations that direct administrative implementation practices.

Accordingly, specifying the legal requirements of EU law has thus mainly been carried out by courts. In this regard, the CJEU's influence has been stronger in relation to habitats conservation than to species protection. The CJEU adopted a less strict and clear conservation level for species protection, so that German courts have – to some extent – developed their own approach to dealing with uncertainties. In particular, administrative decision-makers charged with implementation have been granted the right to use varying methods to approach scientific questions. Such methods, however, must not contradict with the 'generally accepted state of science'. As long as the administrative body abides by this rule, they are free to exercise a margin of discretion.

The Federal Constitutional Court quite rightly pointed out in 2018, however, that the executive will not meet its own constitutional obligations if it does not develop clear guidelines and specific criteria in situations of scientific uncertainty, eg in the form of administrative regulations or binding decrees. The Federal Constitutional Court's call has been answered by the German Government. It is currently drafting a binding regulation that aims to direct the executive in the face of uncertainty and to ensure a uniform implementation of the law throughout the country.

9

Reasoning Styles, the Role of Discretionary Judicial Choices and the Limits of Judicial Review: The Hungarian Courts' Experience with the Habitats and Wild Birds Directives

KATALIN SULYOK*

I. Introduction

This chapter will analytically examine the approach of Hungarian administrative courts to judicial review of risk assessment decisions made by competent national authorities under the Habitats Directive (HD) and Wild Birds Directive (WBD).[1] Such judicial review is rather fact-intensive and intrusive, where courts of first instance have to review the technical assessments of the executive with respect to whether they gathered scientific evidence to a sufficient extent and quality to make well-founded determinations and as to whether they adequately and rationally justified in their reasoning the conclusions reached in light of the technical evidence. This caselaw analysis seeks to identify the steps in the judicial inquiry that are most determinative for adjusting the level of scientific complexities that is entertained by the court in making judicial determinations.

After first depicting the main rules of national implementation of the relevant Directives (section II), the chapter will discuss the institutional structures and procedural powers of the executive (section III, A) and the judiciary (section III, B). This will be followed by taking a closer analytic look at the case law of Hungarian courts with respect to three main questions. Section IV will examine when the courts start doubting the scientific findings of the executive; how much scientific evidence is sufficient to legally establish likely adverse impact; and how

* This publication was supported by the ÚNKP-21-4 New National Excellence Program of the Ministry for Innovation and Technology from the source of the National Research, Development and Innovation Fund.

[1] For full details on these Directives, please see the Table of Legislation or Introduction.

the precautionary principle fits in the court's analysis. The chapter will argue that answers to these questions are not set in applicable procedural rules, hence the extent to which courts will confront scientific complexities in their analysis much depends on subjective choices of respective judges through which they define the science-intensity and the fine-grained limits of their judicial review. Section V will conclude by summarising some broader lessons the approach of Hungarian courts yields for science-intensive adjudication and judicial reasoning styles.

II. The Habitats Directive in Hungary: Domestic Rules and Implementing Authorities

As a newly acceded Member State of the European Union in 2004, Hungary swiftly implemented the HD in the same year by delineating a considerably large proportion, more than 20 per cent of its territory, as Natura 2000 sites. The extensive coverage of Natura 2000 habitats resulted in a high number of conflicts between nature conservation goals mandated by the WBD and HD on the one hand, and the industrial boom fuelled by Hungary's EU accession, on the other hand. Domestic litigation concerning the HD typically featured the permitting process of large-scale industrial activities, such as mining, oil drilling and airport development, clashing with the conservation needs of Natura 2000 habitats and species. A specific subset of such disputes, which closely relates to the topic of interest in this chapter, revolved around the factual and legal requirements of appraising the likelihood of adverse impacts on Natura sites. Such proceedings were noticeably numerous in the first decade of the national implementation of the HD (ie between 2004–2016), which provided an opportunity for the courts to establish their main approach to the requirements of the use of scientific knowledge by lower courts and by administrative agencies.[2]

The HD has been duly transposed into Hungarian law in a standalone government decree,[3] with certain ancillary rules appearing in lower ranking legislation in various sectors, including nature conservation, environmental liability or water governance.[4] The most heavily litigated provision has been art 6 HD, which has been transposed into Hungarian law in arts 10 and 10/A of Government Decree No 275/2004. (X. 8.) concerning areas of conservation of community interest. The essence of these domestic provisions provides that any plan or project not

[2] Since 2018, however, disputes revolving around the finding of likely adverse impacts under the HD have virtually been absent from the case file of domestic courts.

[3] For rules implementing its provisions in national law, see Government Decree No 314/2005. (XII.25.) on environmental impact assessment and the single authorisation procedure. Original language information for all legislation is available in the Table of Legislation.

[4] Eg Decree of the Ministry for the Environment and Water Resources No 14/2010. (V.11.) on areas of land covered by nature conservation sites of European Community importance; Government Decree No 91/2007. (IV.26.) on establishing ecological damage and on the rules of the remedial procedure.

directly connected with or necessary to the management of Natura 2000 sites but likely to have a significant effect thereon, either individually or in combination with other plans or projects, shall be subject to appropriate assessment of its implications for the conservation status of habitats and species protected by the Directive, in view of the size of the area concerned, its location vis-á-vis Natura 2000 sites, and scientific data available on the actual presence of relevant species on such areas. In the light of the conclusions of such an assessment, the competent authorities shall agree to the plan or project only after having ascertained that it will not adversely affect the conservation status of the respective habitats provided that the plan or project does not run counter to the goals of the HD. Plans or projects that adversely affect the conservation status of habitats or species can only be authorised in the absence of rational alternatives and if they serve overriding public interest. Such projects must be carried out with the least detrimental effect possible. Overriding public interest may involve the protection of life and human health, the maintenance of public security and the creation of beneficial impact for the natural environment.

Article 6 HD therefore has been transposed into Hungarian law as a Natura impact assessment procedure. These procedures were conducted by regional Environmental Inspectorates (*Környezetvédelmi Felügyelőségek*), which functioned as standalone authorities during the period when relevant cases have been decided by Hungarian courts.[5] Typically, the Inspectorate administered Natura 2000 impact assessment procedures as part of the environmental permitting process which they conducted. Alternatively, the Inspectorate assessed the likely adverse impacts in other permitting processes (eg mining permit), where it acted in the capacity of a so-called specialised authority. The Inspectorate enjoyed strong procedural powers as a specialised authority under the procedural rules in force at the time, especially because its opinions have been binding upon other public authorities. This meant that the Environmental Inspectorate could veto permits of other state authorities by denying its approval on account of likely detrimental effects on Natura 2000 species or habitats.

Importantly, Environmental Inspectorates had the power to issue binding opinions subject to administrative appeal before the National Environmental Inspectorate, the decisions of which could be challenged before the courts.

[5] This chapter presents the institutional arrangement in force at the time of the relevant court proceedings, which has been fundamentally different from the current administrative rules and set-up. A major reform of the institutional structures and the procedure of administrative authorities was introduced in 2018, due to which Environmental Inspectorates have lost their autonomy and became integrated into Regional Governmental Administrative Agencies. Inspectorates currently function as departments of these agencies, losing their independence and the capacity and powers of a specialised authority. Currently, they are only empowered to give non-binding expert advice to the principal decision-maker, who is the head of the Regional Governmental Administrative Agency. Furthermore, administrative appeal has been cancelled for first instance decisions of the environmental authority, hence such decisions can now only be challenged before administrative courts. Given that the relevant court decisions have been brought under the former institutional set-up and rules of procedure, the current study refers to rules not in force.

If the Inspectorate's binding opinion harmed the legal interest of a party, it could be challenged before the courts in a claim filed against the denial of permit that was based on such an opinion.

This explains the procedural background against which the cases discussed in this chapter were brought before the courts until the 2018 judicial reform, which will be discussed in more depth below. Relevant litigation discussed in the forthcoming analysis has typically featured challenges brought against the scientific subject-matter of the Inspectorate's binding opinion, which gave rise to a refusal of consent to the permit of an activity on account of its adverse impact on Natura 2000 sites.

III. Evidentiary Rules and Procedural Powers of the Executive and the Judiciary

The effectiveness of the national implementation of the HD ultimately hinges upon the procedural powers of administrative authorities to enforce its guarantees, and on the powers of the judiciary to review the legality of relevant administrative acts. The scientific mandates of the judiciary and the executive are therefore of special relevance, as they determine the depth of scrutiny with which the technical findings of the authorities can be challenged. As will be seen below, the ways and the extent to which actors are entitled to engage with scientific evidence vary to a great extent. The reliance on scientific knowledge is subject to detailed procedural rules both in administrative and judicial proceedings, which render technical assessment of cases to be a task primarily falling on the executive (section III, A), although they reserve room for scientific engagement of the courts as well (section III, B). It will also be shown that courts have differing mandates as to the depth of review of technical claims depending upon their position in the judicial hierarchy (section III, C).

A. Scientific Expertise and the Discretion of Executive Authorities

Environmental Inspectorates have been typically endowed with the necessary expertise in environmental matters to conduct Natura impact assessment procedures. Regarding specific aspects of nature conservation questions, the Inspectorate has also sought the expert opinion of the National Park Directorates (*Nemzeti Park Igazgatóságok*) in deciding about the likely impacts of a plan or project on protected habitats, as these entities hold special expertise in nature conservation and the conservation management of protected areas.

Given their special expertise in the technical aspects of impact assessments, the Inspectorates have enjoyed discretion in drawing factual conclusions from the scientific information as to applicable environmental risks and to deny or issue, accordingly, an environmental permit or its consent to other permits. As a result, even though the judiciary has the power to order a new administrative proceeding and can even give instructions to the relevant authority to improve its assessment, courts cannot prescribe a specific content for a specialised authority's opinion to be issued in the repeated administrative proceeding.[6] Courts, however, can review risk assessment decisions if the authority did not establish relevant facts to an appropriate extent, breached procedural rules, or the inferences drawn from the evidence were inadequate or irrational.

Overall, the position and procedural powers of the Environmental Inspectorate ensured the scientific expertise of specialised authorities to be duly integrated into administrative acts. As has been alluded to above, the Inspectorate was involved in permitting processes as a specialised authority, and any decision contravening its opinion or issued without consultation with it was deemed null and void.

B. Constitutional Mandate of Courts: Effective Judicial Protection and Access to Technical Expertise

At the outset it is to be noted that the following portrayal of judicial tasks at different levels of the judiciary reflects the procedural rules in force prior to the judicial reform of 2018,[7] as the relevant cases analysed here have been decided under the Procedural Code of 1952. Under the old system, the judicial review of administrative acts was conducted by the Administrative and Labour Law Courts acting as courts of first instance. Their proceedings concluded with a final and binding judgment in the review of environmental decisions, which could only be challenged before the *Kúria* (the Supreme Court) on the basis of an alleged violation of applicable laws, but not due to an error in the assessment of facts. As opposed to this, following the 2018 judicial reform, regional administrative courts hear such disputes as first instance courts, which bring final and binding judgment in relevant environmental disputes. Such decisions can only be challenged before the Supreme Court in an extraordinary judicial review procedure with reference to a violation of law or a derogation from a published decision of the Supreme Court in a legal issue. While some of the changes in the procedural rules are inapplicable, or are unlikely to be applied, in environmental disputes,[8] some new rules of procedure are consequential for the courts' powers to gather and rely on expert

[6] EBH2004.1160, Kfv.II.39.083/2007/7.

[7] The reform of the procedural code resulted in the creation of a separate code for the procedure of administrative courts. The new rules are set out in Act I of 2017 on the Code of Administrative Litigation (New Procedural Code of Administrative Litigation – henceforth 'New Code') which has been in force as of 1st January 2018.

[8] For instance, the New Code provides for wider powers of courts' *ex officio* investigations in specific cases and ensures reformatory competence to first instance courts in many cases.

evidence. These will be addressed below in more detail. In the following discussion, procedural rules that are no longer in force are highlighted by using the past tense, whereas rules that are still in force under the New Procedural Code are addressed in the present tense.[9]

The constitutional principle of effective judicial protection underlies the functioning of the administrative judicial system. In order to provide effective judicial protection against violations of substantive and procedural rules, the Constitutional Court stresses that courts may review the legality of administrative acts falling within the discretion of the authorities, and that the judiciary is not bound by the factual inquiry of such agencies but may take evidence to establish the relevant facts as it deems fit.[10] The principle of effective judicial protection also requires litigants to be able to submit efficient means of proof, which is of a nature that is capable of substantiating their position under relevant rules of procedure.[11]

Under the free assessment and free weighing of the evidence principles, administrative judges have discretion in evaluating the evidentiary value of expert reports. The Hungarian judicial system does not employ expert judges at administrative courts. Judges therefore must seek expert evidence in matters of technical expertise. Parties may submit scientific reports prepared by their own experts, and the court may also appoint independent experts on the motion of the parties. Court-appointed experts must be enrolled on a government-issued list attesting to their special qualifications in their areas of expertise. Judges are empowered to instruct the independent experts by specifying their mandate and the questions to be covered in their opinion.

While party-commissioned expert reports have been deemed, under the Old Procedural Code, equivalent to the party's statement, *ex curia* experts play a privileged role in the fact-finding of the courts. Most importantly, legally-decisive inferences can only be drawn from reports of court-appointed experts.[12] For instance, courts can only rule in favour of the party challenging the scientific content of a specialised authority's opinion if an independent expert report confirms technical flaws in the scientific findings.[13] The case law addressed in this chapter therefore attests to an extensive use of *ex curia* experts in cases where litigants seek to challenge the technical aspects of administrative decisions.

The old and the new procedural codes mandate different rules governing the use of *ex curia* experts. Under the Old Procedural Code, applicants first had to

[9] Please note that the references to relevant provisions refer to Act of III of 1952 on the Code of Civil Procedure (Old Civil Procedural Code of 1952, henceforth 'Old Code'), which governed administrative court proceedings as well, including the cases discussed in this chapter.

[10] Hungarian Constitutional Court, Decision No 39/1997. (VII.1.) AB.

[11] Hungarian Constitutional Court, Decision No 19/2015. (VI.15.) AB.

[12] Kfv.II.37.099/2014/6. Judgment of the Supreme Court (2014).

[13] Summary report of the Supreme Court's special committee on case law analysis entitled 'Expert Evidence in Court Proceedings' (19 December 2014) 242, available at https://kuria-birosag.hu/sites/default/files/joggyak/osszefoglalo_velemeny_2.pdf.

produce a scientific analysis pointing out technical flaws in the agency's assessment in order to challenge the executive's scientific findings. The court then moved to appoint an *ex curia* expert to decide about the merits of the technical arguments of both sides. The 2018 judicial reform brought significant changes in this respect. Under the new rules, the expert report relied on by the agency in its administrative proceedings is by default deemed equivalent to an *ex curia* expert opinion in the court proceedings. Such an opinion can still be challenged by the opposing party,[14] yet doing so requires commissioning a more detailed *ex parte* expert report, which is capable of *substantiating* doubts about the technical basis of the agency's expert report. This necessitates a more in-depth analysis from the party-appointed expert, which is more costly for the party, and it also requires a higher level of engagement on the part of the judge to understand the scientific aspects of the dispute. If the judge finds that well-founded doubts indeed surround the correctness of the agency's expert opinion, they can appoint another *ex curia* expert to resolve the controversy. Yet, should the court find the plaintiff's technical challenge unpersuasive, it can easily move to uphold the executive's act given that, under the new procedural rules, the agency's expert is to be regarded as a court-appointed expert, whose opinion can serve as a legitimate basis of the judgment. It is important to note that not only spurious technical claims in the expert report, but also a court's unwillingness to entertain complex scientific arguments raised by the plaintiff's expert, can lead to unsuccessful attempts at challenging the expert opinion relied on by the agency. This flags the often hidden and hitherto under-appreciated significance of individual judges' approach toward technical complexities in determining the role scientific knowledge may play in environmental litigation.[15]

Furthermore, the burden of proof lies with the party alleging a fact. As an exceptional rule, if a plaintiff successfully raises doubts about the well-foundedness of an agency's opinion, the burden of proof is reversed and is borne by the agency which must then prove the correctness of its technical assessment before the court.[16] Furthermore, administrative courts are endowed with *ex officio* evidence gathering powers only in exceptional cases, which are not applicable in relation to expert evidence necessary to uncover the scientific bases of a Natura impact assessment.

In sum, the ultimate task of Hungarian administrative courts is to decide the legal controversy on the basis of the scientific evidence put before them. Deciding on the sufficiency of such expert evidence necessitates a judgment call from judges. They employ several principles to guide such an assessment, which will be examined in more detail in section IV.

[14] Opinion of the Supreme Court's Administrative Section No 3/2020. (XI.9.) on the use of experts relied on by the executive in the administrative proceedings.

[15] For a similar proposition on the significant role that the judge's knowledge of substantive issues may play in setting the scope of judicial review in environmental cases, see Helle Tegner Anker et al, 'The Role of Courts in Environmental Law – a Nordic Comparative Study' [2009] *Nordic Environmental Law Journal* 17.

[16] Old Civil Procedural Code of 1952, art 336/A.

C. Scope and Intensity of Review across the Judicial System

In the Hungarian legal system, the first instance courts have 'full' jurisdiction to review the legality of administrative acts. This means that they can hear additional evidence compared to the expert reports contained in the administrative case file. The discretion of authorities only extends to the sphere of normative policy choices, but not to the weighing of facts and evidence.[17] This means that the evidentiary findings of the executive can be reviewed by the judiciary as the factual conclusions of the executive do not bind the court. The court's review of the factual findings assesses whether the authorities appropriately investigated the facts of the case, especially whether they established all the relevant facts, or any gaps in the fact-finding rendered the conclusions inadequate or flawed.[18] Therefore, risk assessment decisions are deemed to be lawful as long as the authority appropriately ascertained the relevant facts of the case, complied with the relevant rules of procedure, and drew rational and logical inferences from the facts established.

The court of first instance evaluates and weighs scientific evidence in their entirety; is obliged to openly discuss the inferences drawn from the facts; and must explicitly lay out its reasoning pertaining to the appraisal of the evidence and the legal conclusions drawn from such facts.[19] A failure to do so can trigger the review of the Supreme Court. Under the old procedural rules, courts of first instance had cassation powers and were only endowed with reformatory powers in exceptional cases not applicable in disputes relevant to this study.[20] Judges therefore had to remand the case to the authority for re-examination if an impact assessment was unlawful, typically for being missing, incomplete or not well-founded in light of the scientific evidence.

In contrast, the Supreme Court had (and still has) cassation powers and conducts only a legality review. It cannot hear new evidence[21] and has to decide cases on the basis of the factual record established by first instance courts and the authority. This also means that the Supreme Court is barred from re-establishing the relevant scientific facts. It can quash administrative acts that contravened substantive laws or violated procedural rules that impacted the merits of the administrative decision.[22] This has typically been the case when the reasoning of the first instance judgment was incomplete.[23] Given that litigation concerning the lawfulness of Natura impact assessment procedures normally features complex and contested scientific evidence, the Supreme Court has often remanded the case for retrial as

[17] Kfv.III.37.582/2016/16. Judgment of the Supreme Court (2016).
[18] Kfv. II. 37.790/2010. Judgment of the Supreme Court (2011).
[19] Kfv.II.37.792/2013/10. Judgment of the Supreme Court (2014).
[20] Old Civil Procedural Code of 1952, art 339.
[21] *ibid* art 275.
[22] *ibid* art 275; New Procedural Code of Administrative Litigation of 2017, art 121.
[23] BDT2004. 1085.

relevant facts were unclear, ambiguous and contested by litigants. The Supreme Court could also, under the old procedures, quash the underlying administrative decisions themselves if there had been a violation of significant procedural rules that could not be remedied by the courts and, therefore, prompted a new administrative proceeding.[24]

The Supreme Court has only limited powers to review the evidentiary findings of first instance courts, as those operate under the free assessment of the evidence principle. As a result, litigants can only challenge the weighing of scientific evidence by first instance courts if the conclusions drawn were manifestly illogical, contradictory or not based on the facts.[25] In other words, the judicial review of the Supreme Court covers a limited scope of whether the fact-finding of first instance courts is sufficient through conducting a manifest error assessment.[26] Save for these limited circumstances, the weighing of rival expert evidence cannot be challenged before the Supreme Court.[27] This also means that the review of the Supreme Court is limited to a scrutiny of the reasoning of the first instance judgment.

Against this background, the Supreme Court can only scrutinise violations of law. Yet such an exercise inevitably implicates a factual assessment to some extent. As will be seen through the case law analysis in section IV, technical questions often cannot be strictly separated from legal appraisals. To take an example, when a party challenges a first instance judgment for not spotting that the executive authority did not evaluate a scientific question in its impact assessment, judges inevitably have to appraise the technical merits of such claims in order to make their legal determination as to remanding the case for re-examination.

Now we shall turn to look at, through deeper analytic lenses, the science-intensive legal questions that courts face in deciding disputes under the HD.

IV. Demarcating Scientific and Legal Assessments and the Limits of Judicial Review

Distinguishing between legal evaluation (which courts should do) and the evaluation of scientific facts (which courts ought not to do but instead should entrust such evaluation to experts) proves to be an intricate task in many cases. The dividing line between law and science often becomes blurred and contestable as the court reaches the subtle layers of its line-drawing exercise. Notably, in environmental disputes answering a legal question often drags scientific facts and considerations

[24] The New Code also accepts such a possibility.
[25] Kfv.III.38.105/2016/7. Judgment of the Supreme Court (2017).
[26] *ibid.*
[27] Judgment BH1998.401.

into the judicial analysis.[28] Detailed procedural rules on fact-finding and judicial review notwithstanding, the present chapter will argue that the exact coordinates of the demarcation line between terrains of judicial analysis and technical assessment depend to a great extent on the subjective choices of the individual judge hearing the case.

For this reason, in order to understand fully how the above-described procedural rules operate in the judicial practice, we shall investigate those instances, where the courts have certain discretion in applying the rules governing their scientific fact-finding and judicial review. The following case law analysis will therefore be organised around three recurring questions emerging in the case law featuring the HD. Namely, when do courts start doubting the scientific findings of the executive? (section IV, A), how much scientific evidence is sufficient to legally establish likely adverse impact? (section IV, B) and how does the precautionary principle fit in the court's analysis? (section IV, C). Common to these queries is that answers to them are not set in legislation and hence are illustrative of the individual judges' approach to defining the limits of judicial review in science-intensive proceedings.

A. When do Courts Start Doubting the Scientific Findings of the Executive?

Under the Old Procedural Code, a party challenging the technical assessment of the authority had not only to merely *allege* the technical insufficiency of the findings as to the likely impacts, but also had to submit scientific reasoning capable of raising doubts about the well-foundedness of the executive's scientific analysis.[29] As discussed above, party-appointed expert reports were sufficient for casting such doubts, yet the court could only declare the authorities' assessment factually deficient, such that it became unlawful, if an independent expert opinion supported such a conclusion.[30]

It is worth recalling at this point that the scientific position of litigants can be presented to the court in varied forms in Natura impact assessment proceedings. Operators seeking permits are required to present Environmental Impact Assessment (EIA) documentation prepared by an environmental consultant, and which therefore reflects the scientific views of the project developer's own experts.

[28] On the peculiarities of international legal disputes characterised by the presence of 'mixed questions of fact and law', see Caroline E Foster, *Science and the Precautionary Principle in International Courts and Tribunals* (Cambridge University Press, 2011) 137–48. On some of the challenges entailed by the interwoven nature of law and science in environmental adjudication, see Katalin Sulyok, *Science and Judicial Reasoning – The Legitimacy of International Environmental Adjudication* (Cambridge University Press, 2021) 38–40.

[29] Kfv.IV.37.196/2007/7. Judgment of the Supreme Court (2008).

[30] Kfv.II.37.099/2014/6 (n 12).

Under the Old Procedural Code, non-governmental organisations (NGOs) and other actors challenging the impact assessment could present their scientific arguments to the court typically by submitting their own expert reports. If the court deemed such scientific arguments capable of questioning the executive's position, it appointed an independent expert and had to contrast these arguments with the opinion of the court-appointed experts.

Against this background, the question arises as to when the courts deem a party's expert position justified enough to be capable of raising doubts about the well-foundedness of the executive's techno-scientific assessment. Furthermore, as a flip side to this query, the courts also had to decide when to dismiss a plaintiff's technical challenge as insufficient and to affirm the authorities' scientific position.

In certain scenarios, declaring the scientific justifications of the executive inadequate could be a relatively straightforward task for lawyer judges. This was typically the case, when the authority's scientific assessment was manifestly incomplete for reasons that could be easily established by adjudicators without a scientific background. For instance, the Supreme Court declared an impact assessment unlawful when the Inspectorate investigated the likely detrimental impacts of building an accumulator factory only with respect to the great bustard (*Otis tarda*), a bird species of community interest living nearby the relevant area, but not with regard to the grassland itself, which was a Natura 2000 habitat.[31] The Court could easily justify finding the assessment deficient with a non-scientific reasoning rooted in everyday logic and hence was put in a rather comfortable position. As any discussion on the impact on habitat was manifestly absent from the agency's decision, the impact assessment procedure could be declared unlawful without a complex scientific assessment having to be carried out by the Court.

Judges may also face a relatively easy task when the technical challenge of the plaintiff saliently lags behind the authority's scientific explanations in level of detail and/or specificity. The courts in such an instance can swiftly dismiss the science-based challenge if that is only vaguely couched and remains on the level of general allegations. This has been the case for instance, when the Court firmly dismissed an appeal launched against the Inspectorate's denial of permit for a pit mine based on an impact assessment that found likely adverse impacts on the great bustard.[32] The plaintiff only vaguely criticised the authorities' assessment of the scientific evidence without, however, submitting scientific data substantiating the incorrect nature of the factual findings. In another litigation, the plaintiff similarly only alleged, but did not support with expert reports, the deficient nature of the technical assessment of the Environmental Inspectorate.[33] Both of these claims were deemed unable by the courts to prevail over the authorities' detailed explanations rooted in scientific evidence.

[31] Kfv.37.240/2007/11. Judgment of the Supreme Court (2007).
[32] Kfv.III.37.282/2012/5. Judgment of the Supreme Court (2013).
[33] Kfv.II.37.165/2011/4. Judgment of the Supreme Court (2011).

Yet, judges face a more intricate task when the plaintiff presents a science-based plea with no manifest errors or gaps in its scope that would stand out even for a judge without scientific training and expertise. This is the context in which court-appointed experts are instrumental for the court to serve as a key point of reference in rubber-stamping one of the scientific narratives as legally legitimate. In other words, highly technical and sophisticated claims seeking to undermine the authority's scientific opinion can only be evaluated by judges with the assistance of independent experts.

Disputes featuring independent experts often necessitate a science-intensive judicial inquiry. In the *bats v underground mining* dispute for instance, the mining authorities denied a permit from a mine on account of the Inspectorate's binding opinion that found likely detrimental impacts on protected bat species and the stone crayfish (*Austropotamobius torrentium*) living on the premises. The plaintiff challenged the scientific assessment of the authorities by submitting an expert report that contested the presence of the species in the area and questioned the possibility of adverse impacts. The Court-appointed expert's opinion corroborated the Inspectorate's scientific assessment by pointing out methodological flaws and gaps in the mining company's impact assessment documentation as to the potential effects on the species. On such a factual basis, the judge dismissed the plaintiff's claim and affirmed the denial of permit.[34] The Supreme Court upheld the judgment, by pointing out that the independent expert opinion justified finding deficiencies in the party's expert report.[35]

The *snails v limestone quarry*[36] dispute also featured close judicial scrutiny of the scientific assessment of the authority's and the company's own expert. The Inspectorate granted an environmental permit to a limestone quarry situated nearby a Natura 2000 site, which was challenged before the Court by an NGO for its alleged detrimental impact on two protected species of round-mouthed snails (*Pomatias elegans* and *Pomatias rivularis*). There was considerable scientific uncertainty surrounding the preferred habitat of the snail species and the size of their respective populations on the quarry's territory, especially concerning the area, where they were both present, giving rise to ecologically rare inter-species interactions. Based on data obtained from scientific literature, the Inspectorate claimed that the snails were absent from the territory. As an alternative claim, should the snails be indeed present in the quarry, the Inspectorate ordered for the manual collection of the specimens in order to relocate them to a nearby forest. The plaintiff claimed that the permit was unfounded as the authority failed to establish the relevant facts to a satisfactory degree, especially the size of the snail populations affected and the project's noise and air polluting effects.

The Court appointed two independent experts and explicitly listed 15 scientific questions it deemed relevant to decide the legal dispute at hand.[37] The *ex curia*

[34] 8.K.28.600/2013/56. Judgment of the Budapest Environs Regional Court (2015).
[35] Kfv.VI.37.085/2016/9. Judgment of the Supreme Court (2016) para.7.
[36] K.27.080/2014/84. Judgment of the Szekszárd Court of Administrative and Labour Law (2016).
[37] *ibid.*

experts cited data from the literature that estimated the density of the snails in the relevant area with a high degree of uncertainty. This was especially relevant given that the estimated monetary value of the adult specimens potentially inhabiting the quarry reached the astronomical range of 2 to 10 billion Hungarian forints. The judgment contrasted the independent expert opinions with the scientific views of the parties. On the basis of a five-page long, extremely science-heavy judicial assessment, the Court identified three main gaps in the factual analysis of the authority, the appraisal of which would have been, in the Court's view, a crucial prerequisite to appraising the likelihood of adverse impacts on snails. In particular, the judge found that the lack of information on the population sizes, coupled with the absence of information on the carrying capacity of the forest where the snails would have been relocated, renders the relocation obligation scientifically unfounded. Therefore, it remitted the case for a new permitting process. These evidentiary findings were upheld by the Supreme Court, which found that the first instance Court's analysis was lawful for it weighed and evaluated the scientific evidence in a thorough manner and drew logical legal inferences from the factual record.[38] This case well illustrates that discharging the judicial task of reviewing technically complex administrative acts sometimes requires a close judicial scrutiny of scientific methodology. Such a judicial inquiry necessitates a hands-on approach for the individual judge hearing the case and shines a light on their willingness to go deeper into the scientific submissions of the parties.

B. How Much Scientific Evidence is Sufficient to Establish Likely Adverse Impacts?

Judges also have to draw a line between facts and law in determining the scope of factual questions that are regarded as legally relevant in finding the existence (or absence) of likely detrimental impacts. In other words, judges ought to assess the scientific aspects of cases when complying with procedural rules regarding the review of discretionary administrative acts. As noted above, a court may only find an administrative decision lawful, if it is satisfied that the executive gathered technical evidence to a sufficient extent and quality.

Importantly, when and how the judge becomes ascertained of the facts of the case remains dependent on an essentially subjective judgment call. This shapes the extent to which scientific complexities implicated in a legal dispute will be appreciated and evaluated by the court. Courts frequently decide about the amount of expert evidence they deem sufficient to establish the relevant factual basis of an administrative act. The court, as a general rule, has discretion in accepting or rejecting the evidentiary motions of the parties as it deems appropriate to establish the factual record.

[38] Kfv.III.38.105/2016/7 (n 25).

A relevant case illustrative of the liberty of judges in governing the fact-finding process concerned the legality of a nature conservation fine imposed on the constructor of a road in a Natura 2000 forest for destroying several specimens of protected flowers, including native orchid species. The number of specimens destroyed could not be established with certainty, as the operator did not conduct a botanical survey of the area prior to the clearing. The authority based its fine on the statement of a ranger attesting to the presence of the flowers, even though the Geographic Information System (GIS)-based floral map of the area did not indicate any orchids on the path of the road. The first instance Court[39] heard the parties' own experts and appointed an *ex curia* expert, yet dismissed the operator's GIS expert, who would have aimed at proving the geographical location of the road's pathway. The Court pointed out that the ranger's GIS device had an error range of two to five meters, due to which the map's content was not fatal to proving the destruction of specimens. As the *ex curia* expert report corroborated that the flowers were indeed living on the area before the construction works, the Court found the fine to be lawful. The Supreme Court upheld the judgment and stressed that the first instance Court had sufficient scientific data on its record to make its determination as to the location of the flowers, and lawfully dismissed the party-appointed expert evidence. Furthermore, it confirmed that the first instance Court drew logical inferences from the facts of the case, and it lawfully weighed the technical evidence.[40]

This proceeding shows that the courts have discretion to set the number of expert reports they deem necessary to ascertain the facts of the case. As long as the first instance Court provides a reasoning that is logical as to its weighing of the expert evidence and provides justifications for its factual findings, the Court's decision as to the amount of expert evidence needed to reach, to its satisfaction, a sufficiently clear understanding of the facts withstands the review of the Supreme Court.

However, as the hotly litigated case of a NATO military radar station confirmed, when scientific facts speak closely to the legal dilemma at hand, courts of first instance do not enjoy unfettered discretion to decide the case by avoiding commenting on the technical dimensions. In this case, the Government wanted to site a radar station on the top of Mountain Tubes on a parcel of land neighbouring a Natura 2000 site. The authorities granted a construction permit, which was challenged by environmental NGOs, local citizens and neighbouring municipalities before the courts for failing to examine the likely adverse impacts on the nearby natural habitat arising from demolition and construction works and from radiation resulting from the radar's operation. They submitted a motion to appoint an *ex curia* expert to appraise such impacts.

The first instance Court, however, dismissed the motion because the plaintiffs did not formally question the opinion of the specialised authority itself, but

[39] 4.K.27.144/2013/31. Judgment of the Court of Zalaegerszeg (2014).
[40] Kfv.II.37.099/2014/6 (n 12).

aimed at commissioning expert evidence regarding the likely impact.[41] The Court regarded such evidence as 'superfluous' and decided the dispute by balancing competing military and environmental interests without hearing expert evidence. In the first instance Court's view, the legal dispute could be decided by way of a proportionality analysis under the constitutional right to a healthy environment. It opined that any possible environmental detrimental effects were outweighed by the military interests sought to be protected, and hence the permit was lawful. Yet in 2010, the Supreme Court overturned the judgment for violating the procedural rules of taking expert evidence. It stressed that the balancing of competing interests raised several questions of fact; and such legal controversies could not be decided by a purely legalistic reasoning, which pays no regard to scientific arguments relevant to the balancing.[42]

Another line of decisions depicts judicial dilemmas in determining whether a party's motion to appoint an independent expert is justified to challenge the authorities' technical findings. As a general rule, courts have to appoint *ex curia* experts whenever the plaintiff offers prima facie substantiated science-based reasons backing up its criticism of an executive's technical assessment.[43] In this vein, the Supreme Court overturned a judgment in 2014, where the Court denied the plaintiff's motion to appoint an independent expert to reveal the likely adverse impacts of an oil drilling station on a grassland protected under the HD.[44] In the material case, the Inspectorate did not consent to the exploration drilling on account of its likely adverse impacts on the grassland. The Court of first instance agreed with the Inspectorate's position that the siting of the drilling infrastructure alone would have inevitably impaired the vulnerable ecosystem; and opined that the oil company's EIA documentation was insufficient to question the existence of adverse effects. For this reason, it found it unnecessary to appoint an *ex curia* expert to examine the adverse impacts. Yet, the Supreme Court held that the first instance judgment was unlawful for the Court conducted, on its own, a scientific evaluation without hearing independent expert evidence. The Supreme Court stressed that first instance courts have a procedural obligation to appoint an independent expert on the plaintiff's motion to assess the science-based challenges against the executive's findings. As only *ex curia* expert reports may induce the court to find an act unlawful, they are the sole effective means of proof available to the plaintiff, and hence they are essential for realising effective judicial protection of their interests. Such a finding also entails that first instance courts are not entitled to choose between rival technical claims of the parties *on their own*, but must first commission an independent expert report and draw legal conclusions from such a more complex factual record.

[41] 10.K.33.033/2006/167. Judgment of the Metropolitan Court of Budapest (2009).
[42] Kfv. IV.37.629/2009. Judgment of the Supreme Court (2010).
[43] See cases discussed under section IV, A.
[44] Kfv.II.37.099/2014/6 (n 12).

Yet, the Supreme Court's practice has not been entirely consistent on this point signalling that subtle and subjective judicial choices are involved in the evidentiary assessments. In a 2008 decision concerning the high-profile development project of a new international airport, the Supreme Court arrived at the opposite conclusion, and upheld a first instance judgment, where the Court dismissed the plaintiff's motion to appoint an *ex curia* expert. An NGO challenged the Inspectorate's environmental permit granted to the project for the likely risks of collision between migratory birds and the airplanes. The authority was of the view that such encounters were not likely due to the planes' trajectory. The NGO submitted a motion to appoint an independent expert to evaluate such risks. Yet, the Court of first instance dismissed the motion and declared the permit lawful without hearing expert evidence on this point.[45] The Supreme Court upheld the decision by stressing that the first instance Court lawfully dismissed the evidentiary motion as the Inspectorate's impact assessment documentation provided an adequate basis for appraising the scientific aspects of the case. In the Supreme Court's view, the Court of first instance legitimately concluded that the project would not exert adverse impacts on birds, even without hearing additional expert evidence as to the risks of collisions and the necessary risk-abatement measures.

The above cases aptly illustrate that setting the *amount* of factual evidence sufficient to establish the technical basis of an administrative act to the court's satisfaction includes a subjective judgment call of judges. In such cases, while exercising legal judgment, courts determine the extent to which scientific arguments and evidence are allowed to enter into their deliberation. This, in turn, often determines the chances of success of the party which relies on technical arguments to make its case.

C. How Does the Precautionary Principle Fit with the Factual Approach of Courts to Tackle Uncertainty under the HD?

As may be clear by now, Hungarian courts regard the notion of adverse impact as a purely factual issue, which ought to be proven on the basis of expert reports.[46] This turns the legality of finding likely adverse impacts to be a matter of contention between competing expert opinions. Although the case law regularly features probabilistic scientific evidence, the precautionary principle is manifestly absent from the courts' reasoning. The primarily factual approach of the courts to cases involving competing scientific evidence leaves little room for weighing normative principles.

[45] K.22.909/2006/71. Judgment of the Court of Fejér County (2007).
[46] K.30.607/2006/24. Judgment of the Court of Hajdú Bihar County (2007).

As seen above, procedural codes have provided elaborate rules for judicial fact-finding and for governing the procedural avenues of litigants to undermine the scientific findings of the executive. In the court proceedings, litigants compete in presenting the court with a more persuasive technical narrative of the facts of the case; and judges have to accommodate scientific uncertainty in the process of clashing rival expert claims. The courts are therefore rather caught up in a battle of experts and solve legal disputes by choosing between competing probabilistic factual narratives rather than factoring in normative principles in exercising their legal judgment.

The courts rarely discuss the requisite standard of proof openly vis-à-vis uncertain scientific evidence. As a rare exception, the first instance judgment in the *snails v limestone quarry* dispute discussed above, touched upon this issue and required the authorities to show the absence of harmful impact with 'certainty instead of assumptions and probabilities'.[47] This may even be read as an endorsement of a strong conception of the precautionary principle, yet the Court's reasoning predominantly focused on comparing rival scientific evidence, and it quashed the permit based on a thorough factual inquiry, without invoking normative principles. In another proceeding, the Supreme Court has also set a high standard of review in relation to expert evidence by requiring litigants to demonstrate a level of certainty precluding reasonable doubt.[48] Yet, it added that such a standard can be met with expert reports containing uncertain and probabilistic elements. The Constitutional Court also confirmed that the final arbiter of the probative value of uncertain technical evidence shall be the court, which has to eliminate any contradictions from the relevant facts before announcing its judgment.[49]

It is also noteworthy that, similarly, the Environmental Inspectorates also neglect to invoke the precautionary principle before the courts in proceedings relating to Natura 2000 sites. The principle appears only sporadically in the reasoning of administrative decisions. Most notably, the principle was explicitly discussed by the first instance authority in a denial of permit for a poultry rearing installation for its likely adverse impact on the Eurasian stone-curlew (*Burhinus oedicnemus*). Yet, the decision was quashed by the second instance authority, which granted the permit with reference to the lack of likely impacts. The case reached the Court because the operator filed a tort claim against the state for an undue delay in concluding the administrative proceedings, which prevented him from using the resources of a financial grant. It was in this context that the appeal Court explicitly noted that the first instance authority acted within its margin of discretion and interpreted the underlying law in a reasonable way, when it gave way to the precautionary principle in denying the permit with regard to likely adverse impacts on the stone-curlew.[50] Therefore, the Court dismissed the claim

[47] K.27.080/2014/84 (n 36).

[48] Kfv.III.37.582/2016/16 (n 17).

[49] Hungarian Constitutional Court, Decision No 30/2014. (IX. 30.) AB, para 71.

[50] P.21.334/2015/34. Judgment of the Court of Szeged (2016) affirmed by Pf.20.815/2016/7. Judgment of the Szeged Court of Appeal (2016).

seeking compensation for the financial damage caused by the actions of the public authority.

What is apparent from the above wording is that the executive has the power to invoke the precautionary principle, but it is not legally obliged to do so in appraising the likelihood of adverse impacts exerted on Natura 2000 habitats. Even though the Ombudsman for Future Generations, who has a constitutional mandate to monitor the compliance of governmental agencies with the right to a healthy environment, clearly argued for the inspectorates' firm reliance on the precautionary principle in making discretionary balancing in EIA decisions,[51] it was exactly the second instance authority, which repealed the first instance decision that was based on a precautionary reasoning by finding it an 'erroneous interpretation of the underlying law'.

Other court decisions also confirm the limited scope of obligations that the precautionary principle entails for the executive's balancing in the context of impact assessment decisions. In the case concerning a permit granted to developing an international airport, discussed above, the precautionary principle has been interpreted by the first instance Court as entailing no heightened scrutiny for assessing the possible adverse impacts of the runaways to be built on the two neighbouring wetlands designated as special protection areas under the WBD. The wetlands were also protected under the Ramsar Convention as important feeding and resting places of migratory birds. Somewhat paradoxically, the Court invoked the precautionary principle to stress that the authority complied with its positive legal obligations when granting the permit without prescribing the use of sensitive radars to detect birds, given that the risks of airplane collisions with protected birds were minimal in view of the authorities.[52]

Moreover, the Supreme Court only stipulates an obligation for state agencies to act in a precautionary manner under the HD outside the scope impact assessment proceedings, specifically, when a human conduct is threatening to cause environmental damage to a Natura 2000 site. The Court reasoned that the authorities in such cases have an obligation to act and may impose fines on the perpetrator before actual environmental damage would emerge.[53] Yet, as another judgment suggests, uncertainty as to the causal link between an allegedly harmful land use and an injury caused to specimens of species of community interest precludes the tort liability of the perpetrator. The second instance Court opined that with regard to environmental damage claims, the requisite causal link between environmentally harmful conduct and the resulting damage must be established with absolute certainty.[54] In the material case, the authorities were only able to estimate, but not to unequivocally prove, the number of protected butterfly specimens that

[51] General Opinion of the Ombudsman for Future Generations No JNO-131/2010.
[52] K.22.909/2006/71 (n 45).
[53] Kfv.III.37.052/2014/4. Judgment of the Supreme Court (2015).
[54] Pf.II.20.375/2016/4. Judgment of Debrecen Court of Appeal (2016).

were allegedly destroyed by a clearing of trees, which were thought to serve as a wintering ground for the species at hand. Scientific uncertainty surrounding the wintering behaviour of the butterfly, coupled with the scarcity of data available on the abundance of the species on the territory prior to the logging prevented the Court from establishing tort liability for destroying possible butterfly habitat.

V. Concluding Remarks: How Deep Do Judges Go when Scrutinising Scientific Complexities?

The present case law analysis has depicted a system of judicial review, where administrative courts conduct an intrusive review into the techno-scientific assessments embedded in the underlying administrative act. Before summarising some of the main analytical findings as to the practical solutions with which Hungarian courts adjust the extent to which they confront the scientific complexities underlying the legal disputes, we shall first address the structure of the judicial review as envisaged by the applicable rules of procedure. Under Hungarian law, first instance courts should appraise whether party-adduced scientific evidence is capable of raising doubts about the well-foundedness of the executive's technical assessment. They also ought to comparatively evaluate the different scientific positions offered by party-appointed and independent experts and be able to make a clear choice between rival scientific positions. Based on scrutiny of the justifications underpinning the findings of the authority, judges must identify and clearly define gaps and inconsistencies in the technical assessments of the executive. They may remit the case to the authorities by explicitly specifying the agency's mandate to clarify certain factual questions in the new proceedings. In the judicial review of impact assessment decisions, such a mandate may involve setting out the types of impact that must be examined by the executive. However, the judiciary cannot give scientific instructions as to the outcome of such an assessment (ie whether or not to find likely adverse impacts established).

The practice of courts suggests that, under the Old Procedural Code, judges appointed an independent expert whenever a party submitted a motion to that effect and offered scientific explanations that at least prima facie suggested voids or deficiencies in the technical assessment of authorities. Courts then aimed to decide cases on the basis of conflicting evidence, where the parties' own scientific narratives had to be contrasted with the opinion of *ex curia* experts. Importantly, administrative courts ought not to decide scientific controversies on their own, but must appoint an independent expert to scrutinise partisan evidence. In other words, Hungarian courts cannot choose between rival scientific claims of the parties themselves, instead they ought to decide the controversy by duly considering the independent expert report as well.

As to the explicit role assigned to scientific uncertainty in the judicial reasoning, the approach of Hungarian courts squares well with those jurisdictions that tend to hide the consideration of the precautionary principle.[55] Courts typically do not comment on applicable sources of uncertainty implicated in a given case, let alone distinguish between different (reducible and irreducible) forms of uncertainty.[56] It is also apparent that both the judiciary and the executive under-utilise normative principles, such as the precautionary principle, in their factual balancing in the face of uncertain science. The legality of finding likely adverse impacts therefore entirely hinges on a battle of rival expert opinions.

The above analysis also demonstrates that scientific uncertainty plays differing roles in the courts' inquiry across different legal contexts. Whereas uncertainty normally precludes finding a causal claim established in a tort law context for the purposes of claiming compensation for ecological damage, it is less disruptive for making legal determinations about the lawfulness of an impact assessment decision.

The task of investigating the technical aspects of impact assessment decisions is primarily left to the executive. Yet, the limits of the agencies' discretion are closely scrutinised by the first instance courts, which can go into the depth of the technical assessments by checking whether relevant scientific facts were investigated to a sufficient extent and whether the agency duly justified its measures in light of the evidence. Both the Old and the New Procedural Code require the courts to scrutinise whether the agency drew rational, non-arbitrary inferences from the technical evidence placed on the factual record. What finally gets legal 'validation' through the courts to a great extent depends on how well the agency explained its technical findings. This points to the crucial role of how the executive satisfies its duty to give reasons for its measures, as the focus of the court's scrutiny ultimately lies in the science-based reasoning of the administrative act.

This study also posits that the extent to which scientific facts will be entertained by the courts in exercising their legal judgments much depends on the discretionary choices of individual judges hearing the particular dispute. The judicial mandate as prescribed by procedural rules can be discharged with differing levels of judicial engagement with scientific evidence and scientific complexities. Put differently, compliance with the relevant rules of procedure, both under the Old and the New Procedural Code, still leaves judges considerable room for manoeuvre to adjust the science-intensity of the legally relevant facts of the case. First instance courts may distance themselves from the technical aspects of disputes by granting a wide margin of discretion to the authorities and allowing only a limited number of expert reports to be submitted and dismissing the parties' motion to appoint an

[55] Joakim Zander, *The Application of the Precautionary Principle in Practice* (Cambridge University Press, 2010); Nicolas De Sadeleer, 'The Enforcement of the Precautionary Principle by German, French and Belgian Courts' (2000) 9 *Review of European Comparative and International Environmental Law* 144.

[56] For a detailed analysis of the heterogeneous sources of scientific uncertainty, the difference of reducible and irreducible forms of uncertainty and the role they play in environmental adjudication, see Sulyok (n 28) 31–37.

ex curia expert on certain contested scientific issues. In contrast, judges may also opt for taking a more hands-on approach to the technical dimensions and can even give specific instructions as to the factual questions the executive must investigate in order to issue a technically well-founded and, therefore, legally sound administrative decision. The high-water mark of such a close judicial management of technical questions has been the first instance judgment in the *snails v limestone quarry* dispute, where the judge chose to closely review the executive's scientific justifications in light of the competing expert evidence and identified inconsistencies in the technical findings of the authority. When first instance courts choose to go into such depths of the technical assessment, they exert epistemic control over the utilisation of expert evidence, and thereby ensure that the judicial findings will not be dictated by expert positions. In addition, such a judicial attitude ensures that plaintiffs can effectively rely on scientific evidence to challenge the technical assessment of the executive. Scientific complexities in this latter case would not bar the court from exercising its judicial function with respect to science-intensive legal claims.

The case law also attests that determining the amount of expert evidence necessary for the ascertainment of the court inevitably involves a subjective judgment call on the part of the adjudicators. This is well illustrated by court proceedings where different numbers of expert reports allowed the court to make a legal determination. As the Supreme Court's special group on case law analysis also notes, the required level of certainty, which the Court must reach before delivering its judgment, is not set either in normative rules or in judicial precedent, but is entrusted to a case-by-case appraisal of judges.[57] This also means that drawing the contours of the legal issues in a dispute, and *vice versa* that of the factual issues that are deemed legally relevant, inevitably involves the judges' subjective judgment calls. Such judicial choices may be informed by an array of individual factors including the scientific literacy of judges or the extra-legalistic values they may hold, as well as the political or economic significance of the project in question. Drawing these lines under the Hungarian law fall within the scope of discretion of the first instance court, as their evidentiary balancing can only be reviewed by the Supreme Court if it is manifestly wrong, goes clearly against the facts established or is otherwise irrational or arbitrary.

The approach taken by courts towards scientific evidence has evident practical implications for the litigants' chances of success, whenever the legal challenge is based on scientific evidence. A judicial analysis that does not normally give way to the precautionary principle, when coupled with the court's unwillingness to engage with technical knowledge in an extensive way, will ultimately erode the chances of success for the party, which is seeking to prompt vigilance about ecological risks based on uncertain scientific results.

[57] Summary report of the Supreme Court's special committee on case law analysis, entitled 'Theoretical and Practical Questions of Certainty in Judicial Decisions' (October 2017) 7.

The willingness of judges to understand the scientific merits of rival claims becomes even more consequential for private parties' chances of winning an environmental dispute under the New Procedural Code. As the new rules set a higher threshold for private parties to substantiate doubts about the correctness of the executive's scientific finding, the litigation will turn on the self-perceived role of the judge whether its task involves going into the scientific depth of technical claims. The striking lack of relevant disputes after 2018 suggests that the procedural reform of administrative courts and the institutional reform of the executive, coupled with severe and lasting underfunding of NGOs in Hungary that were typical plaintiffs in such proceedings, are conducive to a drastic decline in the number of Natura impact assessment cases. This has resulted in constrained opportunities for exerting public and judicial control over the executive's scientific narrative in environmental risk assessment procedures.

Finally, the cases addressed above also reveal that the legality of the evidentiary findings of both the executive and the first instance courts is inextricably tied to the justifications provided for the weighing of evidence. This throws different methods of judicial reasoning into the limelight. As discussed above with respect to concrete case law, sometimes the facts of the case provide an opportunity for the court to engage in a 'descientised', intuitive reasoning to justify their evidentiary findings. Whereas in other cases, courts should interact with scientific knowledge more closely and provide strictly science-based reasoning. Finally, in certain proceedings courts may opt for conducting a purely legalistic analysis, through the normative balancing of competing interests, to interrogate the legality of an impact assessment decision. The present author has elaborated elsewhere on the benefits and potential risks of the different reasoning styles courts may choose from in scientific disputes,[58] thus it suffices here to underline that judicial decisions do differ in terms of their underlying epistemic authority, which confers different benefits and trade-offs for the persuasive nature of their reasoning.

[58] Sulyok (n 28).

10

The EU Nature Conservation Law in Finnish Judicial Review: Various Avenues, Coalescing Case Law?

TIINA PALONIITTY AND HANNA NIEMINEN-FINNE*

I. Introduction

The administrative judicial system in Finland is a close-knit entity where considerations over science and law influence each other at all levels, from administrative decision-making to their review in the administrative courts.

The Finnish judicial review system does not encompass any ostensibly straightforward standards, such as unreasonableness or proportionality thresholds. Furthermore, Finnish courts, in general, control administrative decisions rather intensively. Within the limits of the claim, the factual side of the matter can and must be considered by the court.[1]

Beyond this general point, however, many variations can be observed in the corpus of the case law concerning judicial review of Natura 2000 decision-making. Matters where scientific uncertainty over environmental impacts may occur are indeed funnelled to various administrative courts, and the abilities of these courts to review factual matters vary significantly across this legal landscape.[2]

This chapter examines this diverse landscape and analyses the consequences it has for the dynamics of environmental principles and scientific uncertainty assessments in Finnish case law on the EU Habitats Directive (HD) and Wild Birds Directive (WBD).[3] We begin our chapter from the key constitutional aspects

* The authors would like to thank Kari Kuusiniemi, President of the Supreme Administrative Court of Finland, and Sinikka Kangasmaa, Judge at the Administrative Court of Vaasa, for their invaluable feedback to the earlier drafts of this chapter.

[1] Pekka Vihervuori, *Environmental Law in Finland*, 2nd edn (Wolters Kluver, 2021) [1333]. Finnish judicial review originates from the formation of the nation from the Eastern territories of Sweden. The systems of the two countries still have much in common.

[2] *ibid* [1336].

[3] For full information, please see the Table of Legislation or the Introduction. For the purposes of consistency, our analysis only includes review of matters dealing with the WBD and HD. Finnish nature conservation law also includes conservation sites, doctrines and rules of domestic origin.

(section III.A) and explain the significance of the two avenues – the administrative and municipal appeal – of which either one may be followed in the matters we discuss (section III.B). Thereafter (section IV) we move on to the case law. Analysis of it is divided in two according to the bifurcated avenues, and further divided according to the piece of legislation in question. The procedural and substantial constraints pertinent to each piece of substantial environmental law is explained there too. We conclude (section V) by reflecting on a number of questions. Does the case law reflect the diverse legal topography? Does the courts' reasoning differ in various case types, or do the Directives or prominence of factual considerations and acute uncertainties create a unifying force, equalising the procedural and substantial differences? Does the reasoning across the diverse set of cases reveal when the expert judges were participating in the adjudication?

II. The Implementation of the HD in Finland and the Competent Authorities

The Finnish Nature Conservation Act (*Luonnonsuojelulaki*, 'NCA') was a well-established legal instrument even before the nation became a member of the EU, but implementing the WBD and HD offered a good reason to further develop the instrument.[4] The Natura 2000 network, regulated in NCA 64a §, was established in the 1990s amid a very heated debate resulting in extensive proceedings. Eventually litigation under the Act has been brought before the Supreme Administrative Court (SAC).[5] According to the NCA, causing deterioration of or destroying breeding sites or resting places of protected animals is forbidden.[6] The section includes a rarity in Finnish implementation tradition, a direct reference to a Directive, being the list of species in Annex IV(a).[7]

NCA 65 § requires the assessment of all environmental impacts likely to significantly weaken the protected values of a Natura 2000 site. The appropriate assessment is the developer's responsibility, applicable to all plans and projects. This also applies to developments without the boundaries of a protected site where there is a risk to the conservation value of the site.[8] The administrative authority must ensure that the appropriate assessment is adequately conducted and will require a statement of the assessment from a regional administrative body.[9]

[4] Nature Conservation Act (NCA) 1096/1996; Vihervuori (n 1) [778]. The decision-making process in the HD in general and its relations with the EIA process are explained in Emma Lees, 'Allocation of Decision-Making Power under the Habitats Directive' (2016) 28 *Journal of Environmental Law* 191; see also the first chapter of this volume.

[5] Vihervuori (n 1) [830]. The Court issued almost 700 decisions on appeals from more than 5,000 appellants.

[6] NCA s 49.1.

[7] Vihervuori (n 1) [867].

[8] *ibid* [832].

[9] NCA, s 65.2 and s 65.4.

In Finland, Natura 2000 appropriate assessment is integrated with the formal Environmental Impact Assessment (the EIA): if the plan or project requires an EIA, the appropriate assessment may be connected with the EIA.[10] Neither the statements nor the appropriate assessments bind the administrative authority (eg deciding on a permit) or the court, which may assess the matter independently.[11] This allocation of tasks has been criticised as breaching Union law. As Pölönen notes, according to the case law of the Court of Justice of the European Union (CJEU), the assessment ought to be carried out by the administration, not by developers. Pertinent to our examination, the NCA's Natura-relevant sections do not necessarily fully reflect the precautionary principle along the lines the CJEU has more recently established.[12] Therefore Pölönen has encouraged the decision-makers to embrace the direct effect of the HD 6(3) and consider the principle more extensively than the wording of domestic statutes would allow.[13]

III. The Foundations of Finnish Environmental Judicial Review

A. Constitutional Provisions and Separation of Powers

Since 2000, the Constitution of Finland has recognised the responsibility of public authorities to protect human rights (22 §).[14] In the same constitutional reform, responsibility for the environment (20 §) was incorporated into the Constitution. Section 20 acknowledges everybody's responsibility, instead of acknowledging only public officials' responsibility towards the protection of biodiversity.[15]

Reflecting the legal tradition in force in the country (based on formalistically interpreted written law) this clause was not applied in case law during its first decade because of its open-ended nature.[16] Only more recently have general human rights arguments gained ground in Finnish courts, and simultaneously the significance of 20 § of the Constitution has steadily increased, although it remains admittedly somewhat limited.[17] This might be seen as a manifestation of

[10] *ibid* s 65.2. In these cases the statement of the assessment must be included in the EIA's reasoned conclusions, Vihervuori (n 1) [832].

[11] Ismo Pölönen, 'Mikä Riittää vai Riittääkö Mikään? Natura-arvioinnille Asetetut Vaatimukset Unionin Tuomioistuimen Linjan Mukaan' (2019) 2 *Ympäristöjuridiikka* 10, 24.

[12] *ibid* 29–30, referring to case C-461/17 *Holohan v An Bord Pleanála* ECLI:EU:C:2018:883 [44]–[45].

[13] Pölönen (n 11) 30.

[14] A non-authoritative translation of the Constitution of Finland is available at www.finlex.fi/fi/laki/kaannokset/1999/en19990731.pdf.

[15] Government's Proposal 309/1993 (HE 309/1993 vp), 66; Antero Jyränki and Jaakko Husa, *Konstitutionell Rätt* (Talentum, 2015) 449.

[16] Finnish Constitution s 2.3; Jaakko Husa, *Non Liquet? Vallanjako, Perusoikeudet, Systematisointi – Oikeuden ja Politiikan Välisiä Rajankäyntejä* (Suomalainen Lakimiesyhdistys, 2004) 166.

[17] Hanna Nieminen-Finne, 'Asiantuntija Tuomarina – Tekniikan ja Luonnentieteiden Alan Hallinto-oikeustuomarit Ympäristönsuojeluasioissa' (Suomalainen Lakimiesyhdistys, 2020) 90.

the country's legal culture where open-ended argumentation is an emerging rather than traditional feature. We will return to this aspect in the conclusions as it may explain the scarcity of cases we found.[18]

Furthermore, the section on legal protection (21 §), which has a more established tradition, is relevant to our enquiry. This provision regulates both the duty resting on the administration to comply with the law and the right of judicial review. At the heart of the rule of law, these two sections, 20 and 21 §, set demands for the process and the review itself.[19] In some instances the court may also review whether the administrative authority has complied with the good governance principles enshrined in the Administrative Procedure Act (*Hallintolaki*, APA), such as impartiality, proportionality or protection of legitimate expectations.[20] These considerations have not been central to cases where scientific uncertainties have been discussed, thus we do not discuss them further.

Also relevant to the discussion of the constitutional underpinnings of the courts' approach towards scientific uncertainty is the Finnish interpretation of *trias politica*, or distribution of powers. As mentioned above, the administrative courts and the SAC have a very broad scope and depth of review. Especially for those environmental matters following the administrative appeal avenue, the judiciary significantly interferes with the terrain of the executive.[21] Interestingly, in the domestic discourse on *trias politica* the broad and in-depth court review has not been taken as infringing the separation of powers, not even when elsewhere full deference is often justified as the very option safeguarding the separation.[22]

B. Bipartite Process Dispersed to Various Courts

The aim of Finnish judicial review is investigating the material truth:[23] the facts underlying the decision must equate to the actual facts as much as possible.[24]

The SAC cases arguing with environmental human rights are eg the *Vuotos* case rejecting an artificial reservoir to a heavily modified river in Lapland, SAC 2002:86 (KHO 2002:86 ECLI:FI:KHO:2002:86), and the *Osprey* case on major predatory bird's nesting tree that had not been included to the Natura 2000 network (KHO 2015:3 ECLI:FI:KHO:2015:3, SAC 2015:3).

[18] See text to n 100.

[19] Veijo Tarukannel and Matti Tolvanen, 'Asian Selvittäminen ja Todistelu Riita-asioissa ja Hallintolainkäytössä – Mikä Yhdistää ja Mikä Erottaa?' (2010) 6 *Lakimies*, 934; and Olli Mäenpää, 'Judiciary v. Executive: Judicial Review and the Exercise of Executive Power' (2017) 2–4 *Tidskrift utgiven av Juridiska Föreningen i Finland (JFT)* 243, 245.

[20] Finnish Ministry of Justice, Administrative Procedure Act s 6 ('APA', hallintolaki 434/2003), non-authoritative English translation available at https://finlex.fi/fi/laki/kaannokset/2003/en20030434.

[21] With regards to 'pure' conservation matters, see below text to n 42; Mikael Hildén 'Opportunities and Challenges in the Use of Scientific Knowledge in Environmental Appeal Cases in Finland' in Kari Kuusiniemi, Outi Suviranta and Veli-Pekka Viljanen (eds), *Juhlajulkaisu Pekka Vihervuori 1950 – 25/8 – 2020* (Suomalainen Lakimiesyhdistys, 2020); and Tiina Paloniitty and Sinikka Kangasmaa, 'Securing Scientific Understanding: Expert Judges in Finnish Environmental Administrative Judicial Review' (2018) 27 *European Energy and Environmental Law Review* 125.

[22] Judicial review interferes with the executive powers vested with the administration, yielding constitutional concerns, Mäenpää (n 19) 248, 250.

[23] Administrative Judicial Procedure Act (AJPA), s 79, non-authoritative English translation available at https://finlex.fi/fi/laki/kaannokset/1996/en19960586; Olli Mäenpää, *Hallinto-oikeus*, (Alma Talent,

However, there is recognition of the impact of procedural constraints, such as the limits of the claim and the prohibition of *reformatio in peius*.[25] In general, judicial review is concerned with reviewing the legality of the executive's actions.[26]

In the realm of the HD the available procedural routes greatly define the possibilities and powers vested in the courts. As appropriate for nature conservation law embracing the integration principle, matters relevant to the WBD and HD are scattered throughout different corners of Finnish environmental legislation. The application of the relevant legislation determines the appropriate appeal route.

Finnish judicial review consists of multiple appeal avenues.[27] The two channels of appeal, administrative and municipal appeal impact not only the scope of courts' review, but also the conduct of their proceedings and the choices they can make. Matters following the administrative appeal route can be further divided in two: to matters that are adjudicated with or without expert judges. For clarity we present the two versions of judicial review relevant for our enquiry as bifurcated. It should be noted, however, that this is somewhat of a simplification, since the procedural rules have been fine-tuned to fit the substance of the regulated matter to such an extent that the system can be described as including two 'blended' appeal routes too, in between the municipal and administrative appeals.[28]

Matters dealing with hunting, 'pure' nature conservation (ie matters dealing with the NCA outwith the scope of the Environmental Protection Act (*ympäristönsuojelulaki*, EPA) or the Water Act (*vesilaki*) and logging are adjudicated through the avenue of the administrative appeal procedure without expert judges. These cases are heard by the regional administrative courts.[29] In relation to matters dealing with the EPA and Water Act, a broad and intense review is applied through the administrative appeal procedure with the expert judges and is centralised to the Vaasa Administrative Court (Vaasa Court).[30] In cases concerning land use and planning, finally, regional administrative courts are also competent, but the applicable procedure is that of the so-called 'municipal appeal', which entails several limits to the latitude of powers of the administrative courts.[31]

2018) 979; Olli Mäenpää, *Oikeudenkäynti hallintoasioissa: Hallintoprosessioikeuden perusteet,* (Alma Talent, 2019) 319.

[24] Janne Aer, 'Tuomioistuimen Selvittämisvastuu ja Suullinen Käsittely Hallintoprosessissa' (2009) 5 *Defensor Legis* 761, 762; Anna-Stiina Tarkka, 'Selvitysvelvollisuus ja Todistustaakka – Vertailevia Näkökohtia Hallinto- ja Siviiliprosesseista' (2015) 3–4 *Lakimies* 508, 510–11.

[25] Pekka Vihervuori, 'Muuttuva Hallintopakko' in Risto Nuolimaa, Pekka Vihervuori, and Hannele Klemettinen (eds), *Juhlakirja Pekka Hallberg 1944-12/6-2004* (Suomalainen Lakimiesyhdistys, 2004) 496; Mäenpää, '*Oikeudenkäynti Hallintoasioissa*' (n 23) 457.

[26] AJPA, s 13.1.

[27] Mäenpää 2019 (n 23) 202; Emma Lees and Ole W Pedersen, *Environmental Adjudication* (Bloomsbury, 2020).

[28] Eija Mäkinen, *Kunnallisvalitus – Kiusantekoa vai Tarpeellista Valvontaa ja Oikeusturvaa?* (Edita, 2010) 46; Ari Ekroos and Matias Warsta, 'Selvitys Maa-aineslain Muutoksenhakusäännöksien Kehittämismahdollisuuksista' (Ympäristöministeriön Raportti, 2014) 32.

[29] Nature Conservation Act ('NCA', *luonnonsuojelulaki* 1096/1996).

[30] The legally non-binding English version of the Environmental Protection Act 527/2014 is available at https://finlex.fi/en/laki/kaannokset/2014/en20140527. The legally non-binding English version of the Water Act 587/ 2011 is available at https://finlex.fi/en/laki/kaannokset/2011/en20110587.

[31] Land Use and Planning Act 132/1999, s 188.1; Vihervuori (n 1) [1333] and [1347].

Table 1 illustrates these different routes and the role of expert judges in each.

Table 1 The Two Channels of Appeal and Use of Expert Judges in Different Types of Matter

Piece of substantial legislation	**Administrative appeal without expert judges**	**Administrative appeal with expert judges**	**Municipal appeal**
Hunting Act	x		
'Pure' Nature Conservation cases	x		
Environmental Protection Act		x	
Water Act		x	
Land Use and Planning Act			x

i. The Administrative Appeal Process without Expert Judges

Matters falling under the scope of the Hunting Act or so-called 'pure' nature conservation matters – ie matters dealing with the NCA but outside the scope of the EPA or the Water Act – are heard through the administrative appeal channel. After the decision at the first level administrative authorities, the matters are decided in the regional administrative courts and, on appeal, by the SAC, the court of final appeal in the administrative matters. However, unlike matters falling with the EPA or the Water Act, the procedure does not foresee the presence of expert judges.

The administrative appeal process is reformatory and malleable.[32] In the reformatory process the court has, within the limits of the appeal, the right to not only annull, but also alter the permit conditions. The Finnish administrative courts actively employ this power and it is common for them to alter permit conditions, moulding the planned project so that it passes the acceptable threshold and meets the requirements established in substantive environmental legislation.[33] The scope and depth of examination exercised by the administrative authorities and by the courts in the 'administrative appeal' procedure are traditionally considered more or less equal.[34] The only limitation for the courts is that they cannot *issue*

[32] Vihervuori (n 1) [1333]; Vihervuori, 'Totuudesta Hallintolainkäytössä' 496; Paloniitty and Kangasmaa (n 21) 128–89; Outi Suviranta, 'Hallintovalitus, Hallintotuomioistuimen Tuomioistuinkontrolli ja Tuomioistuimen Ratkaisuvalta' (2005) 2 *Defensor Legis* 231, 235.

[33] Kari Kuusiniemi, 'Ympäristöllinen Päätöksenteko ja Ohjausjärjestelmä' in Kari Kuusiniemi, Ari Ekroos, Anne Kumpula, and Pekka Vihervuori (eds), *Ympäristöoikeus* (WSOY, 2001) 140.

[34] Vihervuori (n 25) 498–99.

an environmental permit or be the first instance to use administrative discretion. For example, if the courts would like to rule on an aspect of the case that the decision-maker did not consider at all, the court ought to remit the case back to the administration instead of using forbidden discretionary powers.[35] Furthermore, the reformatory process is rather permissive when it comes to supplementing the appeal or presenting completely new grounds of appeal, furthering the extent of moulding the matter the court process enables.[36]

ii. The Administrative Appeal Process with Expert Judges

As noted, appeals on cases applying the EPA or the Water Act follow the administrative appeal process sketched out above but, unlike the cases discussed in the paragraph above, they are centralised to the Vaasa Administrative Court.[37] In such cases, an expert judge must be part of the Court's panel.[38] On appeal of these matters to the Supreme Administrative Court, the panel consists of five lawyer judges and two expert members – in other words, cases heard in the Vaasa Court with expert judges, are also adjudicated in the SAC with expert judges.[39] In both courts these expert judges are part of the court chamber, alongside lawyer judges. The expert judges hold a technical or scientific degree and do not have formal legal qualifications.[40] In this multi-professional setting, both the lawyer and expert judges have equal say when deliberating the matter, enabling a thorough review of any scientific questions. The presence of in-house expertise might also explain why the country's judicial review lacks specific standards, as the courts have very wide powers.[41] Expert judges are the country's solution to secure a multi-professional knowledge base within the court, and they impact greatly the depth in which the court can consider science and its uncertainties.

It should be noted that this division amongst environmental cases has been criticised as illogical. The differing treatment, depending upon legislative basis,

[35] Given the complexity of many environmental matters, the question of whether the court has used forbidden discretionary powers is ambiguous and contested, *cf* Tarukannel and Tolvanen (n 19) 944–45; Mäenpää 2019 (n 23) 13.

[36] AJPA, s 41.

[37] See text to n 3.

[38] EPA, s 190.1; Administrative Court Act 430/1999, s 12.2.

[39] The Supreme Administrative Court Act, s 11.1; Kari Kuusiniemi, 'Domstolarna och Experterna: Hur Trygga Sakkunskapen i Miljömål?' in Lena Gipperth and Charlotta Zetterberg (eds) *Miljörättsliga Perspektiv och Tankevanor* (Iustus Förlag AB, 2013) 319, 321. Leave to appeal in environmental matters has not traditionally been demanded but for example as of 1 January 2018 the legislation was amended and leave to appeal is now demanded in the 'environmental' matters (on environmental protection, water use, soil excavation, or land use and building).

[40] On expert judges see Paloniitty and Kangasmaa (n 21) 132–34.

[41] Roberto Caranta has argued that the fact that judges do not hold scientific training may lead them to spot only manifest errors, Roberto Caranta, 'Still Searching for a Reliable Script: Access to Scientific Knowledge in Environmental Litigation in Italy' (2018) 27 *European Energy and Environmental Law Review* 158.

exists for historical reasons and lacks substantial justification. The matter is most pressing with pure nature conservation matters that are not heard with expert judges.[42]

iii. The Municipal Appeal Process

The municipal appeal route is used in planning matters. This procedure, unlike the administrative appeal process, provides, first, strict grounds of appeal. Furthermore, because of the strict rules as to time limits for bringing an appeal provided in the Municipality Act, any grounds presented after the appeal period are not examined.[43] Second, in contrast with the administrative appeal route, in the municipal appeal procedure the court may only quash the earlier ruling or decision, not usually remit it back to the administration, and it does not have the power to alter the decision.[44] Third, planning matters may be quashed only on certain grounds. The decision must have infringed procedural rules; the administration must have exceeded its authority; or the decision must have been otherwise *contra legem*.[45] These grounds for judicial review resemble those applied in England.[46] In planning matters, this more limited review reflects the notion that administrative courts cannot act as an administrative authority. It is interesting that in some environmentally-relevant cases such deference is more prominently applied than in others. The justification – municipal independence prominent in planning in particular – appears weak however if we consider the significant socio-environmental impacts other types of environmental decisions can have in the life of a municipality. Besides the interested parties, all members of the municipality have the right to appeal, standing rights being thus broader than in administrative appeal.[47] This *actio popularis* type of right is meant to balance the otherwise restricted route, and to secure social inclusion and prevent corruption at local level.[48]

The municipal appeal is adjudicated by the administrative courts and, on appeal, by the SAC.

[42] Paloniitty and Kangasmaa (n 21); Hildén (n 21).

[43] AJPA, s 81.2; Municipality Act 410/205, s 135.3, non-binding English translation available at https://finlex.fi/fi/laki/kaannokset/2015/en20150410.

[44] Mäenpää 2019 (n 23) 208, 266.

[45] Municipality Act, s 135.2 and s 135.3; Mäenpää 2019 (n 23) 208.

[46] Explained by Catherine Caine and Richard Broadbent in chapter five of this volume. Interestingly, both nations consider their reviews as legality challenge, even when the Finnish administrative appeal (with expert judges) is almost a polar opposite of the options available in England.

[47] Municipality Act, s 137.1.

[48] Heikki Harjula and Kari Prättälä, *Kuntalaki – Taustat ja Tulkinnat* (Talentum, 2012) 722; Juha Raitio, 'Huomioita Oikeusvaltio-käsitteen Kehityksestä ja Sisällöstä Suomessa' (2017) 5 *Lakimies* 559, 563.

C. Securing Science in Court beyond Expert Judges: The Relevance of Procedural Rules

Expert judges are not the only mechanism in Finnish administrative courts to bring scientific or technical understanding to the attention of the court. All administrative courts can ask for statements from private experts or other administrative bodies (ie not the one who originally decided the matter), regardless of whether expert members are part of the court chamber. Asking for such statements is, however, relatively rare. The passivity of courts in this regard has been thought to reflect the notions of impartiality and non-partisan enquiry, and the fact that, especially in the realm of the EPA, the applicant's duty to examine the matter fully is emphasised in the text of the statutes.[49]

Hearing different administrative authorities is instead a widely used practice by the courts.[50] A question worth pondering is whether frequently relying on the knowledge that administration can provide reflects a notion of such knowledge being 'neutral', something that the legal and judicial decision-maker can safely endorse, when other, private, sources of knowledge would taint the court's deliberations with unwanted tones compromising its impartiality.[51]

Regardless of the avenue in question or the substance of the matter, the *ex officio* principle furthermore characterises Finnish judicial review, but in its less stringent forms. It is the parties' responsibility, and right, to produce evidence and the court only secures that the matter is adequately investigated.[52] Abiding by the *ex officio* principle does not therefore necessarily mean that the court will actively investigate the matter. The principle could be variously expressed as engendering a duty of care; a responsibility to actively investigate; and/or as regulating the court's conduct of the proceedings.[53]

The question of adequate investigation was especially pressing in the cases analysed in this chapter, when the need or accuracy of the Natura 2000 appropriate assessment was often the core of the judicial proceedings. It is worth noting that active investigation, in all its forms, will always benefit some of the parties in, at times also unpredictable ways. This is especially notable in environmental matters with multiple interested parties forming a web of interests.[54] The national

[49] Nieminen-Finne (n 17) 56. An expert witness statement can be acquired on a party's initiative. The legislation reserves a possibility to have hearings, though they are extremely rare in Finnish administrative procedure. (APA, s 43).

[50] EPA, s 42, s 43 and s 196.

[51] In other words, whether certain sources of knowledge would be more objective than others; that by relying on them 'our imperfections as epistemic agents have been effectively averted', Inkeri Koskinen, 'Defending a Risk Account of Scientific Objectivity' (2020) 71 *British Journal for the Philosophy of Science* 1187, 1188.

[52] AJPA, s 39.1; Mäenpää 2019 (n 23) 323–26, 978. Also Government's Proposal 217/1995 (HE 217/1995 vp.) 58–59.

[53] AJPA, s 37.1-2; Mäenpää 2019 (n 23) 322–23, 981; Paloniitty and Kangasmaa (n 21) 128; Aer (n 24) 144.

[54] Nieminen-Finne (n 17) 193, 204; Tarukannel and Tolvanen (n 19) 946.

and EU courts have taken strong stances in supporting the active role the courts have taken in establishing the truth in such a diverse landscape of interests and parties.[55] One of us has argued that because the principle of active investigation is only one of the key principles governing adjudication in environmental matters – others being impartiality and fair trial – less intrusive interpretations of the principle ought to be favoured, stressing the activity of the parties in supplying the court with sufficient investigation.[56]

IV. Case Law Concerned with the HD – Reflecting the Procedural Dichotomy?

Tegner Anker and others have noted the interlinkage between the court's attitude towards its scope of review and their understanding of the matter itself.[57] Building on their conclusions, in the remainder of the chapter, we will probe whether the differences of the avenues, and particularly the variations in terms of the level of expertise at hand, impact the scope and depth of review in our cases. Is the unifying force of uncertainty assessment or effective implementation of the EU environmental law stronger than these differences just described?

Hereafter we focus on the SAC case law dealing with the WBD and HD. In section IV, A we analyse cases that have followed the avenue of administrative appeal, with and without expert judges, and in the ensuing section IV, B we focus instead on the municipal appeal matters. Before embarking on the cases, some preliminary findings.

First, the amount of court rulings discussing scientific uncertainty was surprisingly low. As already noted, Finnish judicial review has seen a move towards more elaborate reasoning in recent years.[58] The increased efforts of open argumentation

[55] C-685/15 *Online Games Handels GmbH and Others v Landespolizeidirektion Oberösterreich* ECLI:EU:C:2017:452 [65] and [68], on a matter on administrative sanction, and SAC 2015:151 (KHO 2015:151 ECLI:FI:KHO:2015:151) on public procurement; Nieminen-Finne (n 17) 193.

[56] Nieminen-Finne (n 17) 204; Mäenpää 2018 (n 23) 990.

[57] Helle Tegner Anker and others, 'The Role of Courts in Environmental Law – a Nordic Comparative Study' [2009] *Nordisk Miljörättslig Tidskrift* 17.

[58] Nieminen-Finne (n 17) 204–205. Recently these conflicting principles have received rare attention. The SAC rejected EPA permits for a major bioproduct/forestry plant in 2019, in part because of uncertainties over its long-term and combined water impacts. The SAC mentioned that the applicant had rejected a temporary permit (as an option to address those uncertainties) during the Court proceedings. In May 2021 the proponent sought for annulment of the ruling on procedural grounds, claiming that the Court had acquired that piece of information in an event that was meant to be only an on-site inspection of the proposed site, not an oral hearing, thus favouring the principle of active investigation over the principles of impartiality and fair trial. At its first ruling in 2022, the SAC rejected the annulment application (SAC 2022:1 KHO 2022:1 ECLI:FI:KHO:2022:1); the annulment application of the Finnpulp company (0034/1/215101, 25 May 2021); Paloniitty and Kangasmaa (n 21) 135; Tiina Paloniitty and Niina Kotamäki, 'Scientific and Legal Mechanisms for Addressing Model Uncertainties: Negotiating the Right Balance in Finnish Judicial Review' (2021) 33 *Journal of Environmental Law* 283, 306–309.

have, however, scarcely been used for contemplating the factual side of the matter, but focussed on legal questions. It is apparent that the SAC is not keen to discuss scientific evaluations at the core of an impact assessment. Even when the topic is debated, the reasoning in respect of factual questions is often shallow. The SAC describes the scientific enquiry it has referred to and after the recount concludes that there is (a lack of) significant scientific certainty justifying certain legal outcomes. Remembering the practical and procedural flexibility the SAC and the Vaasa Court possess in administrative appeal procedures, and the dual nature of the EIA, consisting of both the scientific and the legal side, this modesty in the face of disputes over scientific questions is even more surprising.[59] Though it may be that the courts' decisions are thoroughly discussed in the Court panel, and are only left unwritten within the ruling for cultural reasons, we would be inclined to wish that the ongoing development of open and transparent argumentation would reach the factual considerations too.[60]

Second, the nature of the legal questions the SAC has resolved is interesting. Instead of reviewing the content of Natura 2000 appropriate assessments, the Court has primarily considered whether the assessment is needed in the first place. It may be that this is due to the Finnish solution of coupling the appropriate assessment with the EIA. Such a setting may be prone to situations where the legal question becomes about the need for another type of assessment, or whether the assessment presented in the EIA is adequate. In the concluding section we continue discussing both these aspects, and their significance to our overall analysis.[61]

A. Flexible Administrative Appeals

i. The Environmental Protection Act: The Necessity for an Appropriate Assessment

The Finnish EPA, encompassing all regulation on environmental pollution, leaves ample room for authorities to determine the content of environmental permits.[62] The Act implements the Industrial Emissions Directive, thus revolving around the concept of (significant) 'pollution', defined as harmful environmental impact caused by human activity.[63] In the context of the Finnish EPA, the operator is entitled to a permit as long as the permit conditions are such that the (threat of)

[59] *ibid*, Paloniitty and Kotamäki 306–309.
[60] Paloniitty and Kangasmaa (n 21).
[61] See text to n 100.
[62] EPA, s 48.2. Earlier the Water Act included provisions on water pollution.
[63] EPA, s 1 and s 2; Directive 2010/75/EU of 24 November 2010 on industrial emissions (integrated pollution prevention and control) [2010] OJ L334/17; Elizabeth Fisher, Bettina Lange and Eloise Scotford, *Environmental Law: Text, Cases & Materials*, 2nd edn (Oxford University Press, 2019) 419–20, 430–33.

significant pollution is averted.[64] This brings the (un)certainty of estimated environmental impacts to the fore. Only when the proposed plan cannot be shaped so that the forbidden impacts become unlikely, are there legimate grounds to reject it.[65] Thus even when sustainable development is mentioned as one of the rationales of the Act, the court is permitted to conduct only a legality review, ie considering whether 'significant pollution' is about to take place and broader sustainability – or any other value – considerations are forbidden.[66] The role of the precautionary principle is more nuanced. The principle is mentioned as a general principle guiding all actions encompassing pollution risks, but the section in EPA 48 § defining the limits of the permit conditions does not refer to it (contrary to the concept of significant pollution).[67] The Finnish administrative courts refer to the principle directly in their reasoning – but not excessively. There are legal-cultural reasons for this. Reasoning with principles, environmental ones included, is saved for occasions when the decision-making calls for them and mentioning them in every possible case is not ordinary.[68] In this tradition, the precautionary principle has played a crucial role in the most difficult cases. For example, when there has been significant uncertainty on the long-term and cumulative impacts of major industrial sites, the SAC has relied explicitly on the precautionary principle, though invariably in combination with the legal norms pertinent to the matter.

After these general aspects on the EPA, we embark on analysing two SAC cases where scientific uncertainties of impacts to Natura 2000 areas have been crucial. The *Pansio* case revolved around an established harbour and dock near Pansio village and focused on the need to conduct a Natura 2000 impact assessment because of a site in immediate promixity to the harbour (at the shortest the distance was only 150 meters).[69] Since the harbour had been there from the 1930s, there was empirical knowledge on the impacts.[70] The permit for expanding and altering the harbour had been granted without the need for Natura 2000 assessment. The Vaasa Court had remitted the case back to the administrative authority for the Natura assessment, but the SAC overruled the decision and remitted the case back to the Vaasa Court. The SAC emphasised the established nature of the activity. Also, a Natura 2000 assessment had been conducted in 2001 for planning purposes, and some ensuing studies were at hand, specifically focusing on the sulphur and nitrogen emissions that were not estimated to increase because

[64] EPA, s 49.1, point 2; Ari Ekroos, Anne Kumpula, Kari Kuusiniemi and Pekka Vihervuori, *Ympäristöoikeuden Pääpiirteet*, 3rd edn (Sanoma Pro, 2013) 562.

[65] The reformatory process is explained at text to n 32ff.

[66] EPA, s 1.

[67] Respectively, EPA, s 20 and s 48.

[68] In other words, the courts prefer using other legal mechanisms for promoting precaution without needing to engage directly in the weighing and balancing of principles. Ronald Dworkin, *Taking Rights Seriously, New Imprint with Appendix: A Reply to Critics* (Duckworth, 1978) 187ff.

[69] SAC 2014:37 (KHO 2014:37 ECLI:FI:KHO:2014:37).

[70] The area was listed as both Sites of Community Importance (SCI) and Special Protection Area (SPA), being 852 hectares in size.

of planned amendments at the site. A marginal increase in emissions was not considered as a reason to conduct a new Natura 2000 assessment, especially when other impacts, such as noise, were considered as minor.

The *Pansio* case is one of those matters where the scientific and legal assessments became entangled. In this case the SAC explicitly relied on the precautionary principle. The uncertainty of the impact was acknowledged in the Court's reasoning, though not extensively deliberated. While noting the significance of the protected values – the area being significant to both birds' and habitats' conservation – and the immediate proximity of the site, the Court did not discuss the uncertainties in further detail. It may be that the long history of the harbour was enough to convince the Court that even extended activities would not cause adverse effects to the nearby site. Thus, a long history of operations at the site reduced the scientific uncertainties there might have been had the case been about a novel activity.

The *Lake Suomi* case[71] also discussed the need for a Natura 2000 impact assessment in the context of a peat production permit. Peat production has not only remarkable climate impacts but can cause significant deterioration of water quality in nearby and downstream water bodies. The production had been granted a temporary EPA permit by the administrative authority even though the waters from the site were directed to Lake Suomi, an SPA site. The developer had produced a survey on the impacts of the production site to the Natura 2000 area. The surveilling authority had appealed the matter to the Vaasa Court, which rejected the appeal. The SAC took a stance that the developer's inquiry of the impacts to the SPA site was not adequate. It omitted information of the specific features of the birds' habitats, or the impact the production could cause to them due to the extended or amended water flow. Nonetheless, after taking the water impact and flow enquiry into account, the SAC concluded that gross emissions from peat production were diminishing and since Lake Suomi had been restored, there was no significant scientific doubt left as to the integrity of the protected values. The Court did not find a need for a Natura 2000 assessment.[72]

The Court's logic in the *Lake Suomi* case appears to be that the impacts on the protected values did not need to be investigated when the changes in the medium water flow were not expected to alter the habitat's conditions. By doing so, the Court strictly followed the logic of activity, emission and impact, at the heart of the EPA. If the impact does not extend to the protected habitat, appropriate assessment is not required.

[71] SAC 2017:59 (KHO 2017:59 ECLI:FI:KHO:2017:59). 'Suomi' is the Finnish name for Finland.

[72] In its reasoning the SAC referred to the Commission's guidance documents and the CJEU case law, eg C-127/02 *Waddenvereniging and Vogelbeschermingsvereniging* [2004] ECR I-07405, ECLI:EU:C:2004:482; C-6/04 *Commission v United Kingdom* [2005] I-09017, ECLI:EU:C:2005:626; C-418/04 *Commission v Ireland* [2007] ECR I-10947, ECLI:EU:C:2007:780; C-98/03 *Commission v Germany* [2006] ECR I-00053, ECLI:EU:C:2006:3; C-538/09 *Commission v Belgium* [2011] ECR I-04687, ECLI:EU:C:2011:349; and C-404/09 *Commission v Spain* [2011] ECR I-11853, ECLI:EU:C:2011:768.

ii. Water Law: Weighing and Balancing of Interests

Alongside the EPA, another nucleus of Finnish environmental permits is the Water Law, of domestic origin regulating non-polluting activities relating to waters, such as water construction, hydropower, water abstraction, and so on.[73] Importantly for our enquiry, the Water Act does not share the objective of environmental protection, nor of advancing sustainable development. The Water Act is primarily about weighing and balancing the various interests at stake, environmental good being only one of them.[74]

The Roine Case concerned an artificial groundwater venture that might have impacted a nearby Natura 2000 site.[75] The decision followed closely the rule that the Natura 2000 sites are protected from indirect impacts.[76] The conservation values of the site were closely linked with the site's groundwater levels, and thus were of concern when authorising undertakings outside the area.[77] The Vaasa Court discussed the role of the precautionary principle and scientific uncertainty, noting that neither was a reason as such to disallow the venture. They only obliged the authority to establish such permit conditions that would curb the harmful impact.[78] In taking the case to the SAC, some parties involved complained about the Vaasa Court's reasoning on the certainty of the scientific information used in the impact assessment. The SAC conducted an inspection at the site, and heard a professor as a witness – both rare mechanisms of acquiring understanding of the factual matters. The Court discussed scientific uncertainty by referring to the guidelines set by the CJEU.[79] The Court noted how the scientific assessments did not remove all justified scientific uncertainty on the undertaking's adverse effects surpassing the threshold, and hence the permit should not have been granted in the first place.[80] This was the case in one-third of the plant's planned area, at its edges. Because of this considerable scientific uncertainty, the administration was found to be correct in not allowing the undertaking to extend to those edges. Since the same uncertainties did not apply to the other two-thirds of the area, the SAC

[73] Water Act, s 3:3. Water Law has extensive history in Finland – the land of a thousand lakes – also as a breeding ground for contemporary environmental law. In matters requiring both permits, both permit considerations must be conducted independently even when the processes are integrated, EPA, s 47, Water Act, s 11:12.

[74] Water Act, s 3:4; Erkki J Hollo, Pekka Vihervuori and Kari Kuusiniemi, 'Environmental Law and Administrative Courts in Finland' (2010) 51 *Journal of Court Innovation* 51, 52–53; Pekka Vihervuori, 'Private and Public Ownership of Water Areas – Structures and Implications of the Finnish Model' in Erkki J Hollo (ed), *Water Resources Management and the Law* (EE, 2017) 98.

[75] SAC 2018:121 ('*The Roine Case*' KHO 2018:121 ECLI:FI:KHO:2018:121).

[76] HD, art 6(2).

[77] On the Finnish Natura 2000 implementation, see text to n 7.

[78] *The Roine Case* (n 75).

[79] The SAC referred to the CJEU rulings in C-441/17 *Commission v Poland* ECLI:EU:C:2018:255 [114]; C-258/11 *Sweetman and Others* ECLI:EU:C:2013:220 [44]; and C-387/15 and C-388/15 *Orleans v Vlaams Gewest* ECLI:EU:C:2016:583 [50].

[80] *The Roine Case*, Dealings in the SAC, Chapter 4, subchapter on judicial review.

upheld the Vaasa Court's ruling in that regard.[81] Another key reason was that the area in question was an especially small and sensitive part of the Natura 2000 site. Production in the area might have brought about forbidden adverse effects to the maintenance of the conservation values, especially with regard to the size of the protected area.[82]

Elsewhere one of the authors has used *The Roine Case* as a rare example of the SAC elaborately discussing the details of the environmental models, the tool assessing uncertainties in the case.[83] The Court went into the detail of the scientific method used, groundwater modelling, and explained its legal decision with the specifics of the model. That is rare, also in the matters dealing with the Water Law that otherwise allows for balancing of various interests, encouraging open argumentation. Though this may seem odd, this same reasoning may explain why the amount of Water Law cases was so limited. In Water Law cases there are vast amount of legal arguments to ponder, which can result in the Court relying rather on legal argumentation instead of factual considerations.[84]

iii. Wolv(erin)es and Forestry

The most notorious pieces of Finnish nature conservation law are the two wolves cases the CJEU has decided. Garcia Ureta has discussed the cases extensively elsewhere in this volume at chapter two, and we refer to his insightful analysis on those cases. The saga of settling hunting and conservation needs is, however, enduring, thus we discuss two more cases here. One is an SAC ruling on hunting wolverines from 2020 and another concerns a hunting permit of a whole pack, appealed in late 2020. On top of these hunting cases we discuss a foresty case as our last case following the administrative appeal route.

As Garcia Ureta mentions, exceptions from the protection granted to endangered species can be granted, allowing for the animal's capture or killing in 'small numbers'.[85] In Finland these authorisations for hunting of protected species are at the discretion of the Finnish Wildlife Agency ('FWA').[86] In the *Wolverines* case the FWA had allowed the hunting of two wolverines in the area of two Natura 2000 sites, in both of which the wolverines' habitat was the objective of the protection.[87]

[81] The Vaasa Court had remitted the case back to the administrative authority, showing the limits of the reformatory process, *The Roine Case*, Proceedings in the SAC, Chapter 4, subchapter on judicial review.

[82] *The Roine Case*, Proceedings in the SAC, Chapter 4, subchapter on judicial review.

[83] Paloniitty and Kotamäki (n 58) 304ff.

[84] The situation with Water Law cases in general and matters on groundwater pollution in particular would thus be polar opposites: the strict ban of all groundwater pollution has presumably led to increased reasoning of factual questions, Paloniitty and Kotamäki (n 58) 295ff.

[85] Garcia Ureta in this volume at chapter two.

[86] *Suomen riistakeskus* (Finnish Wildlife Agency), available at https://riista.fi.

[87] SAC 2020:31 (KHO 2020:31 ECLI:FI:KHO:2020:31).

The FWA considered a Natura 2000 appropriate assessment unnecessary due to the limited length and scope of the intervention. A local nature conservation association appealed the case, but the Regional Administrative Court in Northern Finland rejected the appeal.

The SAC considered that the FWA had not appropriately considered the impact of the hunt on the wolverine population at the Natura 2000 sites. The SAC emphasised that it was thus 'not excluded' that the hunting could be detrimental to the maintenance of populations of the endangered species. The SAC also stated that considerations ought to draw on 'accurate and up-to-date scientific knowledge'. In its reasoning, the SAC referred to the fact of wolverines position as an HD Annex II species; the rationale justifying Natura 2000 protection; the scarcity of wolverines; and referred extensively to the CJEU case law and to a Commission guidance document on art 6 HD.[88] The Court did not go further in argumentation or making decisions since the temporal hunting permits were already overdue.

Securing the access to justice in hunting matters seems especially challenging when it comes to wolves in Finland. The FWA's keeness to employ the discretionary powers it holds has resulted in a peculiar game of cat and mouse – nay, hunter and environmentalist – between environmental non-governmental organisations (eNGOs) and the FWA on wolf hunting permits. In fall 2020, the FWA granted rights to disturb and expel a wolf pack.[89] After the regional eNGO's appeal, the Regional Administrative Court had issued an injunction order against this decision. Thereafter the FWA granted a permit to hunt one wolf, which was also successfully done – one day before the Regional Administrative Court issued an injunction against the permit. This pattern was repeated the next month, with the modest alteration of the hunt taking place on the very same day the injunction order was issued. This turn of events resulted in Parliamentary debate over the status of wolf protection in Finland, which indeed seems to require further attention, on top of the guidance the CJEU has provided thus far.[90] Also this example shows that in rural communities, the cultural shift of accepting wolf protection is not yet complete.[91]

The *Lake Oulu* case on logging at a Natura 2000 site was a matter of administrative enforcement and, again, revolved around the need to conduct a

[88] HD, art 6.

[89] The differences between 'expelling' and 'hunting' have been discussed in case law when a snow mobilist had run over a wolverine multiple times, but the animal had not died. The Court ruled the person had attempted to hunt the animal, not just expel it, District Court of Lapland 6 March 2007 no 07/93 R 07/46; Outi Ratamäki and Matti Tolvanen, 'Metsästys ja Pyynti: Rikosoikeudellinen Tulkinta ja Rikoskonkurrenssi' (2018) 2 *Defensor Legis* 167, 174.

[90] Written enquiry, KK 7/2021 vp. 2 February 2021; reply to the written enquiry KKV 7/2021 vp. 19 February 2021.

[91] Pertti Rannikko, 'Suden Salametsästys ja Vaikenemisen Kulttuuri' (2020) 1 *Oikeus* 74, 89–90; on this shift see Outi Ratamäki, 'From Ecological Concerns Towards Solving Societal Problems? A Case Study of the Development of Finland's Wolf Policy' (2013) 2 *International Journal of Information Systems and Social Change* 42–58.

Natura 2000 assessment.[92] In Finland no preliminary permission is needed for logging, only notification of forest use is required. Thus the only legal mechasism to address logging before it takes place is through the procedure of administrative enforcement.[93] The case was brought by eNGOs. The eNGOs considered that the planned logging necessitated Natura 2000 assessment and would cause forbidden deterioration at the site. The SAC overruled the administrative court's decision and remitted the case back to the administration for it to ban the logging until the assessment was conducted. It even advised the administration that it ought to allow the executor of the logging to present such an assessment. Again the SAC referred to the need of having up-to-date and rigorous scientific grounds for decision-making, and referred to the CJEU case law and the Commission guidance documents.[94] The Court stated that it is 'customary legal practice to have the assessment done, unless one can exclude significant adverse effects on objective grounds'.[95] Besides the location of the logging, its extent, representativity, the proximity of the protected habitat, and the manner in which the logging was to be executed, were all significant here.

Both these cases are examples of the Natura 2000 protection taking place outside of the environmental permitting regime. Either there was no administrative decision that would have banned the logging or an authority with prime focus on maintaining the country's wildlife made the administrative decision. The SAC rulings highlight that the rules originating from the EU apply to these 'anomalies' too: the reasons, including in relation to the factual evaluation, must be explicitly written out, or the matter risks being remitted.

B. Constrained Municipal Appeals: Land Use and Building

Our last batch of cases follow the avenue of municipal appeal, the supposedly more restrictive line of appeal reserved for land use and planning cases. The first of these cases is the *Hailuoto* case, discussing a partial master plan allowing the building of a causeway (raised road) between the continent and the Hailuoto island, a major island at the bottom of the Gulf of Bothnia.[96] The plan was to build a causeway through a highly significant conservation area that had multiple Natura 2000 sites in the vicinity, prospectively endangered by the construction work. The appeals were not successful in the administrative court of Northern Finland or in the SAC.

[92] SAC 2020:3 (KHO 2020:3, ECLI:FI:KHO:2020:3).

[93] Forest Act 1093/1996, s 13, legally non-binding English translation available at www.finlex.fi/fi/laki/kaannokset/1996/en19961093.

[94] The SAC cited Commission notice 'Managing Natura 2000 Sites: The provisions of Article 6 of the "Habitats" Directive 92/43/EEC' (21 November 2018, COM(2018) 7621 final).

[95] SAC 2020:3, Ruling of the SAC, judicial assessment, first paragraph.

[96] SAC 2018:49 (KHO 2018:49 ECLI:FI:KHO:2018:49).

In both instances the matter hinged on the adequacy of the investigation, ie the amount and certainty of scientific evidence. The SAC concluded that given that the alleviation measures moderated the impacts of ice erosion, the land use could be carried out without leading to a significant deterioration in conservation terms. The SAC noted that the impacts on the conservation values would also be considered in the ensuing legal processes, such as permit process according to the Water Act and preliminary and final engineering plans according to the Highways Act.[97] The SAC used the phrase 'adequately ensured in advance', thus linking its system-aware decision-making with the precautionary principle. Of the vast amount of evidence in the matter, the SAC specifically mentioned the Natura 2000 assessment and the Ministry of the Environment's statement.

The *Hailuoto* case exemplifies neatly the deference the SAC espouses in matters which follow the municipal appeal route. Though the case revolved around the adequacy of the factual investigation, the SAC relied heavily on the existing Natura 2000 assessment and also referred to the ensuing legal processes, where the acceptance of the impacts would be double-checked.

The *Viikki* case revolved around the building pressure in the capital region, in a northern Helsinki suburb of Viikki, known for its fields still in agricultural use, and for its proximity to wetland that is both a Natura 2000 and a Ramsar site.[98] The parts of the fields planned for building were immediately next to parts that were especially important resting and foraging areas for birds, justifying the Natura 2000 protection. The City Council had accepted the master plan and the Administrative Court of Helsinki had rejected all appeals. The SAC, however, partially quashed the Council's decision. The SAC argued that the fields and the Natura 2000 site comprised an ecological totality where the adverse effects on the fields – such as decrease of area, scenic enclosure, building disturbance – would be echoed on the protected area during and after the building. The SAC relied on authority from the CJEU, referring to the requirement of updated, rigorous or best scientific grounds. The assessment was not appropriate in identifying the number of birds or the adverse effect to each of the bird species, nor was the impact of different building density factors or variation in the execution accurately assessed. For these reasons the SAC did not consider the Natura 2000 assessment appropriate, or adequately dispersing the scientific doubt of tentative detrimental impacts.

Because the matter was a municipal appeal, the SAC could not remit the case back to the City Council but could only partially annul the decision that allowed for building on the fields. The SAC again argued along the lines of 'not having adequately excluded' the adverse effects. The wording implied the Court had

[97] The Highways Act 503/2005, s 17–26, translation into English available at https://finlex.fi/en/laki/kaannokset/2005/20050503.

[98] That is to say, protected under the United Nations Educational, Scientific and Cultural Organization (UNESCO) Convention on wetlands of international importance especially as waterfowl habitat, 21 December 1975, 996 UNTS 245 (Ramsar Convention/ Wetlands Convention). SAC 2018:151 (KHO 2018:151 ECLI:FI:KHO:2018:151).

done a risk assessment and considered the precautionary principle while doing so (though neither, risk or principle, was explicitly articulated). The SAC referred to the Natura 2000 assessment and the surveillance authority's statement on it. The municipal appeal impacted the choices the SAC had at its disposal but less on its reasoning, which was very similar to the approach to reasoning followed in the administrative appeal avenue.

Our final case is the *Porvoo* case on marine wind power.[99] In regional planning the area had been designated to wind power, though the area was comprised of multiple fly ways of migratory birds of national and international significance, the density of birds was the highest of all Finnish wind power areas, and it was a significant nesting, foraging and resting area. After the Regional Administrative Court had rejected the eNGO's appeals, in the SAC the discussion revolved around the need for a Natura 2000 assessment. The SAC referred to the broadness and lack of specificity of the regional plan: it did not entail details of implementation. The SAC argued that lowering the amounts of wind turbines and centralising them far away from the Natura 2000 site could significantly diminish the impacts. The SAC did not consider an appropriate assessment necessary since the ensuing planning phases would produce closer information on the plan.

The case also demonstrates the preliminary phase of the planning decisions, making the reality of deference and broad scrutiny easier to understand. In two out of three planning cases, the process order between planning and permits was decisive, illustrating the role of the precautionary principle in the legal system as a whole. The different steps of decision-making can secure achievement of the principle's objective, when ensuing permits secure the project is materialised thus that no forbidden detrimental impacts occur. The SAC deliberated uncertainties in most detail in the *Viikki* case where the matter dealt with the most detailed planning instrument, the master plan. There the SAC's argumentation resembled the one used in administrative appeal cases. This ricochets also to the role uncertainties had in the Court's reasoning.

V. Conclusion

The most striking finding of the Finnish Natura 2000 cases discussing scientific uncertainties was the lack of them. Though the country's administrative courts often have scientific and technical expertise at hand, and even more often enjoy the liberty broad and deep scrutiny generates, the uncertainties of the scientific assessment are not common arguments in the court reasoning. As mentioned above, we see this as a legal cultural tendency that may be experiencing a transformation

[99] SAC 2020:53 (KHO 2020:53, ECLI ECLI:FI:KHO:2020:53).

at the time of writing.[100] Also interesting is that review of scientific uncertainty is more or less equally thin – or in-depth – in different case types. Summing up the evidence without closer argumentation on details of the factual questions and aspects has been common. Though the situation has improved and appears to be improving further, the totality of our material (or lack of it) results in this conclusion.

From our perspective of scientific uncertainties, the significance of the difference between two appeal routes should not be overemphasised. The difference is retained, but with our demarcations the difference is not as large as presumed. Does it mean that *jura novit curia* trumps the differences? Though the SAC's arguments as to the legal system's multiple entry points for the precautionary principle is accurate, its reasoning on the factual aspects was not so different in the two routes as we had assumed. In municipal appeal matters, especially in case of the most detailed level of planning, the master plan, the Court's reasoning in the municipal appeal procedure did not differ much from its rulings following the administrative appeal route. Thus the lens through which we analysed our material – scientific uncertainties and principles – did not reveal the reasons of the bifurcated system. Planning matters, following the municipal appeal route, are ones where the community decision-makers balance varying, competing, or even conflicting interests. Reaching that balance is a political act and in Finland *trias politica* has been found to call for judicial deference in such matters.

Also, the two avenues seem to be in a state of flux. For historical reasons, matters of soil extraction were heard originally through the municipal appeal route but were moved to the scope of application of the administrative appeal in 2014 (by combining their process with the EPA).[101] Thus earlier soil excavation was a matter of municipal self-governance, but in later years it transformed into a standard 'environmental' matter.[102] There has been national discussion over the need for the municipal appeal route or whether it ought to be abolished altogether.[103] Though we did not find significant differences in the Court reasoning in the two avenues, it is good to bear in mind that our demarcations most likely hid from the view the most 'political' weighing and balancing of interests, inherent to the municipal appeal matters. This emphasises the fact that the triangle of science and

[100] Recently the SAC has decided on matters where a certain scientific method, modelling, has been central, Paloniitty and Kotamäki (n 58) 14–15, 19–22.

[101] Law on amending the Environmental Protection Act 423/2015, Law on amending the Land Extraction Act 424/2015, Government's proposal 257/2014 (HE 257/2014 vp.). Erkki J Hollo, 'Selvitys Maa-aineslupajärjestelmän Yhdistämisestä Ympäristölupamenettelyyn' (Ympäristöministeriön Raportteja 15, 2010) 31; Ekroos and Warsta (n 28) 33.

[102] The process was gradual, though: the rules of appeal were amended on multiple occasions before 2014 so the final change was not as abrupt as it could have been without the preceding steps.

[103] Ekroos and Warsta (n 28) 33; Teuvo Pohjolainen and Veijo Tarukannel, 'Hallinnon Oikeussuojajärjestelmän Kehittämisen Tarpeesta' (2004) 6 *Defensor Legis* 1113; and Olli Mäenpää 'Hallintoprosessin Uudet Haasteet' (2006) 2 *Lakimies* 143, 159. The Finnish Government of 2015–19 had an unsuccessful plan to abolish the municipal appeal for deregulatory purposes. In that attempt the differences in appeal rights between the two avenues were not compensated, *cf* Vihervuori (n 1) [1352]

its uncertainties, politics and law is alive and well in the Finnish administrative-legal system today.

Perhaps too, our findings reflect a reality where scientific uncertainty considerations are so pivotal in this context that – if wanted – they unify otherwise differing aspects of legal culture. In the cases analysed the courts used their decision-making powers in various ways, combining various legal norms and principles, and sources of expert knowledge when reaching decisions. When discussing scientific uncertainty, this usage of the whole extent of 'the judicial toolbox' is understandable: science and its boundaries are intrinsic to environmental matters, permeating every corner of the field. We are also pondering whether, in cases dealt with expert judges, the presence of in-house scientific expertise enables discussing the tentative uncertainties within the court chamber – and if the discussion leads to no relevant uncertainties found, the final decision does not necessarily require extended elaborations on the question. The court can leave reasoning with uncertainties to matters where it is absolutely necessary and, on the other hand, it is likely it cannot use 'scientific uncertainties' as a general argument in complex matters.[104]

[104] Caranta (n 41).

11

The Intensity of Judicial Review in Environmental Litigation in Greek Law with Special Regard to Habitats Sites

KONSTANTINOS GOGOS

I. Introduction

Greek environmental law, which was firmly established in the 1980s, is very much part of Greek administrative law and clearly follows the dogmas established in that field regarding the judicial review of administrative decisions in general. Thus, Greek law on the intensity of judicial review in environmental disputes is more or less an application of general rules on administrative litigation, which are determined by the jurisprudence of the Greek Supreme Administrative Court (*Συμβούλιο της Επικρατείας*: Council of State, CoS) on the basis of a long-standing tradition linking Greek and French administrative law. After an initial stage of judicial activism in the 1980s and 1990s, rules on the judicial scrutiny of administrative decisions in environmental matters overwhelmingly tend to recognise a prerogative for the administration in technical decisions, such as the assessment of a project's impact on protected sites. That is especially true in cases of scientific uncertainty, where a manifest error in judgement cannot be firmly established. Neither the constitutional right to access to justice, nor respective guarantees of effective judicial protection granted by EU law, the European Convention on Human Rights (ECHR) and the Aarhus Convention have had a significant aspect on this viewpoint of the Greek judiciary, as will be shown below.

II. Implementation of the Birds, Habitats and EIA Directives in Greek Law

The birth of environmental law as a branch of public law in Greece may actually be traced back to the implementation of the Environmental Impact Assessment

(EIA) Directive in 1986.[1] The law instituted a special environmental permit (called 'approval of environmental terms') issued at the outcome of the procedure of EIA.[2] The permit ensures that the project is environmentally acceptable under the conditions specified by the permitting authority. This is an administrative decision that may be attacked with an application for annulment by any interested party and is subject to judicial review by the CoS. The rules set in Law 1650/1986 were thoroughly revised by Law 4014/2011[3] with a focus on a speedier public consultation and administrative procedures.[4] Some minor revisions in the same direction have taken effect with Law 4685/2020.[5] Secondary legislation has classified projects according to environmental impact,[6] provided detailed rules on public consultation procedure[7] and specifications for environmental impact assessment studies.[8] Legislation transposing the EIA Directive is implemented by the authorities that are vested with the power to issue environmental permits, ie the Ministry of Environment and Energy in major projects, and the relevant directorate of the regional Decentralised (state) Administration in smaller ones.[9]

[1] Council Directive 85/337/EEC of 27 June 1985 on the assessment of the effects of certain public and private projects on the environment. [1985] OJ L175/40 – current EIA Directive, Directive 2011/92/EU of the European Parliament and of the Council of 13 December 2011 on the assessment of the effects of certain public and private projects on the environment [2012] OJ L26/1. Law 1650/1986, On the protection of the environment, Official Gazette, Part A 160/16.10.1986. For original language versions of legislation, please see the Table of Legislation.

[2] Konstantinos Gogos, *Die Umweltrechtliche Vorhabengenehmigung in Griechenland* [2015] EurUP, 1 ff.

[3] For full details of the Directives, and original language versions of all legislation, please see the Table of Legislation. Law 4014/2011, Environmental permitting of projects and activities, regulation of illicit buildings in conjunction with the establishment of an environmental equilibrium and other provisions within the ambit of the Ministry of Environment, Official Gazette, Part A 209/21.9.2011.

[4] Konstantinos Gogos, 'The Reformation of Environmental Permitting with Law 4014/2011–Five Years After (in Greek)' [2016] *Efimerida Diikitikou Dikaiou*, 183ff.

[5] Law 4685/2020, Modernization of environmental legislation, incorporation of directives 2018/844 and 2019/692 of the European Parliament and the European Council and other provisions, Official Gazette, Part A 92/7.5.2020.

[6] Ministerial Decision 37674/2016, Modification and codification of ministerial decision 1958/2012 – classification of public and private projects and activities into categories and subcategories according to article 1 paragraph 4 of Law 4014/21.9.2011 (OG 209/A/2011) as modified and in force, Official Gazette, Part B 2471/10.8.2016.

[7] Joint Ministerial Decision 1649/45, Concretization of the procedures for delivering opinions by authorities and of the means of informing the public and participation of the interested public in the public consultation in the course of environmental permitting of projects and activities belonging to category A of the decision by the Minister of Environment, Energy and Climate Change No. 1958/2012 (OG A 21), according to the provisions of Article 19, paragraph 9 of Law 4014/2011 (OG A 209), and of every other relevant detail, Official Gazette, Part B 45/15.1.2014.

[8] Ministerial Decision 170225/2014, Concretization of the contents of environmental permitting dossiers for projects and activities belonging to category A of the decision by the Minister of Environment, Energy and Climate Change No. 1958/2012, as in force, according to Article 11 of Law 4014/2011 (OG A 209), and of every other relevant detail, Official Gazette, Part B 135/27.1.2014.

[9] Arts 3 and 4 of Law 4014/2011, Environmental permitting of projects and activities, regulation of illicit buildings in conjunction with the establishment of an environmental equilibrium and other provisions within the ambit of the Ministry of Environment, Official Gazette, Part A 209/21.9.2011.

The Wild Birds Directive (WBD) has been transposed in Greek law by way of the Joint Ministerial Decision 414985/1985.[10] The Habitats Directive was belatedly implemented by Joint Ministerial Decision 33318/3028/1998,[11] following a Court of Justice of the European Union (CJEU) judgment[12] against Greece because of its failure to transpose the Directive in time. This latter Joint Ministerial Decision was modified in 2008,[13] whereas important additional rules regarding habitat protection sites were enacted through Law 3937/2011.[14] The implementation of the rules of the WBD and HD involves different administrative authorities. The administration of protected sites was previously carried out by specialised local 'Management Bodies' set up by Law 2742/1999[15] as private law entities with jurisdiction for a specific site each; these quasi-administrative bodies were merged in a central 'Organisation for the Natural Environment and Climate Change', set up by Law 4685/2020 (art 17). Authorities that issue said environmental permits implement rules on project permitting (arts 6(3) and 6(4) HD), whereas local authorities of the decentralised state administration enforce rules related to species protection from hunting and illicit activities.

An important aspect of HD sites protection is the special, stricter conditions of permitting for projects that might exert a negative influence on conservation objectives. Environmental litigation usually focuses on these administrative permits and other decisions that enable projects in protected sites and are subject to the scrutiny of administrative courts. The following sections present the framework rules on the intensity of judicial review of administrative decisions in Greek law, focusing on environmental disputes in particular and taking into account relevant constitutional rules, such as the constitutional rights to judicial review and protection of the environment, as well as the principle of separation of powers. In that regard, this chapter examines the potential influence (or lack thereof) on the rules of judicial review in environmental disputes of the rights to effective judicial protection granted to litigants by the ECHR, EU law and the Aarhus Convention. In section IV of this chapter we shall examine in greater detail specific decisions of the Greek Supreme Administrative Court on the intensity of judicial review with regard to projects that may have a negative impact on protected sites, spotlighting three groups of disputes that involve wind farms, major tourist projects and mining. Finally, the chapter comes to concluding remarks that sum up our findings.

[10] Joint Ministerial Decision 414985, Management of Wild Birdlife, Official Gazette, Part B 757.18.12.1985.

[11] Joint Ministerial Decision 33318/3028/1998, Determination of measures and procedures for the conservation of natural habitats and wild flora and fauna, Official Gazette, Part B 1289/18.12.1998.

[12] C-329/96 *Commission v Greece* [1997] ECR I-03749, ECLI:EU:C:1997:333.

[13] Joint Ministerial Decision 14849/853/E 103/04.04.2008, Modification of joint ministerial decisions Nos. 33318/3028/1998 (OG B 1289) and 29459/1510/2005 (OG B 992), in compliance with the provisions of Directive 2006/105 of November 20, 2006 of the Council of the European Union, Official Gazette, Part B 645/11.04.2008.

[14] Law 3937/2011, Conservation of biodiversity and other provisions, Official Gazette, Part A 60/31.3.2011.

[15] Law 2742/1999, Spatial planning and sustainable development and other provisions, Official Gazette, Part A 207/7.10.1999.

III. General Introduction to the Greek Legal System Regarding Review of Administrative Action, Especially with Regard to the Rules on Intensity of Review and on Evidence

A. The System of Judicial Review of Administrative Decisions in Greek Law

Greek law distinguishes between two different types of administrative disputes, depending upon the subject matter: i) 'annulment disputes', in which an administrative decision ('administrative act') may be challenged before administrative courts by way of an application for annulment, in the tradition of the French 'recours pour excès de pouvoir'; and ii) 'substantive disputes', in which the administrative decision is subject to an 'appeal' before administrative courts. The distinction corresponds to different procedural rules and, especially, to different standards of judicial control of the reviewed decision.

In 'annulment disputes' the administrative court refrains from investigating the 'substance' of the case, ie the 'evaluation of facts' by administrative authorities.[16] That means that administrative discretion, which is understood quite broadly, lies beyond the scope of judicial review per se in this type of dispute. The court examines the reasoning of the administrative decision and also applies a version of a manifest error control, with the help of a 'common knowledge' and 'common sense' standard. Moreover, the application of non-specific legal terms, as well as terms that demand administrative judgement on technical or scientific matters, is regarded as a case of administrative discretion, subject to the limited judicial review described above.[17] 'Factual errors' of the administrative authority, ie circumstances where the administration has erred in determining (not in evaluating) the facts of the case, fall under the ambit of judicial review in annulment disputes. However, rules on the production and evaluation of evidence by the court are rather rudimentary. The court will not examine evidence other than the documents included in the administrative dossier or presented by the plaintiff before the hearing of the case, unless the production of further evidence is ordered.[18]

[16] *Πρόδρομος Δαγτόγλου* (Prodromos Dagtoglou), *General Administrative Law* (in Greek), 7th edn (Sakkoulas Publishers, 2015) [342]–[356]; Eugenia Prevedourou, 'The Principle of Legality' (in Greek), in Θεοδώρα Αντωνίου (Theodora Antoniou) (ed), *General Principles of Public Law* (in Greek) (Nomiki Vivliothiki Publishing House, 2016) 182.

[17] Dagtoglou, *ibid*; Ευαγγελία Κουτούπα-Ρεγκάκου (Evangelia Koutoupa-Regkakou), *Vague and Technical Terms in Public Law* (in Greek) (Sakkoulas Publishers, 1997) 39 ff; Prevedourou, *ibid*; and Μιχαήλ Στασινόπουλος (Michail Stassinopoulos), *Law of Administrative Acts* (in Greek) (Self-publication, 1951) 256.

[18] Presidential Decree 18/1989, Codification of law provisions on the Council of State, Official Gazette, Part A 8/9.1.1989, art 33.

In 'appeal' or substantive matters, judicial review is more intensive, at least in theory. The court has the power not only to annul, but also to modify the administrative decision. However, the court may only annul the attacked decision and not substitute itself for the deciding authority, if the latter has refrained from using its discretionary powers.[19] In this type of dispute, the judge is generally entitled to investigate the 'substance' of the case, ie both the determination and evaluation of facts by administrative authorities. This, however, applies to technical assessments by the administration only in exceptional cases.[20] Rules on evidence are much more detailed in substantive disputes, yet the courts are generally disinclined to proceed to a full inquiry into the facts of the case. Evidence is based on the documents produced by the parties before the hearing and only in some cases, usually when dealing with damages lawsuits,[21] will the court order a technical expertise or examine technical or other witnesses.

B. The Constitutional Framework of Judicial Review in Environmental Disputes

The central distinction between 'annulment' and 'substantive' disputes is derived, by the CoS, from art 95(1)a of the Greek Constitution. This provides that the CoS has jurisdiction to annul administrative decisions following an application by an interested party. Thus, the Constitution acknowledges, according to long-standing jurisprudence, the aforementioned type of 'annulment disputes' in juxtaposition to 'substantive disputes'.[22] Jurisdiction for 'annulment disputes' belongs by default, according to the same constitutional provision, to the CoS. However, in specific cases, art 95(3) of the Constitution empowers ordinary law to transfer such cases to the jurisdiction of other administrative courts, if that is justified by the nature and the (lesser) importance of the subject matter. On the other hand, 'substantive' disputes generally belong to the jurisdiction of administrative courts of first instance and administrative courts of appeal. The current interpretation of art 95 of the Greek Constitution by the CoS also accepts that enhanced, 'substantive', judicial review is granted only in subject matters that law has qualified accordingly, whereas all other matters involving judicial review of administrative decisions are presumed to be 'annulment' cases.[23] Thus, it is in principle up to the lawmaker

[19] Greek Code of Administrative Process, ratified by Law 2690/1999, Ratification of the Code of Administrative Process and other Provisions, Official Gazette, Part A 45/9.3.1999, art 79 (3) c.

[20] Κλεοπάτρα Καλλικάκη (Kleopatra Kallikaki), *The Comprehension of Technical Issues through Expertise* (in Greek) (2018) *Diikitiki Diki* 552, 554.

[21] See Χαράλαμπος Χρυσανθάκης (Charalampos Chryssanthakis), *Civil Liability of Public Hospitals* (in Greek), 2nd edn (Nomiki Vivliothiki Publishing House, 2020) 31.

[22] Βασίλειος Σκουρής (Vassilios Skouris), *Administrative Procedural Law I* (in Greek), 2nd edn (Sakkoulas Publishers, 1996) 78 ff.

[23] CoS 189/2007 (plenary); 1216/1998; 5820/1996; 3950/1996; 1095/1987 (plenary).

to decide whether a given type of case is subject to the rules on 'annulment' or 'substantive' review.

The CoS interprets the constitutional principle of separation of powers, enshrined in art 26, para 1 of the Constitution, as setting a limit to the powers of ordinary law to enhance judicial review of administrative decisions. According to this jurisprudence, the principle of separation of powers forbids administrative courts from venturing into the full review of discretionary – in the wider sense – administrative decisions; therefore, administrative powers that essentially amount to discretionary judgements, typically involving special technical or scientific evaluations, may not be qualified as 'substantive' disputes, given that an intense judicial review of such inherently administrative powers is not 'opportune', as the CoS remarks.[24] Such disputes must therefore be subject to judicial review according to the limited, 'annulment', standard. Consequently, the CoS decided that the licence to install antennas for mobile telecommunication networks[25] or the administrative allotment of forest areas to mining use[26] may not be subject to full substantive review. Thus, the provisions of the Greek Constitution have been used by the jurisprudence of the CoS in order to limit, rather than enhance, the intensity of judicial review of administrative decisions, even in environmental matters. This follows a long tradition of judicial self-restraint vis-à-vis administrative discretion.

In view of these rules, environmental permitting cases are traditional 'annulment disputes', belonging to the jurisdiction of the CoS.[27] The environmental permit is subject to an application for annulment before the CoS and, thus, to judicial review according to the limited standard. Administrative decisions in areas of scientific uncertainty are not exempt from this dogma of limited review according to the rules of 'annulment disputes'. However, administrative fines imposed on environmental offenders give rise to 'substantive' disputes according to law[28] and are therefore open to (somewhat) closer judicial scrutiny.

It should be noted that the Greek Constitution provides guarantees that might offer opportunities to support a more intensive control of administrative decisions in matters of environmental permitting. Article 24 (1) of the Constitution grants a legal right to the protection of the environment, which includes the right of individuals to demand state action, both of a legislative and an executive nature, aimed at preventing environmental harm. Thus, the general principle of prevention of

[24] CoS 3919/2010 (plenary); 979/2012; 616-9/2013 (plenary); and 3080/2017.

[25] CoS 1015/2018.

[26] CoS 913/2017; 3115/2015.

[27] Νικόλαος Νικολάκης (Nikolaos Nikolakis), 'The Understanding of Processual Issues in Environmental Disputes: The Contribution of Konstantinos Menoudakos to the Shaping of the Jurispudence of the Fifth Chamber of the Council of State' (in Greek) in Elliniki Etaireia Dikaiou Perivallontos (ed), *The Judge, the Law and the Environment* (in Greek) (Sakkoulas Publishers, 2016) 286 ff.

[28] Law 1650/1986, On the protection of the environment, Official Gazette, Part A 160/16.10.1986, art 30(3).

environmental damages is constitutionally enshrined in Greek law.[29] Moreover, the same constitutional provision dictates that state policies having an impact on the environment are bound by the principle of sustainable development. The jurisprudence of the CoS has indeed developed many different facets and various applications of the constitutional right to environmental protection and the principle of sustainability in substantive environmental law.[30] However, the impact of this constitutional provision on environmental litigation is less pronounced. Thus, a wide interpretation of rules on legal standing in environmental disputes has been the main impact of the constitutional protection of the environment.[31] In matters of intensity of judicial control, however, the Supreme Administrative Court has refrained from drawing inspiration from the constitutional right to environmental protection. As will be explained in the following section, constant jurisprudence of the CoS since the year 2000 puts the emphasis on the limitations of judicial review of administrative projections and technical judgements that are associated with EIAs and environmental permitting.[32]

The Greek Constitution also includes, in art 20(1), an individual right to judicial protection of substantive rights and legal interests that encompasses the judicial review of administrative decisions. This guarantee is in many regards similar to the right to judicial protection granted by the German *Grundgesetz* in art 19 IV. The jurisprudence of the CoS on the constitutional right to judicial protection, as well as on art 6(1) ECHR, while accepting that effective individual protection is necessary, has not sought to enhance the intensity of control of administrative action in annulment disputes. The Court has repeatedly stressed that the judicial review normally granted in annulment cases fully satisfies the constitutional and ECHR standards, as it encompasses the full legal review of administrative reasoning, including the examination of eventual administrative errors of fact.[33] Thus, jurisprudence on the constitutional guarantee of effective judicial protection does not question the established doctrine as to the restricted control of administrative discretion and technical assessments in environmental matters.

[29] Ευαγγελία Κουτούπα-Ρεγκάκου (Evangelia Koutoupa-Regkakou), *Environmental Law* (in Greek), 3rd edn (Sakkoulas Publishers, 2008) 46; Γλυκερία Σιούτη (Glykeria Siouti), *Handbook of Environmental Law* (in Greek), 2nd edn (Sakkoulas Publishers, 2011) 52; Κωνσταντίνος Γώγος (Konstantinos Gogos), 'The Principle of Ecological State' (in Greek) in Θεοδώρα Αντωνίου (Theodora Antoniou) (ed), *General Principles of Public Law* (in Greek) (Nomiki Vivliothiki Publishing House, 2016) 251.

[30] Eg in spatial planning and urban development, water resources, energy law, etc. See Gogos (n 29) 249 ff.

[31] Glykeria Siouti and (George Gerapetritis), 'National Report: Greece' in Jonas Ebesson (ed), *Access to Justice in Environmental Matters in the EU* (Kluwer, 2002) 268; Koutoupa-Rengakou (n 29) 135; Βαρβάρα Μπουκουβάλα (Barbara Boukouvala), 'The Judicial Review of Constitutionality of Law in Environmental Disputes in Administrative Litigation' (in Greek) (2020) *Perivallon Kai Dikaio* 179; Δημήτρης Μέλισσας (Dimitris Melissas), *Legal Standing and Time Limits in Environmental Disputes* (in Greek) (Sakkoulas Publishers, 2007) 7; nuanced Nikolakis (n 27) 284.

[32] Leading cases CoS 3478/2000 (plenary); 613/2002 (plenary).

[33] CoS 189/2007 (plenary); 212/2013.

C. The Intensity of Judicial Review in Environmental Disputes in Particular

The current dogma on the restricted intensity of judicial review of administrative assessments of scientific and/or technical nature in environmental matters, firmly established in the year 2000,[34] in the well-known case of the re-routing of the Acheloos river in western Greece, has been steadily repeated in CoS decisions ever since. Relevant issues usually arise in disputes over the legality of environmental permits, issued at the outcome of an EIA procedure. The CoS routinely rules that the Court shall,

> [E]xamine whether the environmental impact assessment study, which is the main means of application of the principles of prevention and precaution, satisfies the legal criteria and whether its contents adequately support the administrative assessment of the environmental impact and dangers arising out of the examined project.[35]

However, the administrative court

> [M]ay not proceed to the direct appraisal of the environmental impact of the project or to a judgement as to whether the principle of sustainability and the other substantive legal principles of environmental protection enshrined by legislation, the Greek Constitution and the provisions of the TFEU have been infringed.[36]

That is because, according to said jurisprudence, 'such appraisals demand the examination of facts, the investigation of technical matters and substantive considerations and evaluations, which lie beyond the scope of judicial review'.[37] Thus, an infringement of the principle of sustainability is only subject to judicial review, if the Court concludes on the basis of the administrative dossier that the project, as is 'plainly evident', causes an irreparable harm to the environment, having such magnitude and consequences that it manifestly breaches said constitutional principle.[38] The essence of this jurisprudence is that administrative courts will control formal or procedural legal requirements of the law relating to EIA and will also examine whether administrative decisions on scientific and technical matters are reasoned adequately and convincingly. The Court will not, however, examine the validity of forecasts on the impact to natural media and other scientific or factual assessments by the administration, restricting itself to a manifest error test.

[34] CoS 3478/2000 (plenary).

[35] CoS 1020/2020; 1761/2019 (plenary); 1305/2019; 1455/2018; 26/2014 (plenary); 2173/2002.

[36] *ibid.*

[37] *ibid.*

[38] On that subject see Βασιλική Καραγεώργου (Vassiliki Karageorgou), 'The Scope of Review in Environmental-Related Cases in the Light of Aarhus Convention and EU-Law' in Jerzy Jendrośka and Magdalena Bar (eds), *Procedural Environmental Rights: Principle X in Theory and Practice* (Intersentia, 2017) 247 ff; Ανδρέας Παπαπετρόπουλος (Andreas Papapetropoulos), *The General Principles of Judicial Review with Respect to the Procedure of Environmental Impact Assessment* (in Greek) (Sakkoulas Publishers, 2003) *passim*.

It has been repeatedly argued in Greek theory that the judicial review of reasoning of administrative decisions in environmental matters, supplemented by a manifest error control of the 'core' of administrative discretion, provides a scrutiny of environmental permitting that is sufficiently thorough and, therefore, well-justified both from a rule-of-law and an environmental point of view.[39] This type of judicial review of administrative discretion is indeed common in legal systems following the French tradition,[40] including the CJEU. The CJEU distinguishes between the 'standard' judicial control of legality of EU acts in actions of annulment according to art 263 of the Treaty on the Functioning of the European Union (TFEU), that basically involves a review of reasoning of discretionary decisions and a manifest error test,[41] and the full judicial scrutiny of administrative discretion ('pleine jurisdiction'), applicable when it is required by a specific provision, as is the case regarding fines by the Commission in competition law cases.[42]

The described model of restricted judicial control of administrative discretion has been sanctioned by the European Court of Human Rights in a number of cases. Even though art 6(1) ECHR demands a judicial review with regard to both law and facts of the case, the Strasbourg Court points out that this provision does not require the courts of the Member States to substitute their own judgment to that of the deciding administrative authority.[43] Furthermore, art 47 of the European Charter of Fundamental Rights incorporates in EU law the same standard of judicial protection granted by art 6(1) ECHR.[44] In this spirit, the CJEU has not cast any doubt on the compatibility, with the right of art 47 of the Charter, of 'legality review' of administrative discretion, as it applies in annulment actions according to art 263 TFEU.[45]

Article 11 of the EIA Directive requires judicial review of the substantive legality of the permitting decision and the CJEU has repeatedly stated that Member States are not allowed to restrict the grounds of annulment that may be raised

[39] Ευαγγελία Κουτούπα-Ρεγκάκου (Evangelia Koutoupa-Rengakou), 'The Contribution of Konstantinos Menoudakos to the Jurisprudence of the Council of State on the Environmental Impact Assessment' (in Greek) in Elliniki Etaireia Dikaiou Perivallontos (ed), *The Judge, the Law and the Environment* (in Greek) (Sakkoulas Publishers, 2016) 69; Boukouvala (n 31) 187.

[40] Astrid Epiney, 'Verwaltungsgerichtlicher Rechtsschutz im Umweltrecht im Rechtsvergleich' (2014) *Neue Zeitschrift für Verwaltungsrecht* 471 ff.; Thomas von Danwitz, *Europäisches Verwaltungsrecht* (Springer Berlin, 2008) 589–90. Also Karageorgou (n 38) 238 ff and 245 ff.

[41] C-160/19 *Comune di Milano v Commission*, ECLI:EU:C:2020:1012 [100]–[102]; C-244/18 *Larco v Commission*, ECLI:EU:C:2020:238 [38]–[39]; AG Kokott, Opinion in C-160/19, ECLI:EU:C:2020:591 [79]; von Danwitz, *ibid*590; Martin Burgi, in Hans-Werner Rengeling et al (ed), *Handbuch des Rechtsschutzes in der EU* (CH Beck, 2003) [105] at 143.

[42] C-199/11 *Europese Gemeenschap v Otis* NV ECLI:EU:C:2012:684 [62].

[43] Cases 55391/13, 57728/13, 74041/13 *Ramos Nuñes de Carvalho et Sa v Portugal* (6.11.2018) [178]; Cases 32181/04 and 35122/05 *Sigma Television v Cyprus* (21.7.2011) [153] and [160].

[44] *Europese Gemeenschap v Otis NV* (n 42) [47]; C-386/10 *Chalkor v Commission* [2011] ECR I-13085, ECLI:EU:C:2011:815 [51].

[45] A statement affirming compatibility with art 47 of the Charter can be found in C-295/12 *Telefónica v Commission* ECLI:EU:C:2014:2062 [57]; see also *Europese Gemeenschap v Otis NV* (n 42) [56]; *Chalkor v Commission*, *ibid* [67].

by plaintiffs against such a permit.[46] However, the CJEU has never ruled that a limited judicial review of technical judgements in environmental disputes, similar to the one practiced by itself according to art 263 TFEU, generally falls short of the required standard. On the contrary, in the *East Sussex County Council* case it was decided that a restricted review of factual issues may be compatible with EU law, if the national court, deciding upon an application of annulment against an administrative decision, is able to apply effectively the relevant provisions of substantive EU law.[47] Finally, up to now the Aarhus Convention Compliance Committee has not initiated a procedure against Greece alleging a breach either of art 9(3) or 9(4) Aarhus Convention in this respect.

In this context, it has been pointed out that the doctrine of limited judicial review of technical judgements and forecasts by permitting authorities in environmental matters would be in line with required standards of judicial protection in EU environmental law, if the deciding court were able to order the necessary means of proof, in order to independently ascertain the factual parameters of such technical decisions.[48] As environmental disputes are generally 'annulment' matters, the judicial control of the factual part of the case in Greek law is limited to the question whether the administration was 'in error' as to the determination of the facts of the dispute. The main source of evidence to be evaluated by the Court is the so-called 'administrative dossier', ie the documents and other evidence collected by the competent authority during the administrative procedure for issuing the decision under review. The litigant authority is required by law[49] to produce the dossier, alongside its opinion on the grounds of annulment put forward by the plaintiff. If the authority fails to comply, the Court will issue an order, commanding the respondent authority to produce the dossier, and in case of repeated failure it will accept the plaintiffs' factual allegations as proven.[50] The plaintiff, on the other hand, is also required to produce evidence to substantiate the grounds of annulment.[51] Such evidence may only be submitted in written form and prior to the court hearing of the case: belated evidence is inadmissible.[52] The Court has the legal power to order independent expertise on a technical issue in annulment disputes, provided that the expertise refers to the determination of the facts of the case and not to their technical evaluation by authorities.[53] In practice,

[46] C-115/09 *Bund für Umwelt und Naturschutz Deutschland, Landesverband Nordrhein-Westfalen eV v Bezirksregierung Arnsberg* [2011] ECR I-03673, ECLI:EU:C:2011:289 [37]; C-72/12 *Gemeinde Altrip and Others v Land Rheinland-Pfalz* ECLI:EU:C:2013:712 [36].

[47] C-71/14 *East Sussex County Council v Information Commissioner* ECLI:EU:C:2015:656 [58].

[48] Karageorgou (n 38) 248 et seq.

[49] Presidential Decree 18/1989, Codification of law provisions on the Council of State, Official Gazette, Part A 8/9.1.1989, art 23.

[50] CoS 1692/1999; 496/1993.

[51] See Βασίλειος Σκουρής (Vassilios Skouris), *The Burden of Proof in Administrative Trials* (in Greek) (Sakkoulas Publishers, 1981) 52 et seq.

[52] Cos 3035/2007; 3035/2007; 696/2004, 2153/2003; 2274/2000 (plenary).

[53] Kallikaki (n 20) 555.

such expertise is hardly ever ordered by the CoS however.[54] That is because factual evaluations and technical assessments are considered the prerogative of the administration and the Court will certainly avoid entering such territory, much like the CJEU does.

IV. Case Law on Scientific Uncertainty in the Fields of Habitats, Birds and EIA Directives

Approximately 21 per cent of the Greek land mass and a considerable part of Greek territorial waters have been classified[55] as protected areas ('Sites of Community Importance') under EU Directive 92/43;[56] a large part of them are 'Special Protection Areas' under the WBD. This means, practically, that most so-called green-field projects – developments taking place in previously undeveloped sites – in Greece are planned in the vicinity or even within protected areas of the WBD and HD. Issues regarding the environmental impact of a project on protected habitats and species arise therefore in many disputes on the legality of environmental permits tried before the CoS. The mere fact that a project is located within a protected site does not rule out environmental permitting, which may be granted depending upon the outcome of an impact assessment on the site's conservation objectives, according to the rules in arts 6(3) and 6(4) HD.[57] It should be noted that environmental permits for projects in or near protected sites are granted in Greece always according to the basic scenario of art 6(3) HD, ie when the EIA indicates that the project will not adversely affect the integrity of the site. It seems that the administration is unwilling to apply the extraordinary conditions set in art 6(4) HD that call for imperative reasons of overriding public interest advocating for the project in case the impact assessment on protected species and sites has had a negative outcome.

There has been a significant quantity of Greek case law on the environmental impact of projects to protected sites and species over the last 20 years. The following narrative focuses on three types of disputed projects that have appeared particularly frequently in the jurisprudence of the CoS: (a) wind parks and other renewable energy projects; (b) major tourist developments; and (c) mining operations.

[54] In the last 30 years the CoS seems to have ordered a technical expertise only in a handful of cases in the 1990s. See CoS 1178/1994, 5267/1995 and 6074/1996 (in the same case), 5220/1997, 190/1998, 867/1998.

[55] Decision 2006/613/EC.

[56] Council Directive 92/43/EEC of 21 May 1992 on the conservation of natural habitats and of wild fauna and flora. [1992] OJ L206/7. Κωνσταντίνος Γώγος (Konstantinos Gogos), *The Environmental Permit for Projects in Natura-2000 Areas – the Rules of Article 6 of Directive 92/43* (in Greek) (Sakkoulas Publishers, 2009) 33.

[57] See CoS 1990/2007 and CoS 1492/2013 (for mining operations), CoS 2038/2019; 1704-5/2017 (on tourist projects).

A. Judicial Review of the Environmental Impact of Wind Parks

In 2008 a nation-wide spatial plan on the development of renewable energy in Greece was enacted.[58] With regard to wind parks, the country was divided up into three regions with varying degrees of density of wind parks to be installed. Parts of the country, eg the eastern mountainous region of Thrace, were classified as a 'priority area' for the development of wind power, due to their high wind potential. Thus, the said spatial plan allowed a high density of wind turbines in such regions, even in sites protected by the WBD as habitats of rare and, in some instances, endangered avian species. The spatial plan provided that wind parks could be permitted in Special Protection Areas subject to a special ornithological study of their impact on the integrity of the site and the protected avian species. Applications for annulment were filed against the spatial plan for renewable energy before the CoS, which, however, ruled in 2013 that the plan was legal and constitutional, as the conformity of installation of wind parks in protected sites with the WBD and HD was to be examined at the later stage of the EIA of each specific project, taking into account the impact of the project on the avian fauna according to the ornithological study to be submitted.[59]

In the wake of this jurisprudence, a great number of court trials ensued, in which the CoS was asked to review the – frequently rather optimistic – estimates of EIA studies on the repercussions of dense wind turbine installations planned in – or directly adjacent to – protected sites upon small and scattered populations of rare avian species (especially predator and scavenger species). Plaintiffs, such as the World Wide Fund for Nature (WWF) and the Greek Ornithological Society, argued that the installation of wind turbines on practically every ridge of the affected areas would act as an impenetrable barrier for avian species, thus greatly enhancing death rates and drastically reducing prospects of survival.[60] Moreover, field observations and other research activities conducted in the framework of ornithological studies submitted by the project owners were criticised as insufficient or methodologically tainted and their results were regarded as untrustworthy by the plaintiffs.

In an early case, the Minister of Environment annulled an environmental permit issued by the regional authorities for a wind park in Thrace in the vicinity of the Dadia National Park (a protected site), as the EIA submitted by the project owner was found to have neglected the cumulative impact of the wind park under review with other, already installed or permitted, wind parks. Furthermore, the

[58] Decision of the Committee for the Coordination of Government Policy in Spatial Planning and Sustainable Development 49828/2008, Approval of the special framework of spatial planning and sustainable development for renewable energy sources and of its strategic environmental impact assessment, Official Journal, part B 2464/3.12.2008.

[59] CoS 1421-2/2013. See also CoS 1358/2018; 47/2018.

[60] See CoS 2306/2016, 2138/2018.

Minister pointed to the negative opinion of the affected National Park Authority and ruled that the special ecological evaluation was not conducted according to appropriate standards as it did not entail a full year's observations on the avian fauna of the affected area. The CoS rejected the application for annulment submitted by the project developer against this decision, ruling that the ministerial decision was duly reasoned.[61]

In most of the following cases, however, in which environmental organisations and/or concerned private individuals applied to the CoS for the annulment of environmental permits for wind parks, be it in Thrace or in other areas of Greece with similar characteristics of environmental vulnerability (such as Euboea, Crete, Andros and other Aegean islands), the CoS accepted the findings and estimates of impact assessments regarding protected and endangered species of avian fauna. The question as to the scientific uncertainty of the impact assessment is not expressly addressed in this jurisprudence. The Court merely examines whether the environmental study submitted by the project owner has concrete answers to the issues raised by the plaintiffs. These court decisions essentially investigate the purely legal question, whether the attacked environmental permit is duly reasoned. If such reasoning is found, the Court will not probe the scientific credibility of the methods and conclusions of the environmental study, as such questions are regarded as belonging to administrative prerogative and thus not subject to judicial review.

The leading case concerned a number of wind parks to be installed within a site protected by both the WBD and HD in Euboea.[62] The CoS reiterated the rule that, as a matter of principle, the inclusion of such protected sites in a 'Priority Area' for the development of wind power by the relevant spatial plan does not infringe upon national or EU law, given that the compatibility with habitat protection requirements will be examined on the basis of impact studies at the environmental permitting stage. In the substance of the case, all allegations against the quality and scientific methodology of field research and the validity of the ornithological impact assessment and its findings were found to be both unsubstantiated and inadmissible. The Court ruled that it does not have jurisdiction to decide upon technical questions and evaluations, which belong to the prerogative of permitting authorities. Moreover, evidence referring to such issues may not be produced for the first time at court, but must be presented to the administration to be evaluated before the challenged decision. Thus, a scientific report on the negative effects of wind turbines on the avian populations of the area, submitted by the plaintiffs, was declared as inadmissible, as it was authored after the issuance of the environmental permit and was not presented to the administrative authorities during the public consultation procedure.

In subsequent cases on the environmental permitting of wind parks, when the plaintiff raised doubts as to the quality of the field investigation and the validity

[61] CoS 2306/2016.
[62] CoS 47/2018.

of the outcome of the environmental impact assessment with regard to the avian fauna, the CoS examined whether the impact assessment report included sufficient answers to the raised questions. The Court tended to reject the plaintiffs' claims either as not adequately substantiated,[63] or as inadmissible, the latter when specific scientific arguments were raised by the plaintiffs, as such scientific argumentation would challenge the administrative decision on a purely technical issue that would fall outside the scope of judicial review.[64] Inadmissibility is pronounced not only when said issues have not been raised in the public consultation procedure,[65] but even when the plaintiffs submitted these objections to the permitting authority prior to the challenged decision.[66] Similarly, objections pointing to alternative, more environmentally suitable construction sites are rejected as inadmissible if they have not been submitted to the permitting authority during public consultation.[67]

On the other hand, in a case concerning the construction of a wind park in an area belonging to the Important Bird Areas (IBA) catalogue in south-eastern Peloponnese, the Court annulled the environmental permit, as it was established that the submitted ornithological study was only based on a relevant bibliography and that no actual field observations and research had taken place.[68] It should be noted that the applicable law provides that field research is usually a necessary part of an ornithological assessment. Thus, easily verifiable methodological defects are viewed as legal issues subject to judicial review.

In a group of recent cases, ecological groups and the highly reputable Greek Ornithological Society applied to the CoS for the annulment of environmental permits of wind parks close to a site protected by the WBD on the Aegean island of Andros. In the first case, a special ornithological study was not conducted by the project owner. However, the environmental impact assessment came to the conclusion that the project would not be harmful to the species of avian fauna in the directly adjacent protected site. The CoS ruled that a special ornithological study was not required in this case, as the project was not planned within a protected site, nor in a site of the IBA catalogue. Moreover, an ornithological study documenting the grave impact of the project on protected avian species, submitted to the Court by the plaintiffs, was deemed as inadmissible evidence, given that the study was conducted after the issuing of the environmental permit and contained scientific data and allegations that were not submitted to the permitting authority in the course of the public consultation procedure.[69] It is clear that the Court does not wish to examine first-hand scientific issues, regardless of the quality of

[63] CoS 2138/2018; 964/2018.
[64] CoS 2138/2018.
[65] CoS 741/2019; 2745/2018; 1358/2018.
[66] See CoS 2138/2018.
[67] CoS 1973/2017.
[68] CoS 1938/2019.
[69] CoS 1403/2019.

evidence produced before it, but restricts its jurisdiction to a moderate control of the reasoning of decisions issued by the permitting authorities.

In other cases of the same group, also concerning wind parks in Andros, the plaintiffs raised doubts as to the scientific validity of the conclusions of the ecological assessment, namely that the permitted wind parks would not endanger a rare local species of eagle. The CoS rejected such arguments, pointing out that even in the ornithological study that was presented by the plaintiffs to the authorities, before the permitting of the project, a general prohibition of wind parks in Andros was not requested. Moreover, the EIA of the project was found by the Court to be duly reasoned. This is somewhat surprising, given that it was initially estimated that the avian species in question was merely transient in the area, whereas later observations submitted by the project owner discovered a nest within 600 meters of the wind turbines. The CoS came to this conclusion because of the small number of turbines to be installed and the fact that the eagle in question was not listed among the conservation objectives of the particular site of Special Protection neighbouring the project.[70]

An interesting question was raised as to the effectiveness of special protective mechanisms to be installed on wind turbines in the Thrace area. Such mechanisms would ensure the avoidance of bird collisions by stopping the rotor, if motion were to be detected nearby. The CoS rejected doubts as to the effectiveness of the method raised by the plaintiff, ruling that such mechanisms, as a matter of common knowledge, prevent collisions with birds, the relevant technical judgement of the permitting authority not being subject to judicial review. Moreover, the Court found contradictions in the evidence produced by the plaintiff and considered as more credible the positive experiences of the permitting authorities with installed mechanisms in other parts of Greece.[71]

B. Review of Planning Decisions Regarding Major Tourist Projects

Large-scale tourist development, usually located in coastal regions, has enjoyed considerable state support in the last 15 years, especially in the form of modern legislation providing new, specialised, spatial planning instruments that make such major projects feasible[72] (which usually combine five-star hotels, residential

[70] CoS 2418-9/2019.

[71] CoS 2138/2018.

[72] Law 4179/2013, Simplification of procedures for the support of tourist entrepreneurship, restructuring of the Greek Tourism Organization and other provisions, Official Gazette, Part A 175/8.8.2013, art 1. On these novel planning instruments for large tourist projects, see Γεωργία Γιαννακούρου (Georgia Giannakourou), *Spatial and Town Planning Law* (in Greek) (Nomiki Vivliothiki Publishing House, 2019) 131–41; and Δημήτρης Μέλισσας (Dimitris Melissas), *The Local Spatial Plan and the Specialised Spatial Plan* (in Greek) (Sakkoulas Publishers, 2019) 309–38.

areas, spa facilities and shopping malls),[73] situated in many cases in privatised government real estate.[74]

In a number of cases, the CoS examined the strategic EIAs of ad-hoc spatial plans issued for large-scale tourist developments. Such is the case of the 'Itanos Gaia' project in Crete, which is planned inside a Site of Community Importance, also classified as a Special Protection Area according to the WBD, and in the immediate vicinity of a number of other protected sites. The Court dismissed the plaintiffs' arguments that the relevant strategic impact assessment did not fulfil the standards of scientific credibility demanded by art 6(3) HD. It was ruled that the submitted environmental study had adequately investigated the impact of the project to all protected sites, both immediately affected by the development and neighbouring it.[75]

A benchmark case concerns a major tourist project ('Kassiopeia Development') situated on the island of Corfu, in privatised state property adjacent to a wetland, which is not protected under the HD nor under the WBD. However, the location of the project has a seafront area facing underwater meadows of the sea-grass species '*posidonia oceanica*', which enjoy priority protection under the HD. In the first related trial,[76] the CoS was asked to review the strategic EIA of the spatial plan specifically enacted for the project. The plaintiffs argued that the neighbouring wetlands were of vital importance for the survival of the endangered species *lutra lutra* (otter) in Corfu, enjoying priority protection under the HD. The Court ruled that the environmental study in question included sufficient documentation and research on otter presence on the island that established that otters merely visited and did not reside in the affected wetlands. Moreover, the impact assessment provided adequate measures for otter protection, especially the prohibition of any development near the wetlands and the isolation of this vulnerable area from the main tourist facilities. With regard to the sea-grass meadows, the plaintiffs argued that the sporting facilities for yachts, which were a planning option according to the spatial plan under scrutiny, as well as the expected clearing of nearby beaches to follow, would seriously harm the protected sea-grass species.

[73] On environmental law problems of so-called 'composite tourist tenements', see Κωνσταντίνος Γώγος (Konstantinos Gogos), 'Composite Tourist Tenements in Forests – Inspired by Council of State Reports 534/2017 and 53/2018' (in Greek) (2020) *Perivallon kai Dikaio* 1 et seq; Νικόλαος Ρόζος (Nikolaos Rozos), 'The Non-Recognition of Certain Townships as Townships: Observations on CoS 234/2017 and 53/2018' (plenary) (in Greek) (March 2019), available at www.nomosphysis.org.gr/category/keimena; Κώστας Σταματίου (Kostas Stamatiou), 'Composite Tourist Tenements as an Instrument of Regulation and Organisation of Tourist Accomodation' (in Greek) (2018) *Perivallon kai Dikaio* 577 ff.

[74] See Law 3986/2011, Urgent measures of application of the mid-term framework of fiscal strategy 2012–2015, Official Gazette, Part A 152/17.1.2011, art 11 et seq. On tourist developments on privatised state property, see Ανδρέας Παπαπετρόπουλος (Andreas Papapetropoulos), 'Spatial Planning in the Islands: The Case of the Spatial Plan of "Afantou" in Rhodes' (in Greek) (2018) *Perivallon kai Dikaio* 570 ff.

[75] CoS (plenary) 1704-5/2017.

[76] CoS (plenary) 3874/2014.

The Court observed that the nearby sea-grass meadows were not included in the protected sites listing under the HD, nor had they been placed under protection according to Greek environmental law. The Court found that the strategic EIA adequately investigated the impact of planned port facilities on the adjacent sea-grass meadows and thus fulfilled the environmental standards of the EIA Directive, given that a detailed impact assessment was not requested at the strategic phase, but would take place at the later stage of eventual environmental permitting of the port facilities. The Court reached this conclusion, even though it acknowledged that the impact assessment study clearly indicated the harmful impact of the port to the aquatic species in question, which was offset, according to the impact assessment, by the avoidance of damages caused to sea-grass by the random anchoring of private yachts that was taking place until then.

In the second Kassiopeia case, the Regional Authority for the Ionian Islands filed with the CoS an application for judicial review against the environmental permit of a specific tourist development project ('tourist village'), including yachting port facilities, that was permitted in Corfu on the basis of the aforementioned spatial plan. The plaintiff claimed that intense human activity (wastewater treatment, desalination and power grid facilities) planned in the vicinity of the nearby wetlands would harm both otter and migratory bird populations that use the wetlands in conjunction with other lakes and water streams of the island as a passage and would lead to the extinction of said species in Corfu. The Court[77] reiterated its findings in the previous Kassiopeia decision regarding the presence of otters on the island and ruled that the EIA of the project contained a satisfactory appraisal of otter presence in Corfu and provided for adequate safeguards. Thus, the plaintiffs' claims that the tourist development would lead to otter extinction in Corfu were held to be unproven. The same ruling was made on the alleged danger of extinction of migratory birds, given that initial plans for activities and construction near the wetlands were abandoned in the meantime and the wetland area would remain intact. As to the yachting port facilities, the Court observed that the affected area of sea-grass meadows was not listed among the protected sites of the HD. Moreover, the Court held that the permitting decision was duly reasoned in finding that eventual damages on the area of sea-grass expected to be used by the port facilities (11,500 square meters) would not adversely affect the ecological integrity of the sea-grass ecosystem, given that said meadows cover a much wider area and that the site chosen was the one with the least impact upon the integrity of the species habitat.

In a more recent CoS decision,[78] the Court examined the EIA for a golf course with adjacent five-star hotel at Ermionida (Peloponnese). The plaintiffs argued that the project, given the lack of water resources in the project area, would endanger both the supply of drinking water to human settlements and agricultural irrigation in the region. The CoS ruled that the EIA and a special hydrological

[77] CoS 1390/2017.
[78] CoS 657/2019.

study submitted by the owner investigated both the existing water resources and the project's needs in detail and demonstrated that these needs could be satisfied through alternative means, especially through the recycling of used water and a desalination plant, without significant repercussions for the environmental media, surface waters and underground water reservoirs, neither in terms of quantity nor quality. Therefore, the plaintiffs' allegations were judged to be unfounded. Further scrutiny of technical evaluations by the permitting authority would lie outside the scope of the Court's jurisdiction.

C. Jurisprudence on the Environmental Impact of Mining Activities

Mining is an important economic activity in Greece, providing major economic and social benefits to the country; eg aluminium production corresponds to 2.3 per cent of the gross domestic product and 10.6% of total industrial exports.[79] It is an activity with a potentially significant environmental footprint, if not environmentally managed properly, and the jurisprudence of the CoS has had to strike a delicate balancing act between the needs of environmental protection and the benefits of mining for the public interest.

The leading case[80] concerned the expansion of bauxite mining in new terrains on mount Gkiona, in central Greece. The environmental permit that was challenged before the CoS authorised mining in new forest areas protected by both the HD and WBD, some of them hosting priority species and habitats. The Court reiterated the rule that mining in protected areas was not generally forbidden by the HD, but was subject to a special assessment as to the impact of the project on the protected habitats and species. Thus, mining activities could be environmentally permitted in Sites of Community Importance, if it were established that the project would not affect the integrity of the protected site. With regard to the specific project in question, the Court ruled that the environmental impact assessment included sufficient data on the expected impact to protected species and habitats and provided adequate safeguards for the integrity of protected sites in most new mining areas, prohibiting mining in certain sites of priority protection. However, the Court annulled the environmental permit with regard to mining in specific sites. Thus, the continuation of underground mining in a Special Protection Area was found to be illegal, since the environmental permit did not provide adequate measures for the protection of sensitive avian fauna. The same was ruled for surface mining in another Special Protection Area. Finally, the continuation of surface mining in certain areas of priority protection, which was allowed by the permitting authority for the reason that the disturbance of the surface area was already

[79] 2017 data; source: http://iobe.gr/docs/research/RES_05_F_27032019_REP_GR.pdf.
[80] CoS 1990/2007; see also CoS 2059/2007 on the same mining project.

almost completed, was annulled by the Court, as the environmental permit did not ensure the restoration of the site in the post-mining era with the same protected flora species that were being removed.

In another interesting decision,[81] the CoS was called upon to decide on the renewal of the environmental permit of a bentonite mine in the Aegean island of Kimolos. The mine is located approximately 400 meters from a protected habitats site that includes the small island of Prassonisi, which is additionally protected as an 'area of exceptional natural beauty' under Greek law. The plaintiffs argued that the mine was illegally occupying adjacent land strips and that it was not respecting the terms of the previous environmental permit, which provided for a zone clear of mining activities surrounding the mine. Moreover, it was alleged that waste materials from the mine were illegally deposited outside the mining area. The plaintiffs substantiated their claims with a series of technical reports and experts' opinions and argued that the piles of deposited mining waste in question could be seen from Prassonisi island, spoiling the natural landscape. The Court observed that such evidence had to be presented to the permitting public authorities first; nevertheless, the Court evaluated these reports and found them not credible, since the photographic material presented by the plaintiffs did not substantiate the claim that the mine was indeed to be seen from Prassonissi, as photographs taken from the island showed a general view of Kimolos without indication of the contours of the mine in question. Moreover, the experts' opinions as to illegal waste deposits outside the mining area were discredited by a previous state authority report to the contrary, presented to the Court by the mine owner. This was one of the occasions in which the CoS chose to directly address the litigants' complaints as to the facts of the case, even though such evidence was hardly admissible according to standard rules of administrative litigation. The Court reasonably chose to address the core of the dispute, given the intensity of the allegations and the magnitude of evidence presented.

In the same case, the plaintiffs argued that the on-going operation of the mine would threaten the habitats of the highly protected Mediterranean seal *monachus-monachus* in Kimolos island, as well as of rare local plant and avian species protected by the HD and WBD, considering that the impact of mining operations on the protected species was allegedly not duly investigated in the submitted environmental study. The Court pointed to documents by the Society for the Protection of the Mediterranean Seal, addressed to the plaintiffs in the previous years, which illustrated that, even though the island's coastline had suffered greatly from mining activities in the past, seal nests were at least 800 meters away from the mine in question and their number had remained unchanged in the previous years. Moreover, the mine was situated at least 50 meters away at all places from the seafront. Given the fact that the mine was well away from both the protected site and the coastline, the Court ruled that an in-depth assessment of the impact of mine operations on the protected seal species was not necessary.

[81] CoS 1964/2015.

In a recent case of major importance,[82] WWF and Greenpeace filed an application for annulment against an administrative decision approving the Environmental Management Plan for a hydrocarbon exploration programme in western Greece. The exploration activity in question entails shallow-depth drilling (11, 500 'shot-holes' with a diameter of 8–10 cm and 10–20 meters in depth, as well as 38 boreholes with a depth of up to 80 meters for the placement of audio receivers) and seismic exploration with the use of explosives along 15 lines, having a total length of 400 km. The lines of exploration crisscross a number of mountainous Sites of Community Importance protected under the HD. Moreover, the area of the project is of particular importance for the conservation of biodiversity because of the great number of protected sites and important species (both fauna and flora) present. The exploration and exploitation of potential hydrocarbon deposits initially underwent a strategic EIA. Following this, an exploration lease was granted, providing that the exploration company should submit for approval by state authorities an Environmental Management Plan for the specific drilling programme it was willing to undertake.

The plaintiffs argued before the CoS, among other things, that the environmental studies submitted by the project owner as the basis of the challenged Environmental Management Plan, were inadequate, based on insufficient data and incorrect as to the impact of the permitted activity on the protected sites and species of the project area. In particular, it was pointed out that the period of observation of protected species did not cover a full calendar year. The Court examined the contents of the submitted environmental studies and ruled that an appropriate assessment of the project's impact on the protected sites, satisfying the criteria of art 6(3) HD, had taken place. As to the flaws of the environmental studies alleged by the plaintiffs, the Court remarked that the methods employed in a scientific study were solely up to the scientists conducting the research and were not subject to judicial review by administrative courts. According to the Court, the examined case studies were conducted by expert scientists, with field observations during springtime, summer and autumn, whereas additional data on protected species was collected from respected recent research. Further scrutiny of a scientific judgement would fall outside the scope of judicial review.

The Court also turned down allegations by the plaintiffs that the ecological study under review was deficient, as it did not take duly into account protected fauna and avian species. The Court noted that the specific locations of protected fauna species were not discovered during field observations. It was also acknowledged, however, that for that reason, the Environmental Management Plan provided that during scheduled monitoring, accompanying the drilling activities, an effort would be made to locate the species in question and, if necessary, micro-adjustments of drilling locations would be undertaken in order to protect the species. As far as protected bird species were concerned, the Court accepted

[82] CoS 961/2020.

that, although the species in question was not observed in the project area, its presence and location had been duly accounted for. Furthermore, the plaintiffs argued that the conclusion of the environmental study that no significant cumulative impact along with other projects was to be expected upon the protected sites was incorrect. It was argued that the assumption of the environmental study – that there were no other significant activities in this natural area – was erroneous given the existing highways and other roads traversing the terrain, the power lines in the protected area and three local waste disposal sites. The Court dismissed these arguments as inadmissible for the reason that the plaintiffs failed both to pinpoint the exact locations of said projects with reference to the location of the permitted exploration activities and to establish in detail the cumulative negative effects of existing infrastructure upon the protected habitats and species in conjunction with the exploratory work in question.

Finally, the plaintiffs complained that the mitigating measures provided were inadequate for the protection of the affected sites and species. The Court ruled that these allegations were unfounded, as the Environmental Management Plan included a total prohibition of exploration activities in certain protected zones, whereas in other zones of vulnerable avian fauna the exploration activities were not allowed in the period of species reproduction. Moreover, according to the Court, the prohibition of helicopter flights in protected areas included in the Environmental Management Plan was not inopportune, because it would not entail the construction of the new access roads, as the plaintiffs alleged, but the already existing road network would be used for exploration purposes in said areas.

V. Conclusions

The Greek CoS must be credited with enforcing environmental law with great diligence in the 1980s and 1990s, applying the newly introduced constitutional right to the protection of the environment and the general principles of environmental law, such as the principles of sustainability and prevention, with diligence and in a ground-breaking manner.[83] However, this jurisprudence has settled ever since the famous 'Acheloos river' decision of 2000[84] on a formula that emphasises judicial self-restraint regarding the review of environmental assessments, that are regarded as, in essence, discretionary decisions. The Court limits the judicial review of such evaluations and assessments by administrative authorities to the

[83] Γεώργιος Δελλής (Georgios Dellis), 'Between Idealization and Realism: Procedural Environmental Rights and their Processual Ramifications from the Point of View of Economic Analysis of Law' (in Greek) in Elliniki Etaireia Dikaiou Perivallontos (ed), *The Judge, the Law and the Environment* (in Greek) (Sakkoulas Publishers, 2016) 257.
[84] CoS 3478/2000 (plenary).

control of reasoning of the environmental permit. This is a strictly legal type of review that focuses on the sufficiency of the reasons given. Thus, the Court will investigate whether the EIA, which forms the basis of the environmental permit, is adequately reasoned, ie it has confronted a particular environmental issue raised by the plaintiffs. If the issue has been addressed in a manner that does not contradict previous administrative assertions in the relevant dossier and the judgement of the administration is not manifestly lacking or erroneous, the Court will, as a matter of rule, reject contrary allegations by the plaintiffs. This type of restricted judicial review of technical and scientific administrative decisions corresponds to a model well known in countries of the French legal tradition and has been adopted by the CJEU in the annulment procedure of art 263 TFEU as well. As was explained above,[85] the compatibility of restricted judicial review of discretionary decisions with art 6(1) ECHR, art 47 of the European Charter of Fundamental Rights,[86] and arts 9(3) and 9(4) Aarhus Convention[87] has not been seriously challenged until now.

The Court avoids a closer scrutiny of scientific evidence produced by the plaintiffs, since scientific and technical judgements by the permitting authority are perceived as falling into the administrative prerogative and lying outside the scope of judicial review. Therefore, evidence submitted by the plaintiffs will, in a number of cases, be declared as inadmissible, especially if it has not been filed previously with the permitting authority in the course of the public consultation procedure. Critical voices in theory[88] maintain that the rejection of evidence which has not been submitted to the authorities in public consultation is not compatible with CJEU case law on art 11 of the EEA Directive, obliging Member States to effective judicial review of environmental permitting,[89] whereas other authors assert that this restriction is well-justified as a deterrent of delay tactics by the plaintiffs.[90]

In a number of cases, the CoS will examine the evidence presented by the plaintiffs, notably if the Court thinks that there is some merit in the plaintiffs' allegations. Nevertheless, this review essentially amounts to the Court decision discussing the parts of the EIA that address the plaintiffs' concerns. The Court will not question the merits or the credibility of the EIA, unless a legal requirement as to the scientific methods to be employed has clearly been breached.

[85] In section III, C.

[86] Charter of Fundamental Rights of the European Union [2016] OJ C202/389.

[87] United Nations Economic Commission for Europe (UNECE) Convention on Access to Information, Public Participation in Decision-Making and Access to Justice in Environmental Matters, 25 June 1998, 2161 UNTS 447 (the Aarhus Convention).

[88] Konstantinos Gogos, 'Die öffentliche Konsultation im UVP-Verfahren zwischen Artikulation der Öffentlichkeit und Verfahrensbeschleunigung – Parallelwege im deutschen und griechischen Umweltrecht' in Ekkehard Hofmann et al (eds), *Demokratisch-funktionale Analyse der Öffentlichkeitsbeteiligung im Umwelt- und Infrastrukturrecht* (Mohr Siebeck Verlag, 2016) 153 ff; Κωνσταντίνος Γώγος (Konstantinos Gogos), 'Towards a Common European Process Law in Environmental Disputes: Judicial Protection Against Environmental Permitting in the Light of Recent CJEU Case-Law' (in Greek) (2015) *Efimerida Diikitikou Dikaiou* 517 ff.

[89] C-137/14 *Commission v Germany* ECLI:EU:C:2015:683.

[90] Dellis (n 83) 273. See also Eftychia Kourakou, 'Öffentlichkeitsbeteiligung im Umweltrecht – die Entwicklung der Rechtsprechung des Griechischen Staatsrates' in Hofmann et al (n 88) 105 ff.

This empirical approach renders a precise separation between questions of law and fact essentially redundant: in either case, the Court will examine whether the reasoning of the environmental permit is adequate and will, at least in principle, not scrutinise any allegations pertaining to 'technical' issues. The Court has the power to investigate 'factual errors' by the administration, but these do not include erroneous evaluations of given facts. Thus, regardless of whether the alleged error of the environmental assessment in question might be qualified as a wrongful application of a legal provision on the facts of the case or as an error as to the environmental assessment, the CoS will generally abstain from questioning the scientific position of the permitting authority. As a matter of rule, the Court does not regard itself as able or legally required to conduct an independent investigation into the technical questions and scientific assessments of the case. Nevertheless, in rare cases of major importance, such inquiries might be conducted by the Court in an informal manner, without traces of these investigations and discussions with technical experts arranged with the parties appearing in the Court's final decision.

For the same reasons, the jurisprudence of Greek administrative courts rarely deals with problems of uncertainty. The CoS takes the validity of administrative technical judgements as given and will not question their credibility. If overwhelming evidence evinces that the environmental assessment is obviously erroneous, then the Court will proceed to an annulment of the attacked environmental permit. However, such an outcome is the result of the Court's conviction that the administrative assessment is not merely questionable, but manifestly mistaken. Thus, very little margin for uncertainty in the assessment of environmental impact upon protected sites is left. The instances in which the CoS has come to the conclusion that the EIA is obviously erroneous have been few and far between in recent years.[91] Especially since the outbreak of the Greek financial crisis in 2010, the Court has taken into account the importance of economic growth[92] and thus tends to have more confidence in the administrative assessment of the environmental impact of permitted activities.

[91] The best known case in this regard being the plenary decision of the CoS 613/2002, on the use of a certain gold extraction method in Halkidiki.

[92] As the member of the CoS, Nikolakis markedly points out:

> 'The Court no longer understands art. 24 of the Constitution (i.e. the right to the environment) in a unilateral fashion, that is as containing a value that supersedes any other public policy or choice by the lawmaker, but as one of many parameters that exert influence upon such policies and choices'. Nikolakis (n 27) 305.

12

The Weakness of the Judiciary and the Poor Implementation of the Habitats Directive: How Judicial Self-Restraint Endangers Biodiversity Protection in France

FRANÇOIS-VIVIEN GUIOT

I. Introduction

As Europe pursues the aim of protecting 30 per cent of its territory,[1] an examination of the French situation illustrates that the implementation of the European legislative framework to protect biodiversity remains insufficient.[2] The reasons for this are linked to the poor implementation of EU legislation and to failures in the practical application of protection measures in the French territory. However, an additional reason might lie with the courts' lack of ability (or enthusiasm) to encourage or provide compensation for the action, or lack thereof, of the administrative authorities.

Are the French judiciary able to ensure strict compliance with the requirement to assess the environmental impact of operations that may affect a Natura 2000 site? From an examination of the relevant literature and case law, one conclusion can be drawn: biodiversity preservation is still difficult to achieve in French law. This observation is true as far as the policy is concerned. Nature protection is not an absolute priority when compared with other political concerns. The same observation applies also to case law. Faced with the technical nature of the issues raised by the Wild Birds Directive (WBD) and the Habitats Directive (HD),[3] this chapter will argue that the ability of the judge to 'unleash' the potential of

[1] Commission Communication, 'EU Biodiversity Strategy 2030', 20 May 2020, COM/2020/380 final.

[2] See the statistics presented by the State of Nature 2013–2018 report, published in *Nature and Biodiversity Newsletter*, 2020, No 49.

[3] For full details, see the Table of Legislation.

these legal controls is not yet fully realised. Bound by an objective conception of legality, the administrative judge 'self-limits' the scope of their reviewing power in relation to purely environmental issues because of their technical (thus, implicitly, 'non-legal') nature. Such issues are classically considered as a matter of administrative discretion, and therefore beyond the scope of judicial review.

This chapter consists of four main sections. Section II briefly considers the difficulties encountered during the implementation of the relevant Directives into the French legal order. Section III offers an explanation of the French administrative judicial review system as well as the various intensities of review used by the French courts. In section IV, an overview of the case law explains the limits of the courts' scrutiny in the field of biodiversity protection. Section V concludes.

II. The Implementation the WBD, HD and EIA Directives in France: A Patchwork of Different Instruments

The Nature Protection Act 1976 and its implementing decrees form the basis of environmental protection in French law.[4] This body of legislation enshrines the obligation to consider the environment in the implementation of public policies and contains a requirement that all development projects be, in principle, subject to impact assessment studies. These provisions also form the basis of the framework for the protection of species and natural habitats in the French territory. These rules were initially seen by the French authorities as largely fulfilling the objectives pursued by the Directives.[5] Subsequently, however, a number of transposition measures – albeit incoherent and scattered – have been adopted.

With respect to the Environmental Impact Assessment (EIA) Directive, France first sought to transpose its European obligations through adjustments to the existing legislative framework (as opposed to new legislation), to the detriment of clarity and effectiveness.[6] This disparate set of provisions was finally codified in the Environmental Code of 2000.[7] The general rules applicable to impact assessments

[4] Law No 76-629 of 10 July 1976 concerning nature protection (Nature Protection Act), JOFR No 162 of 13 July 1976.

[5] According to the information collected by the Commission under the obligation to notify transposition measures, France mentions systematically the Nature Protection Act.

[6] This practice is not sufficient in the light of European case law (see in this respect, Denys Simon and Anne Rigaux, 'Les Contraintes de la Transcription en Droit Français des Directives Communautaires : le Secteur de l'Environnement' (1991) 3 *Revue Juridique de l'Environnement* 290). The Court of Justice has indeed ruled that the transposition in Poland of the European Tissues and Cells Directive, adopted in 2004 by the European Parliament and Council 2004/23 EC, carried out by a multitude of legal acts, was not satisfactory with regard to the requirement of specificity and clarity (C-29/14 *Commission v Poland* ECLI:EU:C:2015:379). Directive 2004/23/EC of the European Parliament and of the Council of 31 March 2004 on setting standards of quality and safety for the donation, procurement, testing, processing, preservation, storage and distribution of human tissues and cells [2004] OJ L102/48.

[7] Ordinance No 2000-914 of 18 September 2000 concerning the legislative part of the Environmental Code, JORF No 0219 of 21 September 2000.

are grouped together in Articles L122-1 to L122-14. Additional provisions have also been integrated into a specific section relating to Natura 2000 (so-called 'Natura 2000 assessments' (Articles L414-4; R414-19 et seq of the Environmental Code)). Despite this codification, adjustments have constantly proven necessary following from infringement procedures or developments in European law (such as the generalisation of the use of impact assessment[8]). The lack of ambitious implementation has thus led to a constant need for reform and to legal instability.

The WBD has faced the same problems of transposition 'method', with added difficulties linked to the political sensitivity of its subject matter. France thus introduced transposition measures very late, and that which was implemented remained clearly contrary to the objectives of the WBD.[9]

Finally, due to be transposed before 10 June 1994, the HD was initially the subject of scattered administrative transposition measures,[10] followed by a few provisions stemming from a Law[11] and a governmental Decree[12] of 1995. However, in 1996, the procedure for establishing sites of Community interest was suspended by the Prime Minister. It was resumed in 1997 on the basis of new circulars which encouraged the listing of only a very small portion of the territory (2.5 per cent of French territory, ie six times lower than provided for by EU law). Because of the violation of the procedural rules provided for in the decree, the Conseil d'Etat (the French highest administrative court) annulled the first lists drawn up by the Ministry.[13] Consequently, the Court of Justice (CJEU) condemned France on two occasions for failure to transpose arts 6(3) and 6(4) HD.[14] It was not until the transposition of the HD into the Environment Code, that French law was brought into line with the obligations contained therein.[15]

[8] Ordinance 2004-489 of 3 June 2004 transposing Directive 2001/42/CE of the European Parliament and of the Council of 27 June 2001 on the assessment of the effects of certain plans and programmes on the environment, JORF No 129 of 5 June 2004.

[9] See on the subject of opening and closing dates for hunting: C-435/92 *Association pour la Protection des Animaux Sauvages and others v Préfet de Maine-et-Loire and Préfet de Loire-Atlantique* [1994] ECR I-00067, ECLI:EU:C:1994:10; C-374/98 *Commission v France* ECR [2000] I-10799, ECLI:EU:C:2000:670; and C-38/99 *Commission v France* [2000] ECR I-10941, ECLI:EU:C:2000:674.

[10] It should be stressed that transposition at this stage has been carried out through the adoption of circulars, whose non-binding legal status does not comply with the requirements for the correct transposition of EU law. See C-239/85 *Commission v Belgium* [1986] ECR 03645, ECLI:EU:C:1986:457.

[11] Law No 95-101 of 2 February 1995 concerning the strengthening of environmental protection, JORF No 29 of 3 February 1995.

[12] Decree No 95-631 of 5 May 1995 concerning the protection of natural habitats and natural species of Community interest, JORF No 108 of 7 May 1995.

[13] CE, 27 September 1999, *Association 'Coordination Nationale Natura 2000'*, req. n°194648; CE, 22 June 2001, *Association 'Coordination Nationale Natura 2000'*, req. n°219995. This annulment justified the second French condemnation by the CJEU for non-transmission of its national list within the time limit.

[14] C-256/98 *Commission v France* [2000] ECR I-02487, ECLI:EU:C:2000:192 and C-220/99 *Commission v France* [2001] ECR I-05831, ECLI:EU:C:2001:434.

[15] Decree No 2001-1031 of 8 November 2001 concerning the procedure of designation of Natura 2000 sites and amending the Countryside Code, JORF No 260 of 9 November 2001, and Decree No 2001-121 of 20 December 2001 concerning the management of Natura 2000 sites and amending the Countryside Code, JORF No 296 of 21 December 2001. The adoption of the regulatory part of the

III. Judicial Review of Administrative Action in France: Some Basic Elements

There are two main 'routes' of judicial review in French administrative law. On the one hand, there is the system of 'full review' (*contentieux de pleine juridiction*), allowing for a comprehensive review of administrative action but with very limited *locus standi* and only available for certain situations, defined in legislation. On the other hand, there is review 'for excess of power' (*contentieux pour excès de pouvoir*)[16] with very flexible conditions of admissibility and available even in the absence of legislative provision. In the 'full review' system, the judge can substitute their decision for that of the administrative authority if the measure is found to be illegal, or even simply inappropriate. In actions 'for excess of power', the applicable test is that of illegality. The grounds for review are lack of competence, error of form or procedure, misuse of power and violation of the law.[17]

The scope of this illegality test is difficult to define precisely. Because of a strict conception of separation of powers, historically, the French judge was only expected to ensure administrative action complied with rules concerning allocation of power and direct violation of the provisions of the law and the explicit meaning of the provisions of the law. What the law left to the administration, the judge could not control in the name of legality. Consequently, review 'for excess of power' included initially only questions of law, ie questions of interpretation of the legal provisions. Questions of fact remained a matter on which the administration had complete discretion. It was only on the basis of a specific legislative empowerment that the judge could overrule the administration's factual evaluations as part of the 'full review' system of control. In these cases, judges act almost as superior administrative authorities, and may therefore also assess the appropriateness of the administrative action.

During the twentieth century, the distinction between questions of law and questions of fact has become more difficult to define. This is because the scope of the test of illegality has broadened. In a decision of 1922, the Conseil d'Etat established that it falls within the competence of the courts to verify the accuracy of the facts mentioned in the reasons given for an administrative decision, based on 'the rule that the administration may not base its decisions in the exercise of discretionary power on materially inaccurate grounds'. The establishment of (simple) facts was therefore considered as falling within the scope of the test of legality.[18] For the same reason, the courts decided around the same time to control

Environmental Code with Decree 2005-935 of 5 August 2005 finally allowed bringing together all the provisions relating to the WBD *a posteriori*. Decree of 5 August 2005 concerning the regulatory part of the Environmental Code, JORF No 181 of 5 August 2005.

[16] CE, Ass., 17 February 1950, *Minister of Agriculture c/ dame Lamotte*, req. n°86949.

[17] This limited list is supposed to define legality ('the whole legality and nothing but legality', as the saying goes).

[18] CE, 14 January 1916, *Camino*, req. n°59619; CE, 20 January 1922, *Trépont*, req. n°68212.

the correspondence of the established facts with the conditions laid down in the legal basis (the so-called 'legal qualification of facts').[19] Finally, when the relevant provisions do not imply a control of the legal qualification or when facts are not simply empirical, the Conseil d'Etat granted itself the power to sanction a manifest error of assessment.[20] Thus, errors in the establishment of facts, manifest errors in the assessment of facts, and errors in the legal 'categorisation' of such facts are now possible grounds for illegality review, depending on the intensity of the judicial review.

When it comes to the correctness of the facts on which the decision was grounded (*contrôle de l'exactitude matérielle des faits*), French courts exercise a control of so-called 'normal' intensity. A different test is applied however for the *assessment* of facts, including in cases involving the qualification or categorisation of such facts. Because of the possible technical or subjective nature of such assessments, or because of the indeterminacy of the law which makes such categorisation of facts uncertain, the courts exercise a control of so-called 'minimum intensity'. In such cases, the court restricts its control to the manifest error of assessment. As a result, only obviously erroneous practices can be sanctioned under this test.

The strengthening of control over questions of fact is a major factor in reducing the discretionary power of the administration. Furthermore, the test of proportionality and the so-called 'cost-benefit analysis' may also serve as control over the exercise of the administrative discretion, challenging the division between assessment of legality *strictu sensu* and assessment of the whole (ie both factual and legal) basis for a decision.[21] The 'cost-benefit analysis' is only applied in cases of expropriation in the public interest.[22] The proportionality test has a more general application. First mentioned in the field of public liberties,[23] it is now a condition of legality of general administrative police measures, administrative sanctions or certain administrative authorisations.

In spite of these evolutions, the general idea, according to which courts should not substitute themselves for the administration, remains largely undisputed. This understanding of the role of courts in 'excess of power' cases forces judges to 'objectify' their scrutiny. They have devised two main ways of keeping their scrutiny limited to the 'objective legality' of administrative action whilst, arguing, increasing the intensity of their gaze.

First, as mentioned above, courts can modulate the intensity of their scrutiny in relation to questions of fact. For example, control over the legal qualification of facts aims to ensure that there is correspondence between a specific set of factual circumstances and relevant legal provisions. This verification is part of the control of illegality of 'normal intensity'. However, this form of control is dependent on the

[19] CE, 4 April 1914, *Gomel*, req. n°55125.

[20] CE, 13 November 1953, *Denizet*, req. n°7423; CE, 15 February 1961, *Lagrange*, req. n°42259 et 42560.

[21] CE, Ass., 31 May 2016, *Mrs. Gonzalez Gomez*, req. n°396848.

[22] CE, Ass., 28 May 1971, *Ville Nouvelle Est*, req. n°78825.

[23] CE, 19 May 1933, *Benjamin*, req. n°17413.

precision of the legal text: the more precisely laws are formulated, the easier the judge's task to control – in an 'objective' manner – the legal qualification of facts by the administrative decision-maker. Second, as discussed above, instead of or prior to the legal qualification, courts may review manifest errors in the assessment of facts under a control of 'minimal intensity'. The emphasis placed by the case law on the 'manifest' character of such a factual error keeps the control of the court within the 'objective' parameters deemed necessary to comply with the principle of separation of powers.

Within this system of 'objective' control of factual assessments, courts rarely question the factual basis of the authorities' discretionary choices. The courts leave the factual debate in the hands of the parties, they do not generally investigate the facts of the case, neither *ex officio* nor with the help of external expertise, even though the French Code of Administrative Justice does foresee such option.

Indeed, according to the Code of Administrative Justice, the court may, either *ex officio*, or at the request of the parties, or of one of them, order, before the judgment, an expert examination to be carried out on the points specified in its decision.[24] Despite the restrictive approach to expert evidence in French law, the Code of Administrative Justice also sets out a comprehensive framework governing the appointment of experts, as well as the right of the parties to object to an appointment.[25] When requested, the purpose of the expertise is to establish the facts and provide technical or scientific answers to the judge, to the exclusion of any question of law. Finally, it should be noted that, in administrative litigation, the burden of proof is on the applicant who challenges the validity of an administrative act.[26] This means that the applicant must, for example, establish the insufficiency of the environmental assessment submitted to the administration. It is only in the event where one of the parties has shown sufficient and concordant clues to raise a doubt that the judge can require an expert report. In most cases, however, the administrative court is satisfied to rule on the basis of the documents submitted by the parties.

IV. The Case Law: A Comprehensive Approach to Scientific Uncertainty

As a preliminary step to analyse the courts' powers in the fields covered by the Directives, it is necessary to draw a distinction in terms of remedies available and powers of the court according to the legal 'routes' used. It is furthermore necessary

[24] Code of Administrative Justice, Art R621-1.

[25] *ibid*, Art R621-6 and following.

[26] According to a constant jurisprudence, administrative acts benefit from a presumption of legality: CE, 2 July 1982, *Huglo*, req. n°25288.

to look at the way in which the judge handles the scientific nature of the legal issues raised before them, concerning the establishment, assessment and legal qualification of facts.

A. Legal Remedies Available in the Field of Application of the Directives

In the context of a claim based on the HD, three possible scenarios can arise. These three scenarios lead to different remedies, and, as will be shown later, to different intensities of review when scientific questions are at stake.

First, claims under the HD might be brought through interim proceedings. In such cases, the applicant must demonstrate the existence of a serious doubt as to the validity of the contested administrative decision.[27] However, under art 2 of the Nature Protection Act 1976, whenever an impact assessment is required, its absence or the presence of extremely basic or imprecise assessment, leads to the automatic granting of a stay of execution by the administrative courts.[28] Art L414-4, IX of the Environmental Code explicitly extended this exception to the enforceability of administrative acts to Natura 2000 impact assessments.[29] Even where such an assessment is provided, it remains possible to request the suspension of an administrative authorisation in the event of serious doubts as to the validity of the decision. Some summary hearings have thus invoked violation of Natura 2000 obligations.[30]

More complex is the question of the distinction between the powers of the judge between 'full review' and review 'for excess of power'. In terms of Natura 2000 litigation, Ordonnance No 2017-80 of 26 January 2017 on 'environmental authorisations' has revised the relevant rules.[31]

Before its entry into force, whenever a special authorisation regime was involved in a project, plan or programme likely to affect a Natura 2000 site, it was necessary to check whether the relevant provisions allowed a 'full review' challenge.[32] This was mainly the case for classified industrial establishments (ICPE),[33] and for those

[27] Code of Administrative Justice, arts L521-1 et seq indicate the conditions applicable to interlocutory proceedings.

[28] CE, 29 July 1983, *Commune de Roquevaire*, req. n°38795.

[29] Law No 2010-788 of 12 July 2010 concerning the national engagement for the environment (Grenelle Law II), JORF No 0160 of 13 July 2010.

[30] The Charter of the Environment, which has been part of French constitutional law since 2001, is the basis for a 'right to the environment' considered as a 'fundamental freedom' likely to justify an urgent application (*'référé-liberté'*). For example: CE, Ord. 27 March 2021, *Sea Shepherd*, req. n°450592. See also TA de Châlons-en-Champagne, Ord. 29 April 2005, *Conservatoire du patrimoine naturel and others, req.* req. n°0500828.

[31] Environmental Code, arts L181-1 et seq.

[32] 'Full review' powers were also applicable to liability claims.

[33] See, eg, an appeal against the prefect's refusal of the authorisation to operate a classified establishment (sand quarry): CAA Bordeaux, 17 December 2008, *SARL SPB*, req. n°07BX01929.

governed by the Water Act (IOTA).[34] Where the law did not specify it, it remained possible to bring a claim 'for excess of powers', but the court could neither make changes to the administrative act, nor substitute its own decision for the contested decision. The court had only the power to annul the original decision.

The Ordonnance aimed to simplify the litigation of 'environmental authorisations' by unifying the litigation regime and by providing a unified authorisation system.[35] However, the scope of this new regime is not perfectly clear. In addition to the ICPE and the IOTA, there is an 'environmental authorisation' under art L181-1 of the Environmental Code in two others cases: when a project is only subject to a declaration obligation before the Prefect, but requires an environmental assessment; and when a project is subject to an authorisation, but falls under 'no specific authorisation or declaration regime'.[36] In the end, the Natura 2000 authorisations do not seem to fall under either of these two new hypotheses. Thus, Natura 2000 assessments remain subject to full jurisdiction litigation, mainly if they are involved in ICPE or IOTA procedures.

The Code also specifies and harmonises the scope of judicial power in such 'full review' cases. Pursuant to art L181-18, 1° and 2°, if a court concludes that the flaw in the administrative decision can be regularised by an amending decision, the court must now render a judgment in advance of the final legal conclusions, in which it sets the terms and conditions, as well as a deadline, for this regularisation.

Given the ranges within the procedural toolbox available to courts, and the absence of limitation on the scope and intensity of judicial review, the limited availability of the 'full review' route in Natura 2000 impact assessment disputes is regrettable.[37]

B. Impact of the Directives on the Intensity of Judicial Review

As a consequence of the limited scope of the 'full review' route, the case law relating to Natura 2000 has developed mainly on the basis of the 'excess of power' review, ie mere legality review. Within this system of control, as mentioned above, the French courts usually adopt the 'minimum intensity' reviewing standard when faced with questions concerning the assessment of the facts or their legal categorisation. As a result, when dealing with environmental matters, they tend to restrict their control to 'manifest errors of assessment'. The control of the qualification of the facts, and *a fortiori* the control of the adequacy of the measures under the

[34] For an example, see TA de Rouen, 19 June 2014, *Sortir du nucléaire and others*, req. n°1201107.

[35] Environmental Code, Art L181-2, 6° specifies that the granting of an 'environmental authorisation' should be considered as 'absence of opposition under the Natura 2000 impact assessment regime pursuant to VI of Article L414- 4'. In this regard, Art 181-3, 5° recalls that the authorisation should ensure 'respect for the conservation objectives of the Natura 2000 site'.

[36] *ibid*, Art L122-1-1, II, al. 2 and 3.

[37] See, eg, for a decision of the judge of first instance, leading to a precise examination of th assessment: TA de Lille, 25 April 2017, *M. X and commune of Heuringhem*, req. n°1401947.

proportionality principle, are exceptional because of the intrinsic technicality of the issues at stake and the imprecision of the relevant legal provisions. The HD could nevertheless have had the potential to strengthen judicial control, at least in relation to analysis of scientific evaluations by the administration. However, French courts have not systematically strengthened their control. In line with the patterns seen across the field of environmental litigation, the courts confer extensive discretionary power to assess the facts and determine the legal consequences of these assessments onto administrative authorities.[38]

Nevertheless, this limited control is not a blank cheque to the administration. This is particularly clear when the courts can find any scientific element to assert (and thus 'objectify') the existence of a 'manifest error of assessment' on the part of the administration. This kind of 'objectification' appears, for example, in the consequences of the annulment by the Conseil d'Etat of the list of sites likely to be considered as being of Community interest. Although the list has lost any legal value, its adoption crystallised the scientific knowledge surrounding the sites involved. Even if scientific matters were at stake, the Conseil d'Etat was thus able to suspend the execution of an administrative authorisation because of a 'manifest error of assessment' with regard to the ecological value of a site, as this value had been scientifically established and previously recognised by this (albeit invalidated) list.[39]

This goes to show that, even within a system of control of 'minimum intensity', the possibility of relying on external scientific evidence allowed the judge impose a significant degree of control over the exercise of the administrative discretion. When doing so, the courts suggest that they are merely drawing inevitable consequences from pre-existing scientific assessments, thus preserving the 'objective', legalistic nature of their control. The fact that the administration contradicts its own previous assessments highlights the unlawfulness of the later decision.

Beyond these general observations on the intensity of judicial control, when examining the case law related to Natura 2000 sites, it is necessary to distinguish between operations that lead to the designation of sites and those that ensure the protection of designated sites. However, as will be shown below, the diversity of the cases, the laconic style of the court decisions, and sometimes the heterogeneity of judicial motivation complicate our analysis.

C. Judicial Review of Decisions Establishing Natura 2000 Site Protection

Where there is doubt over the need to designate a site for protection under the Directives, French courts tend to limit their review to the question of whether

[38] CAA de Bordeaux, 29 November 2007, *Sté Fontaulière and others*, req. n°05BX00528 (about the appreciation of the ecological interest of a species).

[39] CE, Ord., 9 July 2001, *Association fédérative régionale pour la protection de la nature du Haut-Rhin*, req. n°232752.

there has been a manifest error. As a consequence of this hands-off approach, courts usually refuse to engage with scientific questions.

Nevertheless, the court must at least ensure that the administration has considered the relevant available scientific information. By way of example, a prefect's refusal to consult local authorities (which is a prerequisite for site designation) may be challenged on the grounds of an error in the assessment of the facts when the scientific knowledge establishes the environmental interest of the site.[40] As has been held, 'scientific inventories [...] are binding on the prefect as regards the decision to organise the consultation of local authorities'. While the inventory does not *in itself* generate an obligation to classify the site, it may trigger a procedural obligation to at least consider the issue, and thus to engage in consultation.

The importance of the scientific aspects of the decision sometimes encourages complainants to contest the data the administration has considered. But this is almost impossible when it comes to decisions regarding designation of protected sites. There is a public policy of entrusting the establishment of inventories of the state of spaces and species to independent and recognised scientific authorities. In most cases, the scientific expertise and the institutional character of these bodies leads the courts to reject private 'counter-expertise' provided by the claimants.[41] The inventory of natural areas of ecological, faunistic and floristic interest (ZNIEFF) deserves particular mention. This inventory, developed through the National Museum of Natural History, does not have the status of an administrative act of classification and does not produce legal effects *per se*.[42] However, the courts have recognised on several occasions its indirect legal effect. Indeed, it is well-established that 'failure to take into account a ZNIEFF amounts to a manifest error of assessment'.[43] The inventory constitutes an element that the administration must take into account in exercising its duty to identify Sites of Community Interest.[44] In the context of the implementation of the HD, the administrative courts have the same view of all preparatory acts of a scientific nature:[45] although

[40] CE, 16 January 2008, *Minister of Ecology*, req. n°292489. The Conseil d'Etat adds that there is no error of appreciation by the prefect, when scientific expertise is not sufficient or does not provide significant elements to establish the environmental interest of the site.

[41] See for the Wild Birds Directive, CAA of Bordeaux, 2 June 2009, *Fédération départementale des chasseurs des Landes*, req. n°08BX01709 concerning 'areas of importance to bird conservation' and 'Important Birds Areas' inventories drawn up by the French Ministry and the European Commission.

[42] CE, 3 June 2020, *Commune de Piana*, req. n°422182. For the Conseil d'Etat, the inclusion of an area in the national inventory is not an act that can be challenged by way of review 'for excess of power'.

[43] TA d'Orléans, 29 March 1988, *Rommel – Frapec*, req. n°87316.

[44] CE, 16 January 2008, *Minister of State, Minister of Ecology, Sustainable Development and Planning v. Association Manche Nature*, req. n°292489.

[45] When a site has been classified as Natura 2000, the courts seem to attach legal effects to it. The Conseil d'Etat has thus been able to affirm that the lower court did not commit an error of law by simply noting that an area is part of a ZNIEFF and a Natura 2000 site in order to qualify it as a 'remarkable area' within the meaning of Article L146-6 of the Town Planning Code (Decree No 54-776 of 26 July 1954 codifying the legislative texts concerning town planning, JORF No 766 of 27 July 1954) (CE, 3 September 2009, *Commune de Canet-en-Roussillon et Seran*, req. n°306298 et 306468).

they are not binding, they constitute factual elements that both the administration and the judge should take into account and on which citizens can base their arguments.[46]

It can be concluded that, in the case of designation decisions, courts appear to treat existing scientific studies as all-but conclusive as to the establishment of both scientific facts, and of the resulting legal consequences. There is no room in such case law for the analysis of any uncertainties underpinning the factual assessments made by the authorities. When no such studies exist, the French courts still exercise a very limited control over the assessment made by the administration.

D. Judicial Review and Preservation of Natura 2000 Sites

Decisions involving protection measures for existing sites reveal a different picture. There has been consistent criticism of the failure of the courts to provide for a high level of protection for designated sites. Judges rarely annul administrative authorisations of plans, projects or programmes.[47] There is a clear 'sensitivity' to general interest concerns pursued by such decision-making authorities, to the detriment of purely environmental considerations. This is also found in relation to management operations and protection mechanisms for Natura 2000 sites.[48]

This situation seems to clash with EU law for a number of reasons. First, while the courts ensure compliance with the obligation to provide a Natura 2000 impact assessment, case law has sometimes reduced the scope of the applicable provisions. Because of the overlap between different assessment mechanisms under French law, the specific obligations provided for by the HD are only imposed if the planned action or operation may have a 'significant' effect on a Natura 2000 area.[49] Whilst this is in line with the Directive, the CJEU case law has consistently held that it may be necessary to carry out a scoping assessment to establish the possibility of such effects. The French position seems to be rather less strict in this regard.

[46] André-Hubert Mesnard, 'Chapter 4 (folio no. 5460) – Environnement: Protection et Gestion des Espaces Naturels' in *Encyclopédie des Collectivités Locales* (Dalloz, 1999).

[47] Jessica Makowiak, 'Natura 2000 et le Juge Administratif' in Charles-Hubert Born and Francis Haumont (eds), *Natura 2000 et le juge/Natura 2000 and the Judge* (Bruylant, 2014) 83. For a famous case, which exceptionally led the Conseil d'Etat to rule in favour of the environment: CE, 10 July 2006, *Association interdépartementale et intercommunale pour la protection du lac de Ste-Croix et de son environnement*, req. n°288108 e.a.

[48] Jessica Makowiak observes that there is little case law on preventive measures taken under management operations. According to her, this can be attributed to the contractual nature of management measures (Makowiak, *ibid* 246). For a case of annulment of a decree modifying communal urban planning documents in order to allow urbanisation of a Natura 2000 site, TA de Bordeaux, 3 December 2009, *Association les Pechs de Maurissoux*, req. n°0703266.

[49] CE, 7 May 2008, *Association ornithologique et mammalogique de Saône-et-Loire*, req. n°309285: the absence of the obligation to provide a Natura 2000 assessment due to the absence of significant effect of the motorway construction project on the conservation of the corncrake. For other examples, see Makowiak (n 47) 257–58.

In a recent case, the Conseil d'Etat adopted a very 'pragmatic' position on this matter, the conformity of which with European rules is uncertain.[50] The introduction in French law of a 'de minimis rule' regarding procedural obligations seems to conflict with the provisions of the HD if it prevents an open-minded assessment as to the likelihood of significant effects in line with art 6(3).

Second, in accordance with Article R. 414-23 of the Environmental Code, the requirement of proportionality frames the assessment mechanism and consequently informs the court's review. As we shall see, this proportionality test allows courts to assess the content of the impact assessment provided by an applicant when seeking development consent. This proportionality test, which is not present in the Directive, exerts pressures at all stages of proceedings including the litigation itself. Importantly, the information provided to administrative authorities must be *proportionate* with the scale of potential impact of the planned activity (ie the information provided to the administration must be proportionate in its 'bulk'). Even for situations with minimal potential ecological impacts, it is expected that a minimal amount of information will be provided to the administration to ensure the substantiated character of its decision.

In this regard, a ministerial circular provides that 'the level of detail requested by the decision-making authority, particularly in scientific terms, must also be adapted to the scope of the proposed activity and to the conservation issues related to the Natura 2000 site in question'.[51] Here, the administrative authority itself is encouraged to tailor the scope of its consideration to ensure proportionality with the goals of the Natura 2000 network. However, this text also specifies that 'the assessment must deal with all aspects of an activity' and must allow for the verification of the risk of significant harm to the conservation status. The application to the administrative authority, and the impact assessment contained therein, must therefore present the permanent, temporary, direct and indirect effects, cumulated with those of other activities.

The introduction of such a proportionality test is hugely important here and acts in ways far beyond a simple formal and procedural requirement. It has significant legal consequences. This therefore reverberates through the assessment which the courts will carry out. In particular, the judge will ensure that the applicant's impact assessment corresponds to the above-mentioned regulatory requirements

[50] CE, 15 February 2021, *Fédération française de motocyclisme*, req. n°431578.

[51] Circular of 15 April 2010, on Natura 2000 impact assessment. This limitation of the scope of the assessment sometimes leads to questionable solutions. See, eg, CAA de Nantes, 04 October 2019, *Société Quilly Guenrouët Energie*, req. n°18NT00390: pt. 44:

> even if the avi-faunistic study estimated that the impact on two species of raptors, the Common Buzzard and the Kestrel, was strong, these two species are not the ones that justified the designation of the sites 'Grande Brière, Marais de Donges et du Brivet', 'Grande Brière et Marais de Donges' and 'Marais de Vilaine'. It follows from this that the argument that the implementation of the project would undermine the conservation objectives of a Natura 2000 site, in disregard of the provisions of VI of Article LL414-4 of the Environmental Code, is unfounded.

and that the assessment is thus sufficient (as a prerequisite for proportionality). The legal 'character' of the proportionality test means that the French courts move from a review of 'minimum' intensity (linked to the 'manifest error of assessment' threshold) to a review of 'normal' intensity. In other words, the court, whilst unable to assess in-depth the *merits* of the impact assessment can make a full review of the *completeness* of this assessment, based on the proportionality standard. Through this review, the courts verify 'the inaccuracies, omissions or insufficiencies of an impact study [which] are likely to vitiate the procedure and therefore lead to the illegality of the decision taken on the basis of this study'.[52] The judge may therefore verify the formal appropriateness of the provided assessment (scientific references, independence of the author, satisfactory methodology, consistency of the conclusions, etc).[53] Even if an assessment is sufficient in so far as it contains all available scientific data, the existence of persistent uncertainties recognised by the administration will normally lead the court to consider that the project is detrimental to the objectives of protection, and, crucially, therefore cannot comply with the requirement of proportionality because it cannot meet the goals of the Natura 2000 network.[54]

Beyond this review of 'normal' intensity of the formal aspects of the assessment, however, 'judicial control of the actual content of the conclusions [of the expertise] can only remain marginal'.[55] The judges do not necessarily have the competence to detect a possible mistake in the evaluation of the environmental impact in the assessment provided by the applicant and thus in the decision made by the administrative authority. For judicial scrutiny to go beyond obvious errors committed by the authority, or the obvious insufficiency of the study submitted by the applicants

[52] However, it should be specified that these hypotheses of illegality are only operative if 'they could have had the effect of harming the complete information of the population or if they were of such a nature as to influence the decision of the administrative authority' (CE, 20 March 2013, *Compagnie Force 5*, req. n°354115). In the same sense, CE, 7 May 2008, *Association ornitologique et mammalogique de Saône-et-Loire*, req. n°309285 and 323257.

[53] For an illustration, requiring the file to present the 'best scientific knowledge on the subject', see: CAA de Bordeaux, 31 October 2013, *Minister of the Environment*, req. n°12BX00988 (which concerned the inadequacy of the assessment, based on only two nights of observation of chiropterans, and not including an analysis of the significant, temporary or permanent effects).

[54] CAA de Nantes, 6 October 2020, *Association Nature et citoyenneté Crau Camargue Alpilles*, req. n°19NT02389 (concerning the installation of a floating wind farm in the Mediterranean Sea). However, the judge is not always so absolute: CAA de Nantes, 04 October 2019, *Société Quilly Guenrouët Energie*, req. n°18NT00390: pt. 44:

> The mention contained in the chiropterological study, attached to the impact assessment, under the terms of which 'important roosts are found in the remote study area of the project and little is known about the numbers and routes of species with a greater range (migratory species in particular) that could pass through the park' does not allow the existence of reasonable doubt from a scientific point of view as to the existence of lasting adverse effects on the integrity of Natura 2000 sites.

[55] Charles-Hubert Born, 'Quelques Réflexions sur le Mécanisme de Protection des Sites Natura 2000 contre les Incidences des Plans et Projets' in *Mélanges en l'Honneur de Michel Prieur* (Dalloz, 2007) 983.

based on the proportionality standard, the applicant must therefore be able to provide counter-expertise that establishes the existence of reasonable doubts as to the assessment of harm in respect of the conservation objectives of the site.

What is more, judges will most often assess whether there are gaps or failures in the presentation of the scientific information 'on the basis of the evidence in the case file'. They are limited therefore to the evidence provided by the parties and will not readily ask for an independent expert to step in. Judges do not have the technical capacity to assess the intrinsic value or to verify the validity of the factual data at stake. At the same time, they do not use their power of inquiry to solicit competent state agencies (such as the Biodiversity Agency) or other independent expertise.[56] All in all, they merely compare the content of the parties' arguments and so in such cases it may be that neither the minimal control standard, nor the more enhanced standard which relies upon the proportionality test, will result in enhanced scrutiny of the scientific basis of a decision.

The Conseil d'Etat has also endeavoured to regulate the way in which administrative authorities assess the impact assessment provided by an applicant. In particular, the Conseil d'Etat has used the notion of 'error of law' (meaning the misinterpretation of the legal texts) as a tool to control the substance of the assessments and the completeness of the information taken into account. This is similar to the technique employed in using the proportionality test to allow scrutiny of the impact assessment but applies here to the administrative decision, rather than to the quality of the information provided to the decision-maker. As with proportionality, review for error of law is seen as sitting comfortably in the purview of the judge. Through the notion of 'error of law' the courts have been able to evaluate the appropriateness of the criteria used by the administration to make their assessment. This system allows the court to by-pass the traditional understanding of scientific evaluations being a matter of error of fact. For example, the Conseil d'Etat ruled that the Marseille Administrative Court of Appeal had erred in law, holding that the administration rightly considered that a 'concerted development zone' project[57] did not affect the conservation status of the Natura 2000 site on the grounds that this project only involved a very small area.[58] The Court interpreted the law as requiring a concrete and empirical analysis of the environmental impact. By doing so, the Conseil d'Etat prevented the administration from using unlawful criteria or unjustified presumptions, and more generally from making shortcuts in its analysis of the facts.

Finally, with regard to methodological requirements, the courts have tackled two other questions, which serve to illustrate their pragmatic approach. First, with respect to art 6(4) HD, in the context of control of derogations, the administrative courts have underlined the importance of the description of the initial state

[56] More rarely, the judge's reasoning will indicate that the judge's assessment was made 'at the end of the investigation'. However, this does not necessarily imply an active attitude of the judge; it may only refer to the adversarial debates during the court proceedings.

[57] It is an area developed and equipped by the administration with the aim to transfer or concede it later to public or private users.

[58] CE, 13 December 2013, *Minister of Ecology*, req. n°349541.

of the site. This description conditions the possibility of identifying significant effects, but also the definition of compensatory measures potentially required. The Bordeaux Administrative Court of Appeal has emphasised the need to respect minimum and ecologically adequate periods for inventories and field investigations. It thus ruled, concerning a project to extend an open-cast quarry, that one effective day of observation could not suffice to make a satisfactory inventory of the fauna and flora in view of the issues and status of the sites concerned.[59] Minimum requirements are therefore imposed regardless of the scale of the plan, project or programme. While this strengthens judicial review, the conditions for granting an environmental permit are made more flexible by the issue of compensatory measures.

Indeed, administrative practice had emerged in which administrative authorities would take into account mitigation and accompanying measures at the EIA stage.[60] Case law has validated this practice, although the doctrine has criticised it and it is certainly in tension with the approach of the CJEU. According to this case law, if a project has a significant effect, it should only be authorised on the basis of workable compensatory measures, if there is no alternative solution, and only if 'imperative reasons of public interest' justify the operation. Contrary to the jurisprudence of the CJEU,[61] the French courts have considered that the presentation of sufficient mitigation measures can be taken to prevent the plan or programme from significantly impacting the conservation objectives of the site. This practice thereby places the authorisation outside of the scope of the derogations and their specific conditions (provided for in Article L414-4, VII and L414-4, VIII of the Environmental Code). These mitigation measures must be described in sufficient detail for the judge to be able to verify the actual absence of harmful effects and consequently, compliance with the conditions of art 6(4) HD.[62] However, this solution raises the question of the ability of judges to measure the effectiveness of such mitigation measures. Furthermore, compensation measures aim to restore the overall balance of the Natura 2000 network, whereas mitigation measures only attempt to reduce the harmful effects of the project, plan or programme. These two types of measures therefore have a distinct purpose and regime and should not be substituted for each other.

However, it should be noted that there have been cases of annulment of administrative decisions because of the inadequacy of the proposed compensation measures.[63] The courts, for example, have verified whether the compensatory

[59] CAA de Bordeaux, 6 May 2014, *SAS Sablières et travaux du Lot*, req. n°13BX02649.

[60] CE, 9 July 2007, *Association Vivre bien en Aunis and others*. req. n°258014. See also, CE, 27 July 2009, *M. and Mme A and others*, req. n°307206.

[61] The CJEU considers that these measures are not likely to be taken into account during the Natura 2000 assessment, and that they can, if necessary, be qualified as 'compensatory measures' only if they meet the conditions set out in art 6(4) HD. See C-387/15 and C-388/15 *Orleans v Vlaams Gewest* ECLI:EU:C:2016:583.

[62] CE, 14 November 2008, *Communes d'Ambarès-et-Lagrave and others*, req. n°297557.

[63] Compensation measures cannot be challenged directly, but must be challenged indirectly in the context of the appeal against the administration's authorisation decision (CE, 17 October 2016, *Comité de défense du bois des Rochottes et de ses riverains and others*, req. n°388066).

measures presented to the administration and retained to justify the infringement of the conservation objective are likely to maintain the balance of the Natura 2000 network.[64] In this context, it seems that the environmental jurisprudence is moving toward a system of control of 'maximum intensity', meaning that a full proportionality assessment is used to review the choices of the authorities. The constitutionalisation of the principles of prevention and sustainable development in French law since 2004 might be the reason.[65] The principle of prevention in particular entitles the courts to verify as conditions of legality the workability and the proportionality of these compensatory measures.[66] However, to verify these requirements, the review may involve a technical assessment. Again, it is questionable whether the courts will be willing to get involved in these technical issues or whether they will feel bound by the assessments made by the authorities or at least by those presented by the parties.

Furthermore, the courts may have to verify whether there is a public interest sufficient to justify a derogation. The Conseil d'Etat recently handed down the first judgment admitting an 'imperative reason of major public interest' (departing from both the analysis made by the judges at first instance and the conclusions of the *rapporteur public*[67]). It is clear from the case law that the existence of such a reason must be considered on a preliminary basis, *in abstracto*, before examining the other conditions set out in Articles L411-2 and L414-4, VII of the Environmental Code. It is only afterwards that the interest pursued must be weighed against the conservation objective, only by integrating the reduction and compensation measures envisaged into the analysis. As a result, the Conseil d'Etat held that the lower Court,

> [W]as right to rule on the question of whether the project meets an imperative reason of major public interest, without taking into account at this stage the nature and intensity of the damage it causes to protected species, in particular their number and location.[68]

It follows from this ruling that the judges employ a review of 'normal' intensity over the administration's assessment as to the existence of any 'imperative reason

[64] On this issue, it is important to recall the particularly strict doctrine of the European Commission regarding the equivalence between the damage and the compensation provided: Francis Haumont, 'L'Application des Mesures Compensatoires Prévues par Natura 2000' (2009) 10 *ERA Forum* 611–24.

[65] The state promotes an 'ARC' policy, according to which any environmental impact must be avoided, reduced or compensated for, especially when a protected species is endangered. The administrative authorities adopt guidelines to ease the identification of suitable compensatory measures.

[66] See, eg, CE, 12 juillet 2017, *Les amis de la terre France*, req. n°394254.

[67] The *rapporteur public* exercises the same function as the Advocate General before the European Court of Justice. He advises the judges on the solution to adopt in the light of previous case law.

[68] CE, 3 June 2020, *Ministre de la Transition écologique et solidaire et Société provençale*, req. n°425395 e.a. In this case,

> The reopening of the Nau Bouques quarry [white marble] is part of the economic policies conducted at the European Union level which aim to promote the sustainable supply of sectors of industry with raw materials from European sources. The operation therefore constitutes an imperative reason of major public interest.

of public interest' (before considering the respect of the other conditions and in particular the proportionality of the compensation measures). This demonstrates the variation in the intensity of review employed according to the precise question addressed by the administrative authority.

Finally, in the context of the Natura 2000 assessment, special consideration must be devoted to the standard and burden of proof. The position of the CJEU, based on the precautionary principle, is very clear:[69] doubt must always lead to a refusal. The French administrative courts have generally accepted this interpretation and its judicial consequences. In order to obtain an environmental authorisation, it is up to the applicant to prove the absence of any significant effect of the planned operation on the conservation objective. On this basis, the Administrative Court of Appeal of Bordeaux, for example, ruled that the prefect had rightly rejected a project to install a wind farm because of the inadequacy of the submitted assessment and the persistent doubts on the capacity of the compensatory measures to eliminate any risk of impact on the conservation objective.[70]

However, some decisions of the French administrative courts do not fully draw out the consequences of this principle of inversion for the burden of proof. In some cases, environmental permits were given although the impact assessment did not clear up all scientific uncertainties. Furthermore, the courts had applied the general principle of burden of proof in civil litigation by asking the challenger to prove the insufficiency of the file submitted and the manifest error of assessment committed by the administration. This sits in potential conflict with the requirements of precaution. For example, the courts have emphasised in some cases that the person challenging the administrative decision has not established that the transaction would be incompatible with the preservation of biodiversity[71] or that it would prevent the achievement of European objectives.[72] In doing so, they neglected to analyse the illegality from the point of view of procedural

[69] C-127/02 *Landelijke Vereniging tot Behoud van de Waddenzee v Staatssecretaris van Landbouw, Natuurbeheer en Visserij* [2004] ECR I-07504, ECLI:EU:C:2004:482; and C-258/11 *Sweetman v An Bord Pleanála* [2013] ECLI:EU:C:2013:220.

[70] CAA de Bordeaux, 31 October 2013, *Minister of Ecology v Champs Purget wind farm*, req. n°12BX00988: the study did not include an analysis of either the significant temporary or permanent effects that the planned works, structures or developments might have on the conservation status of species present in a Natura 2000 site close to the planned construction site, or of the potential cumulative effects for birds arising from the presence of another wind farm site nearby. See also, TA de Marseille, 24 May 2012, *Ass. Clarency and others*, req. n°1102411 e.a., an assessment which did not establish with certainty the net impact of a project on a protected species is insufficient to grant an authorisation.

[71] CE, 13 July 2009, *Association citoyenne intercommunale des populations concernées par le projet d'aéroport de Notre-Dame-des-Landes*, req. n°314955: 'it has not been established that [the Notre-Dame-des-Landes airport project] would significantly affect the special protection areas located near its perimeter'.

[72] See the references cited by Marie-Pierre Lanfranchi, 'Le Rôle du Juge, Témoin d'une Juridicisation et d'une Juridiciarisation Croissante des Rapports Sociaux?' in Jérôme Dubois et Sandrine Maljean-Dubois (eds), *Natura 2000: De l'Injonction Européenne aux Négociations Locales* (La Documentation Française, 2005) 152.

requirements as discussed above. These solutions are therefore open to criticism, as they weaken judicial review and violate the precautionary principle.

Of course, proof of the absence of an effect is difficult to provide, especially in so far as cumulative effects with other projects or programmes must be taken into account.[73] Furthermore, the imprecision in the 'adverse effects' standard creates a margin of appreciation, even before the applicability of the derogations provided for in art 6(4) is considered. As Makowiak points out, 'the legal notion of significant effects, which is difficult to grasp, is undoubtedly one that is traditionally dedicated to the "experts", ie in concrete terms, to the consultancy firms in charge of carrying out impact studies'.[74]

V. Conclusion

The analysis of the French case law in the field of the HD allows for some concluding observations.

First, as the analysis above has shown, the actual intensity of the administrative courts' rulings is variable and insufficiently harmonised. In some cases, 'minimum intensity' is used. In others, full proportionality reviews are carried out which allow courts a much greater degree of control whilst still sitting under the umbrella of legality review. Much depends upon the precise issue in dispute in the litigation (and the quality of the application filed by the parties' lawyers) – be it the sufficiency of the impact assessment itself, the administrative authority's interpretation of that assessment, or the quality of the resulting decision. As a consequence, a clarification by the Conseil d'Etat as to the correct standard of control spanning the range of Natura 2000 'questions' would be desirable. This clarificatory case law should start by distinguishing all stages of the administration's reasoning with regard to the establishment of protection (for a site or species), and the maintenance of that protection (evaluation, impact assessment, public interest, compensation measures, and so on) and clarify (or possibly harmonise) the intensity of scrutiny required for each of these elements. While the administration can retain a margin of appreciation in the assessment of the facts, there is room for a stricter control of the way in which an environmental evaluation was carried out. Judges should be able also to take an independent stance on the factual arguments of the parties. Such an independent view would strengthen the control of administrative decisions when a significant impact on the environment is at stake.

[73] A dialogue is established between the experts and the state services, which often allows the project to be adapted so that it is no longer considered as having significant effects.

[74] Jessica Makowiak, 'Expertise et Biodiversité: l'Exemple de l'Évaluation des Incidences dans le Cadre du Réseau Natura 2000' (2014) 25 *Journal International de Bioethique* 139–40. The role of private consultancies has also been discussed in Finland; see the chapter by Paloniitty and Nieminen-Finne in chapter ten of this volume, text to n 11.

The studied case law shows similarities with the litigation concerning declarations of public utility, especially when a project, plan or programme of public interest is at stake. There is a discrepancy between the seemingly high standard of control (which is based on the cost-benefit or proportionality analysis)[75] and a more hands-off acceptance of administrative interpretations of the notion of public utility. On the one hand, the courts formally assert a strong form of judicial review. On the other hand, they are particularly sensitive to the role of the administration in determining, preserving, and prioritising public interest. The literature shows that in France, Natura 2000 litigation, and in particular the case law on the adequacy of impact assessments, is seen as 'development-friendly arbitration',[76] to the detriment of biodiversity protection. Commentators stress that courts will often support a conclusion that there is no likely significant impact, meaning that the need for a full assessment is not triggered.[77]

While courts seem to examine more severely the operations of private interest, in French case law it seems that the applicability of an additional protection regime is the decisive element of annulments rulings. In fact, the provisions relating to the Natura 2000 network alone are not very effective at the stage of judicial review. Apart from cases where a formal or procedural defect is raised, authorisations are generally only annulled on substantive grounds in so far as the protection of a Natura 2000 site can also benefit from the application of other protection provisions (town planning rules, coastal law,[78] protection of the remarkable character of a site, nature park status,[79] etc). In the end, 'membership of the Natura 2000 network is only one of several indicators used by the judge to support his decisions'.[80]

Overall, while the literature criticises the use of limited review, this is perhaps not the main problem. Judicial restraint is explicable on the basis of the French interpretation of the principle of separation of powers but review of manifest error can lead to annulment, as can cases where the court considers proportionality in the impact assessment, and error of law in the exercise of administrative discretion. What is more regrettable is the minimisation of European obligations, on the one hand, and the lack of interrogation of scientific information, on the other. The latter is combined too with what appears to be disregard in some cases for the consequences of the precautionary principle on burden of proof.

The development of the route of 'full review' against 'environmental authorisations' since 2017 could have brought improvements with regard to this passive role of the courts. This lever would have significantly strengthened the effectiveness of judicial review, improved judicial engagement with scientific information,

[75] CE, 28 May 1971, *Ville Nouvelle-Est*, req. n°78825.
[76] Lanfranchi (n 72) 159.
[77] Jessica Makowiak 'La Situation en France' in Born and Haumont (n 47) 257.
[78] CE, 3 September 2009, *Commune de Canet en Roussillon*, req. n°306298.
[79] CAA de Nancy, 30 October 2008, *Minister of Ecology*, req. n°07NC01531.
[80] Makowiak (n 77) 261.

and strengthened the impact of the precautionary principle. More fundamentally, judges would have been familiar with the idea of their role in environmental assessment matters. Unfortunately, the narrow scope of the legal concept of 'environmental authorisation' does not allow for systematic use of this second 'route' in Natura 2000 litigations. It is therefore down to the legislator to take up this issue, in order to finally comply with the European requirements.

13

The Habitats Directive in the Romanian Courts: Procedure vs Substance

DACIAN C DRAGOS AND BOGDANA NEAMŢU

I. Introduction

This chapter argues that in Romania, judicial review of the Habitats Directive (HD) revolves around procedure and not substance, due to the reluctance of courts to go into the details of the case which would require environmental or other technical expertise for their complete resolution. We will show in this chapter that the legislation transposing the key EU environmental law Directives – Environmental Impact Assessment (EIA), Wild Birds Directive (WBD) and HD – has been slow.[1] We will argue that, when it comes to practical issues relating to the application of the HD, the case law of the Romanian courts shows a general reluctance to assess the substance of environmental law cases. There is instead a reliance on procedural analysis (eg focussing on the conduct of the EIA). Consequently, there is no real discussion of scientific uncertainty in Romanian jurisprudence and how to approach it. The courts regularly refer back to the administrative authorities when it comes to technical issues that need environmental expertise. Finally, we will show that the issue of uncertainty is dealt with only tangentially, as the courts impose on the decision-makers a duty to assess the relevant facts during the EIA process, seconded by a duty to give proper reasons, and do not order court expertise (except in very rare cases).

The chapter continues with an account of the implementation of the Directives in Romania in section II. In section III it considers the intensity of the judicial review in environmental matters and discusses the scarce case law on scientific uncertainty grouped on different aspects in section IV. Section V discusses the role of the precautionary principles and section VI concludes.

[1] For full detail on the Directives, see the Table of Legislation or Introduction. Original language ersions of legislative provisions are available in the Table of Legislation.

II. The National Implementation of the Wild Birds, Habitats and EIA Directives

In Romania, both the HD and WBD have been transposed mainly through the legislation on protected natural areas, Government Emergency Ordinance No 57/2007 (which is delegated legislation issued by the Government and then validated by the Parliament through a law – hereafter GEO 57/2007).[2] The extended relevant legal framework includes, besides the said ordinance, laws, other Governmental Ordinances, Government Decisions, and various Ministerial Orders.[3]

Between 2008 and 2016, the GEO 57/2007, which transposed the HD in Romania, was the subject of numerous amendments and modifications required by the European Commission. As a result of poor progress in the designation of special protection areas for birds during this period, the Commission undertook the first steps of an infringement procedure. In May 2010, the first letter

[2] Government Emergency Ordinance No 57/2007 regarding the status of natural protection areas, conservation of natural habitats, wild flora and fauna, *Monitorul Oficial al României* No 442 of 29 June 2007; Law No 49/2011 for the approval of the Government Emergency Ordinance No 57/2007 regarding the regime of natural protected areas, conservation of natural habitats, flora and fauna, *Monitorul Oficial al României* No 262 of 13 April 2011.

[3] Law No 95/2016, regarding the establishment of the National Agency for Protected Natural Areas and for the amendment of the Government Emergency Ordinance No 57/2007 on the regime of protected natural areas, conservation of natural habitats, wild flora, and fauna, *Monitorul Oficial al României* No 369 of 13 May 2016; Government Emergency Ordinance No 90/2016 on establishing measures to ensure the management of protected natural areas, *Monitorul Oficial al României* No 990 of 8 December 2016; Law No 204/2017 on the approval of Government Emergency Ordinance No 90/2016 on establishing measures to ensure the management of protected natural areas, *Monitorul Oficial al României* No 863 of 1 November 2017; Government Emergency Ordinance No 195/2005 on environmental protection, *Monitorul Oficial al României* No 1196 of 30 December 2005; Law No 407/2006 on hunting and protection of the hunting fund, *Monitorul Oficial al României* No 944 of 22 November 2006; Ministerial Order No 1964/2007 on the establishment of the protected natural area regime of sites of Community importance, as an integral part of the European ecological network Natura 2000 in Romania, *Monitorul Oficial al României*, No 98 of 7 February 2008; Governmental Decision No 1284/2007 regarding the declaration of special avifauna protection areas as an integral part of the European ecological network Natura 2000 in Romania, *Monitorul Oficial al României* No 739 of 31 October 2007; Ministerial Order No 410/2008 for the approval of the procedure for the authorization of the activities of harvesting, capturing and / or acquisition and / or marketing on the national territory or for export of mine flowers, plant fossils and fossils of vertebrate and invertebrate animals, as well as plants and animals from wild flora and fauna, respectively, and their import, *Monitorul Oficial al României* No 339 of 1 May 2008, modified by Ministerial Order No 890/2009 for the modification of some normative acts that establish tariffs in the field of environmental protection, *Monitorul Oficial al României* No 505 of 22 July 2009; Ministerial Order No 979/2009 on the introduction of non-native species, interventions on invasive species, as well as the reintroduction of native species provided in annex No 4A and 4B of the Government Emergency Ordinance No 57/2007 on the regime of protected natural areas, conservation of natural habitats, wild flora, and fauna on the national territory, *Monitorul Oficial al României* No 500 of 20 July 2009; Ministerial Order No 46/2016, on the establishment of the protected natural area regime and the declaration of sites of Community importance as an integral part of the European ecological network Natura 2000 in Romania, *Monitorul Oficial al României* No 114 of 15 February 2016.

of formal notice regarding the poor enforcement of EU law in one of the most important wetlands in Europe, the Danube Delta, was sent.[4] This concerned the planned development of facilities on the Black Sea coast, in the town of Sulina. The project included the creation of areas for recreation, a dispensary and works on access roads. This area is part of the Natura 2000 network. The Commission found deficiencies in the EIA which failed to prove beyond scientific doubt the absence of a significant negative impact of the works on both habitats and protected bird species. Although the Romanian authorities provided additional information, the Commission considered that there were still doubts about the major negative effects of the proposed work and as such, in January 2015, the Commission sent a reasoned opinion to Romania in the framework of infringement proceedings.[5]

Furthermore, in September 2010, the Commission sent Romania a reasoned opinion for non-compliance with EU legislation in relation to the hunting of birds. The Commission thought that the hunting periods provided for by the Romanian legislation did not guarantee the full protection required by the WBD.[6]

In May 2015, the Commission initiated a new infringement procedure regarding the breach of multiple pieces of EU legislation, such as HD and the Water Framework Directive, through the illegal construction of micro-hydropower plants over several water streams that cross Natura 2000 protected natural areas in the Carpathian Mountains.[7] The infringement procedure by the Commission has come one and a half years after the submission by several representatives of civil society of several complaints to the Commission, which warned about a series of horizontal infringements of European and national water and biodiversity regulations. These referred to the authorisation and construction of energy infrastructures on the territory of protected areas of European interest (Natura 2000) and rivers designated in good and very good ecological condition according to the Water Framework Directive. Other projects continued to be unlawfully authorised or re-authorised as well on other rivers with high ecological value, such as the White River in the Retezat Mountains, located in the Geopark Ţara Haţegului and the Natura 2000 site Strei-Haţeg, or even on the Jiu River and its tributaries, in the area of the Jiu Gorge, inside the Gorge National Park Jiu and Natura 2000 site Jiu Gorge, designated for various species dependent on aquatic habitats, protected at European level. Civil society requested the Commission to intervene urgently in these cases. The Ministry of the Environment, Waters, and Forests did not respond positively to complaints from the World Wide Fund for Nature (WWF) and the

[4] World Wide Fund for Nature (WWF), 'Stadiul Implementarii Directivelor Natura 2000 in Romania' (2016) 8, available online at https://fdocuments.net/document/stadiul-implementrii-directivelor-natura-2000-n-n-primul-capitol-al-acestui.html?page=1. See also SOR (Romanian Ornithological Society) and BirdLife International, 'Danube Delta Natura 2000 Site, Romania: Inadequate Implementation of the EU Nature Directives is Resulting in Site Deterioration and Species Disturbance' (2008).

[5] WWF, *ibid* 8–9.

[6] *ibid.*

[7] *ibid* 8.

Coalition Natura 2000 Federation and, consequently, the case on the White River was brought to the attention of the competent national courts.[8]

In October 2020, new shortcomings had been identified – the Commission warned Romania that the HD had not yet been fully transposed.[9] The Commission sent Romania a letter of formal notice, and our country had two months to remedy the situation. The Commission may still decide to send a reasoned opinion. Among other issues, Romanian legislation does not explicitly mention that the conservation measures included in management plans must take into account the ecological needs of the types of natural habitat and the species present on the territory of the respective sites. This has a direct impact on the quality of management plans, as they may not contain the measures necessary to protect those habitat types and species. National legislation also limits the scope of the main provisions of the HD to activities carried out on Natura 2000 sites. This excludes all other possible causes of damage or disturbance from outside sites. In line with the European Green Deal and the European Biodiversity Strategy, it is essential for the EU to stop biodiversity loss by improving and restoring damaged ecosystems to achieve good environmental status, as the Commission explains on its website.[10]

In addition, meeting the objectives of these Directives requires integration of policies and cross-sectoral cooperation; the creation of appropriate institutional structures for management, monitoring and implementation; sufficient financial resources; and support from stakeholders and civil society. The main problems identified in Romania are the financial constraints in the management of protected natural areas, especially regarding the management and implementation of the necessary conservation measures, together with incomplete scientific data (especially on the species/habitats that are present in Natura 2000 sites) and inefficient communication and cooperation with the public and interested parties/institutions.[11]

A set of institutional arrangements were put in place to implement the HD and other relevant Directives: The National Agency for Protected Natural Areas (*Agentia Nationala a Ariilor Protejate* – ANANP),[12] established in 2016, by Law No 95/2016, operates based on Government Decision No 997/2016.[13] ANANP is a public institution with legal personality, financed from its revenues and subsidies granted from the state budget and operates under the Ministry of Environment. The purpose of ANANP is to ensure unified and efficient administration of

[8] *ibid.*

[9] For more details, please see https://romania.representation.ec.europa.eu/news/romania-proceduri-de-infringement-domeniul-mediului-privind-deseurile-natura-apa-si-calitatea_ro.

[10] *ibid.*

[11] WWF (n 4) 7.

[12] The website of the institution, available at http://ananp.gov.ro/cinesuntem/.

[13] Governmental Decision No 997/2016 regarding the organization and operation of the National Agency for Protected Natural Areas and regarding the amendment and completion of annex No 12 to Governmental Decision No 1705/2006 for the approval of the centralized inventory of goods in the public domain of the state, *Monitorul Oficial al României* No 1070 of 30 December 2016.

protected natural areas and conservation of natural habitats of wild flora and fauna, regulated by the provisions of the Government Emergency Ordinance No 57/2007.

In Romania, as we will show below, assessment within the HD is carried out through EIA assessment, so the case law on the HD directly concerns EIA. The transposition of the EIA Directive in the Romanian legal framework, was carried out rather late: through Law No 292/2018, on assessing the impact of certain public and private projects on the environment[14] (dubbed EIA Law). Moreover, the EIA Law sets a deadline of up to 12 months for the adoption of secondary legislation, which means that the Directive was expected to be fully transposed by the end of 2019, but this secondary legislation was never adopted.

The stages of the EIA procedure remain, in principle, unchanged: however, their duration and characteristics have changed.[15] During *the stage of defining the field of evaluation*, the authorities have a wide margin of appreciation on the additional information they may request from the developer and the level of detail required will also depend on the specific characteristics of the project and the environmental aspects that could be affected. Another novelty is the establishment of a guarantee of the quality of the reports within the EIA procedure, by imposing on the authority the obligation to ensure that it has the necessary expertise to examine the reports submitted by the developer. To this end, for projects of particular complexity, the authority may contract external expertise. However, it remains to be seen how the authorities will be able to fulfil their obligation to employ staff with sufficient expertise in the field in question, given that the explanatory memorandum to the EIA Law does not identify any increase in budget expenditure as a result of the application of this law.

This brief explanation demonstrates the important elements of the legal framework for transposing the two relevant Directives (HD and EIA). We now move to discussing the basics of the system of judicial review before the Romanian courts.

III. The Intensity of Review and the Rules of Evidence before Romanian Courts in Environmental Matters

A. The Scope of Judicial Review in Environmental Matters

The Romanian Constitution does not mandate any specific approach to judicial review of administrative action, apart from a very general provision regarding

[14] Law No 292/2018 on assessing the impact of certain public and private projects on the environment, *Monitorul Oficial al României* No 1043 of 10 December 2018.

[15] Cleopatra Leahu, 'Suciu Popa Partner, Cum se Evaluează Impactul Asupra Mediului în România?' (Business Magazin, 2019) available at www.businessmagazin.ro/actualitate/cleopatra-leahu-partener-uciu-popa-cum-se-evalueaza-impactul-asupra-mediului-in-romania-17835127.

the right of access to court to complain against administrative action (art 52). Consequently, there is no mandated level of scrutiny in cases of scientific uncertainty or a requirement to guarantee effective judicial protection similar to that contained in the German Constitution.

There is debate among scholars regarding the intensity of judicial review and, within the framework of this debate, about the different approaches regarding the relationship between the review of legality in cases of bounded competences and the review of administrative discretion.[16]

Review of legality aims to check the conformity of the decision with the law, while the review of administrative discretion has the role of assuring the conformity of the decision with the goals of the law, which usually are not expressly stated, but implicitly refer to the public interest. Discretion, as understood by Romanian legal scholars, allows public bodies to take decisions within the boundaries of the law by choosing between two or more legal options when enacting decisions, while pursuing the public interest.[17] One speaks instead of a bounded competence (*competence liée* to use the French expression) when the public authority has no choice in issuing a decision. The Law No 554/2004 on Judicial Review[18] introduced review of 'abuse of discretion', following the French model of '*détournement de pouvoir*'.

A wide and rather generic notion of discretion is used by courts. The necessary distinction between policy discretion (weighting the public and private interest); discretion in evaluating complex factual situations; and discretion in interpreting legal rules is not employed by courts.[19] In other words, all matters left to the decision of the administrative authority are subsumed under the umbrella notion of 'discretion', and all that is exercised with bounded competence is covered by the concept of 'legality'.

Overall, Romanian courts tend mostly to adopt a legality review of administrative decisions, and are less inclined to review the ('abuse of') administrative discretion.[20]

In conclusion, legality review is the norm, with exceptional cases where courts review the exercise of administrative discretion, which will be limited to reviewing whether there has been a case of 'abuse of discretion'. This is also applicable to the environmental sector.

[16] Dacian C Dragoş and Bogdana Neamţu, 'Europeanisation of Administrative Law in Romania: Current Developments in Jurisprudence and Legislation' (2009) 2 *Review of European Administrative Law* 87; Antione Iorgovan, *Tratat de Drept Administrativ Vol II* (All Beck, 2002) 49; Tudor Drăganu, *Introducere în Teoria şi Practica Statului de Drept* (Dacia, 1992) 186–200.

[17] Drăganu, *ibid* 186.

[18] Law No 554/2004 on Judicial Review, *Monitorul Oficial al României* No 1154 of 7 December 2004.

[19] See Roberto Caranta, 'On Discretion' in Sacha Prechal and Bert van Roermund (eds), *The Coherence of EU Law: The Search for Unity in Divergent Concepts* (Oxford University Press, 2008) 195.

[20] Cluj Appellate Court, Decision No 3010/2008, unpublished.

B. Procedural Tools and Expertise in Environmental Litigation

The main procedural rules for court-ordered or ex-parte expertise are laid down in arts 330 to 334 of the Code of Civil Procedure.[21] The questions for the expert are usually proposed by the parties, but they have to be approved by the court. The court can rephrase the questions, reject questions or ask additional questions.[22] The experts are selected from a list of authorised experts, kept by the Ministry of Justice and by the Local Bureau for Expert Reports. If the parties do not agree on the appointment of an expert, the court will appoint the expert. The court can appoint an expert to give evidence on questions of scientific facts underpinning an administrative decision, for example.

While theoretically at the disposal of administrative courts, these provisions are rarely used in practice. The administrative courts usually rely on the facts of the case as presented by the parties. When in doubt, the courts prefer to ask the competent authorities for explanations or additional facts and sometimes decide that a procedural stage is missing, ordering the fulfilment of that stage – EIA for instance. Recourse to outside expertise is limited to those exceptional situations in which the court enters into the substance of the decision, beyond a mere legality review. In complex or high-stake projects, this outside expertise has sometimes been ordered.

One such case[23] was front-page news for some time as it involved the authorisation of a 'temporary' waste management facility in a beautiful mountain area, close to people's houses. The facility was intended to replace an old facility, but instead of being authorised for a short period, it was kept going for three years with no sign of being replaced soon by a permanent facility elsewhere. In this case, the study conducted by national authorities in the context of an EIA when issuing the permit was challenged and the Court ordered an independent expert report. The Court relied on an external expert, specialising in waste management, for confirmation that the platform for the realisation of the land represented a controlled landfill of non-hazardous waste. The expert report led to the conclusion that the original decision misinterpreted the legal norms (rather than wrongfully interpreting the facts). Based on the assessment of the external expert, the Court then found that the previous expertise relied upon by the first instance Court – an impact study on the health status of the population drafted by the National Institute of Public Health – had erroneously interpreted the applicable legal norms. The Court consequently reversed the first instance decision and annulled the administrative act.

[21] Code of Civil Procedure of 1 July 2010 (NCPC), Law No 134/2010, *Monitorul Oficial al României* No 247 of 10 April 2015.

[22] See NCPC, art 154. See also NCPC, arts 319 and 321. See Sebastian Spinei, *Evidence in Civil Law – Romania, Lex Localis* (Maribor, 2015) 63.

[23] Cluj Appellate Court, Decision No 3582/100/2017 ECLI:RO:CACLJ:2020:050.00015.

A second case[24] involved the inclusion of a small river into a larger area that is protected from human intervention. The refusal of the Water Administration to chart the small tributary of a larger river as an independent river worthy of protection has been challenged in court by an non-governmental organisation. The judge ordered the engagement of independent technical expertise which confirmed the stance of the public authority that the relevant EU law provisions had been observed; that the Water Framework Directive gave discretion to Member States as to whether or not to chart separately rivers less than 10 km and in permitting such discretion; and that national law had correctly transposed the Directive. The Court relied heavily upon this technical expertise and dismissed the challenge.

This case shows that, in complex technical cases, the courts can rely on expert opinion, and not defer automatically to the expertise of national public authorities. However, such cases are rare. In the majority of situations, the courts trust the initial assessment of the public authorities, or they order a fresh assessment by the same authorities.

IV. Case Law on Scientific Uncertainty in Relation to the HD, WBD and EIA

Before embarking on the discussion of the case law of the Romanian courts, two preliminary general observations ought to be made. First, we could not find cases where the focus of the questions dealt with by the courts is on the assessment made by the competent authorities on the effects of a proposed project on the conservation target in the context of the WBD and HD (eg Special Protection Area/Natura 2000 sites). Most cases found in Romanian jurisprudence concern EIA and the need to conduct a proper assessment of the impact on the environment, including on the birds and habitats in Natura 2000 sites. Indeed, a decision has been made to streamline these processes so that there is no separate appropriate assessment under the biodiversity Directives, but rather these assessments are 'folded into' the EIA.

Second, the body of Romanian case law dealing with the WBD and HD concerns questions which are procedural rather than substantive in nature, and in most of the cases no outside expertise was requested. The analysis of the court mainly deals with the *necessity* of an EIA and thus dwells on the unlawfulness stemming from a lack of EIA. Courts generally conclude that an EIA is needed to assess the impact on the natural habitat, the insufficient assessment of it, or the resuming of EIA after new elements occur.

[24] Cluj Appellate Court, Decision No 129/2020, ECLI:RO:CACLJ:2020:048.000129.

A. The Scope of the HD – The Wolf's Habitat

One case which is critical to the analysis here relates to the expanse of the habitat of the wolf. This case has reached the Court of Justice of the European Union (CJEU) whereby the Court ascertained that the strict protection of animal species provided for in the HD also extends to specimens that leave their natural habitat and stray into human settlements. The capture and relocation of a wolf found in a village could therefore be justified only where such a removal was appropriately assessed as a derogation under national law in compliance with the European standards.

The preliminary question in this case, which was raised by a lower Romanian Court, *Judecătoria Zărnești*, in November 2018, reached the Court in 2019 and lead to a ruling in June 2020.

In 2016, employees of an animal protection association, accompanied by a veterinary surgeon, captured and relocated, without prior authorisation, a wolf that had been present on the property of a resident of a village situated between two major sites that are protected under the HD. The relocation of the captured wolf to a nature reserve did not, however, go according to plan and the wolf managed to escape into a nearby forest. A criminal complaint was filed in respect of offences associated with the unsafe capture and relocation of a wolf. In the context of those criminal proceedings, the referring Court was unclear as to whether the protection provisions contained in the HD applied to the capture of wild wolves on the outskirts of a town or a city or the territory of a local authority.

In its judgment in *Alianța Pentru Combaterea Abuzurilor*, the CJEU ruled on the territorial scope of the system of strict protection of certain animal species provided for in art 12(1) HD.[25] The Court confirmed that this system applies also to specimens that leave their natural habitat and stray into human settlements. In doing so, the Court referred to art 12(1)(a) HD which requires the Member States to take the necessary measures to establish a system of strict protection of protected animal species 'in their natural range', prohibiting all forms of deliberate capture or killing of specimens of these species 'in the wild':

> In order to comply with that provision, the Member States must not only adopt a comprehensive legislative framework but also implement concrete and specific protection measures. Similarly, the system of strict protection presupposes the adoption of coherent and coordinated measures of a preventive nature. Such a system of strict protection must therefore enable the actual avoidance of deliberate capture or killing in the wild of specimens of protected animal species (see, to that effect, judgments of 17 April 2018, *Commission v Poland (Białowieża Forest)*, C-441/17, EU:C:2018:255, paragraph 231 and the case-law cited, and of 10 October 2019, Luonnonsuojeluyhdistys Tapiola, C-674/17, EU:C:2019:851, paragraph 27).

[25] C-88/19 *Asociația 'Alianța Pentru Combaterea Abuzurilor' v TM* ECLI:EU:C:2020:458.

In respect of the territory of said prohibition, because protected animal species which, like the wolf, occupy vast stretches of territory, the concept of 'natural range' is greater than the geographical space that contains the essential physical or biological elements for their life and reproduction, and therefore corresponds to the geographical space in which the animal species concerned is present or to which it extends during its natural behaviour. Consequently, the protection does not comprise any limits or borders, with the result that a wild specimen of an animal species which strays close to or into human settlements, passing through such areas or feeding on resources produced by humans, cannot be regarded as an animal that has left its 'natural range'.[26]

Therefore, according to the Court, the wording of art 12(1)(a) HD, which prohibits the deliberate capture or killing of specimens of protected species 'in the wild', does not allow human settlements to be excluded from the scope of protection under that provision. The use of the word 'wild' is intended only to specify that the prohibitions laid down in that provision do not necessarily apply to specimens kept in a lawful form of captivity. The interpretation that the protection provided for in art 12(1)(a) HD does not comprise any strict limits or borders is also of such a nature as to allow the objective pursued by that provision to be attained.[27]

In summary, the Court affirmed the protection of species concerned not only in restrictively defined places but also specimens of those species living 'in nature' or in the wild which therefore play a part in natural ecosystems. The Court also noted that the development of infrastructure, illegal logging, farming and certain industrial activities contribute to the pressure exerted on the wolf population and its habitat. Consequently, the Court held that the obligation to protect strictly relevant animal species applies to the entire 'natural range' of those species, whether they are in their natural habitat, protected areas, or in proximity to human settlements.

However, the Court did not utilise any scientific evidence to explain this, nor did it consider whether there was any lack of clarity about the 'range' concept. As a result, there was no reference to the issue of 'uncertainty'. The Romanian Court did not refer to scientific assessments being made about the scope of a wolf's natural habitat, either.

B. The Scope of the HD – The Bear's Habitat

The brown bear (*Ursus arctos*) is included in Annex IL (Strictly protected species of fauna) of the Convention on the Conservation of Wildlife and Natural

[26] *ibid.*
[27] *ibid.*

Habitats in Europe,[28] Annex IV HD, and Annex 3 to GEO No 57/2007 (ie the national transposing regulation). More than 6, 000 brown bear individuals live in Romania.[29] At the level of the Ministry of Environment, a decision was made to approve the collection of six brown bear specimens. These were bears habituated to human presence and accustomed to descending into the countryside to get food, endangering the safety and integrity of citizens and their property.

A case was brought to court to challenge six derogations for shooting bears based on art 16(1) HD. The Court held that the derogations were given without actual analysis of the alternative measures to be taken, as required by the legal text.[30] The national Court cited both the Directive and national law (GEO No 57/2007) when stating the requirement to have a proper analysis of such alternatives before granting the exceptions. There was no further analysis of whether the alternatives had not been considered at all or dismissed too quickly. The alternatives were not assessed at all.

The Court cited the case law of the CJEU (*Commission v Finland*) where the CJEU stated that the granting of such derogations 'remains possible by way of an exception where it is duly established that they are not such as to worsen the unfavourable conservation status of those populations or to prevent their restoration to a favourable conservation status,'[31] and that it 'is possible that the killing of a limited number of specimens may not affect the objective envisaged in Article 16(1) of the Habitats Directive, which consists in maintaining the wolf population at a favourable conservation status in its natural range'.[32]

Moreover, the Court recalled that the HD requires full and detailed reasoning as to the absence of satisfactory alternatives able to attain the objectives invoked in such requests for derogation. Consequently, the six derogations challenged were deemed unlawful as they contained only general references to the legal grounds and an opinion of the Romanian Academy that did not regard specifically the specific case at hand. There was no comprehensive explanation of the reasons behind the administrative decision.

Thus, as the law enumerates exhaustively the situations in which such derogations may occur, and the body adopting the derogation was required to indicate in the reasoning justifying the decision both the legal basis and information regarding the concrete, factual situation. The contested decision in this case did

[28] Convention on the Conservation of European Wildlife and Natural Habitats (ETS No 104), Council of Europe, adopted in Bern on 19 September 1979, to which Romania acceded through Law No 13/1993 for Romania's accession to the Convention on the Conservation of European Wildlife and Natural Habitats, adopted in Bern on 19 September 1979, *Monitorul Oficial al României* No 62 of 25 March 1993.

[29] European Commission, 'Conservation of Brown Bear (Ursus arctos) population in Romania', Reference: LIFE13 NAT/RO/001154, Acronym: LIFE FOR BEAR, available at https://webgate.ec.europa.eu/life/publicWebsite/index.cfm?fuseaction=search.dspPage&n_proj_id=5110.

[30] Constanta Appellate Court, Decision No 132/2020, ECLI: RO:CACTA:2020:016.

[31] C-342/05 *Commission v Finland* ECLI:EU:C:2007:341 [29].

[32] *ibid.* See chapter two in this volume by Augustin Garcia Ureta.

not discuss, at least, the relevant factual situation. Moreover, the culling measure was vaguely expressed, as there were no criteria for identifying the 'problem' bear specimens in the decision. From the whole regulation it is clear that such derogations – especially the culling of a specimen – are to be taken only in relation to problem individuals, which must be precisely identified and their 'behaviour' analysed in order to establish the need to eliminate the specimen. However, the contested orders did not identify the individual specimens, but used the generic phrase 'bear'. In this respect, the lack of precise, and verifiable information, about the targets of culling measures led to an uncertainty which was fatal to reliance on the derogation. No analysis was performed to identify a non-lethal solution. Rather the extreme solution (shooting) was chosen first, contrary to the applicable legal framework. The measure ordered by the contested orders was an extreme one, so that, if it were to be executed, it is obvious that serious damage to the fauna would occur and it could not be restored.

This case is an example of how courts review discretion in deciding upon the derogations provided by law. The Court did not enter into a substantive analysis of the factual information relied upon by the Ministry, but reinstated the duty to have a proper reasoning in the administrative decision which justified the final solution envisaged. No external expert opinion was requested by the Court. The Court found the matter to be about 'purely' legal questions. This is one relevant example of how courts do not enter the realm of discretionary administrative decision-making when reviewing environmental decisions.

V. Scientific Evidence and the Precautionary Principle

In this section, we will showcase instances where the courts have made recourse to environmental principles in matters where questions of scientific uncertainty are raised.

In a case regarding environmental permits, the Court[33] stated that the procedure necessary for issuing an environmental permit had not been followed since the contested plan had been adopted before the environmental assessment of that plan. The Court invoked the precautionary principle in decision-making as an argument for the conclusion that environmental assessment must be made *before* the plan to develop the area, and not afterwards. The Court also considered that the public consultation procedure had to be carried out beforehand and not after the adoption of the plan and that, for the plan to be lawful, there must be scientific evidence that there is no harm to the protected species. In the absence of such detailed justifications, the Court concluded that there might be imminent damage to environmental elements, as once the work is done, it is not

[33] Bucharest Appellate Court, Decision No 588/2019 ECLI:RO:CABUC:2019:186.

possible to reverse the effects produced on the protected species. Consequently, the Court concluded that the precautionary principle in decision-making had been infringed by the reversed order of steps in the procedure to approve the development.

The Court went on to stress that environmental assessments must demonstrate that the plan does not diminish the conservation status of protected species and habitats, including by issuing its classification decisions accompanied by all necessary scientific evidence. For example, this can be done by analysing the area where deforestation is proposed in conjunction with the areas where protected species and habitats are located. The Court referred also to the envisaged purposes of art 6 HD as transposed by Romania, and to the fact that the national legislation must be interpreted in light of the Directive and the corresponding CJEU case law, which is regarded as mandatory for national courts.

In this case, it is apparent that the Court did not assess the sufficiency of the scientific information, but only required that such information be the basis of the final decision and that a final decision be taken following a logical succession of steps entailing first the assessment of the environmental impacts of a plan, followed by its adoption. Moreover, the Court held that scientific evidence is needed to demonstrate *the lack of effects on the environment*, which is a rather high standard of review. However, when such evidence is presented, the Court will 'trust' an administrative authority when it says there is no possibility of such effects.

While this ruling seems to point to a rather strict review on the part of the Romanian courts, it should not be overlooked that the decision was – in essence – about a procedural rather than a substantive issue, as the Court did not develop the standard of scientific data that needs to be presented when proving the lack of environmental effects.

In another case,[34] the Court annulled two building permits issued in 2012 and 2016 based on an environmental permit issued in 2003 (before the area was included in Natura 2000). The Court established the need to carry out a new assessment of the impact on the environment at the date of the issuance of the building permits. The Court motivated its position invoking the provisions of art 6(3) HD, and a number of *obiter* comments in the judgments of the Luxembourg Court concerning the application of the HD. The appellant challenged the annulment and, strangely enough, invoked the principles of proportionality, legitimate expectations, and legal certainty *against* the annulment of administrative decisions authorising a project without a proper assessment of the environment.

The Court referred to the CJEU decision in *Commission v Portugal*, according to which 'when adopting the decision authorizing the implementation of the project, no scientifically reasonable doubt must be maintained in the report with

[34] Bucharest Appellate Court, Decision No 4761/2018 ECLI:RO:CABUC:2018:024.

no negative effects on integrity within the targeted site'.[35] Furthermore, it found that in the case at issue, at the time of the authorisation of the project (ie of the issuance and extension of building permits), an assessment had not been carried out to provide the evidence required by EU law to remove all scientific doubts about the negative effects of the project, although it was mandatory according to national and European Union legislation. The project proposed an enormous degree of destruction, entailing practically the total disappearance of the protected area. The argument that the Court should be the one to carry out a proportionality test when it annuls an administrative act was rejected by the Court. It held that it was the appellant who is responsible for the proof that no scientific uncertainties exist at the time of issuing the building permits. However, the Court did not dwell on how the 'no scientific uncertainty' test should be performed. It only provided that this should result from a properly conducted EIA. Commenting on this, one can say that the court can always appoint an independent expert to look at the evidence from the EIA, if needed. Usually, though, in practice, the evidence in the EIA/appropriate assessment is provided by the developer to the administrative authority, as the administrative authority does not have the resources to carry out its own assessments.

The Court also stated that the exceptional situations that would allow a project of general interest that produces a negative impact on the environment in a protected area should be analysed from the perspective of the principle of proportionality. The Court then referred (generally, without citing a specific decision) to the case law of the CJEU that has consistently ruled that these projects can only be implemented after the appropriate assessment has been carried out, in which very strict compensatory measures must be identified to prevent the degradation or extinction of protected species and habitats at the Community level. In no case is it permissible to carry out large-scale projects that have enormous destructive potential on the environment, such as the project in question, without any environmental assessment. Exceptions must also be reported to the Commission, which must give its consent to their implementation, a procedure that had not been followed in the present case.[36]

VI. Conclusion

The few cases discussed above suggest that Romanian courts are reluctant to enter into discussions around scientific uncertainty or certainty and prefer to

[35] C-239/04 *Commission of the European Communities v Portuguese Republic* ECLI:EU:C:2006:665.
[36] *ibid.*

tackle environmental law cases mostly from a strictly procedural perspective. This is a feature of Romanian judicial review in general, not just in environmental law cases.

The Romanian courts do not assess themselves the likelihood of detrimental impacts of a project or the risk of endangering protected species or habitats, nor do they apply the concept of risk, or that of scientific uncertainty. The courts instead rely on administrative authorities (which in turn rely on developers) to carry out such assessments, and they only require that this procedural step be taken and that proof be presented as to the impact on the environment. In other words, the existence of an EIA is mandated and its absence is censored by the courts, but the latter will not venture into controlling its content. This might be a cultural issue that has an impact on the actual proceedings in the court. However, this happens perhaps due to the stack of cases piling up on the judge's desks in the administrative law field, which makes them eager to deal with cases as swiftly as possible. Therefore, in our opinion, lack of time might be more of a structural explanation for the absence of expert witness involvement in environmental court proceedings.

Consequently, there is no real talk of the notion of uncertainty in Romanian jurisprudence. The courts safely limit themselves to a mere procedural review and, with few exceptions, do not challenge the expertise of public authorities. The Romanian administrative courts very much frame the question of uncertainty as a duty to *investigate* the relevant facts seconded by a *duty to give reasons* on the part of the authorities.

In environmental law cases, the precautionary principle may be invoked to request a new EIA or the completion of an already existing one when necessary. In that sense, the imposition on the developer of a duty to show that there are no detrimental effects on the environment based on scientific evidence was considered to be proportionate.

There are no cases where the 'imperative reason of overriding public interest' has been invoked to approve projects. However, it is unlikely that the court's assessment of scientific information would differ when it considers the exception regime, eg whether 'imperative reasons of overriding public interest' are at hand.

The Romanian courts have become accustomed to invoking principles of environmental law, such as the precautionary principle, to request that plans and projects be preceded by a proper EIA. In that sense, a Europeanisation of environmental judicial review is slowly creeping in.

Although this is not discussed either in case law or doctrine, the current scope and intensity of review in our opinion does not comply with EU law and in particular art 47 of the EU Charter of Fundamental Rights as the remedies are not effective. The review is mostly 'on the surface' and only on procedure. When looking at the notion of 'substantive legality' required by the Aarhus Convention (art 9), again, the conclusion is that courts do not provide enough guarantees that administration weighs impartially competing interests when a decision regarding the environment is made, as their focus lies only on procedure instead of substance.

We think that courts should have more audacity to enter the substance of environmental law cases and assess the national decision-making process in light of EU law and standards and challenge the expertise based on which some cases are dealt with at the administrative level. One should not forget that Romanian administration is not yet as fair and public interest-minded as it should be, especially in areas where vested private interests are powerful. The full protection of the environment needs fair and impartial administration seconded by a more effective judicial review by courts.

PART III

Broadening the View

14

Biodiversity in the Court: The Certainty of Contests about Uncertainty

THE HON JUSTICE BRIAN J PRESTON

I. Introduction

Biodiversity loss is a global problem that rivals climate change in its severity.[1] Disputes about biodiversity loss involve considerable scientific uncertainty. Uncertainty arises because of the unpredictability and randomness of natural systems and processes. It occurs on a spectrum from known knowns, to known unknowns to unknown unknowns.[2] While known unknowns can often be identified, managed or even reduced, unknown unknowns always remain and affect the operation of environmental systems. Regulators and courts have, however, developed innovative approaches to manage this type of uncertainty, including use of the precautionary principle. Even known knowns may prove challenging since uncertainty remains even when our knowledge about the state of something is ostensibly settled. This is largely because our systems of knowledge, including science, and settled concepts therein are subject to change and revision over time.[3]

The uncertainties in these disputes can be epistemic, methodological or technological, linguistic and sociological. Epistemic uncertainty is due to inherent variability and natural randomness in ecological systems or processes or the lack of knowledge about ecological systems or processes. Epistemic uncertainty can be reduced, but not necessarily eliminated, by more thorough or comprehensive study and through sensitivity analysis.[4] Methodological or technological uncertainty refers to deficiencies in current methods and techniques used to

[1] William J Ripple et al, 'World Scientists' Warning to Humanity: Second Notice' (2017) 67 *BioScience* 1026.

[2] See Nassim Nicholas Taleb, *The Black Swan: The Impact of the Highly Improbable* (Penguin, 2007).

[3] See Karl Popper, *The Logic of Scientific Discovery* (Routledge, 2002); Thomas Kuhn, *The Structure of Scientific Revolutions*, 4th edn (University of Chicago Press, 2012).

[4] Helen M Regan et al, 'A Taxonomy and Treatment of Uncertainty for Ecology and Conservation Biology' (2002) 12 *Ecological Applications* 618, 618.

describe natural processes.[5] Linguistic uncertainty arises because words used in the description and assessment of ecological systems and processes have different or imprecise meanings. Linguistic uncertainty also arises in the laws and policies that regulate the protection of ecological systems and biodiversity. Finally, sociological uncertainty arises from the exclusion of valid theories or studies as a result of social processes operating in the scientific community.[6]

As a result, in the interpretation and application of laws and policies, there is a (small) core of certainty but a (large) penumbra of doubt. In adjudicating biodiversity-related disputes, courts often need to resolve issues of uncertainty. How have they done so? This chapter examines this question. It does so by primarily drawing on judicial decisions from the Australian state of New South Wales (NSW) and some from other Australian jurisdictions. The mechanisms for reducing uncertainty differ depending on the type of uncertainty involved.

This chapter is structured as follows. Section II highlights the limits of environmental knowledge. Section III discusses the different types of uncertainty. It uses the jurisprudence of the NSW Land and Environment Court to illustrate how these uncertainties might arise. Section IV outlines the different stages in biodiversity conservation and identifies the uncertainties that occur at each stage by reference to Australian judicial decisions. Section V documents how Australian courts have responded to and addressed uncertainty in biodiversity cases. Section VI offers concluding observations.

II. The Limits of Environmental Knowledge

All scientific knowledge is uncertain. However, uncertainty is not a negative attribute. As Feynman observed, 'experience with doubt and uncertainty is important [and] of very great value and extends beyond the sciences'.[7] The value of uncertainty and doubt lie in the fact that they leave open the possibility for further enquiry.[8] Moreover, all scientific knowledge today comprises a body of statements with varying degrees of certainty.[9] Feynman, in short, recognised the importance of 'freedom to doubt'.[10]

Philosophers of science like Karl Popper have observed that science is constantly subject to review, revision, renewal and improvement through iterative cycles of knowledge production.[11] Science can be improved when it is brought

[5] Jacqueline Peel, *The Precautionary Principle in Practice: Environmental Decision-making and Scientific Uncertainty* (Federation Press, 2005) 54; and Adrian Deville and Ronnie Harding, *Applying the Precautionary Principle* (Federation Press, 1997) 31–37.

[6] Peel, *ibid* 54.

[7] R Feynman, *The Meaning of it All* (Penguin, 1999) 26.

[8] *ibid* 27.

[9] *ibid.*

[10] *ibid* 28.

[11] Popper (n 3).

to bear on a problem and through the deductive testing of theories.[12] All knowledge is *provisional*, *conjectural* and *hypothetical* which requires a *choice* to be made between unfalsified theories to determine the best available one.[13] This is not truth creation or the objective representation of reality, but a process which involves subjective choices and strives for approximation to the truth.[14]

A similar project for the refinement and improvement of knowledge exists within the law. Uncertainty affects the law and knowledge limitations are inherent in our legal systems. Judges routinely deal with knowledge limitations and uncertainty. As in science, legal systems have developed mechanisms for reducing and managing uncertainty. The rules of statutory interpretation are designed to address linguistic uncertainty by legislation that is drafted in ambiguous, vague or indeterminate language.

Environmental knowledge is limited by uncertainty. Environmental knowledge can take many forms, including anecdotal information from indigenous and local communities and advanced scientific knowledge.[15] Environmental knowledge provides a crucial foundation for our understanding of nature and the regulation of environmental problems. The process of acquiring knowledge about the environment is dynamic and perpetually evolving, as environmental change is constant. As a result, environmental knowledge is often inchoate, and inherently limited by uncertainty, particularly scientific uncertainty, which can never be fully eliminated.[16] The existence of scientific uncertainty means that it is impossible to get a complete and accurate picture of environmental harm.[17]

In addition, environmental knowledge is limited and shaped by the context within which it is produced. Law and policy are key sources of demand for ongoing knowledge production on the environment.[18] Environmental knowledge is limited because it is produced for particular regulatory purposes, a process referred to as 'regulatory science'.[19]

Finally, the production of environmental knowledge is necessarily limited, because it is often infused with the value judgements of knowledge producers. Experts make value judgements when deciding which environmental problems ought to be studied and addressed.[20] For example, when a scientist expresses their findings in probabilistic terms, such as declaring there is a 20 per cent chance of a particular amount of ozone being present, they are expressing numerically, their

[12] *ibid* 9–10.
[13] *ibid* 22–26, 109.
[14] K Popper, *Conjectures and Refutations: The Growth of Scientific Knowledge* (Routledge, 1963) 236.
[15] Elizabeth Fisher et al, *Environmental Law: Texts, Cases and Materials* (Oxford University Press, 2018) 34.
[16] *ibid* 41.
[17] *ibid.*
[18] *ibid* 34.
[19] Sheila Jasanoff, *The Fifth Branch: Science Advisors as Policy Makers* (Harvard University Press, 1977) 77. See also Elizabeth Fisher et al, 'Understanding Environmental Models in Their Legal and Regulatory Context' (2010) 22 *Journal of Environmental Law* 251.
[20] Fisher et al (n 15) 42.

degree of belief.[21] In addition, the scientist may not have asked the right question to begin with.[22]

Values reflect a considered judgement that an individual makes about what is right, good or appropriate in the circumstances.[23] Value judgements are a fundamental component of environmental decision-making in democratic societies. The principles of representative and open government require sufficient transparency in governmental decision-making processes. Such processes often involve deliberations and debates about the merits of policy proposals. Sax observed that, 'as self-government is at the core of democratic government, and genuine choice is a key to self-government, assuring that risks taken are the product of such genuine choice is fundamental to the legitimacy of environmental decisions'.[24] Thus, environmental decisions must be made by reference to and in accordance with societal norms and values 'under conditions of sufficient knowledge and consideration' in order to reflect a genuine choice that is mindful of the consequences of a risk.[25]

Sound environmental decision-making cannot occur without a significant base of knowledge. In environmental decision-making, a key mechanism for generating information to address knowledge gaps and manage uncertainty is environmental impact assessment (EIA). In democratic societies, EIA is a crucial element in legitimating environmental decisions.[26] Knowledge of environmental impacts requires baseline data, which necessitates extensive and continual monitoring and evaluation.[27] However, scientific statements of fact on their own can never answer the question of what *ought* to be done in a given situation, which lies at the heart of most environmental disputes.[28] Consequently, every stage of EIA is infused with the choices of the decision-maker that reflect and incorporate societal values and preferences.

Sagoff notes that 'a policy, in serving legislated purposes, may be justified primarily on ethical rather than on economic grounds'.[29] For example, the desire to preserve certain endangered species and ecological communities might stem from a societal belief or attitude that they have intrinsic worth and dignity.[30] As Dworkin observes 'we think we should admire and protect them because they are important in themselves, and not because we and others want to enjoy them'.[31]

[21] Lawrence Susskind and Alan Weinstein, 'Towards a Theory of Environmental Dispute Resolution' (1980) 9 *Boston College Environmental Affairs Law Review* 311, 325.

[22] *ibid.*

[23] Mark Sagoff, *The Economy of the Earth: Philosophy, Law, and the Environment* (Cambridge University Press, 1988) 9.

[24] Joesph L Sax, 'The Search for Environmental Rights' (1990) 6 *Journal of Land Use & Environmental Law* 93, 97.

[25] *ibid.*

[26] *ibid* 98.

[27] *ibid.*

[28] Susskind and Weinstein (n 21) 325.

[29] Mark Sagoff, 'On the Value of Endangered and Other Species' (1996) 20 *Environmental Management* 6, 897.

[30] *ibid* 899.

[31] Ronald Dworkin, *Life's Dominion* (Vintage, 1994); *ibid*, 902.

Many economists also agree that biodiversity is a public good that cannot always be reduced to economic valuation exercises.[32] Our need for drawing up conservation lists is not purely driven by economic considerations, but is informed by 'biophilia' which is a form of bias where greater attention and priority is often afforded to larger, more attractive, rare or exotic species.[33] This produces a complex web of values within which environmental knowledge is generated and assessed.

III. Types of Uncertainty

A. Epistemic Uncertainty

Epistemic or epistemological uncertainties are the kind of uncertainties that arise because 'we don't know what we don't know'.[34] They derive from 'limitations of measurement devices, insufficient data, extrapolations and interpolations, and variability over time and space'.[35] They can be summarised into six main categories: measurement error; systematic error; natural variation; inherent randomness; model uncertainty; and subjective judgment.[36]

NSW court decisions on the listing of endangered ecological communities illustrate how scientists and courts grapple with natural variation and indeterminacy, which are forms of epistemic uncertainty that pervade biodiversity cases. These forms of uncertainty often arise in relation to an assessment of whether a particular endangered ecological community (EEC), or threatened species is present. An ecological community is an assemblage of interacting plants, animals, bacteria and fungi sharing a common environment.[37] Uncertainty can arise because an ecological community 'is a dynamic and not a static entity. It is a living entity capable of growth, maturation, senescence and regeneration'.[38]

In *VAW (Kurri Kurri) Pty Ltd v Scientific Committee*, the NSW Court of Appeal observed that 'the intricacy of all ecological communities means that some indeterminateness is bound to arise from the form of expression used to

[32] Sagoff (n 23) 903.

[33] Irus Braverman, 'Chapter 11: En-listing Life: Red is the Color of Threatened Species Lists' in Kathryn Gillespie and Rosemary-Claire Collard (eds), *Critical Animal Geographies: Politics, Intersections and Hierarchies in a Multispecies World* (Routledge, 2015) 5.

[34] Elizabeth Fisher, 'Drowning by Numbers: Standard Setting in Risk Regulation and the Pursuit of Accountable Public Administration' (2000) 20 *OJLS* 1, 115 and 116; Brian Wynne, 'Uncertainty and Environmental Learning: Reconceiving Science and Policy in the Preventative Paradigm' (1992) 2 *Global Environmental Change* 2, 112.

[35] Regan et al (n 4) 618.

[36] *ibid* 619.

[37] Harry F Recher et al, *A Natural Legacy: Ecology in Australia*, 2nd edn (AS Wilson, 1986) 415. Simon C Cropper, *Management of Endangered Plants* (CSIRO, 1993) 150; See also Brian J Preston and Paul Adam, 'Describing and Listing Threatened Ecological Communities under the Threatened Species Conservation Act 1995 (NSW): Part 1 – the Assemblage of Species and the Particular Area' (2004) 21 *Environment and Planning Law Journal* 250, 252.

[38] Preston and Adam, *ibid* 257.

describe them'.[39] The Court's decision recognised that uncertainty is often an intrinsic and unavoidable feature not only in listing ecological communities as endangered but also assessing whether the listed ecological community is present on a particular site. This was the rationale behind the Scientific Committee's rejection of a requirement to specify a minimum number or proportion of species that must be found on land to constitute an ecological community.[40] A determination about the number of species required to indicate the presence of an ecological community on land that is the subject of a development application will typically require evaluative judgments to be made by the decision-maker.[41]

In *Carstens v Pittwater Council*, the Court considered whether the Commissioner (administrative decision-maker) had erroneously concluded that the Pittwater Spotted Gum (PSG) ecological community was present on the land.[42] The parties' experts disagreed on whether the PSG community was present. Epistemic uncertainty arose because the expert evidence revealed that the site was 'an ecotone between the PSG community and the Sydney sandstone gully forest, in which the two communities intermesh'.[43] The Court found that it was reasonably open for the Commissioner to conclude that the PSG community was present based on the expert evidence and his own expertise in the matter.[44]

In *Commonwealth of Australia v Randwick City Council*, epistemic uncertainty affected the Court's determination of whether an EEC, Eastern Suburbs Banksia Scrub, was present on the site. The ecological experts disagreed as to how many of the 46 species listed as characterising the EEC needed to be present. The Court found the site did not contain sufficient of the species to qualify as the EEC.[45]

In *Plumb v Penrith City Council*, epistemic uncertainty arose in relation to the question of whether an EEC, the Cumberland Plain Woodland (CPW), was present on the whole or only part of the school site.[46] The ecological experts disagreed due to differences in the scope of their vegetation surveys of the school site and the fact that the vegetation had been degraded over time.[47] However, all experts found CPW to be present to some degree. The Court accordingly concluded that the 'weight of the evidence establishes that that CPW occurs on the whole of the school site'.[48]

In *Hornsby Shire Council v Vitone Pty Ltd*, the parties' ecologists disagreed on whether an EEC, the Blue Gum High Forest (BGHF), continued to be present

[39] *VAW (Kurri Kurri) Pty Ltd v Scientific Committee (Established under s127 of the Threatened Species Conservation Act 1995)* (2003) 58 NSWLR 631 [9].

[40] *ibid* [233]; Preston and Adam (n 37) 258.

[41] Preston and Adam (n 37) 258.

[42] *Carstens v Pittwater Council* (1999) 111 LGERA 1 [28].

[43] *ibid* [34].

[44] *ibid* [35].

[45] *Commonwealth of Australia v Randwick City Council* [2001] NSWLEC 79 [104].

[46] *Plumb v Penrith City Council* [2002] NSWLEC 223 [25].

[47] *ibid* [26]–[31].

[48] *ibid* [25].

on a site.[49] Unusually, the local council sought to judicially review its own decision to grant consent to subdivision of the site. The basis of challenge was that the development application had not been accompanied by a species impact statement (SIS). An SIS would be required if the proposed development was likely to significantly affect the EEC. The critical issue became whether the BGHF, which had been present on the site, had disappeared by reason of extensive disturbance of the site in the past.[50] Epistemic uncertainty arose because of the lack of data. The considerable disturbance of the site had reduced by half the number of species from the characteristic assemblage of species and had affected the necessary representative structure for the community.[51] The Court considered that 'for a community to exist, enough species must be present on site to allow them to function as an interdependent group'.[52] This was no longer the case.[53]

B. Methodological and Technological Uncertainty

There are also methodological uncertainties.[54] High levels of methodological uncertainty may arise as a result of excessive influence from lay audiences or non-scientific interest groups.[55] Such uncertainty is often attached to risk assessments.[56] Related to these are technological uncertainties, which arise from deficiencies in the technology used to describe the environment and assess and monitor the impact of activities on the environment.

Methodological uncertainty can arise due to the widespread use of models in environmental regulation.[57] As simplifications of reality,[58] models can only serve to provide approximations rather than truths about the natural world, which means that uncertainty always remains. By giving a false appearance of certainty, models can sometimes magnify or mask uncertainty. Scientific uncertainty is inherent in the environmental modelling process.[59] This kind of 'model uncertainty' is often the product of particular choices made in relation to the context to be modelled, how a particular problem is framed, and how the parameters are drawn.[60]

[49] *Hornsby Shire Council v Vitone Developments Pty Ltd* (2003) 132 LGERA 122.
[50] *ibid* [96].
[51] *ibid* [97].
[52] *ibid* [93].
[53] *ibid* [99].
[54] Michael Smithson, 'Ignorance and Science: Dilemmas, Perspectives and Prospects' (1993) 15 *Knowledge: Creation, Diffusion, Utilization* 2, 148.
[55] *ibid* 149.
[56] Fisher (n 34) 116.
[57] Fisher et al (n 19) 252–53.
[58] *ibid* 266; See Paul Krugman and Robin Wells, *Macroeconomics*, 5th edn (Macmillan, 2018).
[59] Fisher et al (n 19) 271.
[60] Jens Christian Refsgaard et al, 'Uncertainty in the Environmental Modelling Process – a 'ramework and Guidance' (2007) 22 *Environmental Modelling & Software* 1543; Laura Uusitalo et al, ɩn Overview of Methods to Evaluate Uncertainty of Deterministic Models in Decision Support' 2015) 63 *Environmental Modelling & Software* 24, 25.

Model uncertainty can arise in relation to the selection of system boundaries, the spatio-temporal scope and choice of outputs, assumptions and variables.[61] It also arises due to the simplification of natural processes and complex natural phenomena and the drawing of parameters in a manner that leads to a narrow examination of the phenomenon.[62] Finally, it can arise as a result of uncertain data inputs due to poor sampling, poorly drawn parameters as a result of insufficient knowledge and numerical approximations.[63]

Hornsby Shire Council v Vitone Pty Ltd is an apt example. The parties' experts disagreed on the appropriate vegetation survey methodology to be used. Each expert alleged that the other's method generated higher levels of uncertainty in the vegetation survey. The developer's expert employed the quadrat method, locating quadrats in each of the discernible vegetation types on the land.[64] The Council's expert criticised the use of this method on a disturbed site.[65] The Council's expert opted for the 'meandering transect' or 'random meander' method, which involves walking across the site several times to identify individual species, and evaluating 'whether or not, given the presence of individual species and the potential for restoration of a greater number and a complex composition of species, the community exists on the site'.[66] The developer's expert criticised this methodology for its failure to provide information on the relative abundance and location of species on the site.[67] He also defended his use of the quadrat method, stating that it was extensively used by the relevant environmental agency.[68] The Land and Environment Court preferred the quadrat method to the meandering transect method. The quadrat method enabled,

> [S]ome objective assessments to be undertaken from which it can be ascertained whether the individual species are reflected in sufficient numbers in identified areas of the site to enable an informed judgment to be made as to whether the community exists.[69]

C. Sociological Uncertainty

Sociological uncertainty arises because technical constructions of scientific logics about environmental risks are not drawn from nature alone, but are socially constructed. They are based on which parameters are considered significant by

[61] Refsgaard et al, *ibid* 1546–47.
[62] *ibid.*
[63] *ibid.*
[64] *Hornsby Shire Council v Vitone Developments Pty Ltd* (n 49) [64].
[65] *ibid* [79].
[66] *ibid* [82].
[67] *ibid.*
[68] *ibid* [80].
[69] *ibid* [83].

scientists and other experts.[70] Sociologists of science have observed that classification exercises for identifying differences or similarities between ecological communities is never a product of nature, but is determined by individual choices made by those studying them.[71] 'Facts' about nature are not there to be discovered but have to be actively read into nature.[72] Scientists employ 'social mechanisms of closure' to delineate and complete certain logical constructions of nature that would otherwise be incomplete.[73]

The drawing up of threatened species lists entails social and value-based choices about which species are worth protecting.[74] This is an unequal process. Specific choices are made by the scientific community, governments and the public about which species are worthy of protection.[75] This is often informed by biophilia.[76] The largest source of bias in listing processes is when scientists want to 'list' their species as threatened in order to attract funding for conservation efforts.[77]

Indeed, the very act of listing certain species and not others creates uncertainty, because it limits our understanding of how particular species might interact with one another as part of an ecosystem. The further the species is ranked away from extinction, the less visible it is and the more likely it is to be ignored or even destroyed.[78] When a species is not listed at all, it remains entirely outside the purview of human societies.[79]

The Land and Environment Court has encountered sociological uncertainty in both biodiversity and climate change cases. These cases have provided a platform for rich sociological debates about environmental degradation and its adverse impacts on a community's sense of belonging and place.

In *Bulga Milbrodale Progress Association Inc v Minister for Planning and Infrastructure and Warkworth Mining Ltd*,[80] the Court considered both the biodiversity impacts and the social impacts of an open-cut coalmine extension project on the community of Bulga. The consideration of social impacts involved a predictive exercise of assessing whether the Bulga community would experience 'solastalgia' – 'the pain or sickness caused by the ongoing loss of solace and the sense of desolation connected to the present state of one's home and territory'[81] – as a result of the proposed development. The term was coined and applied by the community's expert, Professor Albrecht, to denote the concerns of Bulga residents

[70] Wynne (n 34) 122.
[71] *ibid* 123.
[72] *ibid.*
[73] *ibid.*
[74] Braverman (n 33) 5–6.
[75] *ibid* 6.
[76] *ibid* 9–10.
[77] *ibid.*
[78] *ibid* 8.
[79] *ibid.*
[80] *Bulga Milbrodale Progress Association Inc v Minister for Planning and Infrastructure and Warkworth Mining Limited* (2013) 194 LGERA 347.
[81] *ibid* [420].

expressed during interviews he conducted. The miner criticised the methodology used for the sociological assessment, including that the interview respondents were self-selecting and all opposed to the mine. The Court accepted that methodological limitations in recording the concerns of the Bulga residents reduced the weight that could be placed on the assessment of the interview responses, and thus on Professor Albrecht's reliance on the concept of solastalgia. However, this did not mean that the concerns expressed by the Bulga residents in the interview responses should be discounted in assessing the adverse social impacts of the mine.[82] The Court held,

> [T]he objector evidence is relevant to a consideration of impacts on amenity and the public interest more generally where it is more than an expression of subjective fear or concern, and is based in specific, concrete likely effects of the proposed development.[83]

The Court found that although the proposed development would likely have some positive social impacts on the community by generating employment, these benefits would be outweighed by its negative social impacts in terms of adverse noise, dust and visual impacts, as well as adverse social impacts arising from a change in composition of the community.[84]

Similarly, in *Gloucester Resources Ltd v Minister for Planning*, the Court found that a proposed open-cut coalmine, the Rocky Hill mine, would have significant adverse social impacts on the Gloucester community.[85] The concept of solastalgia was again considered by the experts and the Court. The Court found that the proposed development would negatively impact upon the composition, cohesion and character of the community and local people's sense of place, which included the 'cultural and historical connections, and feelings of belonging and attachment to place and the environment'.[86]

While a recently developed sociological concept such as 'solastalgia' may be unsettled and open-textured, it may assist in evaluating a development's social impacts on a community. Both of the cases discussed show that the Court has displayed a preference for using empirical methodologies that canvas public opinion as widely as possible in order to gather evidence from local residents about their sense of belonging and place.

D. Linguistic Uncertainty

Linguistic uncertainty has received relatively little scholarly attention, but may arise in the context of EIAs and 'contribute substantially to the uncertainty surrounding

[82] *ibid* [429].
[83] *ibid* [430].
[84] *ibid* [431]–[433], [434]–[439], [440]–[444], [445].
[85] *Gloucester Resources Ltd v Minister for Planning* (2019) 234 LGERA 257 [270]–[417].
[86] *ibid* [312], [320].

the analysis'.[87] To reduce this type of uncertainty, scientists recommend the use of iterative cycles of re-assessment of the likelihoods and consequences of a risk, and sustained discussion between experts to identify, describe and resolve language-based misunderstandings.[88] The iterative re-assessment approach is routinely used in environmental risk assessments for both marine and terrestrial protected area management.[89]

Linguistic uncertainty can be classed into five distinct types: vagueness; context-dependence; ambiguity; indeterminacy of theoretical terms; and under-specificity.[90] Indeterminacy is not always apparent when a term first comes into use. This is commonly referred to as the open texture of language.[91] This kind of uncertainty is observable in relation to the concept of '*species*' which remains inherently unsettled due to periodic taxonomic revisions.[92] There has been extensive debate in the biological literature about the definition and nature of the concept of species.[93]

Linguistic uncertainty also arises in the interpretation of the legal rules in statutes and statutory instruments. There will be some clear cases where a rule certainly applies, but many where there is doubt as to when and how the rule applies.[94] The language in which legal rules are expressed is often indeterminate and open textured.[95] Rules can never in advance govern every case. Legislation cannot be drafted to cover every case or provide authoritative extra-judicial interpretation.[96] Rules may use very general standards, such as reasonableness, fairness or what is just and equitable, thereby incorporating extra-legal norms into the law. These standards are predicated on 'fact-value complexes, not on mere facts'.[97] The use of these standards enables changes in society's values to be incorporated into the law,[98] and thereby, for the law to be relative and attuned to the time and place.[99]

Corkill v Forestry Commission of New South Wales[100] exemplifies linguistic indeterminacy. The National Parks and Wildlife Act 1974 (NSW) made it an offence to take or kill any protected or endangered fauna.[101] 'Take' was defined to

[87] Janet M Carey and Mark A Burgman, 'Linguistic Uncertainty in Qualitative Risk Analysis and How to Minimize It' in W Troy Tucker Adams et al, *Strategies for Risk Communication: Evolution, Evidence, Experience* (Report, Annals of the New York Academy of Sciences, Volume 1128, April 2008) 14.

[88] *ibid.*

[89] *ibid* 16.

[90] Regan et al (n 4) 621–24.

[91] *ibid.*

[92] *ibid.*

[93] *ibid.*

[94] Herbert LA Hart, *The Concept of Law*, 2nd edn (Oxford University Press, 1994) 123.

[95] *ibid* 128.

[96] Roscoe Pound, *The Spirit of the Common Law* (Transaction Publishers, 1999) 179 and see 174. See also, Roscoe Pound, *An Introduction to the Philosophy of Law* (Yale University Press, 1922) 51.

[97] Julius Stone, *Legal System and Lawyers' Reasoning* (Maitland Publications, 1964) 264.

[98] Julius Stone, *The Province and Function of Law* (Associated General Publications, 1947) 144.

[99] Roscoe Pound, *The Spirit of the Common Law* (n 96) 172.

[100] *Corkill v Forestry Commission of New South Wales* (1991) 73 LGRA 126.

[101] National Parks and Wildlife Act 1974 (NSW) ss 98 and 99.

include disturb or injure.[102] Were the statutory provisions concerned only with the direct and intended consequences of the killing and taking of animals, or did they also include the indirect consequences caused by disturbance of the habitat of the animals?[103] The Court held that these provisions included both the direct and intended consequences of conduct and the indirect consequences such as disturbance of habitat.[104] The Court, interpreting the term 'disturb' in the definition of 'take', applied the natural and ordinary meaning of 'disturb', to interfere or hinder, in the context of the primary objective of the preservation and protection of endangered species of fauna.[105] The Court held that 'disturb' includes 'indirect action, as well as direct physical injury. It covers conduct which modifies habitat in a significant fashion thus placing the species of fauna under threat by adversely affecting essential behavioural patterns relating to feeding, breeding or nesting'.[106] The Court interpreted the terms of these provisions holistically.[107] The decision was upheld by the NSW Court of Appeal.[108]

There is also the potential for linguistic uncertainty to arise in relation to any assessment of 'significant impacts'. What 'significant impacts' means in a given case may differ and be context-specific. Linguistic uncertainty has also arisen in these cases due to the loose employment of ambiguous terms such as 'very highly disturbed remnants' to describe the state of an ecological community on a particular site.[109] Disturbance is integral to ecological communities because they are inherently dynamic and change over time.[110] Linguistic uncertainty that results in the exclusion of certain areas of land at a given point in time because they are 'disturbed' and unlikely to be significantly impacted, may be premature, erroneous and antithetical to biodiversity protection. Such a determination might fail to account for the resilience of ecological communities and their potential to regenerate.

IV. Stages in Biodiversity Conservation where Uncertainties Occur

Uncertainties can occur at almost every stage of decision-making on biodiversity conservation, particularly in relation to EIA and project approval.

[102] *ibid* s 5.
[103] *Corkill v Forestry Commission of New South Wales* (n 100) 136–37.
[104] *ibid* 136–37, 139.
[105] *ibid* 137.
[106] *ibid* 139.
[107] Brian J Preston, 'The Role of the Judiciary in Promoting Sustainable Development: The Experience of Asia and the Pacific' (2005) 9 *Asia Pacific Journal of Environmental Law* 109, 191.
[108] *Forestry Commission of New South Wales v Corkill* (1991) 73 LGRA 247.
[109] Preston and Adam (n 37) 390.
[110] *ibid* 390.

A. Uncertainties in Describing, Listing and Identifying Natural Phenomena

The first stage in which uncertainty can occur is in interpreting statutory powers for the listing of natural phenomena (eg endangered species, ecological communities, ecosystems and natural habitats) for protection. In NSW, the relevant statutory scheme for identifying, listing, protecting and encouraging the recovery of threatened ecological communities has historically been the Threatened Species Conservation Act 1995 (TSC Act) and is currently the Biodiversity Conservation Act 2016. An 'ecological community' is defined as 'an assemblage of species occupying a particular area'.[111] Part 4 of the Biodiversity Conservation Act prescribes numerous criteria for the process of listing threatened species and threatened ecological communities.[112]

i. Describing and Listing Biodiversity

In relation to the scientific classification or description of natural phenomena, there is always epistemic uncertainty. For example, endangered ecological communities (EECs) are by their very nature dynamic and subject to significant variation.[113] *VAW (Kurri Kurri) Pty Ltd v Scientific Committee* is apposite for illustrating such uncertainties. An aluminium smelter (VAW) judicially reviewed decisions of the Scientific Committee to list an ecological community, the Kurri Sand Swamp Woodland (KSSW), as an EEC under the TSC Act. VAW feared that the EEC may occur on its land and constrain its operations. VAW criticised the Scientific Committee's description of the KSSW EEC as lacking certainty and precision.[114] Specific criticisms included that: a majority of the plant species specified as forming the assemblage of species were relatively common and not individually rare; the Scientific Committee had selected only characteristic species rather than a comprehensive and complete list of all species that comprise the assemblage of species for that ecological community; and it had failed to specify a minimum number or proportion of the species specified in the description that needed to be present on any piece of land in order for that ecological community to exist on the land.[115]

The Land and Environment Court rejected these arguments, finding it is not necessary for the species forming an assemblage in a particular area to be

[111] Threatened Species Conservation Act 1995 (NSW), s 4; Biodiversity Conservation Act 2016 (NSW), s 1.6.
[112] Biodiversity Conservation Act 2016 (NSW), Pt 4.
[113] Preston and Adam (n 37) 257.
[114] *VAW (Kurri Kurri) Pty Ltd v Scientific Committee* (2002) 122 LGERA 231; Preston and Adam (n 37) 256.
[115] *VAW (Kurri Kurri) Pty Ltd v Scientific Committee, ibid* [83]–[85].

individually threatened or for the Scientific Committee to specify a minimum number or proportion of species that must exist in order to constitute an EEC.[116]

On appeal, the NSW Court of Appeal noted that the word 'assemblage' in the definition of an ecological community, of 'an assemblage of species occupying a particular area', did not suggest that 'either the nomination of species or identification of an area requires a high degree of specificity'.[117] The Court held that 'the intricacy of all ecological communities means that some indeterminateness is bound to arise from the form of expression used to describe them'.[118] In regard to the criticisms about inclusion in the assemblage of common species and the need for specificity about the number and proportion of species required, the Court found that '[w]hat is relevant in an ecological community is the particular assemblage of species. It is not relevant therefore that a proportion of the species said to form part of the assemblage are commonly found and provide no definitional role'.[119] The Court further noted that:

> To satisfy the requirement of certainty to an appropriate standard, the terms of the Scientific Committee's final determination must enable a citizen to decide whether a specific location falls within it. This does not necessitate the enumeration of the minimum number of species that must be found together to constitute the community, nor the provision of maps indicating where the community may be found.[120]

These judgments indicate that courts do not automatically give uncertainty a negative valence, but rather recognise it is an intrinsic feature of biodiversity. The dialogue between the Scientific Committee and courts in these judgments reveals that the aim is not to banish uncertainty wholesale, but rather to reduce it to a manageable level.

ii. Identification of Biodiversity

The identification of the presence of a particular EEC on a development site can be plagued by epistemic uncertainty as the occurrence of an assemblage of species in a particular area might be patchy or indeterminate. Multiple communities occurring on the same site can constitute an EEC giving rise to complexity and uncertainty in their interaction.[121] For example, in *Carstens v Pittwater Council*, the site was found to be an ecotone between two distinct EECs, the Pittwater Spotted Gum ecological community and the Sydney Sandstone Gully Forest.[122]

In *Newcastle & Hunter Valley Speleological Society v Upper Hunter Shire Council & Stoneco Pty Ltd*, the Land and Environment Court considered whether the

[116] *ibid* [84]–[85].
[117] *VAW (Kurri Kurri) Pty Ltd v Scientific Committee* (2003) 128 LGERA 419 [7].
[118] *ibid* [9].
[119] *ibid* [194] and see [8], [214].
[120] *ibid* [7].
[121] Preston and Adam (n 37) 252–54.
[122] *Carstens v Pittwater Council* (n 42) [34].

project site met the locational and floristic descriptors of one or more EECs.[123] There were competing expert opinions relating to the presence or absence of three EECs. The Court held that resolving these competing expert positions required an interpretation of the description of the EECs in the Scientific Committee's Final Determinations and the application of this interpretation to the project site.[124] The Court recognised that the Scientific Committee's Final Determinations are expressed at a level of generality due to the inherent spatial and temporal variation in natural communities which precludes specificity.[125] The Court observed that while variants of ecological communities are not analogous to genotypes of species, 'conservation of biodiversity encompasses the conservation of the diversity of life at all levels of organisation, which includes variation within ecological communities'.[126] Thus, the Court took a holistic and pragmatic approach in order to maximise biodiversity protection.

Similarly, in *Motorplex Pty Ltd v Port Stephens Council*, the Court found that three EECs were present and co-existed on the proposed development site because they matched relevant locational and floristic descriptors in the Final Determinations.[127] The Court again took a pragmatic approach to addressing the epistemic uncertainty that arose due to the concurrent existence and intergrading of multiple ecological communities on the site.[128]

B. Uncertainties in Relation to EIA and Project Approval

The EIA process is fraught with various kinds of uncertainty at each stage. The stages include: i) the screening process to determine which projects may be subject to EIA requirements; ii) the scoping process to identify the specific environmental issues or concerns to be included in the assessment; iii) the preparation of an impact study, assessment of its adequacy and public consultation and participation; vi) the making of a decision to approve the project; and vi) project implementation.[129]

i. Applying the EIA Screening Test

The screening process involves a determination of whether a project should be subject to EIA requirements. Screening usually has both a statutory (objective)

[123] *Newcastle & Hunter Valley Speleological Society v Upper Hunter Shire Council & Stoneco Pty Ltd* (2010) 210 LGERA 126.
[124] *ibid* [42].
[125] *ibid* [47], [48].
[126] *ibid* [76].
[127] *Motorplex Pty Ltd v Port Stephens Council* [2007] NSWLEC 74 [124]–[125].
[128] *ibid* [121], [122].
[129] Neil Craik, 'The Assessment of Environment Impact' in Emma Lees and Jorge Viñuales (eds), *The Oxford Handbook of Comparative Environmental Law* (Oxford University Press, 2019) 880–81.

and a discretionary (subjective) component.[130] The statutory component involves application of statutory criteria for determining whether EIA is required and, if so, the level of EIA, such as an environmental impact statement (EIS). The discretionary component involves an evaluative assessment of whether a project meets the statutory criteria, such as whether the project is likely to have significant environmental impacts.[131]

Under NSW law, there are two screening criteria to determine whether a higher level of EIA, such as an EIS or SIS, is required: first, whether the development or activity is likely to significantly affect the environment either generally or threatened species or ecological communities, or their habitats, particularly; and second, whether the development or activity is on a list of project categories where significance is assumed, termed 'designated development'.[132] Epistemic and linguistic uncertainties arise in both approaches.

a. Screening Criterion of Likely Significant Effects

The screening criterion of whether a development or activity is 'likely to significantly affect' the environment is open-textured and value-laden. Courts have held that the world 'likely' means 'a real chance or probability' rather than 'more likely than not' and the word 'significantly' means 'important', 'notable', 'weighty' or 'more than ordinary'.[133]

Where the environment likely to be impacted includes threatened species or ecological communities, or their habitats, the assessment of whether there is likely to be a significant effect is assisted by consideration of a multi-part statutory test.[134] The current statutory test under s 7.3(1) of the Biodiversity Conservation Act 2016 (NSW) comprises seven factors that a court may consider, but each of these factors is characterised by uncertainty. There is also uncertainty as to how many factors must be present. A positive answer to any one or more of the factors does not mandate an affirmative answer to the question of whether the development or activity is likely to have a significant effect on particular biodiversity, but equally does not preclude a negative answer to the question.[135] Furthermore, these factors are not exhaustive.[136]

[130] Joe Weston, 'Screening for Environmental Impact Assessment Projects in England: What Screening?' (2011) 29 *Impact Assessment and Project Appraisal* 2, 91.

[131] *ibid* 92.

[132] Environmental Planning and Assessment Act 1979 (NSW), ss 4.12, 4.15, 5.5 and 5.7; Environmental Planning and Assessment Regulation 2000 (NSW) (SI 2000/557), Schs 1 and 2; Biodiversity Conservation Act 2016 (NSW), ss 7.2 and 7.3.

[133] *Oshlack v Richmond River Shire Council and Iron Gates Development Pty Ltd* (1993) 82 LGERA 222, 233; *Newcastle & Hunter Valley Speleological Society v Upper Hunter Shire Council & Stoneco Pty Ltd* (n 123) [84]; *Palm Beach Protection Group Inc v Northern Beaches Council* (2020) 250 LGERA 212 [261].

[134] Biodiversity Conservation Act 2016 (NSW), s 7.3; Threatened Species Conservation Act 1995 (NSW), s 94(3) (repealed).

[135] *Carstens v Pittwater Council* (n 42) [61]; *Plumb v Penrith City Council* (n 46) [36]; *Newcastle & Hunter Valley Speleological Society v Upper Hunter Shire Council & Stoneco Pty Ltd* (n 123) [86].

[136] *Plumb v Penrith City Council* (n 46) [37]; *Newcastle & Hunter Valley Speleological Society v Upper Hunter Shire Council & Stoneco Pty Ltd* (n 123) [85].

Ryan v Northern Regional Planning Panel[137] featured an expert disagreement about the significance of impacts on threatened fauna species stemming from epistemic uncertainty about species' distribution and mobility. The experts disagreed as to whether an SIS was required.[138] The experts agreed that both threatened species were present on the site and would be affected by any vegetation clearance.[139] However, they differed in their assessment of the likely significance of the effects on the species. At the heart of the experts' disagreement were epistemic and methodological uncertainties, including in the experts' individual knowledge about the species,[140] knowledge generally about the species, their behaviour and their habitat preferences,[141] the distribution and mobility of the species,[142] and the methodology used to conduct fauna surveys.[143] Applying a precautionary approach in accordance with the Threatened Species Conservation Act Guidelines (TSCA Guidelines), the Court held that both species were at risk of extinction from short-term and long-term impacts that would be significant and that an SIS was required to accompany the development application.[144]

In *Friends of Leadbeater's Possum Inc v VicForests*, the Federal Court of Australia enjoined a state-owned logging company, VicForests, to halt its forestry operations across 66 native forest coupes.[145] The Court found that VicForests' past and proposed logging has had and is likely to have a significant impact on the habitat of two threatened fauna species,[146] a finding that was upheld on appeal.[147] The substantial expert disagreement was driven by epistemic and methodological uncertainties, including: the level of threat to the species and their habitat; the methods by which impact assessments in relation to forestry operations ought to be conducted; the actual or likely impacts of the forestry operations on the species and their habitat; and the effect of ameliorative or precautionary measures (such as the adoption of new and less intense silvicultural methods) on any impacts.[148] The Court accepted the evidence of the applicant's experts that the forestry operations have had and would likely have significant impacts on both species' habitats such that they would be placed at a high risk of extinction.[149]

b. Screening Criterion of Designated Development

The second screening criterion under NSW law is whether the development is a 'designated development'. Designated development is the term used to describe

[137] *Ryan v Northern Regional Planning Panel* [2020] NSWLEC 55.
[138] *ibid* [2], [74].
[139] *ibid* [72]–[84].
[140] *ibid* [62], [77], [82], [91].
[141] *ibid* [92].
[142] *ibid* [99].
[143] *ibid* [76].
[144] *ibid* [198], [199].
[145] *Friends of Leadbeater's Possum Inc v VicForests (No 4)* (2020) 244 LGERA 92; [2020] FCA 704.
[146] *ibid* [1343].
[147] *VicForests v Friends of Leadbeater's Possum Inc* (2021) 285 FCR 70; [2021] FCAFC 66 at [190], [197], [212], [213], [224].
[148] *ibid* [242].
[149] *ibid* [1431], [1432], [1435].

particular categories of development that are subject to statutory provisions requiring a more detailed EIA in the form of an EIS.[150] Uncertainties arise in determining whether a proposed development falls within one of the categories of designated development. The uncertainties are linguistic (the meaning of the descriptions of the categories) and epistemic (lack of knowledge about the nature, extent and other features of the development and its consequences).

In *Director-General of the Department of Land and Water Conservation v Bailey*, the Court considered whether the clearing of native vegetation to construct a large dam fell within the category of designated development of an artificial waterbody.[151] Linguistic uncertainty arose in relation to the construction of the exemption provisions in the native vegetation legislation and the category of designated development of artificial waterbodies. The Court held that the clearing of native vegetation was properly to be characterised as being for the purpose of an artificial waterbody and it was artificial to sever the clearing from the later construction and operation of the waterbody.[152] The clearing was therefore part of designated development.[153] The Court nevertheless held that because consent had not been obtained under the Environmental Planning and Assessment Act 1979 for that designated development, the exemption did not apply.[154] This aspect of the decision was overturned by the NSW Court of Appeal, which held that the exemption should have been applied.[155]

c. Identifying the Environment Likely to be Affected

The significance of the likely impact of a proposed development or activity will depend on the relevant environment in which it is intended to take place. Linguistic and epistemic uncertainties might arise in relation to what constitutes the 'environment' that is likely to be affected by the proposed development.

This question was considered in *Bailey v Forestry Commission of NSW*, where the Forestry Commission regarded the 'environment' as the whole of the forest and not just the part of the forest in which logging was to occur and as being a working forest rather than a pristine forest.[156] The Land and Environment Court rejected the argument that the environment was the 'whole forest', but equally the environment was not 'merely the individual compartments or land included in harvesting plans whose areas do not appear to follow meaningful ecological or geographical boundaries'. Instead, the relevant environment should be determined 'by reference

[150] Environmental Planning and Assessment Regulation 2000 (NSW), cl 4 and Sch 3; Environmental Planning and Assessment Act 1979 (NSW), s 4.10.
[151] *Director-General of the Department of Land and Water Conservation v Bailey* (2003) 128 LGERA 1.
[152] *ibid* [54].
[153] *ibid* [56].
[154] *ibid* [69], [74].
[155] *Director-General, Department of Land and Water Conservation v Bailey* (2003) 136 LGERA 241 [42]
[156] *Bailey v Forestry Commission of New South Wales* (1989) 67 LGRA 200, 212.

to the area the subject of the licences and the harvesting plans, but considered as part of land to be used for the overall activity'.[157]

In *The Crown v Murphy*, the High Court of Australia held that what constitutes the relevant 'environment' must be ascertained by reference to the person, object or group surrounded or affected.[158] The Court found that sea turtles constituted part of the environment in question, which was a particular coastal strip that served as an annual nesting and hatching site for the sea turtles. The Court held that any use of the resumed coastal land which might lead to a reduction in the number of turtles using that land as their rookery or in the number of surviving hatchlings would constitute a deleterious impact on the environment of the resumed land.[159]

In *Newcastle & Hunter Valley Speleological Society v Upper Hunter Shire Council & Stoneco Pty Ltd*,[160] epistemic uncertainty surrounded the question of 'local occurrence' of the White Box EEC on the subject site due to its widespread distribution and its fragmentation through clearance and disturbance over time. Questions arose as to whether each remaining fragment could be considered a local occurrence of the EEC or whether the collection of fragments in the former range should be viewed collectively as the local occurrence.[161] The Court noted that 'questions of fact and degree are involved in resolving this problem in any particular case'.[162] The Court concluded that the local occurrence of the White Box EEC included the whole project site, but its occurrence beyond the site remained uncertain.[163]

Disagreement can also occur as to the 'study area' that should be surveyed and assessed. In *Ryan v Northern Regional Planning Panel*, the expert ecologists disagreed on their approach to the 'study area', one expert surveying only the subject site and the other expert looking at a wider rezoned area beyond the subject site.[164] The Court accepted the former's approach as it was more closely aligned with the TSCA Guidelines for significance assessments.[165]

d. Identifying the Development

Application of any screening test requires identification of the development or activity proposed in the application for consent or approval. Uncertainty can arise in identifying the nature, extent and other features of the development or activity. In *Ballina Shire Council v Palm Lake Works Pty Ltd*,[166] there was uncertainty as to

[157] *ibid* 213.
[158] *The Crown v Murphy* (1990) 64 ALJR 593, 596.
[159] *ibid* 596–97.
[160] *Newcastle & Hunter Valley Speleological Society v Upper Hunter Shire Council & Stoneco Pty Ltd* (n 123).
[161] *ibid* [96].
[162] *ibid*.
[163] *ibid* [98].
[164] *Ryan v Northern Regional Planning Panel* (n 137) [160], [161].
[165] *ibid* [160].
[166] *Ballina Shire Council v Palm Lake Works Pty Ltd* [2020] NSWLEC 41.

whether the proposed development of a seniors housing development involved construction of access roads, water and sewer infrastructure as well as stormwater and vegetation management works in a nearby creek. The Court held that the environmental impacts of all of those works needed to be addressed.[167]

Uncertainty can also arise about whether ameliorative measures are part of the development. In order to be able to be considered in answering the inquiry of likely impact, the ameliorative measures need to be proposed as part of the application for consent. Ameliorative measures not proposed as part of the application for consent, but which are imposed afterwards, as conditions of consent, are not able to be considered in answering the inquiry as to the likely impact of the development.[168] In *MyEnvironment Inc v VicForests*, the Victorian Supreme Court held that, by reason of the ameliorative measures proposed as part of the logging operations to protect threatened fauna species in the native forests, logging would not constitute a real threat of serious or irreversible damage.[169]

e. Uncertainty in Ameliorative Measures

Uncertainty also arises in identifying which ameliorative measures will be appropriate and effective. In *Bulga Milbrodale v Minister for Planning*, the Court found that there was real risk and uncertainty that the proposed biodiversity offset areas would be rehabilitated to create the intended EECs. There was no current example of a recognised area of the particular ecological community that has been created by rehabilitation.[170] Considerable scientific uncertainty remained as the research programme being undertaken had not progressed to sufficiently establish whether such rehabilitation would be feasible or successful.[171]

ii. Applying the EIA Scoping Test

Once it is determined that EIA is required, the scoping process is used to identify the key issues of concern and the impacts on biodiversity that need to be addressed. Both direct and indirect impacts need to be considered.[172] Cumulative impacts

[167] *ibid* [38].

[168] *Drummoyne Municipal Council v Maritime Services Board* (1991) 72 LGRA 186, 192; *Smyth v Nambucca Shire Council* (1999) 105 LGERA 65 [11]–[13]; *Newcastle & Hunter Valley Speleological Society v Upper Hunter Shire Council & Stoneco Pty Ltd* (n 123) [83]; *Palm Beach Protection Group Inc v Northern Beaches Council* (n 133) [261].

[169] *MyEnvironment Inc v VicForests* [2012] VSC 91, [277], [278], [341], upheld on appeal in *MyEnvironment Inc v VicForests* (2013) 42 VR 456; 198 LGERA 396.

[170] *Bulga Milbrodale Progress Association Inc v Minister for Planning and Infrastructure and Warkworth Mining Ltd* (2013) 194 LGERA 347 [241], [243].

[171] *ibid* [242]. See generally Brian J Preston, 'Biodiversity Offsets: Adequacy and Efficacy in Theory and Practice' (2016) 33 *Environmental and Planning Law Journal* 93.

[172] *Gloucester Resources Ltd v Minister for Planning* (n 85) [494]–[495]; *Ballina Shire Council v Palm Lake Works Pty Ltd* (n 166) [6]; Brian J Preston, 'Contemporary Issues in Environmental Impact Assessment' (2020) 37 *Environment and Planning Law Journal* 423, 425, 429, 442.

may also be a relevant consideration.[173] Uncertainties arise in relation to how such identified impacts will manifest and the extent of those impacts. The identification of impacts is a predictive exercise based on available ecological evidence, which may be incomplete or inchoate, and the different methods chosen by experts when undertaking ecological surveys.

In *Ryan v Northern Regional Planning Panel*, the major impact identified by the expert ecologists was habitat loss. The experts disagreed on the impact of habitat loss, because of differing approaches to the study area. One estimated a loss of 30 per cent and the other 10 per cent of the study area. The Court again accepted the former's opinion, as it conformed with the TCSA Guidelines.[174]

In *Upper Mooki Landcare Inc v Shenhua Watermark Coal Pty Ltd and Minister for Planning*, the screening process established that the proposed development of an open-cut coalmine would significantly affect the local koala population.[175] This habitat loss was identified as a 'critical consequence', with an 'almost certain' likelihood, and was qualified as 'high risk'.[176] Uncertainty remained, however, about how that habitat loss would affect koalas and whether the proposed mitigation measure of koala translocation would be sufficient. The Court held that ongoing monitoring of the koala population and an adaptive management approach (a precautionary approach) were appropriate for managing the uncertainty and risks.[177]

In *Friends of Tumblebee Incorporated v ATB Morton Limited (No 2)*, uncertainty arose in determining the extent to which vegetation clearance on the development site would cause colonisation by a competitive bird species, the Noisy Miner, and thereby adversely impact upon the highly endangered resident bird species, the Regent Honeyeater.[178] The Court observed that 'both experts expressed their opinions in terms of probabilities and potentialities, and not certainties, and that the short-term risk of Noisy Miner colonisation was low'.[179] The Court also identified a number of other scientific uncertainties in relation to environmental damage, including uncertainty as to whether the vegetation cleared is Regent Honeyeater habitat or merely potential habitat; uncertainty as to the long-term effect of the clearing associated with the development proposal on the viability of the local population of Regent Honeyeater; and uncertainty as to the cumulative effect of clearing associated with other approved developments within the locality, and the amount of that clearing.[180]

[173] *BT Goldsmith Planning Services Pty Ltd v Blacktown City Council* [2005] NSWLEC 210 [89]–[90].
[174] *Ryan v Northern Regional Planning Panel* (n 137) [173].
[175] *Upper Mooki Landcare Inc v Shenhua Watermark Coal Pty Ltd and Minister for Planning* (2016) 216 LGERA 40 [20].
[176] *ibid* [16].
[177] *ibid* [144].
[178] *Friends of Tumblebee Incorporated v ATB Morton Limited (No 2)* (2016) 215 LGERA 157 [121].
[179] *ibid* [126].
[180] *ibid* [184].

The Court held that such scientific uncertainty justified the application of the precautionary principle to conclude that the proposed development would likely have an adverse effect on the lifecycle of the Regent Honeyeater such that the viable local population would be placed at risk of extinction.[181]

iii. Preparing the Required EIA

Once it is established that a proposed development or activity is likely to have a significant impact, the requirement to prepare an EIS or SIS is enlivened. An EIS or SIS is an informational tool designed to support and facilitate decision-making under conditions of uncertainty. The environmental legislation prescribes the content requirements for an EIS, including the factors to be considered when preparing an EIS.[182] These factors include environmental impacts on ecosystems; impact on the habitat of protected animals; endangering of any species; long-term environmental effects; degradation of the quality of the environment; pollution of the environment; and cumulative environmental effects.[183] The form and content of an SIS is also specifically prescribed.[184] Information on threatened species or ecological communities must include: a general description; each species or community likely to be affected; conservation status; abundance; distribution; cumulative impacts; location, size and condition of habitats; and ameliorative measures.[185] Epistemic uncertainties will arise in providing this information.

NSW case law in this area illustrates that while the preparation of an SIS goes some way towards managing and reducing uncertainties in relation to the impacts of development on threatened species, some uncertainty will always remain.

a. Adequacy of EIA

A determining authority, in its consideration of an activity, must 'examine and take into account to the fullest extent possible all matters affecting or likely to affect the environment by reason of that activity'.[186] If the activity is likely to significantly affect the environment the determining authority must not carry out or approve the carrying out of the activity unless it had obtained, examined and considered an EIS in respect of the activity.[187] In *Warren v Electricity Commission of New South*

[181] *ibid* [185].
[182] Environmental Planning and Assessment Act 1979 (NSW), s 4.12(8) and s 5.7; Environmental Planning and Assessment Regulation 2000 (NSW), cl 228 and Sch 2.
[183] Environmental Planning and Assessment Regulation 2000 (NSW), cl 228(2).
[184] Biodiversity Conservation Act 2016 (NSW), s 7.20(2) and Biodiversity Conservation Regulation 2017 (NSW) (SI 2017/432), cl 7.6
[185] Biodiversity Conservation Regulation 2017, cl 7.6(2)–(3).
[186] Environmental Planning and Assessment Act 1979 (NSW), s 5.5(1).
[187] *ibid* s 5.7(1).

Wales, the Land and Environment Court interpreted these statutory requirements as 'action forcing', requiring agencies to take a 'hard look' at the environmental consequences of the activity.[188] The test for determining the legal adequacy of an EIS is 'substantial compliance' with the statutory content requirements.[189]

In *Leatch v Director-General National Parks and Wildlife Service*, the Court observed that the same test of substantial compliance applies in relation to a fauna impact statement (FIS) as applies to an EIS, notwithstanding its narrower remit, since the purpose of both documents is to facilitate decision-making and enable public participation.[190] Critically, the Court recognised epistemic uncertainty as an inherent feature of preparing an EIS or FIS due to the dynamism of biodiversity-related phenomena and processes. Accordingly, taking a pragmatic approach, the Court found it to be adequate.[191]

So too, in *NSW Land and Housing Corporation v Campbelltown City Council*,[192] the Court held that the test of substantial compliance was applicable to an SIS. There, the SIS was claimed to be deficient and inadequate on several grounds. First, the lack of targeted fauna surveys resulted in an under-reporting of the presence of the endangered species and inadequate information on three threatened species of bats which were all recorded on the development site.[193] Second, no management plan was prepared for the proposed public reserve lots provided in the proposed subdivision.[194] Third, no compensation strategies were considered.[195] Finally, no monitoring programme was proposed.[196] Moreover, these criticisms of the applicant's SIS were corroborated by two other experts.[197] The Court observed that the test of substantial compliance with the relevant statutory requirements has been long established in respect of an EIS.[198] While the Court acknowledged the expert criticisms, it found that the SIS was not inadequate and upheld its validity on the basis that the content of the SIS substantially complied with the statutory requirements for an SIS.[199] This case aptly illustrates how scientific uncertainties might remain in relation to impacts on threatened species even where a legally compliant SIS is provided.

[188] *Warren v Electricity Commission of New South Wales* (1990) 130 LGERA 565, 570–71.

[189] *Prineas v Forestry Commission of New South Wales* (1983) 49 LGRA 402, 417; *Guthega Developments Pty Ltd v Minister administering the National Parks and Wildlife Act 1974 (NSW)* (1986) 7 NSWLR 353, 361; *Schaffer Corporation Ltd v Hawkesbury City Council* (1992) 77 LGRA 21, 30–31; *Helman v Byron Shire Council* (1995) 87 LGERA 349, 356.

[190] *Leatch v National Parks and Wildlife Service and Shoalhaven City Council* (1993) 81 LGERA 270, 278.

[191] *ibid* 279–80.

[192] *NSW Land and Housing Corporation v Campbelltown City Council* (2002) 126 LGERA 348.

[193] *ibid* [50].

[194] *ibid* [54].

[195] *ibid*.

[196] *ibid*.

[197] *ibid* [55]–[56].

[198] *ibid* [74].

[199] *ibid* [76].

b. Public Participation and Consultation

A planning authority may be obliged to engage in a process of public consultation in respect of a development application.[200] In *Leatch v National Parks and Wildlife Service*, the Court emphasised the importance of public submissions in raising awareness about impacts on the threatened species.[201] On the facts of that case, although the failure to publicly advertise supplementary information deprived the public of an opportunity to participate, the Court held that 'the omission to advertise the further information does not cause the fauna impact statement to be legally inadequate or otherwise fatally flaw the decision-making process'.[202]

In *Helman v Byron Shire Council*, the NSW Court of Appeal emphasised the importance of the statutory duty to engage in public consultation.[203] The Court held that the late lodgement of the FIS after public consultation had already taken place, 'bypassed the statutory requirement that such a document be available for inspection and consideration by the public. Compliance would have enabled relevant and better-informed objections to be lodged'.[204] Critically, the failure of public consultation generated more epistemic uncertainty in the EIA process due to the exclusion of vital information on environmental impacts that might have otherwise been revealed by public submissions.

iv. Making of a Decision

In determining a development application, a decision-maker is under a statutory obligation to consider certain relevant matters, including the impact of the proposed development or activity on the environment. This decision-making exercise is inherently characterised by uncertainty, as the level or degree of environmental assessment, the form in which it must be prepared, and the content of the environmental assessment report will vary depending on the type of development and its environmental impacts.[205] NSW courts have provided substantial guidance to administrative decision-makers on what this task requires.

The requirement for a consent authority to consider the likely impacts of the proposed development:

> [E]mbraces not only site specific impacts, being impacts of the proposed development on the development site, but also off-site impacts. Off-site impacts can be caused not only by the proposed development impacting adjoining or other land in an area of influence, but also some other development provided that the impacts of that development have a 'real and sufficient link' with the proposed development.[206]

[200] Environmental Planning and Assessment Act 1979 (NSW), s 5.17; Biodiversity Conservation Act 2016 (NSW), Pt 9, Div 1, s 9.1.

[201] *Leatch v National Parks and Wildlife Service and Shoalhaven City Council* (n 190) 276.

[202] *ibid* 280.

[203] *Helman v Byron Shire Council* (n 189) 358.

[204] *ibid.*

[205] *Davis v Gosford City Council* (2014) 204 LGERA 71 [30].

[206] *Ballina Shire Council v Palm Lake Works Pty Ltd* (n 166) [6].

The critical factor is that there is a connection between the likely impact and the proposed development. Increasing remoteness in the chain of likely consequences will decrease the significance of an impact.[207]

In *Davis v Gosford City Council*, the NSW Court of Appeal found that the statutory requirement to assess the likely impacts of the development on the natural environment encompasses 'all likely impacts of the development on the natural environment, including on threatened species, populations or ecological communities, or their habitats, and not merely those impacts that attain the threshold of being a likely significant effect'.[208]

In *Upper Mooki Landcare Inc v Shenhua Watermark Coal Pty Ltd and Minister for Planning*,[209] the NSW Planning Assessment Commission (PAC) had granted consent for an open-cut coal mine that would impact on a koala population. To reduce uncertainty and the likely impacts on koalas, consent was granted on conditions requiring preparation of a detailed koala plan of management, monitoring of impacts and adaptive management. The Court dismissed a judicial review challenge to the PAC's decision to grant consent subject to those conditions. The Court found that the PAC did not commit any legal errors in granting development consent, including failing to consider relevant matters about koalas.[210] Whilst there was epistemic uncertainty in relation to the size of the koala population and the potential success or failure of the proposed koala translocation programme, the Court held that the PAC was mindful of these uncertainties and had imposed conditions of consent to address these uncertainties through a regime of adaptive management and monitoring of the koala population.[211]

v. *Implementing the Project*

The Court has recognised that a step-wise or adaptive management approach (a manifestation of the precautionary principle) can be a useful tool for acknowledging and managing uncertainties over time.[212] This adaptive management approach was followed in *Newcastle & Hunter Valley Speleological Society v Upper Hunter Shire Council & Stoneco Pty Ltd*.[213] This approach is inherently pragmatic, as it is realistically attuned to the dynamic and changing nature of a development project over its life cycle and any contingencies that may arise during its implementation.

[207] *ibid* [7], [8].
[208] *Davis v Gosford City Council* (n 205) [74].
[209] *Upper Mooki Landcare Inc v Shenhua Watermark Coal Pty Ltd and Minister for Planning* (n 175).
[210] *ibid* [6], [141]–[145].
[211] *ibid* [171], [181], [182].
[212] *Telstra Corporation Limited v Hornsby Shire Council* (2006) 146 LGERA 10 [164]; See also Rosie Cooney and Barney Dickson (eds), *Biodiversity and the Precautionary Principle, Risk and Uncertainty in Conservation and Sustainable Use* (Earthscan, 2005) 304, Appendix A – Guideline 12.
[213] *Newcastle & Hunter Valley Speleological Society v Upper Hunter Shire Council & Stoneco Pty Ltd* (n 123) [183]–[189].

V. Courts' Responses to Uncertainties

The approach of Australian courts to uncertainty in the different stages of reviewing and determining a development application and its biodiversity impacts can be grouped into three main categories: purposive interpretation of environmental legislation; application of the precautionary principle; and application of other ecologically sustainable development (ESD) principles. Each is discussed in turn.

A. Purposive Interpretation of Environmental Legislation

In order to address linguistic uncertainty in environmental legislation, NSW courts have typically resorted to a purposive interpretation. This approach derives from the particular legal-institutional culture and context in which these courts operate. First, NSW courts are common law courts with a long and robust tradition of interpretation of statutes by reference to common law principles of interpretation as they exist not only at the time of their enactment, but also at the time of their application.[214] Such principles evolve over time. A key common law rule of statutory interpretation, confirmed by Australian federal and state legislation, requires that, so far as possible, courts will give effect to the purpose of the legislative provision in question.[215]

Second, the NSW Land and Environment Court is a specialist environmental court, with a wide jurisdiction to deal with planning, environment and land matters.[216] It was specifically envisaged as a specialist court to 'understand environmental problems, interpret planning and environmental laws, improve the quality of decision-making, decrease delays in decision-making and facilitate the development of environmental laws, policies and principles'.[217]

Third, as state courts, NSW courts are not bound by a strict constitutional separation of powers doctrine as is the case with Australian federal courts. The Land and Environment Court is a hybrid institution which functions both as a superior court of record and an administrative tribunal.[218] For these reasons, the Court enjoys considerable latitude and discretion in interpreting environmental legislation.

Finally, the Land and Environment Court has a 40-year history of generating progressive biodiversity and EIA jurisprudence through the purposive interpretation of environmental legislation. An early instance is *Corkill v Forestry Commission*

[214] Stephen Gageler, 'Common Law Statutes in Judicial Legislation: Statute Interpretation as Common Law Process' (2011) 37 *Monash University Law Review* 2, 1.

[215] Acts Interpretation Act 1901 (Cth), s 15AA; Interpretation Act 1987 (NSW), s 33.

[216] Brian J Preston, 'The Land and Environment Court of New South Wales: A Very Short History of an Environmental Court in Action' (2020) 94 *Australian Law Journal* 631, 632.

[217] *ibid* 633.

[218] *ibid* 632.

of NSW, where the Land and Environment Court declared that the concept of 'disturb' should be given its natural and ordinary meaning in line with the primary statutory objective of preserving and protecting endangered species of fauna.[219] Similarly, in *VAW (Kurri Kurri) Pty Ltd v Scientific Committee*, both the Court and the NSW Court of Appeal held that questions of uncertainty and definition in the description of an ecological community must be addressed having regard to the approach taken by the legislature in the Threatened Species Conservation Act and the way in which an ecological community is defined.[220]

B. Application of the Precautionary Principle

Australian courts have applied the precautionary principle extensively in their biodiversity jurisprudence to manage epistemic uncertainty. In *Telstra Corporation Limited v Hornsby Shire Council*, the Land and Environment Court provided a detailed explanation of the content of the precautionary principle. Critically, it observed that in order for the precautionary principle to apply and for precautionary measures to be adopted, two conditions precedent must be satisfied: there must be a threat of serious or irreversible environmental damage and scientific uncertainty as to the environmental damage.[221] These conditions or thresholds are cumulative. The precautionary principle permits the taking of preventive measures without having to wait until the reality and seriousness of the threats become fully known,[222] but should not be used to try to avoid all risks.[223] Precautionary measures can include a step-wise or adaptive management approach[224] and must be proportionate.[225] Finally, the application of the precautionary principle does not necessarily prohibit the carrying out of development until scientific certainty is attained.[226]

In *Leatch v National Parks and Wildlife Service*, the Court held that,

> While there is no express provision requiring consideration of the 'precautionary principle', consideration of the state of knowledge or uncertainty regarding a threatened species, the potential for serious or irreversible harm to an endangered fauna and the adoption of a cautious approach in protection of endangered fauna is clearly consistent with the subject matter, scope and purpose of the *National Parks and Wildlife Act*.[227]

[219] *Corkill v Forestry Commission of New South Wales* (n 100) 137.
[220] *VAW (Kurri Kurri) Pty Ltd v Scientific Committee* (n 114) (LEC) and *VAW (Kurri Kurri) Pty Ltd v Scientific Committee* (n 39).
[221] *Telstra Corporation Limited v Hornsby Shire Council* (n 212) [128].
[222] *ibid* [156].
[223] *ibid* [157].
[224] *ibid* [163]–[165].
[225] *ibid* [166]–[178].
[226] *ibid* [179]–[181].
[227] *Leatch v National Parks and Wildlife Service and Shoalhaven City Council* (n 190) 282–83.

In *BT Goldsmith Planning Services Pty Ltd v Blacktown City Council*, the Court considered that the precautionary principle was applicable as there was scientific uncertainty in the data, given it was likely to be out of date, regarding how much Cumberland Plain Woodland EEC had been cleared and how much remained.[228] The Court held that a precautionary approach should be applied in the EIA screening process in considering the factors relevant to determine the likelihood of significant impacts on the EEC.[229]

In *Friends of Tumblebee Incorporated v ATB Morton Limited (No 2)*, the Court also applied the precautionary principle in considering the factors for determining whether the proposed development was likely to significantly affect the threatened species, the Regent Honeyeater, so as to require a SIS.[230] Similarly, in *Ryan v Northern Regional Planning Panel*, the Court found that the precautionary principle was applicable to determining whether a SIS was required.[231]

In both *Newcastle & Hunter Valley Speleological Society v Upper Hunter Shire Council & Stoneco Pty Ltd*[232] and *Upper Mooki Landcare Inc v Shenhua Watermark Coal Pty Ltd and Minister for Planning*,[233] the Court applied or upheld a precautionary approach by the imposition of conditions of consent requiring monitoring and adaptive management.

In *Environment East Gippsland Inc v VicForests*,[234] the Supreme Court of Victoria found that the proposed timber harvesting operations of the logging company, VicForests, was likely to have adverse impacts on several threatened fauna species and their habitat.[235] The Court held that VicForests must comply with the precautionary principle when conducting timber harvesting and that application of the precautionary principle required VicForests to conduct field surveys for the threatened fauna species.[236]

In *Friends of Leadbeater's Possum Inc v VicForests (No 4)*, the Federal Court of Australia held that VicForests was under a statutory obligation to apply the precautionary principle to the conservation of biodiversity values in its timber harvesting and other forestry operations.[237] The primary judge's findings on the precautionary principle were upheld on appeal, although the full bench of the Federal Court held that the forestry operations were exempt from the scope of Australia's federal environmental law, the Environment Protection and Biodiversity Act 1999 (Cth).[238]

[228] *BT Goldsmith Planning Services Pty Ltd v Blacktown City Council* (n 173) [72].
[229] *ibid* [73].
[230] *Friends of Tumblebee Incorporated v ATB Morton Limited (No 2)* (n 178) [181], [182], [185].
[231] *Ryan v Northern Regional Planning Panel* (n 137) [145].
[232] *Newcastle & Hunter Valley Speleological Society v Upper Hunter Shire Council & Stoneco Pty Ltd* (n 123).
[233] *Upper Mooki Landcare Inc v Shenhua Watermark Coal Pty Ltd and Minister for Planning* (n 175).
[234] *Environment East Gippsland Inc v VicForests* (2010) 30 VR 1.
[235] *ibid* [777].
[236] *ibid* [15], [506], [777].
[237] *Friends of Leadbeater's Possum Inc v VicForests (No 4)* (n 145) [840]–[847].
[238] *VicForests v Friends of Leadbeater's Possum Inc* (n 147) [130], [183], [190], [197], [224], [225].

C. Application of Other ESD Principles

Under NSW law, a consent authority is also required to consider other ESD principles when determining a development application and assessing its environmental impacts.[239] These include the principle of intergenerational equity and the principle of conservation of biological diversity and ecological integrity. In *BGP Properties Pty Ltd v Lake Macquarie City Council*, the Land and Environment Court held that a consent authority is obliged to take them into account as part of its consideration of the public interest.[240] The Court observed that ESD principles serve to ensure that ecological communities with high conservation value are not lost. The Court subsequently refused the development application, recognising the significant biodiversity value of the Sydney Freshwater Wetland EEC and the intergenerational dimensions and implications of wetland destruction.[241]

In *Upper Mooki Landcare Inc v Shenhua Watermark Coal Pty Ltd and Minister for Planning*, the Court found that the consent authority had not failed to consider the principle of conservation of biodiversity and ecological integrity and, hence, the public interest in determining the development application.[242] By recommending conditions of consent and requiring the collection of baseline data on koalas, a Translocation Management Plan, and monitoring of resident koala health, distribution and population size, the consent authority sought to mitigate and manage the uncertainties.[243]

VI. Conclusion

Australian administrative decision-makers and courts regularly grapple with uncertainty at every stage of decision-making in relation to development projects likely to impact on biodiversity. In particular, the assessment of whether there are likely to be significant impacts on biodiversity is a complex and inherently value-laden exercise that requires the careful calibration and balancing of polycentric considerations and competing interests. While different kinds of uncertainty can arise in the context of biodiversity conservation, the above analysis of Australian judicial decisions reveals that courts have mainly encountered and addressed epistemic, linguistic and, occasionally, methodological uncertainties.

Of these, epistemic uncertainty is arguably the most pervasive form in biodiversity decision-making, as it often arises during the listing process in relation

[239] Protection of the Environment Administration Act 1991 (NSW), s 6(1)(a); *Carstens v Pittwater Council* (n 42) [74]; *Telstra Corporation Ltd v Hornsby Shire Council* (2006) 146 LGERA 10 [121]–[124].

[240] *BGP Properties Pty Ltd v Lake Macquarie City Council* (2004) 138 LGERA 237 [113].

[241] *ibid* [149]–[150].

[242] *Upper Mooki Landcare Inc v Shenhua Watermark Coal Pty Ltd and Minister for Planning* (n 175) [179].

[243] *ibid* [182].

to threatened species and ecological communities and throughout the entire life cycle of the EIA and project approval process. To manage this kind of uncertainty, Australian courts have tended to adopt a pragmatic approach that strongly favours the application of the precautionary principle and other ESD principles. In some cases, this has led to the refusal of a development application where it was found to have likely significant impacts on threatened species or ecological communities. In other cases, courts have upheld the granting of development consent subject to conditions requiring the adoption of ameliorative measures in line with the precautionary principle, such as monitoring and adaptive management regimes that are better attuned to ecological changes over a longer period.

Linguistic uncertainty has also arisen as a result of indeterminate statutory language used in biodiversity conservation. To address this, Australian courts have traditionally favoured a purposive interpretation of legislation, which gives terms their ordinary and natural meaning in a manner that is consistent with and seeks to promote the biodiversity protection objectives of the relevant legislative scheme.

In sum, legal realism is common to all these approaches, since Australian courts have generally recognised that uncertainty can be managed and reduced through iterative processes of knowledge production and information-gathering over time, but not entirely eradicated.

15

Scientific Uncertainty before the Court of Justice and the General Court: Is the Judicial Toolbox Sufficient?

MARIOLINA ELIANTONIO AND MICHAŁ KRAJEWSKI

I. Introduction

The uncertainty of empirical assertions is a pervasive problem in litigation before the EU Court of Justice (ECJ) and the General Court (EGC). It is particularly pressing in environmental law cases. At present, 'science' cannot be plausibly conceived of as a social practice generative of absolute and unchallengeable assertions but, rather, as a never-ending process of verification that leads to a deeper understanding of the studied phenomena that no point claims absolute truth.[1] How does the inherent contestability of scientific assertions affect the role of courts and the process of adjudication? Fuller saw the legitimacy of this dispute-settlement mechanism as stemming from the equal and pro-active participation of the opposing parties in adversarial proceedings which facilitate the impartial adjudicator's 'getting to the truth'.[2] Nowadays, not only must the courts ensure that the administration has taken into account all relevant scientific factors and police the boundaries of methodology, but they must also substantively engage with the rationality of scientific arguments, thereby exercising their own discretion.[3] As demonstrated by Sulyok, however, engaging with the intrinsically probabilistic nature of empirical claims constitutes a particular hardship for non-expert adjudicators on international courts, which may disrupt the social acceptability of judicial decisions in the long run. Put bluntly, 'scientifically poorly reasoned judgments may easily prove unconvincing'.[4]

[1] See chapter one of this volume, by Emma Lees and Tiina Paloniitty, at 20.
[2] Lon Fuller, 'The Forms and Limits of Adjudication' (1978) 92 *Harvard Law Review* 353.
[3] Elizabeth Fisher, *Risk Regulation and Administrative Constitutionalism* (Hart Publishing, 2007) 31.
[4] Katalin Sulyok, *Science and Judicial Reasoning: The Legitimacy of International Environmental Adjudication* (Cambridge University Press, 2020) 367–69.

This chapter examines how the EU Courts navigate between competing narratives and data in cases characterised by scientific uncertainty concerning empirical facts, overcoming the absence of independent specialised expertise. It is based on a study of the annulment[5] and infringement[6] cases relating to the protection of the environment and public health completed by the EU Courts in the five years between 2014–2018. The annulment cases were brought to the EGC by private parties, especially economic operators, and more infrequently by the Member States, triggering judicial review of administrative acts adopted by the Commission and EU agencies based on contentious scientific appraisals.[7] The infringement cases were brought to the ECJ by the Commission against Member States, and they related to national infringements of EU environmental law.

Section II lays down the framework for the present analysis by indicating some of the techniques and tools applied by the EU Courts, as well as international and administrative adjudicators to overcome the problems of scientific uncertainty. The application or non-application of these techniques by the EU Courts is discussed in section III (the apportionment and specification of the burden and threshold of proof), section IV (judicial investigatory tools) and section V (the extent of process-oriented and substantive review). Section VI presents conclusions, summarising problems for enforcement of EU environmental law and the legal accountability of EU institutions and bodies that may arise from the restricted judicial engagement with scientific claims.

II. The Judicial Toolbox

Adjudication as a means of solving disputes between two opposing parties rests on a series of increasingly controversial assumptions, such as the feasibility for adjudicators to achieve epistemic neutrality and construe an objectively correct account of both the empirical reality and the legal interpretation needed to solve the case. As we have seen throughout the country chapters, apart from abstruse scientific terms permeating environmental and other branches of law,[8] generalist judges struggle with gaps in scientific data, their varying quality or unsettled interpretations.

International and administrative adjudicators have developed various techniques moderating or structuring their engagement with uncertain science. One strategy is to set aside the cases in which law-makers have explicitly reserved cognitive (empirical) or volitive (political) appraisals to the expert and politically

[5] Treaty on the Functioning of the European Union (TFEU) [2016] OJ C202/47, art 263.

[6] *ibid* art 258.

[7] The EGC rulings in this procedure may be appealed to the ECJ. However, the ECJ's jurisdiction is limited to the points of law under TFEU, art 256(1), second paragraph, and no ECJ engagement with contentious empirical issues was identified in the said period.

[8] See also chapters two and 14 of this volume by Augustin Garcia Ureta and The Hon Justice Brian Preston respectively on the question of linguistic uncertainty – at 33–34, 298.

accountable administration.[9] In such cases, the courts may wish to abstain from the judicial review of empirical or discretionary issues to respect the law-makers' will and to maintain separation of powers. It is also argued that cognitive appraisals can and should be separated from volitive appraisals, and only the former's accuracy should be subject to judicial review.[10] However, it is well-established that science is a social construct affected by cultural, ethical and political considerations.[11] Therefore, the administration's technical or scientific discretion is always linked to a degree of political discretion.[12] For instance, such discretion is apparent when characterising the level of risk for the environment posed by a particular product or action, or when deciding whether a threshold of proof indicating a new risk has been met through sufficiently reliable and cogent scientific evidence.

The democratic and political accountability of EU institutions and bodies has always been disputed. Hence, the pressure on the legal accountability of their political and expert appraisals has mounted. This pressure has pushed the EU Courts, especially the EGC dealing with judicial review of EU legal acts in the first instance, towards developing a potentially inquisitive technique for the process-oriented review of empirically uncertain and complex matters, which may lead to mixed results.[13] Likewise, in the infringement proceedings the ECJ is frequently confronted with complex empirical evidence. What is at stake in this type of proceedings is the effective enforcement of EU environmental law against non-complying Member States, especially in light of the Commission's scant resources to produce or gather the necessary complex evidence.[14]

Several techniques have been identified by which the EU Courts seek to handle empirical uncertainty. The boundaries between them are not sharply defined, although they allow us to develop an overview of the judicial engagement with science. First, the judges interpret substantive law to allocate and specify the burden and threshold of proof, as well as indicate the legally relevant issues. In EU law, a crucial role is played by the precautionary principle, according to which even incomplete knowledge on the probable risks involved in an activity or a product is a valid cause to restrict or withdraw them to protect public health and the environment.[15]

[9] Joana Mendes, 'Bounded Discretion in EU Law: A Limited Judicial Paradigm in a Changing EU' (2017) 80 *MLR* 443, 451–59.

[10] Miro Prek and Silvère Lefèvre, '"Administrative Discretion", "Power of Appraisal" and "Margin of Appraisal" in Judicial Review Proceedings Before the General Court' (2019) 56 *CMLR* 339.

[11] See chapter one of this volume by Emma Lees and Tiina Paloniitty at 26.

[12] Mendes (n 9).

[13] Giulia Claudia Leonelli, 'The Fine Line between Procedural and Substantive Review in Cases Involving Complex Technical-Scientific Evaluations: Bilbaína' (2018) 55 *CMLR* 1217 (regarding the questionable quasi-substantive review); and Giulia Claudia Leonelli, 'Acknowledging the Centrality of the Precautionary Principle in Judicial Review of EU Risk Regulation: Why it Matters' (2020) 57 *CMLR* 1773 (regarding inconsistencies in the application of the notion of 'all relevant factors').

[14] Martin Hedemann-Robinson, *Enforcement of European Union Environmental Law: Legal Issues and Challenges* (Routledge, 2015) 196ff.

[15] For instance, C-441/17 *Commission v Poland* ECLI:EU:C:2018:255 [112]. The precautionary principle is also used by other international courts. Sulyok (n 4) 274.

Second, the EU judges, just like other international or domestic adjudicators, can, in principle, avail themselves of various investigatory tools to obtain and weigh probabilistic scientific evidence. For instance, they may appoint expert witnesses, commission expert reports or cross-examine partisan experts.[16] As will be discussed further below, the EU judges refrain from using these tools.

Third, any courts can moderate and re-focus the standard of review and level of engagement with complex issues. To ensure the accuracy or, at least, the plausibility, of uncertain empirical determinations, judges may focus on scrutinising the process for reaching the contested measure instead of second-guessing its substance. They may also polish procedural standards such as the right to be heard or the duty to state reasons and make sure that all 'relevant' factors have been appropriately considered.[17] Courts may indeed tackle the substance of scientific issues where they believe to have possessed necessary background knowledge. However, they may also wish to avoid direct engagement with scientific reasoning related to probabilistic causal links between, for instance, a chemical substance and a detriment to human health or the environment. To this end, courts may be reaching for proxies or substitutive considerations. They may seek to circumvent scientific problems by looking for logical inconsistencies in the parties' submissions or invoking one party's burden of proof in the adversarial judicial proceedings to dismiss this party's claims.[18] As regards the EU Courts, they largely employ the process-oriented review, but they also avoid tackling scientific problems directly.

Fourth, courts or court-like bodies capable and willing to delve deeper into scientific reasoning may attempt to verify the reliability of evidence by muddling through the processes and methods underpinning the generation of scientific information. They may also focus on the qualification or impartiality of persons and expert bodies involved in the process. Faced with clashing scientific views, they may try to discern a majority view as a formal signifier of scientific reliability.[19] When it comes to the EU Courts, they increasingly pay attention to the impartiality of experts, but they do not engage with the scientific quality of the evidence.

III. Substantive Law and the Burden of Proof

The interpretation of substantive law allows the judges to frame contentious empirical issues as legally relevant or irrelevant, allocate the burden of proof,

[16] Sulyok (n 4) 47–52.

[17] Joanne Scott and Susan Sturm, 'Courts as Catalysts: Rethinking the Judicial Role in New Governance' (2007) 13 *Columbia Journal of European Law* 565–94; Elizabeth Fisher, Pasky Pascual and Wendy Wagner, 'Rethinking Judicial Review of Expert Agencies' (2015) 93 *Texas Law Review* 1681.

[18] Sulyok (n 4) 52–56. The substitutive considerations and circumvention techniques may also be understood under Sulyok's 'framing' category, ie as a court's decision to exclude a certain scientific problem from the inquiry. *ibid* 11.

[19] Patrick Ky, 'Qualifications, Weight of Opinion, Peer Review and Methodology: A Framework for Understanding the Evaluation of Science in Merits Review' (2012) 24 *Journal of Environmental Law* 207.

and establish the required threshold of proof. In other words, the interpretation of substantive law determines what is to be proven, to what extent and, sometimes, by what means. The burden of proof is a classical legal tool to designate the party which is supposed to justify or rebut legal claims or prove the legally relevant factual circumstances in legal proceedings. Usually, a party initiating legal proceedings is required to discharge the burden of proof, such as a private applicant for a market authorisation or the Commission alleging an infringement of EU law by a Member State.

In infringement proceedings, it is for the Commission to prove the existence of a breach of EU law without relying on 'presumptions or schematic causalities'.[20] The Commission must precisely prove, by adducing concrete elements, with which 'specific obligations' the Member State has failed to comply. In a recent case concerning the Habitats Directive (HD), the ECJ concluded that the Commission had not managed to successfully discharge its burden of proof because it had not produced any material capable of substantiating its allegations, as well as merely referred to documents annexed to its application without providing any specific explanations on how those documents were relevant for the dispute at stake.[21]

The precautionary principle modifies the burden and threshold of proof. Sometimes also EU secondary law rules may re-design its usual allocation[22] or specify the required types of evidence or relevant empirical factors. In annulment proceedings, the EU Courts often operate with several layers of burden of proof rules pointing in opposite directions. While it formally belongs to the applicant (for instance, a private party) to set out legal arguments and adduce evidence, the EU Courts should nonetheless verify whether the defendant EU institution or body has discharged its burden of proof at the administrative stage to impose a restrictive measure on this party. In brief, the application of the burden and threshold of proof is not a straightforward exercise. It results from the interaction of substantive and procedural law and the adjudicators' pragmatic approach. In general, a decision as to when a sufficient threshold of proof has been met is by nature discretionary, especially in cases related to the protection of the environment and public health characterised by scientific uncertainty.

EU environmental law places on the Member States duties to achieve specific goals. The Commission should monitor the implementation of these duties.

[20] C-443/18 *Commission v Italy* ECLI:EU:C:2019:676 [80]. See also C-153/16 *Commission v Slovenia* ECLI:EU:C:2017:275 where the Court made it clear that arguments 'based on mere probability' could not be accepted ([50]–[55]).

[21] C-504/14 *Commission v Greece* ECLI:EU:C:2016:847 [109]–[113].

[22] See, eg, in the context of the Waste Shipment Directive, the rule pursuant to which, when Member States disagree on whether a shipment constitutes waste, that shipment is presumed to constitute 'waste' for the purposes of the legislation. See Regulation (EC) No 1013/2006 of the European Parliament and of the Council of 14 June 2006 on shipments of waste [2006] OJ L190/1. In an infringement case against the Czech Republic, however, the Court does not seem to have applied this rule properly, leading to a further reshuffling of the burdens between the Commission and the Member State. See C-399/17 *Commission v Czech Republic* ECLI:EU:C:2019:200. See further on this point Luca Prete and Ben Smulders, 'The Age of Maturity of Infringement Proceedings' (2021) 58 *CMLR* 285–332, 308.

However, it does not have at its disposal independent investigation resources, so it often relies on the data provided by the Member States themselves. Therefore, the ECJ may be willing to accept fragmentary and not entirely conclusive evidence of a breach and expect the Member State concerned to demonstrate compliance, even though formally the Commission should discharge the burden of proof in infringement proceedings. Indeed, the standard formula used in infringement proceedings suggests that the ECJ will be satisfied with the Commission having adduced 'sufficient evidence' that a breach of EU law has occurred when the alleged breach relates to the law in action rather than just a formal transposition of specific provisions.[23] Where the ECJ finds the evidence sufficient, it falls back onto the Member States to provide a persuasive defence by proving that it has effectively discharged its duties or by challenging in detail the information presented and the inferences drawn by the Commission.[24]

For instance, in a recent case concerning air quality legislation, the Commission alleged that France's plans to improve air quality had been inefficient for several years. France's defence did not convince the ECJ that the samples relied on by the Commission could not have been considered representative. These samples fully complied with the requirements derived by the EU Courts from the applicable legislation. In other words, the ECJ could rely in this case on the legislation to assess the samples' probative value.[25]

In another case concerning Italy's alleged infringement of EU law through its failure to remove plants infected by a harmful bacterium and to monitor and prevent its spreading, the Commission only partly succeeded in discharging the burden of proof. The Commission alleged, among other things, that the inspections were carried out at inappropriate times of the year. Italy counterargued, on purely scientific grounds, that the time it chose was appropriate.[26] The ECJ sided with the Commission for a different reason, avoiding a direct engagement with the scientific problem. Even assuming that the bacterium could be detected throughout the year, the ECJ held that the Italian authorities would have been unable to take any effective measure to prevent the spreading of the disease due to the late period of the monitoring.[27] Thus, the ECJ interpreted the 'appropriate' time in light of the applicable EU measure's objective and found the scientific problem to be legally irrelevant.

Moreover, the Commission alleged that Italy had committed a general and persistent breach of its obligations to prevent the continuous spreading of the

[23] See C-502/15 *Commission v United Kingdom* ECLI:EU:C:2017:334.

[24] *ibid* [24] and the case law cited.

[25] C-636/18 *Commission v France* ECLI:EU:C:2019:900 [44]–[45]. Conversely, in another case against Spain concerning waste water treatment, the Court considered that Spain has submitted sufficient proof of its compliance with EU law by providing the samples complying with the legislative specification whose absence had justified the infringement alleged by the Commission. C-38/15 *Commission v Spain* ECLI:EU:C:2016:156 [37]–[39] and [44]–[46].

[26] *Commission v Italy* (n 20) [49]–[55].

[27] *ibid* [56]–[62].

bacteria throughout the country. Italy counterargued that this spreading was not exclusively imputable to it, as it had to be considered a natural phenomenon, which can only be controlled or slowed down. The ECJ found that the Commission had not presented any specific evidence and Italy's general and persistent breach could not be presumed.[28] Overall, the ECJ navigated around scientific problems through the interpretation of substantive law and the burden and threshold of proof.

The detailed interpretation of substantive law allows the ECJ to indicate which empirical issues are legally relevant, and if need be, to avoid tackling scientific problems. For instance, in an infringement case concerning Germany's alleged failure to take measures against nitrate pollution, Germany and the Commission disagreed on the method of calculation of the concentration of nitrates. Germany used a system of arithmetic average, whereas the Commission employed a system based on weighted average. The ECJ avoided taking a position on which method actually had to be utilised. It shifted the focus towards the deterioration of water quality, which had not been contested by Germany.[29]

EU substantive law may also place duties on producers and marketers to ensure the safety of their products by providing sufficient empirical data.[30] At the same time, the EU administration may be authorised to modify previously issued market authorisations or place additional burdens on producers and marketers, provided that it presents new evidence suggesting previously unknown risks of the relevant products. In the subsequent annulment proceedings, it falls back on the producers or marketers to 'prove' that the EU administration has not considered all the relevant factors. In practice, holders of market authorisations for pharmaceutical products often allege before the EU Courts that they are effectively required to prove the safety of their products once again (the burden of proof being reversed), that the Commission's new evidence and conclusions are 'hypothetical', or that the precautionary principle exempts the authorities from their obligation to provide serious and conclusive evidence.[31]

The precautionary principle steers the EU Courts' evidentiary reasoning. This principle prompts the EU Courts to assign a high value to any reasonable evidence suggesting the absence of complete safety of certain products. As noted by the EGC:

> In view of the precautionary principle, the Commission may … merely provide serious and conclusive evidence which, without ruling out scientific uncertainty, gives

[28] *ibid* [78]–[84]. In the context of the HD see also *Commission v Poland* (n 15) [158]; *Commission v Greece* (n 21) [29]; C-141/14 *Commission v Bulgaria* ECLI:EU:C:2016:8 [58]; C-461/14 *Commission v Spain* ECLI:EU:C:2016:895 [77].

[29] C-543/16 *Commission v Germany* ECLI:EU:C:2018:481 [61].

[30] For instance, the REACH Regulation is based on the principle 'no data = no market'. Regulation (EC) No 1907/2006 of the European Parliament and of the Council on the Registration, Evaluation, Authorisation and Restriction of Chemicals (REACH) [2006] OJ L396/1.

[31] T-783/17 *GE Healthcare v Commission* ECLI:EU:T:2019:624 [55]–[56]; T-115/15 *Deza v ECHA* ECLI:EU:T:2017:329 [172]–[173]; T-672/14 *Dr August Wolff v Commission* ECLI:EU:T:2016:623 [116], [121] and [133].

> reasonable grounds for doubting the harmlessness of the medicinal product concerned, its therapeutic effect, the existence of a favourable risk-benefit balance or the qualitative and quantitative composition declared …[32]

Although substantive law shoulders the Commission with the duty to provide evidence of risk, the precautionary principle may still have the effect of reinforcing the producers or marketers' duties and curb legal certainty associated with prior authorisations for the sake of public health or the environment. In practice, the producers or marketers may be obliged to provide more data to refute 'sufficiently' probable risks indicated by the Commission.[33]

For instance, in the annulment case *GE Healthcare* the EGC had to decide whether new evidence on the accumulation of a previously authorised substance in the brain, in the absence of data on concrete clinical consequences and neurotoxicity of this substance, were sufficient to state a risk. The applicant alleged that the Commission's evidence was theoretical and hypothetical as there was simply no clinical evidence demonstrating a causal link between the substance and some neurological issues. However, the EGC was satisfied with the Commission's evidence relating to the substance's more substantial accumulation in the brain than previously estimated. It also noted studies *suggesting* an interrelation between the substance in question and some adverse effects on health.[34] In reaching its conclusion on the threshold of proof required from the Commission, notably, the EGC invoked the precautionary principle.[35]

IV. Empirical Investigations in Judicial Proceedings

Investigatory inactivity of the EU Courts has long been discussed in the literature.[36] The EU Courts have at their disposal a complete set of investigatory tools.[37] However, they refrain from appointing independent expert witnesses, commissioning independent expertise, or even hearing and cross-examining expert committee members who have assisted or participated in the contested EU decision-making

[32] *GE Healthcare v Commission*, *ibid* [47]–[49]; *Dr August Wolff v Commission*, *ibid* [181].

[33] The Commission's discretion in this regard may be limited, for instance, with a duty to present 'new' data, ie data that emerged after the prior authorisation has been made. Hence, the Commission cannot simply change its mind on the previously available evidence. *GE Healthcare v Commission* (n 31) [63]–[64]; T-584/13 *BASF Agro v Commission* ECLI:EU:T:2018:279 [114]ff. However, the previously available data may be used to buttress the interpretation of new data, *GE Healthcare v Commission* (n 31) [64].

[34] *GE Healthcare v Commission* (n 31) [66]ff. See also, *Deza v ECHA* (n 31) [172]–[173]; *Dr August Wolff v Commission* (n 31) [116], [121] and [133].

[35] *GE Healthcare v Commission* (n 31) [43].

[36] Eric Barbier de la Serre and Anne-Lise Sibony, 'Expert Evidence Before the EC Courts' (2008) 45 *CMLR* 941; Alexander Fritzsche, 'Discretion, Scope of Judicial Review and Institutional Balance in European Law' (2010) 47 *CMLR* 361.

[37] Arts 63–75 of the Rules of Procedure of the Court of Justice [2012] OJ L265/1; Arts 91–102 of the Rules of Procedure of the General Court [2015] OJ L105/1.

in view of clarifying the contentious issues of scientific interpretation. Several explanations have been proposed regarding why the EU Courts avoid using the investigatory measures: a concern about protracted proceedings, their increased cost, or a loss of judicial authority in the face of unsolvable scientific disputes in the courtroom.[38] There is, however, a difference between relinquishing judicial power to independent experts and directing questions to partisan experts. EU officials could be summoned to be subject to cross-examination by the parties, thereby further clarifying and defending their scientific findings and helping the judges ascertain the meaning of scientific evidence.[39]

Instead, the EU Courts rely merely on written, partisan evidence annexed to the parties' submissions. In the annulment proceedings, it is incumbent upon the applicant to prove the unlawfulness of the contested measure by adducing relevant evidence, even though the EGC is formally bound to verify the comprehensiveness and reliability of the contested measure's factual basis and the reliability of conclusions drawn from it. In infringement proceedings, it is generally incumbent upon the Commission

> [T]o prove the allegation that an obligation has not been fulfilled, by placing before the Court all the information required to enable it to establish that the obligation has not been fulfilled, without the Commission being entitled to rely on any presumption.[40]

The Commission cannot apply to the ECJ for commissioning a 'neutral' expert opinion on the matter.[41] However, the Commission's own investigatory resources and measures are minimal. The Commission relies on the data provided by the Member States, based on the principle of loyal cooperation, and by individual complainants, including non-governmental organisations (NGOs). Considering the scientific uncertainty involved in most evidence relating to environmental law cases, more research is needed into the operation of mechanisms through which the Commission obtains and verifies the evidence.[42]

In annulment cases, the EGC tends to dismiss the applicant's motions for more robust measures of inquiry. It justifies these dismissals perfunctorily. At the same time, the ECJ recognises the EGC's broad discretion in this respect and does

[38] *GE Healthcare v Commission* (n 31) [43].

[39] A similar option is used by the European Chemicals Agency (ECHA) Board of Appeal which allows for the representation by non-lawyers. In practice, the appellants and the ECHA are represented before the Board of Appeal by a whole group of lawyers, consultants and scientists who all clarify their positions and even directly engage with each other. Michał Krajewski, *Relative Authority of Judicial and Extra-Judicial Review: EU Courts, Boards of Appeal, Ombudsman* (Hart Publishing, 2021) 133–136.

[40] C-502/15 *Commission v Czech Republic* [23].

[41] C-141/87 *Commission v Italy* [1989] ECR 00943, ECLI:EU:C:1989:165.

[42] Recently, a group of Romanian scientists wrote an open letter questioning the reliability of evidence regarding the extent of illegal logging in Romania submitted to the Commission by several NGOs that led to the letter of formal notice in Case 2020/2033 C(2020) 651 final. Rectorul Universităţii Transilvania din Braşov, 'Referitor la: EuroNatur, Agent Green et al., Open letter to Romanian President and Government – Natural Forest Heritage' (14 April 2020), available at www.fern.org/fileadmin/uploads/fern/Documents/2019/NGO_letter_to_Romanian_President_and_Government.pdf.

not require it to provide detailed motives for these dismissals.[43] For instance, in *Bilbaina* the applicants requested the EGC to commission an expert report. The case turned out highly contentious on scientific grounds as it concerned the factors relevant for assessing the aquatic toxicity of a substance.[44] The EU Courts received criticism for potentially misrepresenting the scientific issue.[45] Notably, in this case the EGC had rejected the request for an expert report as it had considered that 'it has sufficient information available to it and is, therefore, able to understand all the relevant scientific issues'.[46] Similar brief statements can be found in other cases.[47]

Exceptionally, where the degree of complexity and uncertainty seems manageable for the judges, they may address the parties with written questions for the hearing to explain further and clarify contentious scientific issues. For instance, in *Paris, Bruxelles and Madrid v Commission*, the EGC requested the parties to provide further clarification as to the technical differences between the on-road and laboratory tests of car emissions to comprehend the operation of the Commission's correction factors introduced for on-road vehicle tests.[48]

V. The Techniques of Judicial Engagement with Science

A. The Process-Oriented Review

In infringement proceedings, where the ECJ largely relies on the scientific evidence submitted by the Commission, it seeks to ensure the Member State's right of defence within the administrative stage which crystallises the contentious issues including the scientific ones. Thus, the ECJ rules on issues that have been already thoroughly discussed by the parties. In particular, sending a letter of formal notice before the point on which a failure of a Member State to comply with EU law obligations can legitimately be alleged will result in the inadmissibility of the action, as shown by an infringement brought by the Commission against Spain in the context of the Waste Framework Directive.[49]

Furthermore, the ECJ carefully checks whether the Commission has complied with its duty to clearly specify the allegations against a Member State in the administrative stage of the proceedings. The ECJ has specified that:

[43] C-490/15 P and C-505/15 P *Ori Martin v Commission* ECLI:EU:C:2016:678 [108].

[44] T-689/13 *Bilbaína de Alquitranes et al v Commission* ECLI:EU:T:2019:69 [21].

[45] Leonelli, 'The Fine Line between Procedural and Substantive Review' (n 13).

[46] *Bilbaína v Commission* (n 44) [21].

[47] The EGC expects the applicant to justify the application for a measure of inquiry in detail. T-208/16 *Graziano Ranocchia v ERCEA* ECLI:EU:T:2018:68 [142]–[51].

[48] Joined Cases T-339/16, T-352/16, T-391/16 *Paris, Bruxelles, Madrid v Commission* ECLI:EU:T:2018:927 [136].

[49] C-642/18 *Commission v Spain* ECLI:EU:C:2019:1051.

> Although the reasoned opinion provided for [in Article 258 TFEU] must contain a coherent and detailed statement of the reasons which led the Commission to conclude that the State in question has failed to fulfil one of its obligations under the Treaty, the letter of formal notice cannot be subject to such strict requirements of precision, since it cannot, of necessity, contain anything more than an initial brief summary of the complaints. There is therefore nothing to prevent the Commission from setting out in detail in the reasoned opinion the complaints which it has already made more generally in the letter of formal notice.[50]

As a consequence, the reasoned opinion may expand on the letter of formal notice and make specific points more explicit, but it must, in principle, be founded on the same grounds and submissions as the initial letter of formal notice, since the rights of defence of the Member State concerned would otherwise be violated.[51]

The reasoned opinion may be regarded as a final crystallisation of the breach alleged by the Commission. This means that the Commission cannot amend the substantive content of the submission if and when it brings its application to the ECJ. If new grounds have arisen after the sending of the reasoned opinion, or if the parties wish to bring new elements to the ECJ's attention, the art 258 procedure must be re-initiated. However, this is not necessary when later evidence is of the same kind as earlier evidence and is included only to support the original argument. This might be the case in scientifically complex proceedings where producing evidence might be time consuming. For example, in an infringement case against Ireland, the Commission was allowed to produce new evidence which went to show that the earlier breach concerning the application of the Waste Water Directive had been part of a general and persistent pattern of breaches.[52]

Process-oriented review may also be a technique allowing courts to moderate their standard of review, as is frequently the case in the annulment proceedings. Rather than second-guessing the substance of scientific appraisals, courts may opt to scrutinise the decision-making process for reaching the contested decision. There is a certain inconsistency between the process-oriented standard of judicial review officially proclaimed by the EU Courts and its practical application in the annulment procedure. According to the official standard, not only must the EU Courts, *inter alia*,

> establish whether the evidence relied on is factually accurate, reliable and consistent but also whether that evidence contains all the information which must be taken into account in order to assess a complex situation and whether it is capable of substantiating the conclusions drawn from it.[53]

[50] C-279/94 *Commission v Italy* [1997] ECR I-04743, ECLI:EU:C:1997:396 [15]. See also C-191/95 *Commission v Germany* [1998] ECR I-05449, ECLI:EU:C:1998:441 [54]. Recently in the context of the HD, see C-461/14 *Commission v Spain* (n28) [28]–[29].

[51] C-166/82 *Commission v Italy* [1984] ECR 00459, ECLI:EU:C:1984:43 [16].

[52] C-494/01 *Commission v Ireland* [2005] ECR I-03331, ECLI:EU:C:2005:250.

[53] C-12/13 P *Commission v Tetra Laval* ECLI:EU:C:2014:2284 [39].

Also, the EU Courts verify whether 'the competent institution has examined carefully and impartially all the relevant aspects of the case …'.[54] These formulas may suggest the EGC's pro-active approach in assessing the reliability of the contested measure's empirical basis and the inferences drawn from it. On top of that, the EU Courts enforce the right to be heard of the persons adversely affected by the envisaged EU measure,[55] as well as police the administration's duty to state comprehensive reasons for its legal acts.[56]

In practice, however, the EU Courts only respond to the pleas in law and arguments formulated by the applicants.[57] The applicant is ultimately required to demonstrate to the judges that the EU administration's scientific reasoning was faulty or that a relevant factor was missing. The EU Courts may have difficulty deciding whether a specific factor is relevant from the scientific point of view.[58] Due to potential differences in established methodologies and interpretations, the EU Courts may be merely able to verify whether the EU administration's conclusion drawn from scientific data appear reasonable of whether it is probable rather than objectively correct. The assessment of reasonability involves discretion. Admittedly, it has been argued that the reasoning underpinning scientific methodologies and interpretation is no different from general practical reasoning.[59] As such, it should not remain beyond the intellectual reach of courts and lawyers.[60] However, it could be counterargued that acquiring necessary background knowledge in a specific field to autonomously assess the relevance of empirical factors in a given case requires time and resources that generalist courts lack. Whether a specific empirical factor is 'relevant' may seem intuitive but turn out implausible from the scientific point of view.[61]

For instance, in the *Bilbaína* case, the EU Courts might have inadvertently quashed the Commission's and the ECHA's precautionary approach to assessing the aquatic toxicity of a chemical substance used in industrial production. By formally applying a process-oriented review, the EU Courts indicated a 'relevant' scientific factor that the Commission and the ECHA had not sufficiently considered. The methodological approach opted for by these bodies did not encompass the low

[54] Recently, *Deza v ECHA* (n 31) [164].

[55] For instance, T-296/12 *The Health Food Manufacturers' Association v Commission* ECLI:EU:T:2015:375 [97].

[56] For instance, T-630/13 *DK Recycling und Roheisen v Commission* ECLI:EU:T:2014:833 [102]–[113].

[57] Krajewski (n 39) 87ff. Only a violation of the duty to state reasons can be raised by the EU Courts on their own motion.

[58] Hans-Peter Nehl, 'Judicial Review of Complex Socio-Economic, Technical and Scientific Assessments in the European Union' in Joana Mendes (ed), *EU Executive Discretion and the Limits of Law* (Oxford University Press, 2019).

[59] Deirdre Dwyer, *The Judicial Assessment of Expert Evidence* (Cambridge University Press, 2009).

[60] Herwig Hofmann, 'Interdependencies between Delegation, Discretion and the Duty of Care Regarding Facts' in Mendes (n 58) 220-236, 225.

[61] The common sense approach might have turned out sufficient in T-100/15 *Dextro Energy v Commission* ECLI:EU:T:2016:150 [32]ff, where the Court found that one of the relevant factors to be considered while authorising food claims is the negative impact of a high consumption of sugar on human health, even though this factor was not clearly indicated by the applicable legislation.

solubility of the substance in question. However, the inclusion of this factor – required by the EU Courts[62] – might have had the effect of changing the methodological approach to the risk assessment from one that had overestimated the risk, being more protective of public health and the environment, to one that would underestimate the risk, being more protective of the industry's economic interests. It was argued that the EU bodies had actually exercised their political discretion by opting for the precautionary approach due to the scientific limitations of existing methodologies, whereas the EU Courts exercised a quasi-substantive review and quashed the precautionary approach despite the existing methodological constraints and the resulting uncertainty of risk.[63] It is uncertain to what extent the EU judges could properly assess the relevance of this specific factor and its consequences for the assessment in question and the precautionary principle.

At the same time, the EGC applies a light-touch 'intelligibility' review of scientific opinions by independent committees that form the empirical basis of EU administrative measures.

> The courts may only examine whether the recommendation and the opinion contain a statement of reasons from which it is possible to ascertain the considerations on which the recommendation and opinion are based and whether they establish a comprehensible link between the medical or scientific findings and their conclusions …[64]

In such cases, the EGC does not delve into the data or studies' methodological nitty-gritty.[65] Instead, it inspects the reasoning of scientific committees for potential answers to the applicant's arguments.

In the already mentioned *GE Healthcare*, the question was whether new evidence on the accumulation of the substance at issue in the brain without any clinical data on its persistence was sufficient to state a neurological risk. The applicant argued that three hundred million doses had been administered since 1988, and there were still no traits of clinical problems. In response, the EGC picked up several factors indicated by the competent scientific committee that might indirectly suggest the existence of risk, even though no direct evidence was available. In accordance with the precautionary approach, the cumulative analysis of multiple indirect pieces of evidence was enough in the absence of direct evidence.[66]

[62] *Bilbaína de Alquitranes et al v Commission* (n 44); C-691/15 P *Commission v Bilbaína de Alquitranes et al* ECLI:EU:C:2020:284.

[63] Leonelli, 'The Fine Line between Procedural and Substantive Review' (n 13).

[64] *GE Healthcare* (n 31) [51].

[65] Regarding more in-depth review by the Board of Appeal of the European Chemical Agency see, Michał Krajewski, 'Judicial and Extra-Judicial Review: The Quest for Epistemic Certainty' in Mariolina Eliantonio, Merijn Chamon, Annalisa Volpato (eds), *The Boards of Appeal of European Agencies: A New Paradigm of Legal Protection?* (Oxford University Press, 2021).

[66] Similarly, in *Deza v ECHA* (n 31) [189]ff. In case of inconclusive scientific studies, the Court verified whether the Commission had mentioned which studies had been relevant but did not require the Commission to specifically justify why certain studies had been considered 'of some relevance' (possibly in light of the precautionary principle as only some studies have shown endocrine disruption). The Court seemed to be satisfied with the 'amount' of evidence presented and the fact that the applicant had not contested many studies (193ff).

Likewise, in *Dr August Wolff*, the scientific problem related to the safety of a cream intended for local use leading to an increase in blood concentration of estradiol. According to the expert committee, estradiol concentration in the blood after using this product was higher than after using other comparable products dedicated to local exposure. The committee recommended limiting this product's use due to generally known risks related to the use of products containing estrogens. The EGC verified the intelligibility of the committee's reasoning, including the evidence demonstrating a higher concentration of estradiol as a result of using the product.[67] However, the applicant provided medical literature assuming higher limit values than those accepted by the committee. The EGC dismissed this argument by simply arguing that the applicant had not sufficiently demonstrated that this information alone should change the committee's assessment.[68]

The question remains to what extent generalist judges, as not specialists, can appraise the actual weight of such indirect evidence without access to independent expertise and time and resources to acquire background knowledge.[69] The precautionary principle allows for or even requires administrative action despite scientific uncertainty, but it assumes that the EU administration nonetheless relies on 'serious and conclusive evidence' or 'solid evidence' and 'reasonable grounds'.[70] Although the threshold of proof for the EU institutions to take precautionary action may be, as a matter of principle, very low, with their discretion being extensive,[71] the role of judicial review is still to filter out 'manifestly unreasonable' grounds. The dividing line between unreasonable and manifestly unreasonable scientific interpretations may turn out blurred in practice.

B. Substantive Review and Engagement: Getting around Scientific Inquiries

Beyond the process-oriented review technique, the EU Courts declare applying the substantive review for a 'manifest error of assessment' in annulment cases. However, they rarely find such errors. Nonetheless, the degree of cases' complexity

[67] *Dr August Wolff v Commission* (n 31) [151]–[163].

[68] *ibid* [160].

[69] In T-201/13 *Rubinum v Commission* ECLI:EU:T:2015:311 [64]–[65] and [73]–[75], the scientific question was whether the detection of a gene usually linked to resistance to antibiotics in bacteria used in food supplements means that this food supplement may cause resistance to antibiotics. The applicant argued that the evidence the committee had relied on was inconclusive and lead merely to hypotheses, but the EGC expected the applicant to clearly demonstrate a 'manifest' error in the committee's assessment.

[70] *GE Healthcare v Commission* (n 31) [55]; T-229/04 *Sweden v Commission* [2007] ECR II-02437, ECLI:EU:T:2007:217 [161].

[71] Giulia Claudia Leonelli, 'Balancing Public Health and Environmental Protection and Economic Stakes? Bayer Crop-Science and the Court's Defence of the EU Socially Acceptable Risk Approach' (2021) 58 *CMLR* 1845, 1867–68.

and uncertainty fluctuates. The EU Courts may decide to engage with issues that seem technical at first sight when the required degree of background knowledge is manageable for them.

For instance, in *Bruxelles, Paris and Madrid*, the question was whether the Commission could introduce 'CF pollutant conformity factors' in an implementing regulation.[72] These factors had effectively legalised exceeding the limits on emissions of nitrogen oxides laid down in the Euro 6 standard. The Commission argued that these are mere 'statistical and technical corrective elements' as on-road vehicle tests – as opposed to 'pure' laboratory tests – resulted in 'uncertainties'. However, the EGC noted that the on-road tests were supposed to reflect better the actual level of emissions rather than only double-check the results obtained in a laboratory, which was clear from the preamble of the applicable EU regulation. The EGC was also capable of conceiving alternatives. It noted that it was conceivable to introduce corrections to the measurement on the road itself in order to better ensure the tests' representativeness. Instead, the Commission opted for effectively amending the Euro 6 standard. The issue of emission limits did not seem that abstruse. Hence, the applicants could elucidate the problem for the EGC through specific examples of the emissions produced by different vehicles to illustrate the actual effects of the Commission regulation. Overall, the EGC appears able to form its own view on the probative value of complex evidence and the soundness of expert reasoning, if sufficiently specific arguments and background knowledge is provided by the parties.[73]

However, in a significant number of cases involving more abstruse and uncertain empirical issues, the EGC looks for ways to circumvent the scientific problem by pointing out inconsistencies or deficiencies in one of the parties' submissions or invoking the burden of proof resting with this party. Generalist judges have limited background knowledge on what kind of inferences can be drawn from uncertain scientific data, whereas in many cases, a dispute between an applicant and the EU bodies concentrates on interpreting such data correctly or at least plausibly. In such cases, there is no question about which evidence or legal arguments are more comprehensive or convincing, but rather, what legitimate conclusions can be

[72] *Paris, Bruxelles, Madrid* (n 48) [121]ff. In this case, the Court undertook the assessment under the plea of the 'lack of competence' on the side of the Commission to modify the essential elements of EU legislation (Euro 6 limits) and it did not invoke the usual formulas of limited review.

[73] *ibid* [134]. Likewise, in T-80/16 *Shire Pharmaceuticals Ireland v European Medical Agency* ECLI:EU:T:2018:165 [62]–[65], the EGC was able to assess by itself whether two medicinal products were or not in fact the same product, on account of containing the same active substance but different excipients, administration methods and partly different effects on patients. In T-204/11 *Spain v Commission* ECLI:EU:T:2015:91, based on scientific articles, reports and data provided by the parties, the EGC was able to autonomously assess if the new chemical method for identifying marina toxicity was less protective of public health than the previous biological method due to its cost, efficiency and inherent properties. In *BASF Agro* (n 33) [130]–[136], the EGC confidently assessed the difference in the quality of data coming from the field studies and monitoring studies. In T-135/13 *Hitachi Chemical Europe v European Chemicals Agency* ECLI:EU:T:2015:253 [74]–[77], the EGC has dealt with relatively straightforward methodological deficiencies of a scientific study.

derived from data that are in principle not contested by the parties. Such disputes might be effectively resolved by neutral experts possessing sufficient background knowledge of the relevant scientific discipline and its methodologies to sort out the wheat from the chaff and choose the more plausible scientific interpretation, if at all possible.

In such cases, the EGC may be inclined to side with the Commission as the representative of the public interest and require the applicant to 'prove' the Commission's error. In *TestBioTech*, one of the arguments related to the use of glyphosate and pesticides with some genetically modified organisms. The Commission found some statistical evidence of unintended effects to be irrelevant. An environmental NGO challenged the Commission's interpretation of the data considering that the underlying risk assessment of the European Food and Safety Authority had not been sufficiently prudential and that, due to the degree of uncertainty, the case merited further investigation. The EGC dismissed the plea, requiring the 'evidence' of a manifest error. However, this part of the dispute related only to conclusions that could be legitimately drawn from the existing data rather than the completeness of evidence.[74] Therefore, the applicant alleged on appeal before the ECJ that the EGC had imposed an impossible burden of proof on it. However, the ECJ disagreed with this plea.[75]

The EGC applied a similar science-evasive technique in *Deza*. The applicant, in that case, questioned an explicitly uncertain assumption made by a scientific committee that found a specific substance to be carcinogenic by itself rather than due to a certain impurity, a low level of which was present in the tested sample. Shouldering the applicant with the burden of proof, the EGC emphasised that proving uncertainty does not suffice to prove a 'manifest' error of the committee.[76] It is unclear whether the EGC was able to assess by itself the degree of plausibility of the committee's assumption. In the same case, the applicant argued that the carcinogenicity study involved administering the substance in unnaturally high quantities to the tested animals. However, the EGC held that,

> The applicant had not established that the method of directly applying high quantities of any substance was not a recognised and established scientific method. In this respect, the applicant merely makes a general assertion without providing any specific evidence calling into question the reliability of the method.[77]

[74] T-177/13 *TestBioTech eV v European Commission* ECLI:EU:T:2016:736. Giulia Claudia Leonelli, 'GMO Authorisations and the Aarhus Regulation: Paving the Way for Precautionary GMO Governance?' (2019) 26 *Maastricht Journal of European and Comparative Law* 505, 513–15. See also for cases in which the EGC requires the applicant to demonstrate 'manifest' errors, *Hitachi, ibid* [59]–[60], [67], [95]–[96] and [115]. Also, in *BASF Agro* (n 33) [164], instead of inquiring into the way in which the Commission applied the precautionary principle and proportionality, the EGC focused on the lack of evidence of prior impact assessment.

[75] C-82/17 P *Test BioTech et al v Commission* ECLI:EU:C:2019:719 [67].

[76] *Deza v ECHA* (n 31) [198]–[199].

[77] *ibid* 199.

The EGC referred in this case to the allocation of the burden of proof and the adversarial judicial setting rather than autonomously verifying whether the scientific method applied had been 'manifestly' implausible. However, the question remains about the objective accountability of the EU administration for its science-intense decision-making in case the applicant is in no position to prove that a specific scientific method is not recognised.

The EU Courts may also decide to circumvent the scientifically complex issues when the case lends itself to an 'easy way out' from the scientific conundrum, mainly by dint of logical inconsistencies in the parties' submissions. For example, in an infringement case concerning shale gas extraction in Poland, the Commission had submitted several scientific studies confirming the high environmental risks of shale gas extraction, which implied the need to conduct an environmental impact assessment before such extraction would be authorised. Poland instead maintained that the local geological conditions were such that shale gas extraction was not liable to have considerable effects on the environment. The Commission rebutted this allegation by claiming that the diversity of geological conditions rendered a case-by-case analysis necessary. As Poland did not contest this fact, the ECJ had an 'easy job' in siding with the Commission and solving the scientific problem in the latter's favour.[78]

Similarly, in *Paris, Bruxelles, Madrid*, the EGC supported its reasoning by pointing out inconsistencies in the Commission's reasoning. The Commission argued that some correction factors to on-road tests for vehicle emissions were necessary to account for uncertainties produced by laboratory tests. However, the EGC pointed out the internal inconsistency of the Commission's reasoning:

> Without claiming to be a technical expert, the Court observed that the RDE [on-road vehicle] tests have 'matured' over a long period, since the Commission states, in its written submissions, that the work on those tests began in January 2011 …. In those circumstances, it would be surprising if the Commission had not had the time to clarify and standardise the RDE tests sufficiently so that they are representative of real driving conditions on the road.[79]

The same type of 'logical inference' used to avoid delving into scientific questions can also be identified in infringement proceedings. For example, in a case against the United Kingdom concerning the alleged violation of its obligation to ensure the collection and treatment of urban waste water in several agglomerations, the Member State sought to defend itself by proving that the system it chose to ensure compliance, although not entirely successful, was in line with the 'best technical knowledge not entailing excessive costs' concept foreseen by the relevant EU law measure and that, despite its delay in completing the works to put this system in place, it could not be censored for having – in essence – chosen the best possible

[78] C-526/16 *Commission v Poland* ECLI:EU:C:2018:356 [69]–[71].
[79] *Paris, Bruxelles, Madrid* (n 48) [142].

option to comply with EU law. Instead of assessing whether the technique chosen by the Member State concerned was indeed the best available one, the Court noted that the United Kingdom had embarked upon a large programme of works, a fact which proved, in the Court's view, that there were other technological solutions in order to overcome the problems of compliance with EU law.[80]

Likewise, in the abovementioned case against Italy, revolving around the alleged omission to remove infected plants, the question at stake concerned the determination of a 'suitable' moment to conduct inspections so that the presence of the bacterion could be detected. Italy and the Commission disagreed, as the Commission claimed this was a specific period of the year, while Italy claimed that inspections could be carried out throughout the whole year. The ECJ refrained from taking a position and shifted the focus towards another, related obligation imposed on the Member States by the relevant EU legislation. It stated that if inspections are conducted later in the year, they may identify the bacterion, but that point in time would be too late to remove the infected trees.[81]

This 'shifting technique' could also be identified in an infringement case against Poland and its alleged failure to comply with air quality legislation through the air quality plans submitted. Instead of tackling the complex question of the 'adequacy' of the plans to reduce the PM10 concentrations, the ECJ focused on the fact that the plans adopted set the expiry of the periods prescribed for putting an end to the PM10 exceedances between 2020 and 2024, which made it possible for Poland to put an end to such exceedances only in 10 or even 14 years after the date on which those exceedances were recorded. In the ECJ's view this fact in itself constituted a violation of the requirement that Member States ensure that exceedance periods be as short as possible.[82]

A case was also identified in the examined period in which the EGC explicitly refused to settle what it considered a purely scientific issue. In *GE Healthcare*, one of the applicant's arguments related to the alleged benefit of its product to other contrast agents for myocardial perfusion imaging. The relevant committee had perfunctorily dismissed this argument. The EGC held that

> The applicant bases its arguments relating to the benefit of Omniscan for myocardial perfusion imaging on medical considerations, which the Commission disputes with similar arguments, and on scientific literature … the Court cannot substitute its own assessment for that of the [competent committees] and its power of judicial review is exercised only over the lawfulness of their operation, and over the internal consistency and reasoning of their recommendations and opinions. Consequently, the Court cannot examine whether the applicant's statements are well-founded.[83]

It is arguably more common for the courts to camouflage their 'scientific' evaluations with juridical discourse (eg the duty to consider all 'relevant' factors[84]) rather

[80] *Commission v United Kingdom* (n 23) [44].
[81] *Commission v Italy* (n 20) [56]–[62].
[82] C-336/16 *Commission v Poland* ECLI:EU:C:2018:94.
[83] *GE Healthcare* (n 31), [98]–[99] and [118]–[119].
[84] Leonelli, 'The Fine Line between Procedural and Substantive Review' (n 13).

than explicitly withdraw from any engagement with scientific evaluations and entirely defer to the challenged institution, which bears dangerous resemblance to the denial of justice on the dispute's crucial element. As noted by Sulyok, such techniques downplay the importance of scientific considerations underlying legal disputes run the risk of undermining the acceptability of judicial decisions.[85]

C. Verifying the Quality of Evidence

Courts may choose to guarantee the quality of scientific evidence, without going into its substance, by polishing the standards relating to the potential conflicts of interest, the professional qualifications of experts and expert groups. As already mentioned, the EGC attaches a strong presumption of correctness to scientific opinions issued by expert committees assisting EU administration.[86] Therefore, the applicants may challenge EU experts' impartiality in elaborating the empirical basis of EU administrative action.

In *GE Healthcare* the applicant alleged that a Commission expert had assisted lawyers who brought an action for damages against the applicant. The EGC dismissed the claim relating to the lack of impartiality as the minutes of the expert group meeting indicated that this expert had not had a decisive influence on the committee's position.[87] The ECJ recently raised the bar in *Dr August Wolff*. In that case, the allegation was that the expert committee's reporting member had been an expert of the national body that had triggered the procedure for verification of market authorisation. Therefore, he acted as both a 'prosecutor' and a 'judge'. The EGC held that the reporting members' nationality and her work for the national authority were insufficient to cast doubt on her objectivity without more specific proof. Moreover, it noted that other reporting members had been involved in the procedure and that the decision was unanimous.[88] However, on appeal, the ECJ highlighted the requirement of 'objective impartiality', which implies institutional guarantees that should dispel any reasonable doubt as to a potential bias. The ECJ noted that the reporting member had a significant role in the decision-making process within the committee, which by default determines the Commission's decision. Moreover, the litigation as to the rejection of national authorisation for the product at issue, involving the national authority the member of which was the contested expert, was still ongoing. These facts generated a reasonable doubt as to the impartiality of the EU decision-making process.[89]

[85] Sulyok (n 4) 269.

[86] See examples where such strong presumption of correctness was attached: *Dr August Wolff v Commission* (n 31), [121]–[132]. *Hitachi* (n 73) [59]–[60]; T-400/17, *Deza v ECHA* (n 31) [46]–[49], [73]ff.

[87] *GE Healthcare* (n 31) [179]–[184].

[88] *Dr August Wolff v Commission* (n 31) [86]ff.

[89] C-680/16 P *August Wolff and Remedia v Commission* ECLI:EU:C:2019:257 [24]ff.

On the other hand, the EU Courts do not in principle delve into scientific studies' methodological correctness, unless specific allegations in this regard are made by the parties.[90] Nor do they check whether they have been subject to peer review or whether they remain in line with the majority's opinion on contentious issues within the scientific community. Occasionally, one of the parties may use methodology-related arguments to contest the use of a specific study by the other party. But it remains uncertain to what extent the generalist EGC is capable of solving more advanced methodological controversies.[91] In any case, its epistemic capacity depends on the persuasiveness and clarity of the arguments presented by the parties.[92] On the contrary, specialised and quasi-judicial boards of appeals operating in certain EU agencies may prove capable of delving into the methodological nitty-gritty of scientific studies and thus carry out more intense extra-judicial review. They have been set up to limit the number of complex cases reaching the EU Courts and to provide more thorough review in fields such as the risk regulation of chemicals. Nonetheless, the relation between the two routes – the judicial and extra-judicial – is not yet clear as in many cases, despite a different label, the EU Courts and boards of appeal may apply a similar type of review.[93]

In infringement proceedings, the ECJ relied on annual reports submitted by the national authorities and did not question their validity or reliability, possibly because they were not contested in Court and corroborated by the Commission's arguments.[94] The ECJ regularly holds that 'any official document' issued by national authorities may be considered a reliable source of information.[95] However, other types of information, though partisan, such as information obtained through the press or video reports, have also been considered acceptable by the Court if corroborated by more official sources, such as a report from the relevant environmental agency.[96]

VI. Conclusions

The presented analysis demonstrates that the EU Courts' toolbox to deal with the science underlying contested EU measures or infringement disputes remains limited. While the EU Courts apply the precautionary principle to bridge the gap between law and intrinsically uncertain empirical appraisals, doubts arise

[90] See, eg, *Spain v Commission* (n 73).

[91] For instance, in *Hitachi* (n 73) [74]–[77].

[92] It is also uncertain which controversies should be classified as more advanced. See T-115/15 *Deza v ECHA* (n 31) [198]–[199], where the EGC expected the applicant to demonstrate evidence calling into question the reliability of the method of applying high doses (in the applicant's view – unnaturally high doses) of a certain substance to animals under laboratory conditions.

[93] Krajewski (n 39).

[94] *Commission v France* (n 25).

[95] C-104/15 *Commission v Romania* ECLI:EU:C:2016:581 [85].

[96] *ibid* [55]–[57].

regarding their epistemic capacity to scrutinise the boundaries of EU institutions and bodies' discretion in justifying their precautionary measures. By the same token, the Member States may be willing to take advantage of the ECJ's weakness in this regard and seek to avoid repercussions for EU law infringements. Notably, the Commission is in a comparatively weaker position as it has to rely on the Member States for the provision of data on their compliance with EU law. A question arises whether the EU Courts can carry on their current relatively passive judicial practice without considering recourse to more incisive procedural tools in science-intensive cases. Even the potential of the process-oriented review technique encounters inherent limits in disputes revolving around a choice between conflicting interpretations of scientific data. Without specialised background knowledge, the generalist EU judges may not be able to assess the coherence and plausibility of such interpretations. The ECJ has, for now, circumvented a need to engage with purely scientific assertions, but its self-restraint in this regard may also have an impact on the type of environmental infringement cases brought to it by the Commission, uncertain of its chances for success, with concomitant risks for the protection of the environment in the EU. The lack of direct and transparent engagement with science by the EU Courts, despite the growing docket of science-intensive cases on their desk, may also, in the long run, affect the authority of their decisions in the eyes of the Member States and private parties alike.

Conclusions

MARIOLINA ELIANTONIO, EMMA LEES
AND TIINA PALONIITTY

I. Introduction

In drawing conclusions from this study we cannot but zoom out to consider the landscape as a whole. It is clear from the chapters that there are subtle and important variations in the operation of the Directives across Member States. These variations happen in a number of dimensions. The form of the administrative decision-maker is not homogenous: neither is the approach to judicial review of decisions emerging from this range of bodies. In putting together this collection we expected to unearth variation, but the degree and causes of it were in some places unexpected in their complexity and nuance. In drawing together these threads it is possible to identify three main sources of differentiation which mutually influence each other and which operate to different degrees in the various legal systems we considered.

The first source of these differences lies in the administrative decision-makers themselves. This has not been the focus of our study, but it is important to engage with this as a backdrop to what follows. The second source is the operation of the courts, both in terms of the substantive law of judicial review, and in terms of the process in court. The final source relates to 'environmental' substance – that is, the ways in which the courts engage with environmental standards per se. Indeed, the level of protection for sites clearly varies through the Member States notwithstanding the apparent homogeneity of the underpinning law. This affects not only which cases end up in court, but also the kinds of uncertainties and evidence-bases that the courts are required to handle and reason with. It should also be noted that we encountered a significant variation in the volume of case law. Whilst this is notable in itself, it has consequences for the robustness of our conclusions. In jurisdictions with little case law, eg Romania, it is more challenging to draw concrete patterns. Nevertheless, this conclusion explores these three dimensions in turn.

II. Decision-Making Process

Neither in national courts, nor in the courts of the European Union, do Habitats Directive (HD) decisions operate in a vacuum. In all cases they emerge from challenges to administrative decisions of one form or another. Any comparative study of how courts handle these challenges must therefore acknowledge that not only do the courts vary in their approach, so too do administrative agencies in respect of which a challenge emerges. This is critically important. Administrative variation influences outcomes. It also sets the foundation for the judicial review that follows. The role of developer, administrative authority and interested parties, and the way in which power is allocated between these three, sets the backdrop against which the judicial action takes place.

This backdrop is not homogenous: it may also be obscure or, worse, entirely opaque, even to those highly familiar with the national context. For our comparative study this has important consequences. We cannot divorce how the courts handle and reason about scientific evidence relating to the HD from the way in which the administrative authority came to reach its own conclusions as to the factual evidence. In many instances, however, that process will be partly hidden in the reasoning of the court. Nevertheless, before we can map our comparative conclusions regarding judicial process, it is important to sketch out at least some critical aspects of the administrative landscape revealed in this book which frame judicial reasoning.

A. Sources of Evidence

First, we can consider from a comparative perspective the respective role of developers as a source of facts within the process. In some jurisdictions, such as the UK, developers and their scientific advisors are the primary source of the evidence relied upon in administrative decision-making. Romania and Finland too exemplify this approach. Whilst authorities have legal responsibility for the decision made, and are able to request more information from developers to substantiate this approach, the developer provides the information. However, in Romania, in contrast to the UK, such information is then reviewed by a specialist agency with legally guaranteed expertise, meaning that for especially complex decisions the agency itself may seek specialist advice.

In Ireland, in decisions involving the Planning Board, the Board itself carries out the appropriate assessment and information in this respect may come from a range of sources. Here the Board decides whether the developer and other sources combined provided sufficient information. The same is true for the specialist Lithuanian State Service for Protected Areas which is able to use consultants if the agency itself lacks expertise. The consequence of this diversity of sources of information is that (a) it minimises the degree to which the developer shapes the evidential 'pathway' which a decision follows and (b) shifts responsibility onto the shoulders of the administrative agency to weigh and contest conflicting evidence. Another way to express this is to think of the administrative authority as gatekeeper and guardian of information. It determines what information, and in what form, is relevant to the court because of how it phrases its decision in the first place. The source of the information is relevant to the way in which that information is presented.

B. Constitution and Role of Administrative Agencies

Second, it is important to consider the constitution and role of the administrative authority in question. Indeed, in cases where such an agency is required to weigh evidence as explained above, their make-up and expertise become critical in the final 'form' of the evidential picture as presented to the court. In some jurisdictions decisions lie almost solely with dispersed and decentralised non-specialist agencies (perhaps in consultation with a specialist advisor): in other jurisdictions the agency is specialised and centralised. In others still the agency is centralised without scientific expertise.

Ireland is a particular case in point here. Rather than relying on an administrative agency alone, the Planning Board in terms of its form and status sits between judicial and administrative authority. This Board can make first instance decisions and when sitting as an appellate body from decisions of regional planning authorities is entitled to hear decisions *de novo*. However, the decision-making process of this Board is very different from that of a local planning authority in the UK, for example (and deliberately so). Indeed, scientific expert Board Inspectors, sitting in a quasi-judicial role, themselves prepare the report allowing or not allowing consent. The decision-maker here is somewhere between judicial and administrative in their function, and has specific scientific expertise. Both the form and the internal processes of the Board are very different even from other specialist agencies.

In other jurisdictions, decisions regarding protected sites are administered by single specialist agencies which operate with purely administrative functions. Here we can include Romania (National Agency for Protected Natural Areas) and Lithuania (State Service for Protected Areas). In Greece, environmental permitting for development is centralised in the Organisation for the Natural Environment and Climate Change, whereas decentralised state authorities deal with species protection.

In such cases we can see that the degree of specialisation of the agency, its scientific competencies, and its relationship with political actors and the public as democratic subjects will vary. In general terms this influences the constitutional understanding of separation of powers. In specific terms it influences the way in which scientific information is analysed in the administrative decision, who has control over that information, and how that is then framed in any reasoned outcome challenged before a court. Indeed, the critical background importance of agency form is best exemplified by the example of Hungary, where the change from regional Environmental Inspectorates operating as independent specialist agencies, to the same operating as advisors to the centralised (and politicised) Regional Governmental Administrative Agencies, is clearly significant in how decisions in Hungary are made.

C. Administrative Decision-Making and the Precautionary Principle

The final layer to consider *within* the administrative decision which forms the backdrop for the judicial process, is the moment at which and the way in which an administrative decision-maker will invoke the precautionary principle. As we discuss below, the principle itself can mean many different things depending upon the context of its use: it can be a tool to assess the quality of *evidence*; it can create rebuttable presumptions of fact; and it can be used to interpret the meaning of a legal standard. It does all of these things in different places in the operation of the HD.

However, when we look at the translation point between the administrative and the judicial, as this collection does, it is clear that different actors may be relying on the principle to perform a range of roles. In the context of the HD, where an administrative decision-maker concludes that a permit cannot be granted *on the basis of the precautionary principle*, they may have reached (at least) three similar, but not identical, conclusions.

First, they may have decided that there is insufficient evidence upon which to base their decision because the test for 'sufficiency' in evidence is filtered through by the principle, meaning that instead of 'clear' they need 'certain' evidence. Thus, they may have decided that the *quality* of the evidence provided is not good enough to meet a precaution-driven sufficiency standard. In this case precaution becomes a means of assessing whether an evidential base is sufficiently convincing. Second, they may have decided that the evidence they have is indeed high-quality evidence, but that it does not cover the entirety of the questions surrounding a plan or project. Thus, it may be certain that the plan will have effect x, but that does not tell us anything about the possibility of effects y and z. In this case, precaution says that the *quantity* of evidence is insufficient – precaution encourages the identification of missing information. In this case then precaution becomes a means of assessing whether the evidential base is sufficiently comprehensive. Finally, the decision-maker may have concluded that they have both convincing and comprehensive evidence, but that they have to decide, for example, whether harm is 'likely' for the purposes of the Directive. Likely, as a spectrum term must be interpreted and precaution transforms, in line with the Court of Justice of the European Union's (CJEU) ruling in *Waddenzee*, a likelihood into a possibility.[1] In this case it is the legal standard that is changed. Indeed, in any particular case the principle may operate in all three ways creating a three-fold precautionary effect. Once the decision comes before the courts, which of these three uses underpinned the administrative decision will shape how the court then reasons with the precautionary principle in its own judgment. Not only does this understanding therefore vary from jurisdiction to jurisdiction, but also from case to case.

D. Conclusions on Administrative Decision-Making and Scientific Uncertainty

Thus, our comparative study has revealed much about the process once a dispute regarding the use of scientific evidence in a decision relating to the HD reaches a judicial forum. But it has also shown the importance of what has gone on before. The idiosyncratic ways in which Member States have integrated HD decision-making into their existing administrative structures has a profound influence on the ways in which agency decisions are reviewed in court.

The internal processes, form, and understanding of the administrative agency as regards its task as actor in habitats and species protection are very important. All decisions in this context are made on the basis of evidence. That evidence emerges from a package of factual material laid before the decision-maker. The source of the material relied upon to determine the robustness of the evidence is not neutral: the material comes from somewhere and is provided by someone. In some states it is provided by a developer. In others it is provided through a range of sources, collated by an administrative agency. Furthermore, that evidence must be interpreted, reviewed, weighed and understood. This task is completed by the administrative agency and that agency may be scientifically literate or not; may have an intimate connection with the landscape or population of a particular region; and may be subject to political pressures, be that other administrative actors or be that the exigencies of popular votes. The composition of that agency determines, in part, what values and priorities become integrated into that weighing of evidence. Finally, in all cases involving the HD precaution is the watchword. However, what precaution means, and how it works, will vary from agency to agency. This means that the starting point for any judicial intervention already encompasses this dimension of variation.

[1] C-127/02 *Landelijke Vereniging tot Behoud van de Waddenzee v Staatssecretaris van Landbouw, Natuurbeheer en Visserij* [2004] ECR I-07504, ECLI:EU:C:2004:482.

III. The Procedural Eco-System

The great variation in the ways in which HD decision-making takes place at the Member State level also appears when looking at both the procedural rules on judicial review as well as at the scope and intensity of review used by national courts when reviewing decisions taken on the basis of the Directives. Our comparative investigation revealed that 'traditional' labels commonly used in comparative administrative law to describe the approach towards judicial review of administrative action are largely a matter of semantics rather than concepts able to capture the reality of the intricacies of judicial review practices. This is the case with respect to the traditional distinction between legality and merits review: while all legal systems provide a (sometimes constitutionally guaranteed) mechanism of legality review, and understand it as a cornerstone of the rule of law, merits review sits more uneasily with the *trias politica* and is therefore either left out from the jurisdiction of administrative courts or admitted only within clear limitations. However, beyond these principled distinctions, matters become more blurred when a thorough control of administrative discretion within the legality review comes 'dangerously' close to a merits review.

Furthermore, our comparative analysis showed that national understandings of seemingly pan-European notions, such as proportionality or the duty to give reasons, may differ widely, and with them the consequent intensity of judicial review performed by court. What is encompassed under the 'umbrella' of proportionality – despite the same wording being used in France or in Germany – is very different, and brings about a different intensity through which national courts will be able or willing to control the administrative discretion afforded to national authorities by the Directives.

Finally, in turn, the intensity of judicial review is linked to the epistemological possibility of national courts to access and understand the scientific knowledge necessary to control administrative decision. Here also there is great variation in national approaches, though – perhaps counterintuitively – our analysis showed that broader possibilities to understand the scientific underpinnings of national administrative decisions do not *per se* lead to a more thorough control of these decisions. In turn, seeing that these decisions are taken within the scope of application of both EU law and the Aarhus Convention, it is questionable whether certain national arrangements comply with international and supranational obligations applicable at Member State level.

A. Access to Scientific Knowledge in Environmental Litigation

The legal systems covered in our volume differ greatly when it comes to both the rules concerning the existence of specialised environmental courts (or o specialist judges within generalist administrative courts) and the possibility and practical occurrence of resorting to experts in cases concerning the HD.

Finland is the only system where expert judges form part of the court, but only with respect to certain types of environmental cases. In Ireland, there is no specialist environmental court, although there are plans for a new 'Planning and Environmental Law Court' to be managed by 'specialist judges' and there is an *ad hoc* element of specialisation through assigning certain environmental cases to judges assigned to a specific List in the High Court. Similarly, in Germany there are 'environmental senates' within generalist administrative courts, while in England and Wales some environmental cases are adjudicated by a Planning Court where there are specialist judges without – however – there being a difference in which evidence is scrutinised when compared to generalist judges in the High Court. Whilst some statutory appeals are also heard through the tribunal system, the judges within the First-Tier and Upper Tribunals are themselves generalists to a greater or lesser extent.

In all other legal systems (and this is also partially the case for Finland, England and Wales, and Ireland), it is generalist judges – without specialist knowledge of environmental law – who are called upon to adjudicate cases falling under the scope of the HD. The question of whether and to what extent these judges can resort to experts to understand the scientific underpinnings of a dispute is of crucial importance.

Most legal systems do foresee systems of appointing or hearing experts in various shapes and forms (and sometimes also attached specific legal consequences to expert evidence in terms of evidentiary weight), but our comparative investigation revealed a large lacuna when it comes to the actual occurrence of experts featuring in environmental cases in practice. Indeed, in most legal systems (with the notable exception of Hungary, where recourse to expert evidence is fairly common), the proceedings remain largely adversarial without the courts regularly engaging in autonomous fact-finding activities, unless the evidence is clearly inconclusive or contradictory. A rather unique construction is to be found in the Netherlands, where scientific and technical knowledge can be obtained from the Foundation of Independent Court Experts in Environmental and Planning Law, which works on behalf of courts and the Council of State as independent advice-provider.

Interestingly, as the next section will reveal, there is no clear – and principled – correlation between the presence (through a court member or an external expert) of specialist knowledge and a more thorough scrutiny of administrative decisions under the HD.

B. Intensity of Review

The legal systems which we have covered in this volume range from a very 'hands-off' approach towards the judicial control of administrative discretion, to a very intense system of review. Ireland and England and Wales are the systems with – at least seemingly – the weakest form of control, because of the applicable standard being that of 'unreasonableness' under the *O'Keeffe* and *Wednesbury* doctrines, respectively. The approach is of deference to the decision-maker when assessing environmental decisions. However, this test is vague and flexible (when is a choice of the administration 'unreasonable'? When it is instead 'disproportionate'?). For this reason, this limited review has not prevented Irish courts from engaging with a fairly close analysis of the substance of the decision and the choices of the administration. This has been less the case in England, where the Higher courts have consistently emphasised that they are not best equipped to review scientifically-loaded choices of the administration. By contrast, in the Tribunal system where the adjudicator is authorised to intervene more closely into the merits of a decision, extensive and in-depth review of both the scientific evidence and the methodology of scientific expertise relied upon by either party to a dispute, is the norm.

A second set of legal systems seem to go beyond the threshold of unreasonableness to control 'manifest errors' in the discretionary choices made by the administration. This is the case, for example, in Italy, France, Lithuania and Romania (with the omnipresent national 'variations'). It is questionable, however, whether this different and formally more intense scrutiny leads in practice to an increased control on the part of the courts: in most cases courts remain anchored to a very 'hands-off' approach and do not question the technical and scientific choices of the administration in their substance. Although in some cases the courts have looked for techniques to question the underlying material on which HD decisions have been based (for example, through the 'objectification' of judicial control in France), courts remain wary of entering into the examination of how the authorities drew the conclusions from the existent material (and of using, therefore, the procedural tools at their disposal to do so).

At the other end of the spectrum lies Finland, where there are – in principle – no standards of review such as unreasonableness or proportionality and, within the limits of the claim, courts are supposed to consider thoroughly every aspect of the dispute. However, it is only in certain environmental cases, that in Finland a true 'reformatory' process applies, which allows judges to not only annul but also modify the disputed decision. At the lower level of courts, the same approach of thorough control applies before Hungarian courts (and as discussed above in the relatively narrow role accorded to the Tribunal system in the UK). Also in Germany, the 'inquisitorial principle' requires that courts 'make all reasonable efforts' to investigate the facts of the case and are required to make use of all possibly relevant sources of evidence.

Interestingly, the analysis of the case law showed that neither the presence of expert judges nor the availabilities of a wider remedial toolkit caused Finnish courts to more thoroughly review HD decisions. The opposite is true in Hungary and Germany, where administrative courts conduct a rather intrusive review of the scientific assessments underlying administrative decisions.

C. Role of Procedural Principles

One element of our comparative investigation where relatively little variation has been found concerns the vital importance of principles of procedural nature to extend the review of courts – often beyond the more straightforward 'province of legality'.

In several legal systems, which also have different attitudes towards judicial review of administrative action (such as the Netherlands, Italy, Ireland or Lithuania), procedural principles (and in particular the duty to give reasons) have been powerfully used by courts to look at the substance of the case. The need for the administration to provide adequate reasons, able to substantiate and justify the decision adopted, emerges a chief technique for courts to look into the content of HD decisions, and, albeit somewhat indirectly, also into the scientific underpinnings thereof. However, as section IV will show, also the use of seemingly similar procedural principles does not necessarily lead to a similar level of protection in HD-related cases.

D. Conclusions: Compliance with EU Law and the Aarhus Convention

As decisions taken by national authorities under the HD fall within the scope of application of EU law and the Aarhus Convention, a pertinent question is whether procedural rules concerning expert evidence, or the presence of expert judges, as well as the different approaches to judicial review may fall short of the requirement to ensure effective judicial protection under Article 47 of the Charter of Fundamental Rights of the European Union and to provide a 'procedural and substantive review' of decisions under environmental law under Article 9 of the Aarhus Convention. While no procedural arrangement seems in principle to fall below these standards, certain doubts can be raised with respect to legal systems where a very deferential approach to the control of administrative discretion is adopted, such as in the case in England and Wales or Lithuania. While this matter is under the scrutiny of the Aarhus Convention Compliance Committee at least with respect to the English unreasonableness test, no conclusive answer can be given. However, it remains to be said, as Áine Ryall argues in chapter three with respect to equally deferential Irish standards, the applicable tests are so vague and therefore flexible that they could be rather easily adapted to meet a possibly heightened scrutiny needed under EU law and the Aarhus Convention.

IV. The Level of Protection

These administrative and procedural aspects serve as 'entry points of diversity' in understanding how and why judicial approaches to the Directives, and the use of scientific information in adjudication, vary. However, variation in substantive outcomes, and, as a result, in the level of environmental protection achieved, does not follow in a straightforward fashion from these variations in legal technique. In this last part of our comparative analysis, we consider what the variation we have revealed means for the goals of the Directives, and for environmental protection. This section considers first, the substantive focus of the courts' rulings. Second, we consider the role of precaution in the package of reasons expressed to justify the courts' decisions, and third, we bring together the findings to consider the consequences for environmental protection in the EU.

A. Substantive Focus

The first source of variation is how the courts select the object of their enquiry in matters often complex in science, technology, and law (or, in many systems, how the parties frame their dispute thus guiding the line of enquiry pursued by the court). In line with the aspects considered above, the courts in England and Wales have adopted a rather limited scope and they restrict themselves to securing whether an appropriate assessment was required to be and has been carried out (a threshold which encompasses not only the existence, but also the sufficiency at a *threshold level*, of the assessment). This allows the courts to opt out from detailed engagement with scientific underpinnings as the level of detailed scrutiny demanded of the administration is low. The Irish courts have, until recently, taken a similarly hands-off approach focusing on the 'threshold adequacy' of an assessment rather than looking in detail at, for example, the methodological approach taken by an administrative authority to the scientific evidence. However, in both England and Wales (in cases involving the Tribunal system) and in Ireland following extensive references to the CJEU, there is clearly pressure within the system for the higher courts to deepen their level of engagement. In essence, this means that the substantive focus of these courts however is not whether the goals of the Directive have been met in any instance, but in allocating power between different organs of the state.

The Netherlands also has extensive case law relating to the appropriate assessment but contrary to England and Wales that review is more intrusive and does not limit itself to whether appropriate assessment was carried out but also how it was carried out and how the authorities considered and weighed different factors in their decision-making. Examination of the scientific uncertainties is thorough. Originally a 'quantitative' approach, the Dutch judicial technique has more recently evolved into a qualitative one, focusing on certainty along the lines the CJEU has established. Similarly, in Finland and Hungary the review is fact-intrusive with a substantive focus (although it is likely that the extensive reforms in Hungary not covered yet in the case law will change this picture), covering both legal and factual questions and revolving around the impacts to the protected site. In France it is that the proportionality test that allows courts to assess the content of the impact assessment and so here the focus of the court will be the perceived benefits between carrying out a more intensive assessment, and the likelihood of this generating more certain or more relevant information.

In Germany, the object of the scrutiny is also a substantive one, but the *risk* included in the proposed plans (rather than their impact) is in the limelight. Germany has established the tradition of reviewing the role of scientific uncertainties in assessing the risks the project might include. More recently the matters dealing with EU conservation law have been discussed in terms of best available scientific knowledge and development of binding standards for the assessment of scientific uncertainties. Thus, in all of these jurisdictions, the choice to focus on the process followed by the administrative authority; the evidence considered by such authorities; the benefits to be obtained by more extensive reviews; or the scale of the risk being considered, will modulate the application of the Directive. Importantly, the Directive itself, and the case law of the CJEU, in focussing on the substantive standard to be reached (ie no uncertainty based on the best scientific knowledge) tells the Member State courts nothing about how to check whether that standard has been met. Different courts will, in reliance on what they are used to and what is deemed appropriate within the system as a whole, select different techniques for judging these environmental tests.

B. Precaution

The second source of variation lies in the reasons underlying the courts' examination of the way in which the authority considered the scientific uncertainty at stake and in particular, in the way in which the *court* conceives of precaution. In England and Wales, as the courts reject the idea of reviewing the substance of the matter, as mentioned above, and the focus is on securing procedural legality, the role of precautionary principle has been minimal: it is used only to mediate the question of reasonableness. Similarly, Irish, Italian, Lithuanian, Greek and Romanian courts, because of their general reluctance to consider technical or scientific matters, their uncertainties included, have not significantly engaged with the principle as a means to consider scientific evidence. However, in all of these cases it should not be assumed that the precautionary principle does not play an important role in the system. Indeed, precaution is used to shape the *interpretation* of the legal standards at play, either directly, or indirectly through compliance with the jurisprudence of the CJEU. In such instances precaution appears at the level of the substantive test, not as a means to review evidence.

In other legal systems, despite the more substantive engagement with the scientific uncertainties considered by the authorities, courts may avoid engagement with the precautionary principle as a tool to assist in interpretation of either evidence or of law. For example, Hungarian judges independently assess the different and or rival expert positions, identify and clearly define gaps and inconsistencies in the technical assessments of the executive. However, they do not advise the administration as to which conclusion *should* be reached when they remit the matter back to the executive to decide; if deciding the matter by themselves, they must do so by the guidance of a court-appointed expert. The uncertainty assessment is therefore treated as a matter of evidence on the balance of probabilities, to which there is no further need to add a layer of precaution. The Dutch courts also extend this review to the depths of techno-scientific considerations, including the acceptability of the chosen scientific method. However, they rarely mention the precautionary principle in their reasoning.

The outlier amongst the legal systems we have considered is Finland, where precaution and techno-scientific uncertainties are commonly referred to. The courts in Finland discuss scientific uncertainties and consider their role in the potential impact on the protected values. Although the normative setting of the Wild Birds Directive and HD is very diverse, this sensitivity to uncertainties permeated through the field. If we return to the divisions above, therefore, regarding the possible understandings of what role the precautionary principle should play (interpretive, evidential or substantive), the majority of courts treat the principle as a tool to assist in interpretation. They do not – and this is somewhat surprising – treat the principle as a principle of *evidential quality or quantity* per se: rather, the lack of evidence means that the decision may not cross a reasonableness threshold, or may disclose a manifest error.

C. Consequences for Environmental Protection

The CJEU repeatedly states, as chapters two and 15 of this volume show, that certainty in evidence is required if the tests in the Directives, themselves interpreted in a broad, purposive manner, are to be met. Member State courts, albeit in different ways, seem to pull back from the full consequences of this approach because of the unsettling potential of this test to shift the balance of power between organs of the state. Whether the court system allows the court to assess the evidence through its own scientific advisors, to request more information from the parties, or requires them to rely only on what was provided, in all cases pre-existing constitutional balance has a profound influence on how far the court will step into the shoes of an administrative authority and what it means for it to do so. This has consequences for the level of environmental protection achieved given the complexities of the relationship between administrative authorities, the priorities of national government, the democratic mandate of such authorities, and where the environment sits in its decision-making matrix. In this final section we consider in very general terms the tentative conclusions we can draw from our study for environmental protection. In other words, we ask now whether the goals of the Directives are met, not *how* the Member States go about addressing them.

There are some jurisdictions where there are clear indications that the courts, albeit using a range of techniques, see their constitutional role as being partly about upholding the goals of the Directives. For example, the French system is traditionally very deferential to administrative discretion but when it comes to HD case law, French judges seem to have been willing to 'step up their game' *within* the traditionally acceptable parameters to ensure a rather high level of environmental protection. Similarly, Irish courts, which might have been expected to be very deferential when technical questions are at stake, have in recent years, led by a Supreme Court which is keen to enter dialogue with the CJEU, engaged with such questions rather vigorously. In Italy too if one reads between the lines of a formally weak scrutiny, one can see that a high level of protection was ensured by the courts' case law. Italian courts have been capable of identifying when precautionary action is needed, resulting in most often securing the conservation aims. That is not to say that these jurisdictions are achieving model outcomes, but rather that the courts have shown a willingness to work purposively within the wider legal culture to achieve environmentally positive outcomes.

By contrast, some jurisdictions have maintained rather more rigidly the traditional divisions of their judicial review standards. For example, the German courts have a long experience of reviewing the risks involved and discussing the best available technique and have both a procedural ecosystem and a judicial culture which allows for thorough review of administrative decisions: however, in HD-related cases, their review does not seem to go beyond the manifest error level.

In Lithuania and Romania the current standard of review does not secure effective biodiversity protection either. In some countries the road to non-satisfactory substantive outcome has been through limiting access to courts. Hungary has chosen to mould the procedural norms and structures so that the number of cases has declined drastically; the Dutch have followed the German solution of narrowing the standing rights, restricting access to courts and in effect hampering biodiversity protection. Elsewhere fragmentation of the legal landscape hinders the fulfilment of the Directives' aims: in Ireland, the fragmented legal landscape undermines the effectiveness of environmental laws in practice, as it does in France.

V. Conclusions

Based on the analysis conducted throughout this volume, therefore, there are justified reasons to be concerned over the uniform application of EU conservation law and of its effectiveness in practice in terms of environmental protection.

The technique of a Directive is of course to mandate a goal to be achieved whilst leaving the mechanics to the Member States. This is designed to chart a course between the maintenance of idiosyncratic legal cultures on the one hand, and the effectiveness and harmony of EU law on the other. In the case of the WBD and HD what we see is that the levels of variation in *how* Member State courts decide cases relating to these Directives produces variation not just of process – administratively and judicially – but also of substance. Furthermore, the guidance from the CJEU, which is all about the level of protection to be achieved and the required level of evidential certainty, leaves Member States free to decide the techniques they can and cannot use to assess whether there is evidential certainty in any particular case. In short, there is a gap in harmonisation, a deliberate gap into which legal culture steps.

INDEX

www.ingramcontent.com/pod-product-compliance
Ingram Content Group UK Ltd.
Pitfield, Milton Keynes, MK11 3LW, UK
UKHW020230290926
15470UKWH00002B/446

9 781509 9481